Divisions
of Labor

Divisions
of Labor

Globality, Ideology, and War
in the Shaping of the Japanese
Labor Movement

Lonny E. Carlile

University of Hawai'i Press

Honolulu

Library of Congress Cataloging-in-Publication Data

Carlile, Lonny E.
    Divisions of labor : globality, ideology, and war in the shaping of
the Japanese labor movement / Lonny E. Carlile.
        p. cm.
    Includes bibliographical references and index.
    ISBN 0-8248-2456-3 (hardcover : alk. paper)
1. Labor movement—Japan—History—20th century. I. Title.
    HD8726.C37 2005
    331.88'0952—dc22

                                        2004017240

Designed by the University of Hawai'i Press Production Staff

Printed by The Maple-Vail Book Manufacturing Group

To Walter G. Carlile
and the late
Masako M. Carlile

Contents

Part III: Beyond the Cold War

Acknowledgments

This book had exceedingly long periods of gestation and metamorphosis during which I received invaluable help from more people than I can possibly recognize in a short acknowledgment. I therefore name here only a few of the individuals to whom I am indebted and express my implicit appreciation to those I do not have the space to mention.

Inspiration for the book is owed above all to Masumi Junnosuke, who, by allowing me to translate two of his books—and, in the process, to probe deeply into his mind and his incredible scholarship—provided the spark that ignited my interest in the history of the Japanese labor movement, along with help, advice, and generous hospitality over the years. This book is also an outgrowth of my doctoral dissertation (on business associations, no less), for which I received invaluable help and guidance from Chalmers Johnson, Robert Scalapino, and Tom Smith, at the University of California at Berkeley. I am exceedingly grateful in particular to Professor Shibagaki Kazuo for his generosity and assistance over the years, and to Baba Hiroji, Kato Eiichi, Hara Akira, and Miyajima Hideaki, among other superb mentors and colleagues, during my stint as a visiting scholar at the University of Tokyo Institute of Social Science under the sponsorship of the US-Japan Fulbright Program. I thank Takemae Eiji of Tokyo University of Economics for his generous assistance and support in my gaining familiarity with Japan's Occupation period, and Koseki Shoichi and other members of the Occupation History Study Association.

I received valuable help from Frank Langdon, David Edgington, and Terry McGee, among other colleagues connected with the University of British Columbia Institute of Asian Research, including Gonnami Tsuneharu of its Asia Collection. More recently, Sharon Minichiello and my associates at the University of

Hawai'i Center for Japanese Studies, along with Ric Trimillos and various colleagues in the university's Asian studies program, provided much-appreciated support; Tokiko Bazzell of the university library's Japan Collection was wonderfully accommodating in helping me gain access to required sources.

Professor Takagi Ikuro of Japan Women's University graced me with unsurpassed generosity, sharing his expertise, his contacts, and his sources; without his assistance, completion of the project would not have been possible. I would also like to thank Patricia Crosby and the staff at the University of Hawai'i Press, for making it possible to publish this book, and Karen Weller-Watson, for her skillful editorial work.

Finally, I extend special thanks to my wife, Laura Noda, for her constant support over the years, and for her patience with a project that seemed never to go away.

Introduction

A double entendre embedded in the title of this book encompasses two of the three core themes that tie this work together and two key characteristics of labor movements throughout most of the twentieth century. "Divisions of labor" refers both to the ways in which competing ideologies divided labor movements into competing partisan groups, and to units of military organization, in the sense that workers were organized and mobilized in "wars" of various kinds via these ideological groupings. These "wars" include not only armed conflicts among states and nations but, in the broader sense, prolonged and intense political competition among social categories (class war) and more abstract competition over ideology and international hegemony (e.g., cold war).

The third core theme of the book is the globality of the process out of which the contemporary Japanese labor movement—the primary focus of this work—emerged. That is, the movement's evolution is presented as part of a larger geopolitical process shaping labor movements in Japan and other parts of the world during the years that stretch from World War I through the Cold War era that began in the late 1940s. The global dimension is especially significant because political forces of this period impinged with particular intensity on national-level labor movements.

The processes described here established the ideological and organizational attributes of the labor movement in Japan and other so-called advanced industrialized countries of today, thus setting the basic institutional and political parameters within which labor movements would continue to operate.[1] By focusing on the globality of the Japanese movement and its connection to the "divisions" of labor as described, we have an analytical frame of reference that helps us isolate those forces and circumstances critical to the dynamics of labor politics in a particular national context. Put another way, this book offers a globally contextualized comparative history of the Japanese labor movement.

Inspiration for approaching the task in this way came from the sense of déjà vu I experienced when reading works on Western European labor-movement history after having gained a general familiarity with Japan's labor history. It was not simply that familiar characters and plot devices kept reappearing in the different national narratives as if they were put together out of the contents of a Hollywood scriptwriter's toolbox; there were also astonishing simultaneities in the timing of key developments in histories that were separated geographically by the world's largest land mass and an ostensible "East-is-East, West-is-West" cultural divide. The close proximity and easily observable concrete evidence of the intertwining trajectories of national labor movement histories within Europe has encouraged a global—or, alternately, contextualized comparative—approach. European labor movement history is thus often written as a Europe-wide history or as compendiums of multination case studies. The resulting accumulation of explicitly and implicitly comparative studies has fostered a cognizance of the international and global nature of the forces that have shaped the histories of labor movements. By contrast, despite a number of initial stabs (moreso in works published in Japanese than in English), comparative analysis of Japanese labor-movement history has not been undertaken to anywhere near the extent that it has of European labor history. One of the main reasons for this has been Japan's isolation as the only independent industrialized country in a historically nonindustrialized, largely colonized, part of the world. Also, for the non-Japanese scholar and student of labor history, linguistic hurdles must be overcome in order to access the relatively numerous publications and source materials that are essential in the study of the Japanese movement.[2] In light of this, a subsidiary purpose in writing this volume is to begin to bridge the gap between the two sets of literatures by systematically comparing developments in Japanese labor-movement history with those of three leading countries in Western Europe—France, Italy, and West Germany.

Having said this, several provisos are in order. First, although the effort here is meant to highlight the "globality" of Japanese labor history, strictly speaking, the framework of analysis adopted is interregional rather than global. Nonetheless, the interregional context implicitly meters global forces. This is because the three Western European countries and Japan shared contiguous political-historical "spaces" in the global system during the period in question in the sense that all four were countries near the epicenter of the transition from Allied-Axis to Cold War East-West conflict in the international system. Precisely because of this "location," their respective labor movements were impacted powerfully, and in systematically similar ways, by this global-level transition. Thus, although the empirical coverage is admittedly far from global in its scope, by connecting developments in the labor movements of these specific countries to the regional manifestations of a global phenomena, we are able to recognize the global dimension of the local-level histories covered, and may even be inspired to extend the analysis to labor histories in other "locations" in the global system.[3]

A second proviso is that, although it does engage in extensive comparative analysis, the book is primarily a *Japanese* labor-movement history. It departs from the standard practice of a single-country study (i.e., only tangential coverage of other countries), but it does not conform to the standard format for a conventional comparative study either (i.e., more or less equal weighting of all countries covered). In terms of format, discussions of each subperiod begin with an extended discussion of broader developments in the international system, in the international labor movement, and in the three Western European cases, which is then followed by a more extensive and detailed discussion of counterpart phenomena in Japan. From a conventional standpoint the book may include too many pages discussing other countries or, alternatively, may give too much weight to a single country. When read, however, with the proper intent in mind, the logic of this "imbalance" should be apparent.

A third proviso is that this is not labor history in the sense of a history of the working class or a history of industrial relations. The term "labor movement" is used here in the wider, European—rather than the narrower, American—sense. It is this that Adolf Sturmthal referred to when he stated, "A multitude of organizations—varying from country to country and from one historical period to another—come under that common heading. These are unions, of course, but also political parties (which can be associated in a variety of ways with trade unions), workers' educational organizations, cooperatives (mainly consumer cooperatives), mutual insurance organizations, workers' sports organizations, and so on, all the way to workers' stamp collectors groups."[4] This study concentrates on the first two—trade unions and political parties—among these various interrelated organizations, along with the councils and other associations they spawned.

Fourth, my treatment focuses also on the thought and strategy of labor movement leaders. Until about a quarter century ago, labor historians generally dealt with matters like the ideological currents, the ways in which labor movements were organized nationally, and how these ideologies and organizational arrangements mediated relationships between and among the working class and capital and the state. More recent work has consciously attempted to broaden the focus in an effort to better grasp working-class history in its full panoply. This has led to an eclectic profusion of studies on a variety of topics, including industrial relations inside factories, working-class culture, role of gender in working-class lives, consequences of inter-ethnic relations on work life, and local-level union and working-class community organizations, to name just a few. In this sense, my book may be old-fashioned, but through this kind of elite- and thought-focused analysis, I hope to demonstrate the key elements of the globality of the period's labor history.

Finally, the book was written bearing in mind such dictums of Charles Tilly's as that "we should build concrete and historical analyses of the big structures and large processes that shape our era," and that our "analyses should be *concrete* in having real times, places, and people as their referents and in testing the coherence of the postulated structures and processes against the experiences of real times, places, and people." Tilly maintained in particular that these "should be *historical* in limiting their scope to an era bounded by the playing out of certain well-defined processes." We need to recognize, he adds, that *"when* things happen within a sequence affects *how* they happen."[5] Not intending a political-science-style universal model of global-local interaction in labor movements, applicable across time and space, my working premise is that these global forces—namely, the spread of particular types of working-class ideologies and particular alignments in the international-state system—were, if not unique, certainly distinctive during the period and were not present beyond it.

Part 1

ROOTS

Chapter 1

Labor Movements in Western Europe, 1920-1945

D uring the 1920s the seeds of labor movement entanglement in Cold War politics in Western Europe and Japan were sown, most importantly in the forms of the sharpening of differences over labor movement strategy and a corresponding linking of ideology and organization in labor movement politics. The differences over principles that would divide labor movements in the 1920s were fundamentally the same ones that would divide them during the Cold War years. It would be somewhat of an overstatement to say that these issues were identical to those that split the world into two competing camps during the 1950s, but there was considerable overlap, and it was the particular combination of dovetailing and disjuncture between the global and the national that determined the warp and woof of labor movement history in these countries during the Cold War years.

In the interim, between the 1920s and the Cold War, global politics and labor politics interacted in ways that would reshape the place and function of labor movements in national polities. Therefore, as a prelude to our later narrative and analysis, this chapter traces in broad strokes the trajectory and dynamics of labor movements in Western Europe prior to the end of World War II. Chapter 2 provides narrative and analysis relating to parallel developments in Japan during the same period. The discussion is then extended forward in chapters 3 through 5 to developments in the immediate post–World War II, pre–Cold War years.

Interwar social democracy, communism, left socialism, and Christian trade unionism

The appearance of industrial society in Continental Europe over the course of the nineteenth century was accompanied by the spread of ideas about how the newly emergent class of industrial workers might best advance its interests under the socioeconomic and political conditions and constraints it confronted in that society. The most influential and by far the most pivotal of these were the ideas associated with Karl Marx. The essence of Marxian socialism as it came to be understood in the popular mind (as opposed to the subtle and manifold content of the actual writings of Marx)—what Sassoon has labeled "vulgar Marxism"—can be described as consisting of the "trinity" of propositions listed in table 1. As Sassoon notes, "the first proposition embraces the Marxist theory of economic exploitation; the second the so-called materialist conception of history; while the third, not really elaborated by Marx, was the product of the ideas and political practice of European socialism (especially in Germany) after Marx's death." In the context of the time, these provided a powerful and compelling case for the use of class and class interests as the points of reference for organizing and promoting movements aimed at improving the lot of industrial workers. Its pivotal significance for the evolution of European labor movements stemmed primarily from its being embraced and applied by individuals who were active in the leadership of labor organizations and thus its serving as the motor for the development of class-oriented forms of labor activism. Secondly, its spread and the emergence of movements based on its tenets stimulated efforts aimed at counteracting and redirecting its influence, such as attempts by incumbent elites to forestall, repress, or co-opt class-based labor movements in order to avoid what were perceived to be the negative consequences of their rise, as well as the encouragement of alternative forms of labor movement organization that rejected the class-based basic tenets of vulgar Marxism. Historically, the most widespread of these in the European context was that promoted by the Catholic Church. Third, certain ambiguities in Marxism itself encouraged internal differentiation and division within the movements based on its tenets. Because of the centrality of these ambiguities to an understanding of the dynamics of twentieth-century labor movements, it is helpful to review them in some detail.

One source of internal tension in Marxian-socialist thought grew out of differing positions on the question of whether the labor movement should be "reformist" or "revolutionary" in character—that is, focused on working toward beneficial changes within the confines of the existing regime or oriented toward overthrowing and replacing wholesale the existing socioeconomic and political order. The sociopolitical context of early twentieth-century Europe provided justifications for both positions. On the one hand, the very fact that trade unions and working-class political parties had, despite resistance and obstacles, gained footholds in the politics and economies of some of the countries where industrialization was most advanced lent credence to assertions concerning the possibility of incremental advances toward socialism within existing democratic capitalist orders. On the other hand, there were still formidable institutional barriers in all countries that blocked the attainment of working-class interests as well as ruling elites who were willing to engage in drastic measures to prevent labor movement advances. This line of thought led to the conclusion that the appropriate strategy for the labor movement was either to wait for the emergence of or to precipitate those conditions that would lead to the collapse of the existing political economic order. Reforms, in this view, would only lengthen the life span of capitalism.

A second internal tension had to do with the relationship between trade unions and political parties, which had by then become the labor movement's primary organizational forms. Should there be a division of labor and relative independence between the two, with trade unions specializing in economically oriented activity and political parties devoted exclusively to political functions? Or should one be subordinated to the other? Prior to World War I, the most visible cleavage in the labor movements of Continental Europe was that which divided the Marxian labor organizations from the Christian labor organizations formed in reaction to them. The former was by far the larger of the two. Although the kinds of tensions described were apparent inside Marxian organizations, and they occasionally precipitated organizational splits, for the most part Marxian-socialist

Table 1. Propositions of "vulgar Marxism"

Proposition 1	The present capitalist system is unfair. Its fundamental relation, the wage relation, is based on a contract between juridically equal parties, but this disguises a real inequality: the capitalists "cheat" the workers by appropriating far more than they pay in wages and other necessary production costs. This special and statistically unquantifiable appropriation, called "surplus-value" by Marxists, gives the owners of capital great wealth and control over the economic development of society. They thus appropriate not simply wealth but also power.
Proposition 2	History proceeds through stages. Each stage is characterized by a specific economic system to which corresponds a particular system of power and hence a specific ruling class. The present capitalist stage is not everlasting, but a transient historical phenomenon: the present ruling class will not rule forever.
Proposition 3	Workers are a fundamentally homogeneous class, regardless of differences which may exist among them. All workers are united "in essence" by similar interests: to improve their conditions of life under capitalism; to struggle against the existing social order; and to overcome it by bringing about a new stage of history in which there can be "real," and not merely formal, equality. It follows that workers must organize themselves into political parties and trade unions and reject any attempt to divide them.

Source: Adapted from Donald Sassoon, *One Hundred Years of Socialism: The West European Left in the Twentieth Century* (New York: New Press, 1996), p. 6.

movements were able to sustain organizational solidarity through face-saving compromises.

Developments during and following World War I, however, intensified the ideologically based tensions among the competing streams to the point that they were transformed into open organizational rivalry.[1] Several factors were involved. On the one hand, a number of major political developments in Europe during the period reinforced the case for the reformist line. Prompted by the need to obtain labor's cooperation in wartime mobilization, extant regimes found themselves forced to recognize and work with labor unions, and as a consequence, the power and influence of the working class and its representative organizations expanded dramatically within these regimes. In other instances—Germany is a prime example—labor movement influence was enhanced by the outright collapse of staunchly conservative regimes and their replacement by more inclusive, democratic ones in which labor and socialist organizations served as founding parties. The establishment of electoral democracies grounded in universal suffrage across Europe dangled before the labor movement the prospect of advancing the interests of the working class through the ballot box.

On the other hand, these very same years also generated conditions that seemed to confirm the correctness of the revolutionary position. The massive carnage, destruction, and social dislocation wrought by World War I, and an unprecedented wave of radical worker actions—general strikes, factory takeovers, and so on—that enveloped Europe in 1918–1919 served as a perfect backdrop for claims that the collapse of the capitalist order was imminent. On top of this, an ostensible proletarian revolution had occurred in "backward" Russia, pointing to the possibility of a much wider geographic applicability of Marxian precepts than had been previously assumed. Although the wave of postwar worker unrest eventually subsided, those who were revolutionarily inclined could easily interpret these developments as signaling the validity of a centralized, elite-led, conspiratorial revolutionary line.

The post–World War I years marked a watershed for the Christian workers' movement as well. Martin Conway notes in his history of interwar Catholic politics that "the experiences of the war years contributed to the new-found vitality of the Catholic faith during the 1920s." This was because "in religious terms, the manifold uncertainties and sufferings of the war provoked a rise in the intensity of religious practice. Not merely at the front line but also among the civilian populations, there was a return to Catholicism as people sought solace and reassurance in the structure of religious faith."[2] The advent of mass democracy, furthermore, made it imperative for the Catholic Church and other confessional denominations to create mass organizations of their own to defend their interests and advance their own particular visions of a Christian society. The interwar years were thus marked by a significant rise in Christian political activity in all of the major countries of Western Europe, with activity in the labor movement being an important pillar therein.[3]

The pervasiveness of these intensified divisions within European labor movements was readily apparent at the international level. By the mid-1920s all of the leading ideological currents save one had managed to establish an international association of its own.[4] Serving as the global voice of the communists were the Comintern (the Communist, or Third, International), formed in 1919, and its associated labor organization, the Profintern, or Red International of Labor Unions (RILU). Emphasizing the ripeness of revolutionary conditions globally, the international communist movement established the Moscow-headquartered Comintern as the nerve center of a unified supranational movement. Undergirding the communist current was the belief that the fomenting of proletarian revolution required the talents of a well-trained vanguard thoroughly committed to the revolution and able to direct the movement in fine-tuned fashion in light of changing revolutionary conditions. Reflecting the primacy that Marxian doctrine granted to the working class as a vehicle for sociopolitical change, trade unions, as the primary organizational form adopted by the working class, were seen as critical agents in the revolutionary process. But, they were also perceived to be unwieldy and politically immature. For this reason, it was a basic tenet of the communist movement that a vanguard communist party should steer the unions in accordance with a revolutionary strategy. Comintern affiliates were thus required to accept the following principles:

> Every party . . . must carry on systematic and persistent Communist activity inside trade unions, the workers' councils and factory committees, the cooperatives, and other mass workers' organizations. Within these organizations Communist cells [committees of party members] must be organized which shall by persistent and unflagging work win the trade unions, etc., for the Communist cause. . . . The Communist cells must be completely subordinated to the party as a whole.[5]

In exercising its leadership over a world-scale proletarian revolutionary movement, the Comintern issued pronouncements and country-specific guidance that local parties were expected to follow. Special status was granted to the national interests of the Soviet Union on the grounds that, as the site of the global proletarian revolution's initiation, it constituted the revolution's home base and thus needed to be protected at all costs.

Social democrats were represented internationally by the Socialist, or Second, International and the associated international trade union organization loosely associated with it, the International Federation of Trade Unions (IFTU). In contrast to the centralized Comintern and Profintern, and in line with their differing sensibilities, the locus of power and influence in the social democratic labor-move-

Table 2. International labor organizations 1929

Organization	Established	Estimate of annual budget (1929)	Membership (1929)	Number of countries with members (1929)	Notes
SOCIALIST					
Amsterdam International: International Federation of Trade Unions (IFTU)	1919	n.a.	13,000,000	28	Germany held largest national membership; Western European union organizations predominated
Socialist International: Labor and Socialist International	1923	$25,000	6,500,000	36	
COMMUNIST					
Comintern: Communist, or Third, International	1919	$345,000*	1,800,000	50+	Of total membership distribution 3/4 in Soviet Union, 150,000 in Czechoslovakia, 125,000 in Germany, 52,000+ in France
Profintern: Red International of Labor Unions (RILU)	1921	n.a.	17,000,000	50	Of total membership, 10,000,000 in USSR, 2,000,000 in China, 500,000 in France, and 200,000 in Czechoslovakia
CHRISTIAN					
International Federation of Christian Trade Unions (IFCTU)	1920	$10,000	1,500,000	15	Of total membership about half in Germany, 25% in Belgium and Holland. Membership also in France, Czechoslovakia, Poland
SYNDICALIST					
International Workingmen's Association (IWMA)	1923	$9,235	162,000	9	Membership in Germany, France, Holland, Denmark, Norway, Sweden, Mexico, Argentina, Uruguay

*1927 figure

Source: Lewis Levitzki Lorwin, *The International Labor Movement: History, Policies, Outlook* (New York: Harper, 1953), pp. 118–162.

ment organizations resided at or below the national level. Accordingly, social democratic internationals were loosely structured federations devoted primarily to liaison work. The basic operating principle of the Socialist International was a voluntarism in which international stances were to "grow naturally from the process through which [national level] Socialist parties get adapted to one another."[6] Its declared agenda was decidedly decentralized and incrementalist: "Its ideal was a world society composed of independent socialist nations cooperating for the general improvement of the conditions of mankind. It regarded the coming of socialism as a gradual and peaceful process, for the success of which a violent revolution was neither necessary nor desirable. Capitalism, in its view, would be modified in a socialist direction through the extension of 'workers' control' and 'industrial democracy,' that is, through the growth of economic councils, by means of which the workers would acquire a greater share in management and an increasing influence in the making of economic policy."[7]

Politically, the social democratic movement was committed to nonviolent parliamentary tactics and democratic procedures. Indeed, by the 1920s the social democrats were prone to value democratic institutions even more highly than socialism, as this statement by an Austrian social democrat illustrates:

> We want to preserve the rights of freedom, and the guarantees of personal and intellectual freedom for which the best of mankind have died on the funeral pyres of the Inquisition, in the Bastilles of absolutist tyrants, and on the barricades of countless revolutions. We do not want to abandon these values in exchange for Socialism, but we want to draw inspiration from these values in our struggle for Socialism. We cannot renounce democracy to win Socialism; you must make democracy the very basis and instrument for building up a Socialist society.[8]

With regard to union-party relations, the social democratic camp endorsed a general principle of autonomy between the union and party spheres. This principle was expressed organizationally at the international level in the delegation of important elements of international trade-union work to various formally independent trade-union secretariats in specific industrial sectors (e.g., the International Federation of Transport Workers, the International Miners' Federation, and the International Union of Woodworkers). This arrangement, and the principles and values that animated it, could not have been farther in spirit from that of the Comintern.

The conflicting unionisms espoused by the Socialist International/IFTU and the Comintern/Profintern brought the two sides into a programmatic conflict. Comintern affiliates were told that "every party belonging to the Communist International is obliged to wage an unyielding struggle against the Amsterdam

'International' of the yellow trade unions."[9] The demand that communists should struggle against the social democrats remained a constant theme throughout the 1920s, though the prescribed format changed on several occasions. At the outset, communists were called upon to undercut the social democratic movement by engineering splits in the latter's organization that paralleled the breaking off of the Third from the Second International. In 1922 the tactic of choice shifted to that of a "united front from above" in which communists were urged to amalgamate with the social democrats and take control of the new, integrated organizations. In 1928 it was to establish a "united front from below," or to win rank-and-file workers away from social democratic organizations and mobilize them through separate counterpart communist organizations. Although rhetorically the hostility of the social democrats toward the communists was usually expressed in less-shrill language, they nevertheless rejected proposals from communists for organizational amalgamation and vigorously fought against communist infiltration. The differences and infighting between the two camps produced bitter, emotionally tinged internal conflict in the labor movements of virtually all of the industrialized countries.[10]

Overshadowed and falling in between these competing currents was left-socialist unionism. Left socialism grew out of the lingering sentiment among a segment of the socialist working-class movement that the balance of class power remained the primary determinant of the political and economic standing of the working class.[11] However, unlike the communists, left socialists felt that the conditions faced by the working class varied significantly from country to country and that these variations needed to be taken seriously in formulating strategy. This fed into a stream of labor movement thought, the essential parameters of which were perhaps best described in the founding statement of the soon-to-be-defunct "Vienna International" in 1921. "In order to fulfill this task [of promoting socialist revolution]," the declaration stated, "the workers' International must consider the variety of objective conditions of the struggle in the various countries. It must not hamper the freedom of any particular Socialist party in adapting its action to the conditions of its particular country. It must not restrict the proletariat either to using democratic methods only, as is done by the so-called Second International today, nor prescribe the mechanical imitation of the methods of the Russian peasants' and working men's revolution, as the Communist International would like to do."[12] Given that left socialists tended to perceive as high the social and political obstacles to the promotion of worker interests, great stress was placed on forging a "united front" among labor organizations.

In the context of an unbridgeable rivalry between the social democrats and communists, however, it proved difficult for the left socialists to maintain a coherent organizational identity of their own. Left socialists themselves were prone to divisions over whether to align with the communists or the social democrats as a first step toward broader solidarity. Many left-socialist groups ended up affiliating with the Socialist International simply because of that international's more open membership policy. The direction of coalition building on the part of left socialists, however, was not uniform and there were notable exceptions, such as the Italian Maximalists who, though rejected by the Comintern, refused to join the social democratic internationals. Debates over differences of stance between the more numerous social democrats and the left socialists continued to inform both the meetings of the social democratic internationals and the domestic debates of the left.

Rejecting the fundamental premise of all three from a religion-based perspective was the International Federation of Christian Trade Unions (IFTCU). Christian trade unionism objected vehemently to the very notion of class struggle as a basis for resolving the problems faced by working men and women. While there was Protestant involvement, the majority in the Christian trade-union movement was Catholic and looked to Vatican pronouncements for guidance, with the 1891 encyclical entitled Rerum Novarum particularly influential in this regard. Rather than conflict among classes, the Christian trade-unionist position was rooted in an organic interpretation of society. That is, "Christian trade unionists recognized that the workers formed a distinct social class," but this recognition "did not, in their opinion, imply a recognition of 'class struggle.'" They rejected the proposition that a solution to the problems of the working person required socioeconomic transformation. "The task was not to fan the flames of class conflicts, but to harmonize differences and make possible the peaceful cooperation of all classes for the common good." Thus:

> In accordance with their general principles, the Christian trade unions advocated a system of industrial relations based on harmonious cooperation between capital and labor. Under private property, they said, the owners of capital and the entrepreneurs should carry the pecuniary risks of enterprise and should receive a reasonable reward for this as well as for their managerial efforts. Capital should also have freedom to exercise the rightful functions of organizing and directing production. But capital must keep in view that it was not superior to labor and that labor was the lifegiving factor of production. Capital should not claim an exclusive right to control production and distribution, but should recognize the right of labor to share in such control.
>
> In its turn, labor should do its best to make industry fulfill its economic and social ends. In return for his efforts, the worker was entitled to compensation which would enable him to live the life of a civilized human being. Labor was not to be treated as a commodity subject to the laws of supply and demand, but as the embodiment of human personality. The workers should be protected against everything which might impair his health, stunt his personal development, or injure his moral life.[13]

Finally, one can point to the continuing existence of the anarcho-syndicalist movement as a declining, but nonetheless distinct, fifth current in the international labor movement during the 1920s. Given their abhorrence of the state and their preference for localized organizations and direct action, it is not surprising that the syndicalists were not particularly effective in building national or international organizations and were quickly eclipsed by the newly emergent international communist movement as the most prominent current on the radical end of the labor movement. They were nonetheless successful in establishing the small International Workingmen's Association in 1923. Despite some expansion in membership, anarchists' influence in domestic-level labor movements was on the decline during the interwar period, having been crowded out by their more vigorous social democratic and communist counterparts.

The experiences of the Western European labor movements at the national level during the 1920s refracted in varying patterns the dynamics of the labor movement exhibited in a more purified form at the international level. Although the experiences varied considerably from country to country, a number of generalizations are nevertheless possible about European labor movements. As it did for the international labor movement, the end of World War I and the immediate postwar years marked a period at the national level when differentiated organizational identities reflecting the prevailing ideological currents emerged. Conflict was most pronounced between the social democrats, who placed highest priority on the defense of democratic institutions, and the communists, whose tactics shifted in accordance with dictates from the Comintern. Caught in the middle were the left socialists, who consistently rallied, generally unsuccessfully, for solidarity. The general trend was for syndicalism to decline precipitously in influence, though Spain was a notable exception in this regard. Christian laborism was handicapped by the general hostility toward Christian unionism on the part of the class-oriented labor-movement activists and by the continuing ambivalence of the Church toward democratic institutions.[14]

A brief overview of the situations in Germany, France, and Italy helps to illustrate the varying patterns by which communist, social democratic, left-socialist, and Christian currents structured the labor movements of Western Europe during these years. The ideological cleavages were manifested in near archetypal form in the German labor movement. Its social democratic, left-socialist, and communist wings took on organizationally separate identities in 1917 when the German Social Democratic Party, Sozialdemokratische Partei Deutschlands (SPD), divided over what tactics to adopt vis-à-vis the collapsing regime of the kaiser.[15] The breakaway elements of left socialists and communists formed the United Social Democratic Party (Unabhängige Sozialdemokratische Partei Deutschlands, or USPD), but the communists, under orders from the Comintern, split off again, to form the German Communist Party (Kommunistiche Partei Deutschlands, or

KPD) in 1918. Trade unions were similarly split along ideological and denominational lines. Social democratic and left-socialist unions were aggregated under the General German Federation of Labor (Allgemeiner Deutscher Gerwerkschaftsbund, or ADGB) aligned with the SPD. Christian trade unions maintained a corresponding umbrella organization in the form of the German Labor Federation (Deutscher Gewerkschaftsbund, or DGB). Catholic trade unions in the DGB maintained links to the Catholic Center Party, while Protestant labor organizations tended to align with the nationalistic German National People's Party (Deutschnational Volkspartei, or DNVP). Both of the Christian parties were cross-class parties that drew much of their support from outside the working class. During the 1920s, German communists devoted considerable energy to infiltrating organizations within the ADGB, although there were points at which independent communist organizations were set up. Syndicalism, by this time, was of very little consequence in the German labor movement.

In France a communist party (Parti Communiste Français, or PCF) was formed in 1920, when the existing French Socialist Party split.[16] The PCF was able to take with it the greater share of the latter's membership and electoral votes. A parallel division in the trade unions occurred in 1921, when the communists in the Confédération Générale du Travail (CGT) split off to form the Confédération Générale du Travail Unitaire (CGTU). Discontentment with the social democrat's moderation and the PCF's external control and lack of consideration for national conditions led to moves among this group to coalesce in an independent third pole. The French communists and their organizations rapidly lost support and by mid-decade the moderate social democrats clearly overshadowed the communists by a wide margin, inducing the left socialists to merge with their moderate counterparts. Throughout all of this, the previously strong French syndicalist current waned.

In Italy after World War I the three-part division of communist, left-socialist, and social democratic influences manifested in the competing political groupings of moderate social democrats (the Minimalists), left-socialist Maximalists, and the Communists in the Partito Communista Italiano, or PCI. The center of gravity lay with the left socialists, who at one point were affiliated with the Third International but split from it over the latter's refusal to countenance a greater degree of autonomy of action for the Italian party. Italian Catholics were represented via their own party, the Popular Party (Partito Popolare). Although struggles among the social democrats, left socialists, and communists were incessant, the pre–World War I Italian trade-union organization Confederazione Generale del Lavoro (CGL) managed to hold together until it was forcibly dissolved in the mid-1920s by Mussolini's Fascist regime. Other, smaller trade-union organizations represented currents outside of the socialist mainstream, such as the anarcho-syndicalist Unione Sindicale Italiana (USI). Two union organizations representing corporatist inclinations were also present. Both were formed in 1918 in reaction to the upsurge of worker radicalism in Italy following the end of World War I. These were the Catholic Confederazione Italiana del Lavoro (CIL) and the national socialist (fascist) UIL (Unione Italiana del Lavoro). The fundamental premise of the latter organization was that "the nation was more important than the class, and that class collaboration among the various classes of a nation was preferable to, and more feasible than, class collaboration among different nations." In line with its nationalistic orientation, the UIL clearly rejected internationalism on the basis that "international unions were an absurdity as long as there were 'have' and 'have not' nations."[17] In any event, these differences became somewhat moot with the establishment of Mussolini's Fascist state. This regime proceeded to consolidate all independent labor associations into corporatist organizations under the close guidance of the state, and all competing political parties were banned.

Facing fascism: from disarray to resistance

If it is the cross-national permeation of rival Christian, social democratic, left-socialist, communist, and—to a lesser extent—syndicalist ideas, with its divisive consequences for national labor movements, that captures the central dynamic of labor movement history in industrialized countries during the 1920s and early 1930s, then the counterpart dynamic for the period between 1935 and 1945 is the movement toward political and organizational unity at both the domestic and the international level. The primary catalyst for this reversal of direction was the threat of fascism, a term that I use somewhat loosely here to refer to the hyper-nationalist totalitarian and quasi-totalitarian regimes that came into being in Germany, Italy, and Japan, along with movements elsewhere that espoused similar principles. In countries where fascist regimes were in power, and in countries under Axis occupation, the independent labor unions were broken up and workers were forcibly incorporated into authoritarian labor fronts, and the political parties associated with them were either driven underground or incapacitated through repression. Fascist repression of labor movements, however, set in motion a dialectic that caused the movements to be transformed into broad antifascist coalitions—appropriately referred to in the European context as the Resistance. Participation in a common struggle against fascism took a significant portion of the energy that had earlier gone into internecine struggle and redirected it first against the common enemy of fascism and then, once fascism was defeated, into a program of postwar reform and reconstruction combined with a vigilance against reaction.

It was symptomatic of the character of the European labor movements that their ineffectiveness against the rise of fascism was not the result of nonrecognition of the threat posed—for it was acknowledged very early in the game—but rather the consequence of mutually contradictory interpretations of how to deal with it. Social democrats placed utmost priority on the maintenance of parliamentary democratic institutions and were willing to countenance major political sacrifices in defense of these democratic institutions. The more combative left socialists, by contrast, emphasized the need to hold a firm "class" line and to mobilize a united front against the fascists. The communists, believing fascism signaled capitalism's demise, saw value in hastening its spread. Christian trade unions tended either to stand aloof or to welcome the perceived corporatist inclinations of fascism, thereby further undercutting unity in the labor movement.

Internal divisions among labor movements and the resulting dysfunctionality and vulnerability in the face of fascist threat had been demonstrated early on in Italy, where internal bickering and hesitancy on the part of the large and influential socialist movement paved the way for the rise to power of Benito Mussolini and his Fascist movement in the mid-1920s. With the consolidation of Mussolini's Fascist dictatorship in 1922, independent trade unions disappeared from Italy proper, and the respective wings of the labor movement were forced to pursue in exile what activities they could. If the paralysis stemming from social democratic–communist rivalry in the working-class movement facilitated the rise of Italian fascism, the same rivalry led to outright communist complicity in the rise of Nazism in early 1930s Germany. The KPD (Communist Party) defined the "social fascism" of the SPD (Social Democratic Party) to be a greater threat to the working class than were the Nazis, and it was this argument that provided the rationale for a KPD vote against the SPD-supported government that set the stage for Hitler's dictatorship. Conditions in France made the threat of fascism less severe, but the social democrats, the communists, and the Christian labor movement there nevertheless differed dramatically in their interpretations of what fascism represented.[18]

It was Hitler's repression of the left and the threat of Nazi-German territorial expansion across Europe that helped initiate a decade-long trend—shaky and reversible at first—toward unity in Western European working-class movements. Initially, the most visible signs of a turnaround were in the international labor movement. The subject of what the Labor and Socialist International should do in response to the establishment of a fascist regime in the center of Europe was considered at its Paris conference in August 1933. Following extensive debate, the social democrats and left socialists in the LSI ironed out a common position that was codified in a resolution entitled "The Strategy and Tactics of the International Labour Movement during the Period of Fascist Reaction." The resolution was structured around two themes. First, referring to the various state-interventionist economic reforms that were adopted in leading countries in response to the Depression, the resolution posited, "The world crisis has already profoundly changed the structure of the capitalist economy. The liberal and individualist phase in the evolution of capitalism has come to an end. Under the pressure of the crisis a controlled, organized and monopolized capitalism is developing with increasing rapidity." This development, it argued, constituted a historical opportunity. That is, "the new forms of state-controlled and organized economy may serve to prepare the transition from capitalism to Socialism." However—and this was the second theme stressed in the resolution—it also emphasized that, "as an effect of the economic crisis, democracy has been severely shaken in those countries where it had not yet become firmly rooted before the war." The "terrorist despotism" that had been constructed in Germany was cited as the prime example of this phenomenon. Although restricted at the time to just two countries in Europe, fascism was characterized as a much broader—indeed, global—threat: "Fascism tends to gather together all the national forces under the direction of a tyrannical power in order to marshal them against other nations. This increases the danger of a new world war, which would involve the complete downfall of civilization." The LSI resolution called on "all peoples to join the International in this struggle against Fascism, against War and against what is at the root of Fascism and War—the inhumanity of the capitalist regime."[19] The resolution, in short, marked an important watershed in that it identified fascism as a direct threat to labor movements worldwide and articulated a tendency in labor movement thinking that would become increasingly pronounced in the ensuing years—namely, the fusion of the struggle against fascism and the effort to reform capitalism.

For all the alarm expressed, however, the measures in the resolution were decidedly moderate in nature. For instance, there was nothing more concrete relating to assisting the German working class in a "revolution" against the Nazi regime than that "all the socialist parties are to give expression to their solidarity with the victims of Fascism" via relief work and a "moral and material boycott of Hitlerism." A large amount of text was in fact devoted to encouraging labor movements to take measures that would avoid war at all costs. "The workers of the democratic countries must not submit to the temptation of the ideas of war," the resolution stated.[20] As the subsequent fate of diplomatic appeasement policies toward Hitler would show—policies for which social democrats were prime backers—the responses put forward by the LSI would prove to be ineffective.

The realization by the Soviet leadership under Joseph Stalin that Hitler constituted a threat to the Soviet Union itself pushed the international communist movement over the threshold to the point where the threat of fascism began to be perceived as greater than that of the social democrats. Indications that a shift was under way in the international communist movement were already apparent in the autumn of 1934 when the communists began emphasizing left-wing unity in the wake of the republican uprising in Spain. The emerging stance was formalized at the seventh Comintern congress, in July 1935. A resolution adopted there replaced the preceding line of giving priority to the fight against the social democrats' "social fascism" with one calling for "a new kind of United Front tactics" in which "the greatest and most pressing duty of the international labor movement in the recent period of history is to restore workers' unity in action."[21] The key elements in this "new kind of United Front tactics" were threefold. First, the new "front" would expand beyond the traditional base of working-class socialist and communist movements to include various other "democratic forces" opposed to fascism. Ideologically, the new strategy would involve postponing the goal of revolution, at least until the immediate task of defeating fascism and reaction were achieved. And with respect to tactics, revolutionary rhetoric was to be toned down and communists were urged to actively cooperate with other groups in the "popular fronts."[22]

Among the earliest and most significant fruits of the Comintern's change of policy was the advance of the so-called Popular Front (Front Populaire) in France. The Popular Front encompassed Socialist and Communist Party affiliates, socialist and communist trade-union federations, a wide range of other mass organizations, and prominent intellectual and cultural figures. Formally inaugurated at an anti-Fascist mass demonstration in July 1935 on the anniversary of the storming of the Bastille, the roster of groups participating in the French Popular Front seemed to highlight the potential effectiveness of a social democratic–communist alliance as a mobilizing device.[23] The subsequent inauguration of a Popular Front coalition government under the Socialist Leon Blum, and the consequent passage of a wide range of pro-labor socioeconomic reforms under Blum's Popular Front government, seemed to further confirm the viability of socialist-communist unity. At the level of the international labor movement, social democrats and left socialists in the Socialist International and the IFTU were divided over how to respond to the new Comintern policy and its promotion of popular fronts. Eventually a resolution rooted in the long-standing principle of national party autonomy was settled upon. It was declared that popular fronts should be countenanced where such actions were deemed appropriate by the national organizations involved.

In August 1939 Stalin abruptly reversed course and signed a neutrality pact with Hitler. This was followed by an equally abrupt abandonment of the popular front by communist parties and trade unionists throughout Europe. The advance toward greater social democratic–communist unity was resumed, however, once communist policy reversed yet again with the German invasion of the USSR, in January 1941. With this, Soviet policy shifted to one of wholehearted cooperation with the Allies. At the national level, communists now participated in antifascist popular fronts with even greater enthusiasm. As Continental social democrats and communists were now fighting on the same side in a full-fledged war, the stage was set for further consolidation.

The impact of these developments was readily apparent in the international labor organizations.[24] Hitler's invasion of neighboring nations made it impossible for the social democratic organizations of the Continent that had previously dominated the IFTU to continue playing an active leadership role, and the IFTU headquarters was moved to London. This naturally increased the role and voice of the British trade-union movement. Unlike most Continental trade-union movements, the British unions had not divided into separate social democrat and communist organizations, and for that reason the British social-democratic-dominated Trades Union Congress (TUC) had, in the words of one observer, "fewer inhibitions than their European counterparts when it came to working for international links" and had even at one point during the 1920s approached Soviet trade unionists with a proposal for a joint organization.[25] Once the war began, it was initiatives on the part of UK, US, and Soviet trade unionists—all of whom had previously either not participated in (US and USSR) or stood somewhat aloof from (UK) the IFTU and were being encouraged by their respective governments to strengthen ties with Allied unionists—that set the stage for unification of the international labor movement across ideological boundaries. During the war, initiative in the international relations arena in the American labor movement that had earlier been dominated by the staunchly anticommunist (and arguably anti–social democrat) American Federation of Labor (AFL) began to be shared with the AFL's more left-leaning rival, the Congress Industrial Organizations (CIO). The Soviets were altering their stance vis-à-vis the capitalist world. Perhaps the most symbolic gesture in this regard was Stalin's dissolutions of the Comintern and Profintern, in 1943.

The coordinated effort of trade-union representatives from the three countries resulted in invitations being sent for an international trade-union conference, scheduled for June 5, 1944, in London. At this conference, which was attended by 63 organizations from 46 countries, representing an estimated 60 million rank-and-file unionists, the decision was made to establish a world trade-union federation that would encompass all competing labor-movement currents. The upshot was the inaugural congress of the World Federation of Trade Unions (WFTU), held in Paris in September 1945. The WFTU claimed to represent some 67 million workers from labor's political spectrum. The selection of French left-socialist Louis Saillant to head the new organization symbolized where the ideological center of gravity in the international labor movement had come to rest. Given the developments leading up to its creation, it was entirely appropriate that one of the key figures involved described the establishment of the WFTU in the following manner: "The progress of the common struggle of the United States, Britain, the Soviet Union and the other Allies . . . had given rise to a sentiment of international unity; feelings of allied solidarity were strengthened and a great hope swelled in all men's hearts."[26] The sentiments in favor of labor movement solidarity were supplemented in the WFTU by a requirement that only one organization be allowed to represent trade unionists in a single country.

The same geopolitical forces that were reshaping the international labor movement were also reconstituting labor movements at the national level, but in a way that varied in accordance with a nation's geopolitical location and historical trajectory. In France the PCF's turn to a pro-Hitler stance led to the Communists being kicked out of the CGT in September 1939. While most social democrats urged resistance against Hitler, the communists remained passive. The Germans invaded France in May 1940. The pro-fascist Vichy regime, established in the wake of the German invasion of France, abolished the CGT and replaced it with a closely supervised labor-front organization. Certain social democrats began setting up an underground resistance at this time. It was not until after the German invasion of the Soviet Union in early 1941 that French communists established a separate resistance organization. The Catholic Church, in the meantime, maintained a cooperative stance vis-à-vis the Vichy regime.

The sociopolitical milieu of workers in occupied France was one in which, in the words of one study of the labor movement in the coal mines, "patriotic sentiment became inextricably connected with class struggle" as the connection between the harsh wartime working conditions and political repression made apparent "the linkages between economic exploitation and political collaboration."[27] To the extent that they were able to function, the trade unions operating illegally and underground acted as de facto arms of a guerrilla movement while displaced workers joined the ranks of the Resistance armies. When the Germans began forcibly transporting French workers to German factories, this watershed decision, perhaps more than any other during the war, sent great numbers of French workers into the maquis. The power of the nationalism being fostered was such that even members of the Christian wing of the labor movement proved willing to turn their backs on the pro-Vichy dictates of the Catholic Church. Not surprisingly, it was the Communists, with their acculturation in a movement devoted to fomenting insurrectionary revolution, who were most effective in taking political advantage of these conditions. In the process, the PCF evolved over the course of a few short years from a discredited and marginal force into a major presence in the French Resistance.

As the Resistance expanded, its variegated political components began to meld, albeit not to the point where class and ideological identifications disappeared. A unified umbrella organ for the French Resistance, whose "membership ranged from the far left through the centre to the patriotic right," was established in May 1943 in the form of the Conseil National de la Resistance (CNR). In March of the following year, the CNR, as a self-proclaimed government-in-exile, adopted a program for postwar reconstruction based on a Socialist draft.[28] As for the trade unions, social democrat and communist cooperation in the Resistance laid the groundwork for an "annulment" of the 1939 expulsion of the Communists from the CGT and through this the CGT once again became a unified organization that encompassed both the Communists and the Socialists. Following the Allied forces' advance in the wake of the Normandy landing, the CNR was installed as the de facto government of France, in 1944, and it was the CNR's reconstruction program drafted by the Socialists that was eventually implemented by the coalition.

As previously noted, following World War I the Italian socialists fissured into three competing streams with the January 1921 formation of the Communist Party and the October 1922 expulsion of the party's reformist wing. The Italian labor movement proved defenseless in the face of Mussolini's advancing Fascism. However, as one observer of the Italian situation described it, "after such a disaster the disagreements over ideology and tactics which had been the cause of the schism became insignificant when, under conditions of exile, the task was clearly to mobilize all anti-Fascist forces in the struggle against the regime in Italy."[29] In a development in 1927 that presaged the formation of a similar coalition in France, exiled left socialists, social democrats, middle-class Republican figures, and representatives of the Italian trade-union federation formed an antifascist coalition based in Paris. In 1930 the left socialists reunited with the social democrats in a single party-in-exile that affiliated with the Socialist International. An initial linkup with the Communists was attained via an August 1934 agreement on "united action" following the Comintern's adoption of its popular-front line. Like other popular fronts established at that time, the Concentrazione Antifascista collapsed temporarily, following the conclusion of the Nazi-Soviet pact, in the summer of 1939.

As in France, the dislocations and severe conditions that workers faced in Italy set the foundation for their mobilization into the underground Resistance, while the German occupation of northern Italy beginning in September 1943 provided the catalyst for a sharp jump in numbers.[30] The Committee for National Liberation (Comitato di Liberazione Nationale, or CLN), the counterpart of the French CNR, based in the "liberated" southern half of the country, was established on July 26, 1943, and encompassed all of the wings of the active Resistance. As was true of the CNR, the CLN brought together the Socialists, the Communists, the Christians, and the bourgeois anti-Fascist parties. A formal "pact of alliance" was concluded between the Socialists and the Communists a year later. In the German-occupied northern part of the country, joint strikes, sabotage, and guerilla warfare were directed against the Germans by Socialist, Communist, and Christian Democratic partisans. Unity in the trade-union movement was attained with the establishment of the Confederazione Generale Italiana del Lavoro (CGIL), in June 1944, as a common labor federation encompassing the Socialist, Communist, and Christian unionists.

The German variant

A distinguishing feature of the German situation early in this period, by contrast, was the absence of a resistance movement comparable to that in France and Italy. There were, to be sure, anti-Nazi German partisans in exile, and there were inside Germany sporadic acts of resistance to the Nazi regime, but none of this was on the scale of, for instance, the estimated one-to-two-hundred-thousand-strong partisan forces active in Yugoslavia and Italy.[31] This difference had much to do with Germany's differing geohistorical location. Totalitarian fascism manifested itself in Germany in its most extreme form, and during the 1940s the country was the pivotal Axis power. Through such brutal tactics as the arrest, incarceration, and murder of tens of thousands activists and suspected activists, the Nazis had by the mid-1930s preemptively suppressed virtually all organized mass resistance by the Socialists and the Communists, who in the past had together attracted more than 40 percent of the German electorate's support. The severity of the Nazis' suppression of different wings of the labor movement also happened to correlate with the degree to which these elements actively participated in the armed Resistance elsewhere. Thus, the Communists, the pivotal force in the post-Resistance polity elsewhere, "became the object of the most merciless and radical persecution by the Nazis."[32] Beyond this, one can point to the isolation of Jews in concentration camps and the methodical execution of an estimated 6 million of their number as a further instance of systematic and ruthless suppression of a potential popular base for a mass resistance movement. The consequence of this suppression was that "by the end of this period, the risks involved in resistance, or even in offering the most passive aid to the resistance, had become so great that the hardy political activists still willing to put their lives on the line had been effectively cut off from the bulk of their former supporters." As a result, "this split between class and cadre was to remain the central structural feature of the workers' resistance until 1945."[33] All of this forestalled the development in Germany of precisely the kinds of ties between partisans and labor unions that defined the basic character of the postwar labor movement in France and Italy.

Of similar consequence was a second reason for the relative underdevelopment of the German resistance movement. Whereas elsewhere in Europe the Resistance was directed against foreign occupiers and their domestic collaborators, any German resistance movement constituted by nature internal resistance. This denied the German movement the ability to capitalize on nationalistic mass sentiment. (On this point, one might note that the Italian Resistance did not take on a truly mass quality until after the Germans expanded their occupation of that country in the fall of 1943.) It was precisely for this reason that those individuals who were active in the German anti-Nazi movement referred to their activities at the time as "opposition" rather than "resistance."[34] As Charles Maier argues, whereas in other parts of Europe clandestine resistance was accompanied by "bonding" and "fraternity," for German resistors the same activities were "atomizing," and were characterized by "loneliness" and "a separation from one's countrymen." Germany's sociopolitical milieu was thus not conducive to forging political alliances of the sort that characterized the Resistance coalition era of France and Italy.[35]

The German political-historical situation, furthermore, was such that postwar initiatives paralleling in spirit those of the Resistance in France were prevented from belatedly being translated into concrete institutional renovations. So-called "antifa" (antifascist) movements rooted in the same sociological and political categories that had constituted the base of the French and Italian Resistance arose in Germany in the wake of the advancing Allied armies in 1945. Unlike their French and Italian counterparts to whom the advancing Allied armies handed over the reins of government, the German antifa groups were subjected to a ban on political activity and prohibited from forming political groups.[36] This action, as Diethelm Prowe argues, affected elements among the anti-Nazi movement differentially. Specifically, it "hampered political organization primarily on the left" and favored moderate, established politicians because it "hit precisely where the left's greatest strength lay, namely in the mobilization of masses." Within the left, this policy hit the Communists the hardest since as we have seen, systematic, party-directed mass mobilization, particularly in the labor movement, was at the heart of the Communists' method of expanding their influence.[37] The policy was somewhat less catastrophic for the German social democrats since many had managed to insert themselves into the political establishment during the Weimar years and were thus among the pool of experienced administrators that the military governments favored when appointing officials to staff local administrative and advisory offices. The ban on political activities was not lifted until late in 1945, and only at the local level even then, while the country as a whole was divided into four independent Allied military government sectors. Given these substantial differences in context, it is hardly surprising that the structure and dynamics of the German labor movement in the immediate postwar years, though stemming from similar political-historical roots, should diverge in critical ways from that of France and Italy.

Chapter 2

The Labor Movement in Interwar and Wartime Japan, 1920–1945

Prior to World War I, the Japanese labor movement—or, more accurately, Japanese workers and their would-be leaders— resided outside the sphere of influence of the Marxism-centered labor unionisms around which the labor movements of Continental Europe evolved. Until about half a century earlier Japan had existed outside of the realm of Western European civilization and thus well beyond the boundaries of European labor-movement ideational influence. This relative isolation from Western civilization disappeared during the latter half of the nineteenth century as Japanese elites engaged in a concerted effort to modernize the country through the systematic importation of Western science, technology, and selected social institutions. Even under these circumstances, however, there were factors that worked against the importation and application of those modes of thought associated with European labor movements. Prior to World War I there was relatively little of the interaction between social- ist parties and trade union organizations that had served as the sociopolitical soil in which European Marxian socialist practice flourished. Unions had appeared in Japan as early as the 1880s but did not take lasting root. One contributing factor here was the timing of industrialization in Japan, which prior to World War I was still an overwhelmingly agrarian country with limited manufacturing and a demographically small working class. Instead of male factory workers and skilled craftsmen, who were the mainstay of the labor movement in Europe, workers in Japan's factories were mostly young, single females who maintained ties to their homes in the villages in the countryside and typically quit factory work upon marriage.[1] However, Japan's late industrialization was clearly not the sole reason for the nondevelopment of a Marxian-oriented labor movement since, as the Eastern European and Russian experiences make clear, ideas could spread and impact societies even in the absence of an identical, material base. A more proximate reason one could point to is the controls placed by the state on ideology and organization that constrained the spread of the kinds of ideas and practices found in European movements at the time. Specifically, socialist thought had been introduced into Japan in the late nineteenth century but remained largely a subject of academic research. There was a social gap separating Japanese socialist intellectuals and the working-class base that discouraged the dovetailing of ideology and organization. Article 17 of the 1900 Peace Police Law outlawed labor unions and potentially subjected all working-class political activity to severe state sanctions. Ever-vigilant state authorities were quick to stamp out any moves to translate socialist ideas into political action, as occurred when the first socialist political party was forcibly disbanded a year after its establishment in 1907. Even greater repression followed in the wake of the Great Treason Incident of 1910, in which a group of anarchists were alleged by authorities to have plotted to assassinate the emperor.

To the extent that there was an influential body of thought in the labor sphere, it was the Christian humanism imported via individuals returning to Japan from the United States. A considerable number of the most important leaders of the early Japanese labor movement were Christians despite the fact that the number of Christians in Japan was miniscule. One factor at work here, no doubt, was the perception by Meiji state officials that Christian activists were a moderate and benign group who did not pose the kind of threat to the existing state-centered sociopolitical order that socialists and anarchists did. Furthermore, as was true in Western Europe, Christian doctrine and thought resonated well with traditional, preindustrial ethics, and there was a comforting parallel between the organic conception of class relations associated with Christian views and the paternalistic conception of industrial relations being advanced by the Japanese state and business community.[2] In any event, in the absence of a framework of discourse through which to comprehend the new reality, and without the outlet of formal institutions for political participation and organizational vehicles for pressing demands in the workplace, the primary modalities for the collective expression of worker grievances were periodic spontaneous strikes, and mass gatherings and riots of the "urban crowd."[3]

World War I precipitated changes, however, that brought both the socioeconomic base and the ideological environment of the Japanese labor movement closer to those of its leading Western European counterparts. With regard to the former, the war resulted in a dramatic leap in industrialization as Japanese manufacturers jumped to fill the void left in Asia by European exporters overwhelmed by the war effort at home. Secondary-sector employment jumped from 4.9 to 6.3

million (out of an employed population of 27.1 million) between 1915 and 1920, with the highest rate of increase in the heavy- and chemical-industry sector.[4] Economic growth induced the movement of population from the countryside to the city. Growth was particularly conspicuous in the male blue-collar segment in large modern factories, and in the transport and communications sectors, both of which have been among the most hospitable sectors for trade-union organization worldwide. The number of labor disputes increased dramatically over the course of the war years and culminated in the peak that marked 1919–1920. Unions were now frequently involved. The number of unions, in turn, grew despite their technical illegality, and as time passed, they consolidated into more inclusive units. All of this was facilitated by the loosened grip of the Meiji oligarchy over the polity and society, which allowed for initiatives from the bottom up.

For the same reason, the years immediately following World War I were also a period of great ferment intellectually, as new ideas relating to the organization and strategy of working-class movements began to be more widely disseminated and applied. By this time the Meiji government's initiation of universal primary education was beginning to bear fruit in the form of a literate population. Newspapers became widely available by the end of 1921, and there was a veritable publishing revolution that allowed for the mass distribution of imported ideologies. Various flavors of social and political thought imported from the West—ranging from liberalism and conservatism on the right to communism and anarchism on the left—circulated widely. And in contrast to their earlier isolation, intellectuals took an increasingly active role in the leadership of the trade-union movement.[5]

At the core of the Japanese labor movement's emergence as a true mass movement, but never fully encompassing it, was the Yūaikai. At its point of origin, the Yūaikai exemplified the qualities of pre–World War I Japanese labor. Established by Suzuki Bunji, a Christian and a graduate of the elite Tokyo Imperial University who had personal connections with the political and business establishments, it began as a "friendly society" devoted to worker education, self-improvement, and the mediation of labor disputes. It started out in 1912 with just thirteen workers and mushroomed to 30,000 by 1919.[6] Two groups were particularly critical in engineering the transformation of the "friendly society" into a bona fide trade-union organization. One of these consisted of socialistically oriented intellectuals ranging from "veteran" socialists of the 1900s to students from political study societies at Tokyo and Waseda universities who joined the Yūaikai and began to play a prominent role in its national leadership. Individuals in this category who would subsequently become key figures in the pre– and post–World War II labor movements include the left socialist Takano Minoru and the future communist Nosaka Sanzō. The other was a group of new leaders among the "genuine" workers in the organization, who began to actively involve themselves in the labor movement during the expansionary years of World War I. Nishio Suehiro and Matsuoka Komakichi, both of whom would become prominent leaders in the Japanese social democratic camp, were the most prominent individuals in this category.

Infusion of these elements into the Yūaikai catalyzed the melding of political ideology and trade-union organization into a bona fide mass-based movement comparable to the mainstream of Western Europe's unionism. Organizational restructuring of the Yūaikai in 1919 transferred power from Suzuki to a larger group of trade-union leaders, accompanied by a change in name from Yūaikai to Sōdōmei, with the full designation of Nihon Rōdō Kumiai Sōdōmei Yūaikai, or General Confederation of Labor-Friendly Society. The "friendly society" (Yūaikai) designation was dropped entirely from the full name two years later as the organization put forward a class-conflict-oriented vision, which was succinctly described in a widely quoted passage of the 1922 Sōdōmei platform: "We believe that the worker and capitalist class cannot coexist. Through the strength of trade unions we shall press for the complete emancipation of the working class and the construction of a new society of liberty and equality."[7] The language of transformative socialism infused not only the leadership of the labor movement but also the day-to-day thoughts and expressions of the rank-and-file industrial workers.[8] This opened the way for Sōdōmei and other union organizations of varying stripes to coalesce in a loose umbrella organization, the Rōdō Kumiai Dōmeikai, or Labor Union League. It was during this same period that a coalition of individuals therein attempted to establish a political arm, Shakaishugi Dōmei, or Socialist League, although police repression prevented it from developing into a very active organization.

The transition from a relatively inclusive but tentatively united mass labor movement to one characterized by competition between social democratic and communist ideologies proceeded rapidly between 1920 and 1925, and by the end of the decade, one could easily identify in Japan's labor movement the same ideological currents that were animating Europe's. Details of this transition are well-documented elsewhere and are therefore presented here only in skeletal form.[9] The first step in this transition involved a break with anarcho-syndicalist elements inside Sōdōmei, which was more or less completed by 1922, when anarchism had disappeared almost completely as an active organized component of the movement. Following the demise of the anarchists, schisms in the movement during the 1920s and 1930s were centered around the social democrat–communist rivalry. A major split occurred in May 1925 with the expulsion of the communists from Sōdōmei, spearheaded by Japanese social democrats. The communists went on to form their own union organization, the Hyōgikai. This occurred just as the Comintern was about to direct communist infiltration of Sōdōmei, subsequently leading to attempts by the Japanese communists to forge a united front with Sōdōmei. In the meantime, a group of left-socialist unionists bolted from Sōdōmei and formed a national organization of their own called the Nihon Rōdō

Kumiai Dōmei (Federation of Japanese Labor Unions) during the summer of 1926. The upshot of all of this was separate unions associated with social democracy (Sōdōmei), left socialism (Nihon Rōdō Kumiai Dōmei), and communism (Hyōgikai).

The one element of the European labor movement that on the surface appears to be missing from the Japanese stage at that time was a readily identifiable Christian current. But, as noted, Christian unionists were active in the social democratic camp well in excess of their share of the general population. One important background factor at work was the absence in Japan of an independent and influential clerical hierarchy clearly associated with this mode of thought and, as a product of this, the absence of a heritage of clerical-anticlerical confrontation of the sort that had animated European society and politics for nearly a century by then. This difference allowed for a much easier coexistence of moderate social democracy and corporatist tendencies in the Japanese case. In line with this, it is possible to detect within the social democratic wing of the Japanese labor movement an ideological tendency that favored a class-collaborative, corporatist form of labor-capital relations paralleling in spirit that of the European Catholic movement.[10]

The formation of a "labor party" became a highly topical issue after legislation was finally passed in 1925 granting all males the right to vote. This presented to respective wings of the labor movement opportunity to pursue their goals through the ballot box. Despite universally voiced support for the principle of a single working-class party, the existence of separate union organizations and the severity of ideological rivalry made this all but impossible. Four separate ostensibly proletarian parties emerged that represented the social democratic persuasion, a moderate left-socialist persuasion, a second more radically oriented left-socialist group, and an underground communist party. These were the Social Mass Party (Shakai Minshūtō), the Japan Labor Farmer Party (Nihon Rōdō Nōmintō), the Labor Farmer Party (Rōnōtō), and the Japan Communist Party (Nihon Kyōsantō), or JCP, respectively (see table 3). The social democrats, wary of a communist commandeering of a common proletarian party, had initiated the schism by creating the Social Mass Party based on staunchly social-democratic principles. The communists, whose previous efforts to launch a permanent political party had been nipped in the bud by the Japanese police, continued trying under the guidance of the Comintern. Ongoing repression, however, made this exceedingly difficult, and the Japan Communist Party remained an on-again, off-again underground organization. Japanese left socialists, as was true of their counterparts in Europe, found themselves whipsawed by the ongoing confrontation between the social democrats and the communists. One group—referred to in Japan as the center faction of the proletarian movement—parted company with the dominant social democrats in Sōdōmei and the Social Mass Party and coalesced around a middle-ground left-socialist party known as the Japan Labor Farmer Party.

Another group of left socialists parted company with communists loyal to the Comintern over the issue of creating a bona fide communist party. In their interpretation, coalescence around a party openly associated with the international communist movement would simply invite counterproductive repression that would delay progress in advancing the working-class movement. What they argued for instead was a confrontational "legal left" strategy that would pursue radical tactics within the limits of the law both inside and outside Japan's national legislature, the Diet. The rallying point for this group of left socialists was the Labor Farmer Party.

Like their counterparts elsewhere, the Japanese social democrats eschewed revolutionary politics and adhered to a political line that emphasized working for reform within the confines of the existing order. As in Europe, this was based on the perception that the "liberal" and "democratic" tendencies of the regime offered reasonably promising opportunities to attain working-class goals. However, it deserves pointing out that certain features of Japan's political institutions encouraged a brand of reformism on the part of Japanese social democrats that was less exclusively wedded to the defense of parliamentary democratic institutions than was the norm in Western Europe. This was because the "democratization" of the interwar Japanese polity occurred without a fundamental change in the preexisting institutional structure of emperor-centered bureaucratic rule. From a comparative standpoint, this was no doubt due to the fact that thanks to its sociopolitical distance from the battlefields of World War I, Japan had not experienced the regime-overturning turmoil of the sort that Germany, for instance, had. The social and political disturbances were significant but containable for the time

Table 3. Union-party alignments in Japan late 1920s

Alignment	Ideological category			
	Social democratic	Left socialist		Communist
Union	Sōdōmei (Japan General Confederation of Labor-Friendly Society) and others	Nihon Rōdō Kumiai Dōmei (Federation of Japanese Labor Unions)		Hyōgikai (Council of Japanese Trade Unions)
Party	Shakai Minshūtō (Social Mass Party) *120,039	Nihon Rōdō Nōmintō (Japan Labor Farmer Party) *85,698	Rōnōtō (Labor Farmer Party) *193,047	Nihon Kyōsantō (Japan Communist Party) JCP underground

*Numbers refer to votes received in the 1928 general election.
Source: Nishida Yoshiaki, "Labour and Farmers' Movements in Prewar Japan," in *The Political Economy of Japanese Society: The State or the Market?* ed. Banno Junji (Oxford and London: Oxford University Press), 1: 238.

being through delimited reform within the framework of the emperor-centered authoritarian regime based on the Meiji constitution. The result was quite appropriately characterized by one historian as "imperial democracy."[11] Thus, although the influence and role of political parties represented in the Diet expanded dramatically under imperial democracy, the Diet's powers remained significantly circumscribed, and the imperial bureaucracy and spokesmen for the throne remained in a position to circumvent legislation passed by the Diet. As a consequence, the survival of a liberal- or reformist-policy orientation among bureaucratic agencies was as—if not more—important in assuring the advance of working-class-oriented reform than was access to a parliamentary majority. In Japan the incompleteness of representative democracy thus made it sensible for the social democrats to concentrate on their prior objective of squeezing out of the system institutional reforms that would give the labor movement a meaningful voice.[12]

Internally, in a manner characteristic of post–World War I European social democracy, Japanese social democrats argued for a relationship of relative independence between the trade unions and the proletarian parties. As one source ably summarizes the Japanese social-democratic position: "The duties of labor unions . . . were to improve working conditions, obtain wage increases, demand protection against unemployment, secure adequate labor legislation, and tackle the problems of old age and retirement. . . . Ample strike funds had to be accumulated, and the loyalty of the workers had to be secured. Though unions should engage in politics, the functions of unions and political parties should be kept separate and distinct."[13] A rigid anticommunism, forcefully expressed in the expulsion of communists from Sōdōmei in 1925, was a further key component of the moderated unionism that the Japanese social democrats pursued.

Despite these parallels in ideological orientation, it is noteworthy that Japan's social democratic organizations were not affiliated with the Second International or the IFTU. One obvious obstacle was the expense—substantial, but by no means insurmountable—of maintaining links with a movement headquartered half a world away. Beyond that, the Second International did not actively court non-European movements, owing to the continuing belief that a true socialist movement could not be expected in preindustrial societies of the sort that characterized Asia generally.[14] Japan, of course, was the notable exception to this general Asian condition. But as George Totten suggests, Japanese social democrats were reluctant to openly affiliate, fearing mistrust on the part of the Japanese government upon whose good faith they increasingly relied, in a context where representative democracy had not been fully institutionalized.[15] The Japanese social democrats did, however, consistently support and participate in the International Labor Organization (ILO), which was a relatively safe venue because access to the tripartite organization was mediated by the Japanese state.

The Communist International's stance toward relations with Asian labor movements contrasted sharply with that of the Second International. The Comintern had from its inception declared its support for the anticolonial movements in Asia and pursued various initiatives specifically aimed at fostering and assisting these movements. Japan was given particular stress in the Comintern Asia policy because it was considered "to be in a revolutionary key position in the Far East." In the words of Comintern president Grigori Zinoviev: "If Marx had once said that without a revolution in England any revolution in Europe would be no more than an insignificant storm in a tea-cup . . . , then we must say that, without a revolution in Japan, any revolution in the Far East must remain only a local concern, a relatively unimportant storm in a relatively small tea-cup."[16] Unfortunately for the international communist movement, there were formidable obstacles to the effective integration of the Japanese communists into the global movement, the biggest being the severe, legally sanctioned state suppression of communist activity that dogged the party from its inception.[17] The first Comintern-sanctioned party was secretly established on July 5, 1922, and its first "congress" was held ten days later, at which point the party had a membership of forty. However, that party was effectively destroyed by mass arrests in June of the following year. Although already substantial, the legal mechanisms at the disposal of the Japanese state in attacking the communists were strengthened tremendously by the 1925 Peace Preservation Law. The law imposed stiff sentences on anyone advocating a "modification of the national polity" (interpreted at the time as advocating destruction of the imperial institution) or the abolition of private property, both of which were central pillars of the JCP platform. The Peace Preservation Law opened the way for further massive arrests of communists and suspected communists on March 15, 1928, and in April the following year. Although clandestine party activity continued, these arrests dealt the party a severe blow.[18] Beyond outright repression by the state, the party's development was hampered by the Comintern itself through its miscommunications, misunderstandings, and miscues. As Comintern directives to the Japanese branch zigzagged in response to changes in the political situation in Moscow, the JCP alienated would-be supporters and undercut the effectiveness of the Japanese communist movement.[19]

Reflecting Comintern policy, the Hyōgikai took the offensive not only against the social democrats but also potentially sympathetic left socialists as well. In the words of one affiliate, the party was "opposed to the skeletal social democracy of the Sōdōmei, but . . . also opposed to labor movements like that sponsored by the Rōnō Taishūtō (the left socialist Labor-Farmer Mass Party), which spoke like the Left but dedicated itself to the anti-CP cause."[20] Internally, the communists preferred the top-down "democratic centralist" mode of organization and communication, with communist cells in unions and other mass organizations operating in accordance with directives from the party. Unions and strike activity were valued by the Hyōgikai and the JCP for their political educational function rather than as vehicles for attaining concrete gains "within the system."

Of the respective currents, left socialists were the most heavily laced with intellectuals. Among the prominent left socialists who would subsequently play important roles in the post–World War II labor movement were Yamakawa Hitoshi, Arahata Kanson, Suzuki Mosaburō, and Katō Kanjū. Thanks to prolific publishing, their public influence and presence far outstripped their meager organizational base. Like the communists, the Japanese left socialists believed that the consciousness of the Japanese masses was backward and that it was the role of a well-attuned vanguard to devise ways to "channel the most radical sections of labor and the tenant farmers into legally permissible courses of action."[21] Unlike the communists, however, they were staunch advocates of the principle that national conditions varied, and for that reason appropriate revolutionary strategy had to be derived not from the directives of the headquarters of an international movement but from a careful analysis of the distinctive conditions of Japan. Another characteristic that Japan's left socialists shared with their European counterparts was the belief that a more powerful stimulus than simply working within the parliamentary system was required to bring about the desired sociopolitical transformation. They felt that under current Japanese conditions it was sensible from a tactical perspective to restrict activities primarily to technically legal means.[22] Whereas the social democrats tended to be staunchly anticommunist, the left-socialist emphasis on the need for a "united front" allowed for the inclusion of communists when circumstances were judged to be appropriate for such an alliance.[23]

As in Europe, precisely who the priority partner should be in the ongoing feud between the communists and the social democrats was a matter of controversy among Japanese left socialists and provided fodder for complicated factional realignments. In the Japanese context, the left socialists tended to subdivide into two identifiable groupings that reflected the pull of the two poles of social democracy and communism—the social-democratic-leaning "center" and the communist-leaning "legal left." The left socialists were a small enough group that personality issues at the leadership level profoundly affected organizational arrangements within the current. As a consequence, the left-socialist tendency in Japan was manifested in a wide and fractious collection of groups that resulted in a shifting kaleidoscope of separate right-leaning, left-leaning, and independent groups.

By the end of the decade following World War I, then, a Western European labor activist dropped into the middle of the Japanese labor movement milieu would have found the terrain rather familiar. The ideologically based divisions that were characteristic of the leading Western European labor movements had taken root in Japan, setting in motion similar political and interorganizational dynamics, including shared modes of conceptualizing, strategizing, and organization. Having said this, I hasten to add that Japan of the 1920s gave a distinctive cast to the labor movement and its environment. First, Japanese industrialization was more limited than that of France, Germany, and even Italy, thus the relative demographic significance of the working class for the nation's politics and economy was less. Even at its peak in 1931, union density, or the percentage of the workforce that was unionized, was just 7.9 percent, and even that number tends to overstate the breadth of the labor organization. Just over 40 percent of Japan's organized workers were in the transport and communications sector, whose 29.8 percent union density marked the highest of any sector. Nearly three-quarters of these workers were members of the Seamen's Union (Kaiin Kumiai), which had attained a closed-shop contract with the Shipowners Association in 1926. If one excludes the seamen, then union density in the sector drops to around 10 percent, with the biggest bloc of the remaining unionists consisting of streetcar workers in the major urban centers. Union density in the manufacturing sector was just 8 percent, with a fifth of this group associated with the management-oriented "company unions" of the state armories.[24] In the Diet, the proletarian parties captured around 5 percent of the vote in national elections held during the decade between 1925 and 1935. With less than 2 percent of the seats in the Lower House of the Diet, these parties were hardly in a position to play the kind of central role in parliamentary politics that the social democratic parties of France, Germany, and Italy did.[25] Even had they obtained proportionate Diet seats the circumscribed nature of parliamentary democracy in Japan at the time would have profoundly limited the effectiveness of labor movement influence. And when compared to counterpart movements in Western Europe, the connection between the Japanese movement and the international labor movement was considerably looser. Finally, in part due to the absence of a pattern of Church-state tensions like those found in Europe, and due as well to the greater centrality of the Japanese state in the process of identity formation and development and the consequence to the underdevelopment of democratic institutions, the corporatist labor stream in the Japanese labor movement during the 1920s was less hampered by a connection to a particularistic religious outlook and arguably more strongly tied to the state than in Western Europe at the time. All of these have implications for the subsequent fate of the Japanese labor movement in the decade that followed.

The Japanese labor movement and fascism, 1930–1945

As in Europe, the arrival of the Great Depression and the rise of fascism in the early 1930s onward were interpreted by the respective wings of the Japanese labor movement in remarkably similar ways to their Western European counterparts.

In the eyes of many left socialists, the times required the consolidation of class power and influence via a broad united front. For the communists, what was required was heroic, radical actions that would disrupt the capitalist order and galvanize the working class into spontaneous revolt. By contrast, the dominant Japanese social democrats, though agreeing that capitalism was in crisis and that socialism was desirable as a future goal, were fearful that the conditions wrought by the economic crisis had given rise to a delicate situation in which overly aggressive action on the part of the labor movement would invite a dangerous reaction. Instead of confrontation, they advocated "the politics of compromise with capitalism and liberalism to help solve the momentous problems of the Depression." Tactically, they reacted in a manner that parallels that of the German social democrats' reaction to fascism—that is, they made painful compromises in an attempt to salvage what they could of the liberal character of the regime.[26]

The differing context of the incumbent regimes, however, led to a behavioral pattern that was somewhat different from the Western European norm. As discussed earlier, the liberal tendencies that were of greatest significance to the labor movement were not found in the Diet—where the basically antilabor Seiyūkai (the more conservative of the two "bourgeois" political parties that controlled the Diet) had gained a majority—but in the state bureaucracy and in particular in the reformist vector of the renovationist movement.[27] The essence of the resulting social democratic stance has been captured succinctly by Sheldon Garon: "Put simply, the labor leaders appropriated the language of the patriotic Right, asserting that the needs of national unity demanded that the state place unions on an equal level with capitalists. Although Sōdōmei and the Social [Mass] Party publicly opposed 'fascism,' they found the doctrine of national socialism useful in practice." Initially, the strategy was intended as a way of assuring the survival of independent labor organizations.[28] However, as the 1930s unfolded and the militarist ideology became official state doctrine, the autonomy and independence of all wings of the labor movement receded to the point that independent unionism disappeared altogether.

If passive acquiescence and incremental incorporation into the fascist order constituted the dominant trend in the Japanese labor movement, it was not the only one, and, in fact, initiatives were pursued that paralleled those that gained expression in the French Popular Front. Thus, in the early 1930s, in the midst of the Depression and amid waves of ultranationalist terrorism, a group of left socialists led by Katō Kanjū and Suzuki Mosaburō tried to use the newly organized National Labor Farmer Mass Party (Zenkoku Rōnō Taishūtō) to construct a broad antifascist united front that would resist militarism domestically and Japanese expansionism abroad.[29] When this failed as a consequence of defections, key leaders associated with this effort took refuge in a series of labor councils that eventually solidified, in the spring of 1931, into the National Council of Labor

Unions, or Sōhyō (later, Zenpyō).[30] A subsequent drive to create a broad party-based antifascist front, this time stimulated in part by communication with the French Popular Front, appeared in 1936 and evolved into the Japan Proletarian Party (Nihon Musantō). This effort, too, was frustrated, by a lack of support from mainstream social democrats and by state suppression through mass arrests of those involved in the so-called Popular Front Incident (Jinmin Sensen Jiken).[31] Consistent with the existence of left-socialist currents, then, an initiative on behalf of intercurrent unity was pursued enthusiastically by the left socialists in Japan as well. A key difference between Europe's and Japan's conditions was that the communists remained an inconsequential political force in Japan in the 1930s. A differing set of situational incentives induced the social democrats, on the other side of the would-be coalition, to eschew participation and adopt cooperation with the regime. Furthermore, to several prominent left socialists who broke away from Suzuki and Katō's popular-front initiative, the statist inclinations of fascist elements in the army and bureaucracy were read as indicators of a progressive force, inducing them to cast their lot with the militarists. For these reasons, the popular front in Japan was unable to gain momentum anywhere approaching that of the French Popular Front.

Crushing of the popular-front initiative was followed by accelerated displacement and eventual elimination of autonomous labor-movement organizations. Processes that were essentially identical in character to the forceful dismantling of the labor movement in both its trade-union and partisan dimensions in areas of Continental Europe controlled by fascist regimes occurred in Japan under the guise of the so-called Sampō, or Industrial Patriotic Associations. Ideologically, the Sampō movement, modeled after the Nazi Labor Front, was built around a systematic denial of the legitimacy of class interests in favor of a "labor-management unity" in which "both the enterprise owner and the employee become one" in pursuing "the ultimate mission of industry," which was "to contribute to prosperity of the Empire." The organizational expression of the Sampō movement was a hierarchy of "industrial patriotic associations" *(sangyō hōkoku kai)*. Mandatory at the plant level and consisting of appointed representatives from labor, management, and other areas of the enterprise "community," the Sampō organization constituted an archetypal "administered mass organization" whose aim was to undercut the influence of autonomous organizations that might interfere with the implementation of state policy and to assure the state the opportunity to mobilize a segment of the populace unobstructed.[32] A threshold point in the rise of the Sampō movement was reached in 1940 when an "economic new structure" *(keizai shin taisei)* was declared and the remaining autonomous trade unions, including the venerable Sōdōmei, were forcibly dissolved along with all independent business associations. These were replaced by 54,000 "industrial patriotic associations" encompassing 4.5 million members set up in firms and prefectures throughout the country. In practice, the Sampō associations functioned primarily as organs for exhorting workers to produce more. A parallel process unfolded in the arena of partisan politics with the rise of the administered mass organization in that sector, the Imperial Rule Assistance Association, or Taisei Yokusankai, and the tandem elimination of all independent political parties, including the Social Mass Party.

Wartime mobilization increased in intensity following the outbreak of war with China in 1937, and with it direct state administration was extended into a wide range of areas that were previously the province of either managerial discretion, the labor market, or, occasionally, collective bargaining. The National General Mobilization Law of 1938, in particular, granted extensive discretionary authority to state agencies to "control human and material resources." It ushered in a period of bureaucratic "rule by ordinance" during which the state took de facto control of the labor market through active intervention in corporate personnel recruitment, technical training and the setting of wages, work hours, and welfare. In addition to eliminating whatever limited influence autonomous unions had managed to gain in these areas, the process also systematically narrowed the range of independent authority exercised by management.

In the end, a distinguishing feature of Japan's condition at the time of its surrender on August 15, 1945, was the absence of a resistance movement such as those that had emerged in France and Italy. There was even less "space" for the development of a viable resistance movement with a mass working-class base in Japan than there was in Germany. As an industrialized island nation off the coast of a largely nonindustrialized and colonized continent, Japan's geographic location was not one that encouraged international linkages among comparably industrialized countries of the sort that sustained the Western European Resistance movements in exile. More proximately, the Japanese state's wartime containment and then repression of potential resistance to the regime was extremely thorough. Japan's communist party had for all practical intent and purpose been eliminated as a viable organization by the early 1930s, and its leadership languished in jail. The social democrats and left socialists who were allowed to operate prior to the complete dissolution of an organized opposition in 1940 did so under increasingly tight constraints. In this sense the Japanese situation was similar to Germany's, but in contrast to Germany, the dropping of atomic bombs on Hiroshima and Nagasaki in early August 1945 resulted in Japan's surrendering without an invasion of Japan proper. This meant that there was no opportunity to activate and mobilize latent resistance into a political-military force as happened in France and Italy and began to happen in Germany. The one exception of a sort was the small band of Japanese communists under Nosaka Sanzō that operated out of the

Chinese Communist base camp in Yenan. Though both the JCP and Nosaka would subsequently play an important role in the postwar labor movement, their impact on the course of events prior to Japan's surrender was negligible.

The conditions faced by the Japanese labor movement during the war thus resembled most closely that of its counterpart in Germany. The atomization that it experienced has been cogently described as follows:

> Although there were a few labor movement leaders and activists . . . who continued to be active even after the dissolution of the unions, most were unable to actively operate and spent their wartime days at their respective work sites, areas, and battlefronts. These were people who did not lose their consciousness as unionists, and there were many instances where they secretly or openly maintained contact with one another. In this sense, the heritage of the prewar movement did not disappear even during the Asia-Pacific War. However, at the same time, there is no denying that under the fascistic repression they remained inactive.
>
> As the degradation of living conditions progressed as a consequence of air raids and so on, spontaneous resistance spread among workers, but it was an extremely rare occurrence for the scattered activists to have harnessed, in the form of a movement, this dissatisfaction extant among the masses. Almost all Japanese workers experienced surrender on August 15, 1945, with virtually no subjective preparation.[33]

As in Germany, following Japan's surrender the country was placed under Allied occupation and this meant that the ultimate disposition and direction of postwar reform would be determined by the policies implemented by Allied occupation officials. Having said this, it must be stressed that there were important divergences in the way in which the two occupations were administered. First, Japan was occupied as a unit. A single power—the United States—was given virtually single-handed oversight of occupation administration in light of the overwhelmingly dominant role that American forces had played in the fighting in the Pacific. Japan therefore did not experience the kind of balkanization and decentralization of post-surrender reform and reconstruction that characterized the German experience. Even moreso than in the German occupation, it was American sensibilities about what was appropriate that set the general tone and parameters of the postwar reform process in Japan. A second difference was that the occupation of Japan was indirect rather than direct. That is, rather than having foreign military organizations take on the functions of government, Allied authorities chose to govern Japan indirectly, through the existing Japanese governmental apparatus. There were a number of reasons for this decision, although the primary one was shortage of personnel with requisite knowledge of Japan and ability in the Japanese language. The result, when leavened with the characteristically American emphasis on the democratic process, was a peculiar domestic political context in which the Occupation Forces, after an initial flurry of "democratization" reforms and demilitarization measures, encouraged "democratic" forces in Japanese society to mobilize politically against the old order. Political prisoners were released, restrictions on political activity were lifted, and trade unions were encouraged. Put in a conceptual language closer to that which held sway in the labor movement at the time, the reforms implemented by the Occupation Forces represented a uniquely incomplete "democratic revolution" in which the revolutionary subject deliberately stepped aside midway through the process.

Third, as a consequence, and in contrast to the German occupation experience, labor movement activists in Japan were in a position to—indeed, were encouraged to—organize and operate on a national scale. In part by intent and in part as a latent consequence of policies pursued for other purposes, the Americans also provided the Japanese labor movement with a target against which to direct its political energy. Specifically, the Americans considered the authoritarian Meiji constitution to be inappropriate for a newly democratized Japan and wanted a new, democratic constitution to be adopted, but in characteristic fashion, they wanted the process of its adoption to be "democratic." For that reason the Occupation Forces initially insisted that the Japanese themselves draft the new constitution. However, the several drafts that the Japanese government came up with failed to meet expectations and officials from the Supreme Commander of the Allied Powers (SCAP) Government Section ended up writing the new constitution themselves.[34] All of this took some time, and it was not until May 1947, twenty-one months after surrender, that the new constitution with its democratized state apparatus went into effect. In the meantime, the old constitution and the authoritarian state structure associated with it remained in effect, and the system, not surprisingly, produced conservative (reactionary from the labor movement's perspective) governments similar to those that dominated the prewar system. Thus, although the arrest of war criminals and SCAP-directed purges gradually relieved government ranks of "militarists," the Japanese cabinet remained headed by conservatives appointed by the emperor and associated with the prewar regime, and they were not directly responsible to the popularly elected Lower House of the Diet.

The underdevelopment of a resistance movement at the time of surrender, the continued survival of the old regime staffed by prewar conservatives under conditions where left-wing forces were allowed to mobilize freely, as discussed in greater detail in subsequent chapters, gave rise to a distinctive sociopolitical environment in post-surrender Japan in which key elements of the Western European wartime resistance situation were transposed onto the Japanese postwar context. It was in this distinctive milieu that the postwar Japanese labor movement was born.

Chapter 3

Labor Movements in Post-World War II Western Europe, 1944–1947

The end of World War II transformed the geopolitical map of Europe, strongly marked by the way in which the military campaigns had unfolded and by the structure of international alliances of those years. The war saw Soviet troops advance on Germany from the east, and US and British troops from the west and through the Italian peninsula from the south. This meant that when Germany surrendered in May 1945, if one excludes neutrals like Sweden and Switzerland, Europe was divided in half, with the eastern portion under Soviet occupation and the western half controlled by Resistance or non-Soviet Allied occupation forces. In the western half, whether or not a country was under Resistance control or Allied occupation correlated with the status of that country within the Allied-Axis alliance structure. Resistance-based coalition governments took power in countries where fascist regimes were the product of a German invasion, like France. Germany was placed under Allied occupation because of its status as a former core Axis power. Also a former core Axis power, Italy represented a kind of halfway house by virtue of its having generated a Resistance movement as the Germans withdrew. In Italy the general rule was for control to be handed over to Resistance forces as Allied troops advanced, but there also existed a small number of provinces in which Allied occupation was maintained until 1947.

The social and political dislocations wrought by war gave rise to a situation where the power and influence of the labor movement had increased enormously throughout Western Europe.[1] In those parts of Europe that had escaped Axis occupation, the modulations of democratic electoral politics translated rising popular sentiment in favor of drastic socioeconomic reform into newly installed, trade-union-backed social democratic governments, as in the United Kingdom, or else strengthened the hold of existing ones, as in Sweden. In those parts of Europe that had fallen under Axis rule, there was the wholesale replacement of wartime political regimes by popular fronts led by partisan activists, along with, it might be added, a transformation in the organizational format of the labor movement itself. Thus, in France, Italy, and Belgium, between 1944 and 1947, political coalitions derived from the Resistance that stretched from conservative bourgeois nationalists on the right to communists on the left took power. Discredited by their association with the wartime regime, the governing elites and the bourgeois interests that were at the core of the prewar regimes lost legitimacy and influence. In their place quasi-militarized labor movements and the working-class interests that they ostensibly represented became a primary mass base as well as an ideological point of reference for the newly installed resistance coalitions. It was these coalitions that shouldered the task of establishing a new postwar order from the state's constitutional foundation on up. Because working-class parties were numerically dominant, such reforms generally carried a socialistic orientation, although in keeping with the notion of the resistance representing a broad popular coalition encompassing interests beyond the working class, they were geared toward modifying rather than replacing capitalism. By contrast, in those parts of the Continent under Allied occupation (Germany, Eastern Europe), even though popular sentiment had swung decisively toward labor's preferences, it was the policies and preferences of external occupiers that ultimately determined the extent and character of any postwar reforms that might be undertaken. The sensibilities of the Americans and Soviets, the dominant occupiers, often proved to be different from those of the political forces representing the local populations.

This expansion of labor movement influence occurred in a context in which social, economic, and political conditions propelled two topics into the heart of public discourse: the recovery of production and institutional reform.[2] The concern with economic recovery is easily understood when we consider that the production of goods and services had dwindled to fractions of prewar norms in these societies and sheer physical survival was problematic. There was a pressing need to replace destroyed housing, to redirect industrial production from servicing the military to meeting civilian needs, and to rebuild damaged transportation and distribution infrastructures. It was readily evident that social and political order was critically dependent on the recovery of production. Reform was topical because faulty institutions were understood to have given rise to the chain of events that led to the recently experienced cataclysm. Socialization and the institutionalization of economic democracy were viewed as essential in the process of institutional repair. Socialization—or some form of collective control over the means of production—was sought to ensure that the resources needed for recovery would be mobilized in equitable and socially beneficial ways. Nationalization, economic planning, and regulatory controls of various sorts were all seen as the appropriate vehicles for achieving socialization, as well as constituting one component of a broader framework of economic democracy, or worker participation in the process of managing industry and enterprise. Institutionalization of economic democracy was considered necessary to counteract the oppression and deprivation associated with capitalist hierarchies. Giving workers a voice in the management of industry would help to assure that firms and factories were run in a manner consistent with the workers' interest. In addition to works councils and factory committees for worker participation in management at the plant level, a variety of mechanisms for assuring participation at the company (e.g., codetermination), industry, community, and national levels were put forward, ultimately with varying degrees of success.

The embrace of socialization and economic democracy, it might be noted, marked a retreat from—or perhaps more accurately a fine-tuning of—earlier Marxian-influenced ideas that had permeated labor movement thinking about the political and economic institutional arrangements that the movement should seek and support. No doubt due to the fact that a fundamental socioeconomic transformation seemed so far off, Marxian thought did not initially pay much attention to what the nature of economic organization might be as a society made the transition from capitalism to socialism or, for that matter, how long the period of transition might be. Over time, however, individuals associated with the social democratic camp in particular—Eduard Bernstein being a prominent example here—began to address this issue and came increasingly to the conclusion that it would be acceptable to reform or incrementally modify capitalism rather than eliminate it right away. Political economic developments during the Great Depression gave further impetus to this trend as the dire economic distress of the early 1930s led to major innovations in economic management in leading capitalist economies. This changing attitude was reflected, among other places, in a 1933 Socialist International resolution: "The world crisis has already profoundly changed the structure of the capitalist economy. The liberal and individualist phase in the evolution of capitalism has come to an end. Under the pressure of the crisis a controlled, organized and monopolized capitalist is developing with increasing rapidity." This development, it argued, constituted a historical opportunity. That is, "the new forms of state-controlled and organized economy may serve to prepare the transition from capitalism to Socialism."[3] This changing orientation gave further impetus to developing concrete applications of this line of thinking in socialist intellectual circles and was embraced by socialist politicians and union leaders.[4] The communists' adoption of the popular-front strategy of forging a broad coalition of political forces to extend well beyond the working class, which was occurring in tandem with this rethinking, worked in the same direction since such a coalition would by its very nature require the party to abandon its maximal agenda of replacing capitalism with socialism.

France

The postwar French trade unions grew rapidly from the kernel of the Resistance. According to one estimate, 85 percent of French nonagricultural wage and salary workers were union members in 1945–1946.[5] The reported membership of the CGT (generally taken to be somewhat inflated) had surpassed its prewar, Popular Front–era peak of 5 to 5.25 million in 1945 and then increased further to 6 million in 1946. At 700,000, the Catholic Confédération Française des Travailleurs Chrétiens (CFTC), which regrouped after the war, also grew well beyond its prewar peak.[6] As during the war years, the communists were the most effective at expanding their influence in the labor movement in the fluid postliberation environment. The PCF was able to place its members, and individuals sympathetic toward it, in key CGT leadership positions, and it eventually forged a dominant position in the French union movement.

Thanks to its presence in the Resistance, the labor movement, through its affiliated parties, was a core presence in the postliberation governments. Individuals associated with the Christian, social democrat, and communist wings were represented in the provisional Resistance government established under Charles de Gaulle following the initiation of the August 1944 Allied invasion of France, which remained in power until late 1946. Postwar elections produced a governing coalition of three parties, which were each tied to a particular wing of the labor movement and which were nearly equally balanced in terms of the number of votes and parliamentary seats each received. Specifically, in the October 1945 elections of the national assembly, the communist PCF received 26.2 percent of the vote, the Christian Mouvement Républicain Populaire (MRP) 23.9 percent, and the social democratic–left-socialist Section Française de l'Internationale Ouvrière (SFIO) 23.4 percent. As a centrist party and in keeping with the ethos of a Christian party, the MRP spanned both "bourgeois" and proletarian bases of the Catholic electorate. Table 4 provides a schematic rendering of these alignments.

The phrase "the spirit of 1944" has been used to refer to the distinctive mix of resistance, reform, and recovery that permeated the postliberation French labor movement ethos.[7] The conceptualizations were from the beginning influenced by the state-centric visions of modified capitalism that had taken hold in the labor movement since the Depression. State planning, nationalization of key industries, and institutions of worker participation were essential components of this economic vision. The postwar Resistance coalition proceeded to take concrete steps

Table 4. Government, union, and party blocs in immediate postwar France and Italy

Bloc	Ideological category			
	Christian (cross-class)	Social democratic	Left socialist	Communist
FRANCE				
Government	CNR (Conseil National de la Resistance)			
Union	CFTC (Confédération Française des Travailleurs Chrétiens)	CGT (Confédération Générale du Travail)		
Party	MRP (Mouvement Républicain Populaire)	SFIO (Section Française de l'Internationale Ouvrière)		PCF (Parti Communiste Français)
ITALY				
Government	CLN (Comitato di Liberazione Nazionale)			
Union	CGIL (Confederazione Generale Italiana del Lavoro)			
Party	DC (Democrazia Cristiana)	PSI (Partito Socialista Italiano)		PCI (Partito Communista Italiano)

to implement this state-centric vision of socialized capitalism. The auto industry (Renault), banking, electric power, and gas, insurance and coal mining were all nationalized, giving the French state control over strategic sectors of the economy.[8] The embrace of economic planning culminated in the ambitious economic-modernization program embodied in the 1947 Monnet Plan. State control over labor markets and consumption were achieved by keeping in force Vichy-era controls on wages and prices. The state also took on a greatly expanded role in assuring social security by establishing state-administered social insurance schemes in the areas of health, maternity, unemployment, old age, disability, and death.

The collapse of the authority and legitimacy of owners and managers, many of whom were purged for their collaboration with the Germans, meant that upon liberation the functions of maintaining order and of continuing the operation of grassroots productive enterprises devolved by default to organizations of workers. A variety of "experiments in worker control," including a takeover of as prominent an enterprise as the Paris metro transport network, were conducted around the country. Throughout France, a variety of workplace committees, many working closely with local CNR organs, were formed to oversee plant operations.[9] These ad hoc impositions of grassroots "economic democracy" were subsequently given a formal foundation or otherwise expanded upon by the Resistance coalition governments. For instance, in February 1945 an ordinance was issued that mandated the creation of "enterprise committees" *(comités d'entreprise)* in companies with more than ninety-nine employees. Parallel innovations occurred at higher levels of administration. Oversight of the social welfare system was granted to a set of state-established councils on which worker delegates sat. Nationalized enterprises were administered by tripartite boards consisting of worker, state, and consumer representatives and were promoted as a socialistic measure that would establish "popular" control over sectors vital to economic recovery. At the industry level, various tripartite state-sponsored planning commissions were created. In a similar vein, a National Economic Council, dubbed the "fourth house" of the legislature, was formed as an institution in which key producer groups were represented at the national level in decisions relating to economic planning. Topping this structure was, of course, the Resistance coalition government itself, which spanned parties representing both bourgeois and proletarian interests.[10]

Despite the initial forays into the creation of institutions of economic democracy, as Adam Steinhouse details in an important recent work, the conditions that prevailed in Resistance coalition France—conditions wherein economic decision making tended to be centralized in state organs, and parties prevailed over unions in the labor movement—failed to provide sustained support for these new institutions, with such neglect being most pronounced at the workplace level. While there was some support for a greater emphasis on promoting workplace economic democracy in certain parts of the French labor movement—notably in the CFTC—the attention of the increasingly PCF-dominated CGT was focused on developments at the center, and in particular on the national "battle for production." The role of the French Communists was critical in this regard. Secretary General Maurice Thorez exemplified the PCF's stance in a widely publicized mid-1945 admonishment to striking French miners:

> To produce, to mine coal, is today the highest form of your class duty. . . .
>
> Yesterday, our arms were sabotage and armed action against the enemy. Today that arm is production, to frustrate the plans of the reactionaries, to manifest your class solidarity towards the workers in other areas whose work depends upon your efforts. . . . The slightest weakness on your part will aid the campaigns of the enemies of the people against you, against the working class, against nationalization, against democracy, against France.[11]

In line with this, the PCF directed great energy and zeal into restraining rank-and-file militancy. As the party on the far left of the coalition, its support for the more moderate reform program served to contain demands for more radical change at a moment when the restraint and cooperation of the working class on behalf of production recovery was badly needed.

The flip side of the PCF's—and through it the CGT's—emphasis on promoting the battle for production as a means to secure a position in government was an inattention that effectively condoned the withering away of the institutions of economic democracy that had taken tentative root in the immediate postliberation period. As Steinhouse puts it, "the focus and the structure of the CGT were adapted to an interventionist strategy in the state along well-established lines. There was little inclination or flexibility within the CGT structure to deal with the possibility of new decision-making capacities at the level of the workplace, which would be more difficult to control or politicize in the interests of a party that thought in terms of state power and the systematic subordination of cells (soviets) to party control."[12] Over time employers at the enterprise level, with the increasing complicity of a Resistance coalition in a hurry to increase production, regained control over the workplace and ran their firms without engaging in the consultation that the committees were supposed to foster. At higher levels, state planners tended to consult primarily with industrialists and ignored the committees involving union representatives. In parallel with this, elections to fill the enterprise-level committees that had been established by law were turned into contests for seats among the various currents in the labor movement, and their actual impact on enterprise operations was quite limited.

A similar dynamic had comparable effect on the development of collective bargaining. While legislation was passed that was ostensibly intended to carve out an arena of labor-employer interaction independent of the state, in practice the state's control of wages and prices and its intervention in the settlements made collective bargaining effectively meaningless. An observer of the French scene captured the mechanics of the situation: "When the government put through the collective bargaining law of December 1946, it still kept wages under control. The law, moreover, imposed priorities in agreements, with national agreements required to precede regional, and regional to precede local; and any agreement was subject to governmental approval; after approval, it was extended to all employers and employees in the trade and area covered. The excessive degree of state intervention, the exclusion of the major issues, wages, and the interminable debates among the unions as to 'the most representative organizations' stultified negotiations under the 1946 law." It is thus not surprising that between 1946 and 1950, the years in which it was in effect, only four national agreements were successfully negotiated under the provisions of this law.[13]

Since the state pegged wages well below prewar levels in real terms and was unable to effectively control the distribution of food and other necessary commodities (meaning that workers were forced to buy essential livelihood commodities at inflated prices on the black market), worker resentment and dissatisfaction was widespread. Not surprisingly, this created severe tensions inside the labor movement.

Italy

The postwar Italian labor movement, like that of France, was a product of the transition from Resistance guerilla warfare to Resistance coalition governance. As in France, a Resistance coalition linking working-class and "bourgeois" parties and spanning a broad ideological spectrum emerged during the period of fighting against the Germans and the coordinative organ that they created—the Committee for National Liberation (CLN)—became the embryo for postwar Resistance coalition governance.[14] The format for political-party organization among ideological currents in the Italian Resistance coalition was remarkably similar to that in France (see table 4). Working-class political parties divided along Christian (the Democrazia Cristiana party, or DC), social democratic–left-socialist (the Partito Socialista Italiano, or PSI), and communist (Partito Communista Italiano, or PCI) lines.[15] One key difference between France and Italy can be seen in the way that the Italian labor movement was able to create a single organizational umbrella for the union segment of the movement, the Confederazione Generale Italiana del Lavoro (CGIL), that transcended the Christian-Marxian divide. One contributing factor is that the CGIL was even more of a top-down creation of the parties than the French CGT. That is, the CGIL was created by representatives of the Resistance parties at a meeting in June 1944, just prior to the Allied liberation of Rome, or well before the Resistance had control over the German-occupied industrial heartland in the northern half of the country. Worker organizations that emerged in the north as part of the clandestine resistance effort were incrementally incorporated into the CGIL framework only after this, as the established Resistance forces advanced. It was thus literally true that "the leadership of the three major parties set up the CGIL as an extension of their activities within the working class."[16] Nevertheless, the CGIL's unity, like the French CGT's, was such that the partisan identities and outlooks ran strong. This is illustrated by, among other things, the CGIL's practice of making sure that officials representing all of the parties were installed in each of the local labor chambers (*camera del lavoro*) and in each CGIL industry-level or "category" subunit.

Not surprisingly, Italian labor movement activities were centrally focused. Various relatively generous and comprehensive (on paper, at least) state-administered social security arrangements were either carried over from earlier periods or were newly established from the top down by the Resistance coalition government.[17] Employment security in industry was proclaimed via a government decree freezing employment in the north.[18] In the Italian case, in contrast to that of France, collective bargaining did play a significant role in mediating industrial relations. Here, too, however, as is consistent with the top-down Resistance coalition model, there was a high degree of centralization: Italian wages were subject to centrally negotiated agreements between the CGIL and Confindustria, the private-sector industrialists' employer association. The agreements, furthermore, were rigid and detailed and set wages and benefits for all of Italy. Several factors account for the adoption of this system. First, Mussolini's Fascist regime had established a system of comprehensive nationwide state-supervised labor-management agreements that it used to attain state policies in the industrial-relations arena. Under the conditions of postwar Italy, both the CGIL and Confindustria found it convenient to retain this framework. Furthermore, Italy, unlike France, had the unified associations of labor and capital that were needed to conduct this kind of negotiations. For all of the shortcomings about which there has been much subsequent observation, it is noteworthy that in keeping with the political context and policy tenor of the time, these agreements did feature "socialistic" provisions. For instance, wage packets contained a variety of allowances that caused the compensation to diverge in principle from wages reflecting the market value of the labor provided. Allowances included a "bread bonus," a Christmas bonus, and a family allowance. Of primary consequence were cost-of-living allowances tied to the inflation rate, which constituted well over 50 percent of total worker wages by 1948.

As in France, the flip side of centralization for the Italian unions was weak institutionalization of unions at the lower levels. A number of institutions designed to extend the worker voice at the workplace were established in the initial postwar years. The most important were workplace National Liberation Committees (CLNAs), which were considered factory-level organs of the Resistance coalition's broader CLNA structure; the internal commissions *(commissioni interne)*, which were worker councils comparable to the French enterprise committees that were elected by all workers in a factory irrespective of union membership; and management councils *(consigli di gestione)*, or joint labor-management committees, which were intended to provide a worker voice in the management of production and other areas that had earlier been considered the prerogative of management.[19] As Tom Behan details in his micro-level history of developments in Milan, during the initial postliberation period, the CLNAs, like the French CNRs, played a particularly critical role in organizing the work at the factories while assuring that workers' basic survival needs were met. As some semblance of normality set in, however, the CLNAs tended to recede into the background in favor of the newly created (technically, newly revived) internal commissions and management councils. The CGIL granted the internal commissions legitimacy in 1943 by signing an agreement with Confindustria that called for the creation of such commissions in all establishments employing over twenty workers and granted to the committees a broader range of functions that included "acting as liaison between the unions and the workers, seeing that collective agreement was scrupulously carried out, attempting to mediate individual labor disputes, negotiating local collective agreements, expressing their opinion on the factory rules and regulations and making suggestions of a technical nature to improve the efficiency of production."[20] According to the CGIL-Confindustria agreement, managers were required to consult with internal commissions in advance of layoffs. The CGIL's 1945 congress, however, retracted these powers in favor of an arrangement that granted local CGIL organs strict union supervision of factory agreements, thus effectively pulling the rug out from under the internal commissions. The effect was to turn the internal commissions from being representative organs of the labor movement into sites of contestation between the different partisan factions. This might have played out as a mechanism for effecting local-level worker representation had the CGIL been effectively decentralized. In fact, however, local-level Italian "unions," an American observer notes, were "best described as loose associations of workers who belong to a similar occupational category, such as metalworkers, port workers, bus and tram drivers, local employees of governmental agencies, hospital workers, bakers, and so on." He continues by noting that:

> These units are generally not comparable to the union local that is characteristic of American trade unionism. It is one of the sources of weakness in Italian trade unionism that plant-level organizations do not exist and that the unions and leagues, organized as they are on zonal or community-wide basis, provide only the barest minimum of associative integration. In most instances neither local unions nor leagues maintain headquarters, nor do they evolve complex bureaucracies, preferring to achieve what strength they can by joint action with other like units that are members of a local chamber of labor—or through affiliations with unions organized at the provincial and national levels.[21]

Simultaneously, the CGIL seems to have lost interest in the management councils, thereby allowing management to effectively ignore the councils in the administering production site.

Ideologically, the center of gravity in the Italian Resistance coalition was further to the right of its French counterpart. Whereas the political parties in the French Resistance coalition tended to be more or less evenly balanced in terms of their electoral strength, in Italy the Christian Democrats outdistanced the other parties by a substantial margin. In the June 1946 election, for instance, the DC took 35.2 percent of the vote against the PSI's 20.7 and the PCI's 19.7 percent, with the bulk of the remainder going to conservative and centrist parties that were willing to work with the DC.[22] One reason for this was that the influence of the Catholic Church among the general population in Italy was substantially stronger than in the more secularized France. Satisfying a partner like the DC required a drastic scaling back of the traditional demands of the left. The PCI's Palmiro Togliatti, who returned to Italy from Moscow in March 1944 to head the party, proved up to the task and served as the glue that held together the Italian Resistance coalition. The compromises that the PCI under Togliatti struck for the sake of sustaining the Resistance coalition were at times breathtaking. The Communists, for instance, agreed to support the short-lived monarchist government of Pietro Badoglio. They allowed the restoration of an unreformed central state bureaucracy. Agrarian land reform was postponed and diluted.

The PCI was, as in France, at the forefront in urging workers to exercise restraint and sacrifice on behalf of the "struggle for production." It acquiesced to a gradual whittling away of various protections that had been attained for workers. A six-month "salary truce" was signed in by the PCI-dominated CGIL with Confindustria. In defiance of a constitutional provision of the principle of equal pay for equal work, differential pay scales were set for women and youth, as well as for different regions of the country.[23] In spite of—and at times because of— these policies, the PCI grew impressively as a mass party during these years. Party membership reached over 1.7 million after liberation and 2.2 million by 1947.[24] Thanks to its superior organization and discipline, the Communists obtained the support of over 40 percent of the delegates in the first CGIL congress, in January 1945. This figure rose to 57.8 percent at the 1947 congress, with Socialists receiving 22.6 percent and Christian democrats 13.4 percent.[25] There were a number of reasons behind the Communists' ability to gain control of the CGIL. In addition to the superior organizational discipline that was a characteristic attribute of the Communist movement, as in France, the Communists gained tremendous prestige as a consequence of their strong record of resistance. This was particularly true in the industrialized north, the regional core of Italy's labor movement, where Communist partisans had taken on an active role in organizing several general strikes against the Germans, and large numbers of party members had been killed or jailed. The party's coffers, deepened with Soviet funds, assured that its activists enjoyed a "relative economic security" that the other parties were unable to duplicate. Where the other parties' activists tended to rely on outside jobs and occupations to finance their activities—and these rapidly disappeared in the economic turmoil of the postwar years—the PCI was willing and able to supplement the incomes of the party-affiliated in the union movement. As a result, "when there was work to be done, it was often a communist who did it. When there was a business trip to be taken, it was usually a communist who took it, traveling on party funds when the union coffers were empty. In this way the communist labor leaders were not only more active, but they had the best contacts with Rome and with each other." A further reason was that as the war wound down to a close, the other currents lost their most well-known and respected labor leaders; as a consequence of murder at the hands of the Germans in the case of the Socialists' Bruno Buozzi, and cancer in the case of the Christian Democrats' Achille Grande. This left the Communist Giuseppe Di Vittorio as the one nationally prominent labor-movement leader with prewar roots.[26]

Thus, the Italian case highlights, even more so than does the French, the tension between the coexisting centripetal and centrifugal impetuses built into the post-Resistance experience. The Italian Resistance brought into being a postwar coalition that encompassed a broad spectrum of politically diverse social groups. Like that of France, the Resistance of Italy cemented into place a left-of-center reform-and-recovery agenda, though the political center of gravity was located somewhat to the right of that in France. In both France and Italy the Resistance experience spawned a centralized organizational structure in the labor movement based on a fusing of variegated partisan identifications. The extreme diversity and plurality of the social forces and political outlooks in the Italian coalition worked against legalization of the corresponding institutions and policies, and what emerged in the absence of relations mediated through the state was a centralized but informal and directly *bargained* accommodation between labor and capital. This difference in the location of the political center of gravity in the Italian post-Resistance coalition and in the format for the institutionalization of the reform-and-recovery effort would subsequently contribute to an extreme polarization of the Italian political environment and the Italian labor movement once global currents shifted in 1947.

Germany

As was true of their French and Italian counterparts, the the West German labor movement's vision of the postwar political economic order in the early postwar years comprised a mix of socialization and participatory economic democracy. Within German domestic society, the balance of power had clearly shifted in labor's favor. German employers had been severely discredited by their cooperation with fascism, and it was widely believed that economic recovery could come about only if German labor were appropriately mobilized on behalf of "battle for production." Also true of their counterparts elsewhere, the West German movement's theme of unity across political tendencies was widely embraced. In the German case the prevailing ideal was expressed as "a single general union *(Allge-*

meine Gewerkschaft) to which all working people, regardless of rank, salary, job, industry or geography, would belong." The idea was to have "this general union . . . conduct all negotiations with the employers, both private and public. Whatever sub-division there might be—and the advocates of this particular form of union organization left no doubt that the fewer there were the better for the working class—they would simply act as supplementary bodies to the all-encompassing union and never constitute autonomous entities in any respect."[27]

Ironically, the strong political and organizational constraints on its action in the immediate postwar years allowed the German movement, over the longer term, to come closer to the attainment of this ideal than the French and Italian labor movements did. The absence of a Resistance milieu was extremely important in this regard, as was the extended Allied occupation of Germany. In contrast to the French and Italian situations, Germany's limited Resistance and the Allied ban against political parties allowed union identity and union organizational integrity to take root before partisan identities and broader political and organizational imperatives did. This had the effect of diverting the energy- and institution-building efforts of the West German labor movement into a nonpartisan trade-union organizational structure. The inhospitableness of the Western occupation zones as an environment for the Communists pressed in the same direction. The West German Communists were not presented with the opportunity to rebuild their organizations and reputations through participation in a resistance, which their French and Italian brethren were able to exploit so effectively. While in the Soviet zone in Eastern Germany Communist hegemony in the labor movement was established with the backing of Soviet occupation authorities, the KPD was unable to make much headway in Western Germany. Since it was the Communists who most readily and systematically politicized trade unions, the impetus toward union politicization was that much less powerful in the largely social democratic/left-socialist and Christian West Germany. More fundamentally, the Allies' direct military governance in Germany meant that there was no "state" to serve as the axis of party-led centralization.

As for policy, it was official Allied policy to encourage "free trade unions" in Western Germany. Allied authorities saw local-level union organizations as the appropriate vehicle for creating unions of this type. In the words of the US military government officials in Germany, unions "should first be local in character and should be extended no faster than the proven capacity for democratic responsibility and action."[28] In line with this policy, the three military governments in the Western zones opposed the "one big union plan." For the Americans, the opposition was philosophical. In the words of General Lucius Clay, the commander of the military government in the American occupation zone: "Whereas the Soviet Military Administration created the type of organization it desired by first establishing Communist leadership, it was our policy to permit the unions to develop from the ground up through democratic processes. We wanted them, in forming a federation, to keep some degree of autonomy and to retain some control of their own finances, thus making it more difficult for unscrupulous leadership to use the movement for ideological and political purposes. . . . We insisted . . . that the membership of local trade unions be permitted to decide the type of organization they wished to have without having it imposed on them from above."[29] The type of union organization that Clay was railing against was, of course, precisely the kind of organization that the Resistance movements had created. The British attitude was similar. In the British view, "democracy somehow had to grow spontaneously, from the bottom upwards."[30] A fear of revived German power, rather than any philosophical difference with the Germans, seemed to be the motivating force behind the French reluctance to allow centralized unions. Ultimately, it was not until the creation of the Federal Republic, in 1949, that German unionists were presented with the opportunity to consummate their organization-building on a national scale. By that time, as will be discussed in some detail in chapter 6, the social and political context had changed dramatically.

It is noteworthy that the degree of antipathy in US occupation-force policy toward even some of the milder varieties of social democratic unionism might not have been as great had it not been for the presence of the AFL. The AFL had set up the Free Trade Union Committee (FTUC) as an organ devoted to averting the spread of communism by engaging in the highly political task of spreading the gospel of "apolitical" business-unionism abroad. The association between "free trade unions," which were based on this business unionism, and anticommunism was conceived as follows: A "decisive role" could be played by the "free trade unions" because "they were built on voluntary action by their members, on contractual relations with employers, on freedom from state intervention in their affairs, and on the principle of raising living standards by peaceful action." They were, in short, "by their very nature opposed to government domination and totalitarian ideas" that the AFL saw as the heart of the "Bolshevik bureaucracy." The AFL considered developments in Germany to be critical because it viewed Germany as "the key to the reconstruction of Europe and to the establishment of world order and peace."[31] US military government officials in Germany, with the help of AFL-affiliated advisers, actively encouraged German labor leaders to adopt a decentralized structure more in keeping with "free trade unionism" of the AFL variety.[32]

The consequences of this American antipathy toward what the European left considered basic institutions of economic democracy is well illustrated by the fate of multiple initiatives to effect these on the German side. As was true in other parts of Europe, the fall of fascism spawned spontaneous worker organizations—"works councils" in the German context—to fill the administrative void left by the disappearance or discrediting of management. As described by one student of the phenomenon, "it was mainly the locally developed, indigenous and independent works councils at the factory level which took the first steps" not only in organizing workers but also "in restarting the production process in Germany's devastated industries." By virtue of the fact that they "filled a political vacuum left as a result of the delegitimation of many employers for supporting the Nazis," such "works councils occupied a strategic position in German industrial life which furnished them with extraordinary powers on the community level."[33] Under conditions where Allied officials were slow to recognize their status, works councils—the organizational counterpart of the plant-level organs in France and Italy—emerged as "a political fact in search of a legal identity."[34] In addition to factory-level works councils, company-level "codetermination," or some kind of arrangement where worker representatives would be eligible for participation on company supervisory boards, was institutionalized at labor movement initiative in the coal and steel industries in the British zone as an outgrowth of a "deal" in which representation was granted to labor in exchange for its cooperation with company managements in lobbying against Allied proposals to dismantle these companies' plants for reparations and antitrust purposes. German labor organizations sought to make these informal power-sharing arrangements permanent and to universalize their coverage by granting them formal legal status as a further mechanism for extending economic democracy and labor movement influence. A 1946 Allied occupation "law" in fact tentatively granted works councils legal status. A comparable tentative legal status was granted to company-level codetermination arrangements in the British zone in 1948. However, American policy ultimately frustrated the effort to consummate this drive on a Germany-wide basis. The proper vehicle for labor-management relations in the American understanding was a system of "private" collective bargaining that guaranteed the bargaining parties as much latitude as practicable to structure their relationship in any format that they chose. General Clay expressed the implications in the context of occupied Germany in this way: "There was a tendency on the part of German trade unions to have the rights of labor enacted into law. This seemed to me unwise and contrary to their own interests. Their constitutional rights were clearly established. To insist that they be further specified in legislative acts implied that they could be denied by such acts. Collective bargaining gave the trade unions the opportunity to establish the rights of works councils and other rights, and Military Government had authorized and urged its use by both employee and employer."[35]

The concrete initiative that the labor movement put forward as a means of realizing economic democracy beyond the firm was the "economic council," which would consist of representatives from business, unions, consumers, local governments, and/or other interests. Local-level economic councils were in fact set up throughout the Western zones to assist in the coordination of food rationing, production recovery, and any number of other basic economic activities that were required to get the population through the dire economic conditions of the war's aftermath, and German unionists and labor parties backed these initiatives aimed at giving these councils formal legal standing. The British and French were accommodating but the Americans were not, and behind the American response once again were fundamental philosophical differences with the German social democrats over the appropriate relationship between private interests and the state. On the one hand, "the fact that legislative initiatives were taken in almost all West German states and that laws for power-sharing economic chambers [*Landeswirtschaftsrat*] were actually passed by the overwhelming majorities in Germany's key political and economic centers, Berlin and North Rhine-Westphalia, indicates the centrality of this form of democratization" in German thinking. However, "the corporatist conception of democratization that stood behind the Landeswirtschaftsrat ran clearly counter to the American ideal of a representative democracy based on direct elections and a separation of politics and economic organizations. . . . For Americans, the kind of power sharing represented by the economic councils was fundamentally undemocratic and quasi-Fascist." In the American way of thinking, public and private spheres needed to be clearly differentiated, and the latter should in principle be as free from state intervention and structuring as possible. In February 1947 chambers of commerce and labor organizations in the British zone decided to establish a centralized zone-wide business-labor council to help coordinate policy and its implementation. Similar councils were established at the *länder* level in the French zone. In contrast, in areas under American control—including Hesse, Wüttemberg-Baden, Bavaria, Berlin, North Rhine-Westphalia—these were vetoed. And when the Western zones were combined into a single zone, a German effort to legalize economic councils throughout the combined zone was stopped at the initiative of the dominant Americans.[36] A similar scenario unfolded in West Germany with regard to a further mechanism that was widely pursued in Continental Europe as an ostensible means of democratizing the economy, namely nationalization.[37]

One can see in the preceding overview of developments in the German labor movement in the Western occupation zones a process in which tendencies that were present in the French experience were redirected in the German case into rather different channels. As we shall see, a somewhat different arrangement of comparable variables led to a parallel but distinctive process in Japan.

As outlined in the preceding, European labor's confrontation with fascism altered the environment and the character of the Continent's labor movements. This was particularly evident in the countries discussed in this chapter. Fascism virtually destroyed the independent labor movements of France, Italy, and Germany. To the extent that these movements survived, they were forced to do so in drastically altered form, first as clandestine movements or movements in exile, then as part of a military force of resistance against incumbent regimes or foreign occupiers, and, eventually, as proto-governments in newly liberated national territories. This experience altered the relationships among the competing political wings of these movements and reshaped the associated organizational structures. As in the creation of the WFTU internationally, this reshaping was in the direction of a fusion of union organizations, but the degree to which this was consummated varied depending on specific national conditions. It was an experience that pushed these movements toward centralization and unity even while, paradoxically, reinforcing narrower ideological and political identities derived from the interwar years.

It was also the case, however, that geopolitical factors—specifically, those relating to a country's "location" in the international system during the period of Allied-Axis conflict—played a role in mediating this impact. In France and Italy, the fact of German occupation and the subsequent disposition of these countries after the war's end were such that the logic of participation in the Resistance was played out relatively unadulterated. The postwar labor movements of both countries were essentially top-down creations of the Resistance "partisans." One effect of this was a centralization of the union organizations and a correspondingly weak institutionalization at the local level. Another was the strong association of competing wings of the labor movement with specific political parties. In Germany, however, the postwar occupation rechanneled these impetuses in an alternative direction.

The resistance experiences and the postliberation situations provided the context for the establishment of the ideational and institutional framework for postwar industrial relations in these countries. The Resistance was not simply about defeating the Germans but understood by those involved to be a fight against the old sociopolitical order, and the implementation of its visions of reform were striven for once the fighting ended. A passage from an anonymously authored 1944 political manifesto by an Italian partisan captures the way in which the antifascist struggle came to be transmuted in the popular mind—in an interpretation that defined the ethos of the immediate postwar years—into a struggle of a cross-class coalition on behalf of "reform" against the forces of reaction:

> The enthusiasm of the struggles has been projected everywhere beyond its immediate objectives toward the new society that must arise from the ruins of Fascism. The sense of anti-Fascism as a European revolution has been brilliantly confirmed in the devastation of a war that had opened as a simple struggle among the powers. . . . Every event tends to demonstrate that the social contrasts are those of a war deepened sufficiently to become a true civil war. A civil war characteristically reveals the disintegration of the dominant classes, the shattering of their internal solidarity, and the

necessity on the part of the parties to seek their salvation by appealing to yesterday's enemy, i.e., to the popular masses.

The manifesto goes on to describe the consequences of this mass-elite solidarity forged by the Resistance experience: "the mobilization of the masses and the formation of democratic governments follows an accelerated rhythm; the monarchs, generals, landlords, and industrialists have come to understand, regretfully, that to save themselves from Hitler they must appeal to peasants and workers, even with the consequences that may follow."[38]

Postwar economic conditions were such, however, that reform had to be tempered by the need to foster economic recovery. The most politically impactive feature of the Resistance ethos was its remarkable ability to forge a sense of common purpose, though not necessarily programmatic coherence or consensus, among groups subscribing to divergent and contradictory ideologies, on the one hand, and a willingness to entertain drastic reforms of groups in society that under normal circumstances would have adamantly fought for the status quo, on the other. In both France and Italy the center of gravity in the resulting Resistance coalitions was left of center. Reflecting this, and the fact that this was a time of institutional reconstruction, a variety of "socialistic" or "modified capitalist" arrangements were put in place. Of particular importance for the labor movement were the institutions of economic democracy that took the form of councils for representing workers inside the firm. In the partisan-oriented context of postwar France and Italy, however, these did not become the sites for establishing a unified voice for workers in the factory, but sites of competition for support from among the competing partisan streams.

In Germany, as noted, geopolitics served to prevent this logic of the Resistance milieu from being played out. To begin with, the strength of the fascist thrust in Germany and the ruthlessness of its suppression of the labor movement made the very formation of a resistance movement difficult, and its scope and strength were correspondingly weak when compared to that of France and Italy. Given that it was under Allied occupation, furthermore, the preferences of the occupation powers had a decisive impact on both the structure of the postwar labor movement and the institutions of postwar industrial relations. In the Soviet zone, East Germany was molded along Stalinist lines. In the Western zones, with three occupying powers, the situation was more complex; but in the end it was US preferences that tended to have the strongest impact. Whereas the "natural" impulse of the German movement appears to have been one that favored centralized unionism and the legalization of the institutions of economic democracy in a way that paralleled that in Italy and France, American occupation preferences were different. In particular, functional representative bodies of the sort sought by German labor leaders were anathema to the Americans. The occupation ban on politics muffled the impetus for partisan politicization, and German unionists in the Western zone were effectively forced to construct their organizations from the bottom up. The upshot of this was the emergence of labor organizations in which political-party identification was suppressed, and unions strongly rooted in local-level and industry-level organization. It also meant that German labor during that time was without the institutionalized representative organs (legally established works councils and codetermination) that it so strongly desired.

As in France, Italy, and Germany, the experience in Japan of confronting fascism, the geopolitics of World War II, and the postwar international order would profoundly reshape its labor movement and its environment. It is to the situation in Japan that we now return.

Chapter 4

Uniting the Front, 1945–1947

In key countries of postwar Western Europe, such as France and Italy, socialist-communist cooperation in the labor movement served as the anchor for a broad center-left coalition that stretched rightward to encompass sympathetic groups and organizations representing other, presumably less "progressive," social categories. As noted in the preceding chapter, these "popular fronts" were forged in the white heat of the antifascist resistance and after liberation became the political foundation upon which postwar governments were constructed. These Resistance-based popular-front governments, in turn, shaped the character of the postwar institutional-reform process and also provided the mobilization framework for the "battle for production." It was noted in chapter 2 how the Japanese political-historical context did not allow for development of a comparable wartime resistance movement. Nevertheless, the *idea* in Japan that addressing the problems of reform and production through a popular front rooted in socialist-communist cooperation was a powerful one, and it played a major role in the politics of Japanese labor during the first eighteen months or so following surrender. The disjuncture between the ideal (socialist-communist-based popular front) and reality (the absence of a resistance coalition) meant that the energies of the labor movement would be directed toward the creation of just such a popular front. The complicating factor was that by virtue of Japan's status as a former Axis power, this needed to occur, as in Germany, in the none-too-conducive context of a US-dominated Allied occupation. In the end a coalition faintly reminiscent of the Resistance on the European continent was established a year and a half

61

into the occupation. The fact that this unfolded under peacetime rather than wartime conditions, and was subject to periodic interventions by the occupation forces, left a deep impression on both process and outcome.

Initial reconstruction of the labor movement

The scope and breadth of the Allied occupation's ambitious reform agenda did not become apparent to Japanese labor-movement activists until October 1945, or nearly two months after Japan's August 15 surrender, when the Supreme Commander of Allied Powers (SCAP), General Douglas MacArthur, began to unveil the specifics of the "democratic revolution" that he intended to oversee in Japan. During the interlude between surrender and the start of the occupation reform program, the initiative to reestablish the Japanese labor movement was taken by surviving social democratic and left-socialist leaders of the prewar movement, since the surviving communists remained locked in their jail cells and were expected to remain there indefinitely. Considering the fact that wartime suppression had scattered and atomized the personal networks that had previously sustained the labor movement, and wartime bombings and neglect had wrought severe damage to Japan's communications and transportation infrastructure, the work of reestablishing the labor movement unfolded with amazing rapidity. As in Europe, the guiding impetus was unity, and like their counterparts in Germany, Japanese labor leaders spoke of creating "one big union" that would bring together the competing ideological currents.[1] By early October, in fact, matters had progressed to the point that a national conference was convened to discuss the establishment of just such a unified national labor-union organization. It was decided at that meeting that the new organization would be christened with the name of the most prominent prewar labor organization, Sōdōmei. Work was simultaneously conducted on establishing a working-class political party, and here too, unity was the watchword. Like the proposed Sōdōmei, the party was to be one that transcended the prewar ideological divisions. The inaugural convention of the new party, dubbed the Japan Socialist Party (JSP), was convened on November 2, 1945. The party that was established at that time consisted mainly of incumbent and former Diet members associated with the prewar proletarian parties and union officials active in the Sōdōmei preparatory committee, with a good many of the participating delegates falling into both categories.

Arguably, the task of establishing unity in the Japanese context at that time was less forbidding than that which confronted labor leaders in Europe, since the Japanese movement did not have to contend with the polar antagonisms associated with having a Christian wing on the right and a communist wing on the left. Despite this, continuing differences stemming from the incompatibilities in worldview remained alive beneath the veneer of organizational unity, stemming in this case from the differences that divided the social democrats and left socialists. At the Sōdōmei October preparatory labor conference, for instance, there was a fierce debate over whether the new union's program should be built around labor-management cooperation or class conflict. While organizing at the local level, the two wings frequently established competing branches in a district. With respect to organization policy, the social democrats tended to be restrictive in their screening of potential union members in order that they might root out suspected communists and to ensure tight vertical control, while the left socialists strove to create organizations that were as broad-based and inclusive as possible.[2] The JSP's inaugural convention was marked by a bitter argument between moderate social democrats and Marxian left socialists over the status of the emperor.[3] The dissension extended even to the party's name and it is noteworthy that the debate over whether the new party should be called the "Social Democratic Party" or the "Socialist Party" was framed by references to European examples. Advocates of "Social Democratic Party" argued that socialist parties in Europe were associated with pro-communist elements and therefore the name should be rejected, while proponents of "Socialist Party" maintained that international historical experience showed "Social Democratic Party" would define the ideological coloring too narrowly and identify the party too closely with reformism. In the end "Socialist Party" won the day by just one vote.[4] In a context where these currents had not had the opportunity to develop a common set of objectives, it proved impossible to consolidate opinion sufficiently to draft a party program. A platform was ultimately adopted that consisted of just three sparse lines declaring the party's support for democracy, socialism, and peace. Furthermore, the party was unable to agree on who should become party chairman and for that reason started out under the direction of a temporary central executive committee. In both the union and the party, however, the social democrats unambiguously dominated the organizational apparatus.

This tenuous labor-movement unity was subsequently disrupted further by a totally unanticipated development. On October 10, the occupation forces' General Headquarters (GHQ), in a measure intended to jump-start the democratization process that it had outlined for Japan, had Tokuda Kyūichi, Shiga Yoshio, Miyamoto Kenji, and other leaders of the prewar Japanese Communist Party (JCP) released from the prisons where they had been incarcerated for as long as eighteen years. Ironically this occurred on the very day that the prewar left socialists and social democrats were holding their national organizational conference in which Sōdōmei revived as the ostensible kernel of the nation's "one big union."[5] As befitted a self-described party rooted in the working class, the JCP set to work immediately on the task of organizing labor unions of its own.[6] The party set up the Labor Union Promotion Association (Rōdō Kumiai Sokushinkai)—a body that was in fact little more than a name printed on the business cards of JCP organizers—and began assisting workers in their efforts to establish unions in direct competition with the socialists. For the JCP, union building overlapped with party building to an even greater extent than it had for the social democrats and left socialists.[7] The party's position on labor unions was formally articulated in a document entitled "Resolution Regarding Labor Unions" approved at the JCP's fourth party congress held between December 1 and 3, 1945.[8] This document highlighted the importance of working-class organizations to the success of Japan's "democratic revolution," which was designated as the party's mission. All party members were required to join unions and to promote unity in the labor movement. They were told that overly "mechanical and formalistic tendencies" on the part of JCP cadres in the past had contributed to splits in the labor movement and, in light of this, were warned to take care to avoid these tendencies. At the same time, however, the party's labor union division chief Kamiyama Shigeo made it a point to emphasize that at all times party organizers were to operate under the direction of the party.[9]

Initially, the most successful JCP ventures in terms of the scope of influence were not unions per se, but factory delegate councils *(kōjō daihyōsha kaigi),* or liaison bodies that brought together representatives from factories in a given district. The organizational format and functions performed by these councils were quite similar to those of the local liberation committees that operated in the initial postliberation period in France and Italy. That is, the delegate councils were inclusive affairs to which all factories in a given area were encouraged to send representatives irrespective of their political party or upper-level labor organizational affiliations. The councils were used not only to assist in unionization efforts and support workers in disputes with employers, but also to lead extra-parliamentary protest marches and demonstrations on issues that were of concern not just to the factory workers but also to the general population of a district, such as delayed food rations. The first factory council was created in Kanagawa prefecture in mid-December 1945 and consisted of delegates from twenty-one factories. This was followed by the creation of a number of similar district-level factory councils in the Tokyo-Yokohama area and then by the creation in January 1946 of the Kantō Region Labor Council (Kantō Rōkyō), which consolidated all of the district-level factory councils in the greater Tokyo area. Similar processes led to the formation of regional councils in the Hokkaido, Tohoku, and Osaka regions.[10]

The sudden emergence of a communist presence in the labor movement under conditions in which the noncommunist left was still in the process of working out its own objectives for the postwar movement proved highly disruptive, and the social democrats and left socialists produced very different readings of its implications. To the staunchly anticommunist social democrats, SCAP's release of the communists signaled that Japan's "democratic revolution," which it had wholeheartedly supported up to that point, had suddenly turned into a "revolution gone too far" *(yukisugita kakumei)*. Nishio Suehiro recalled the thinking among the social democrats at the time as follows:

> What was most important for Japan at that stage was to first firmly implant the fruits of our received democratic revolution. There needed to be no further destruction or confusion. Along with the defeat of the old forces, we had to prevent the destruction that would result from a revolution that went too far and to steadily strive for the rebuilding of Japan. . . .
>
> Even now I am overwhelmed by the weight of the historic responsibility that was cast on our shoulders as we came to the near religious conviction that in this instance we were the only ones who could fulfill the mission of toppling the old forces on the right while preventing dangerous communist revolution on the left.[11]

This was not the language of working-class solidarity but that of a recrudescence of the prewar social democratic stance toward the communists.

The left-socialist reaction was different. The left socialists argued that the rapidity and externally imposed character of the reform process was such that the consciousness and organization of the Japanese working class and other social elements lagged far behind the pace of institutional reform. This lag, they feared, would make the reforms vulnerable to a revival of reactionary forces.[12] Given the primacy that they attached to the popular front as a vehicle for precipitating sociopolitical change, the left socialists were amenable to a linkup with the communists under the right conditions. In fact, in a manner of thinking that paralleled GHQ's jump-start democratization thesis, the left socialists, who were fearful of the "bourgeois" tendencies of the social democrats, saw the communists as representing a countervailing force that would help assure the progressiveness of the postwar democratic revolution. The communists in fact courted the socialists once they had managed to establish their postwar priorities. On several occasions they proposed the setting up of a common organization—something that would presumably have resulted in a framework resembling the CGT or CGIL—but in each instance vehement opposition on the part of the dominant social democrats assured that these initiatives would not bear fruit.[13]

Organizing unions

Yet another set of developments set in motion by the occupation forces' intervention complicated efforts to attain unity and coherence in the postwar Japanese labor movement. On October 11, SCAP ordered Japan's government to engage "in the encouragement of the unionization of labor." Along with a rapidly deteriorating economic situation and the December Labor Union Law, passed at SCAP's insistence, which put labor unions on a firm legal foundation for the first time in Japanese history, the order spurred a massive and extremely rapid process of unionization. By December, the number of unionized workers—officially zero at the time of surrender—had grown to 380,000. Surpassing the prewar peak of unionization at some point during that or the following month, the total six months later had increased nearly tenfold, to 3.75 million. Rapid growth continued through the ensuing two years, and by 1948, union density peaked at 55.8 percent.

The rapidity of Japanese unionization far exceeded the capacity of the prewar activists to incorporate the unions into their organizations using existing strategies. Virtually all of the newly created unions were enterprise unions, or units whose memberships comprised employees of a single plant or company. Rather than serving as vehicles for a "battle for production," these unions were created in the midst of disputes with employees over dismissals, wage hikes, and personnel policies. In the absence of external guidance, enterprise unions represented a "natural" grouping for workers at the grassroots level, since for most workers the plant or company was a social context in which they regularly interacted with fellow workers.

As in Western Europe, the communists proved to be particularly adept at adjusting to the postwar circumstances, and this greater adaptability allowed them to overtake Sōdōmei in the number of union members under their wing. In early 1946 the JCP established an office devoted to facilitating the creation of industrial unions and, appropriately enough, named it "preparatory conference on national industrial unions." Hosoya Matsuta was one of two individuals commissioned by the party to organize and operate the office. Hosoya recalls what happened when they opened for business in the Yūrakuchō section of Tokyo, also describing the distinctive dynamic that MacArthur's top-down encouragement of unionization produced:

> Once we set up the secretariat it was reported in the newspaper that the . . . office had been established. The next day the crowds were like those you find at the bazaars in front of a temple. People seeking to form labor unions arrived in droves. Since there was a huge crowd and only one desk and a chair, we had them line up but were still in no position to service them all. It is all rather hilarious when you think about it now. It just shows how high union organization fever had risen. Workers from all sorts of enterprises and shops were in a hurry to organize. However, they had never seen or heard of an actual labor union. How do you start one? How do you operate one? Where did our organization fit in? They came thronging to us with questions of this sort.[14]

In contrast to Sōdōmei's attempts to strictly enforce predefined organizational principles (something at which it was not completely successful), the JCP organizers adopted a pragmatic approach that gave wide latitude to unit enterprise unions for establishing their organizational format. The result was that the unions usually formed industry-level organizations in which the locus of sovereignty (i.e., decisions over the calling of strikes and control over union finances) remained at the enterprise union level. In other words, they tended to form industrial *federations* rather than true industrial *unions*. Furthermore, the scope of coverage of these organizations (their "industry") was more often than not a specific product group rather than an industrial sector—for example, steel and electrical-machinery workers instead of the more inclusive metalworkers. The conspicuous exception to this general tendency toward decentralized industrial federations occurred in the public sector, where the existence of state monopolies ensured that an enterprise union could easily constitute a de facto industrial union. The JCP-led staff under Hosoya, working with the party, encouraged these budding industrial federations to join together in a national center while in the interim the party did what it could to establish a presence in the individual industrial federations through the classic device of establishing party "cells" and "fractions"—organizational units of communist party members inside a nonparty organization that operated at the behest of the party with the aim of steering the larger organization in a desired direction.[15] The party successfully penetrated the upper ranks of such strategically important organizations as the seamen's union (Kaiin Kumiai), which was Japan's only major true industrial union, the national railway workers' union (Kokurō),[16] the electric power workers' union (Densan), the postal and communications workers' union (Zentei), and the teachers' union (Nikkyōso). The degree of influence attained by the party varied from organization to organization, with party hegemony attained (though this was not always publicly known) in Zentei and Densan. The party's grip on Kokurō and Kaiin Kumiai was more problematic. Interestingly, Hosoya and others consulted with GHQ and received guidance from a number of CIO-affiliated officials who did not trust the prewar social democrats and were delighted to see a Japanese organization in the works that appeared to them to be based on the same organizing principles as the CIO.

These initiatives on the part of the JCP changed the character of its party-union relations. Where earlier its penetration of unions tended to be localized at the rank-and-file level, the party now began to concentrate its cells in the leadership ranks of the biggest national unions and industrial federations, thereby allowing it to move toward the archetype of a "transmission belt" relationship with the labor unions. Party directives generally ran directly from JCP headquarters to the cells in the headquarters of a specific industrial union, and a single party-headquarters official was assigned to oversee a given union. But the arrangement was not without its shortcomings. Party oversight was not as effective as the party might have hoped, since JCP headquarters was chronically understaffed. Party officials active at the time describe Yoyogi (district of Tokyo in which the national party office was located, used as a synonym for "party headquarters") as a veritable beehive of frenetic activity. Furthermore, the party's autocratic chairman Tokuda is said to have insisted on making policy decisions personally, but since he also held a seat in the Diet and later the Central Labor Relations Board and had a penchant for engaging in fiery impromptu agitational speeches, he was frequently away, thus decisions were often not made in a timely manner. A party official described the typical situation of party officials charged with overseeing cells in labor unions: "Although one might have a tentative grasp of the situation from spot checks conducted while waiting for [party] directives, when it came to the actual details of a dispute the best we could do was leave matters to the central struggle committee [of the union] and try to ascertain that there wasn't a divergence from party policy."[17]

With the JCP's adoption of a new labor union strategy built on fostering a national organization of industrial federations, the Japanese labor movement found itself with two separate projects aimed at amalgamating the budding population of labor unions into a comprehensive national umbrella. Even as the respective leaderships continued to claim publicly that they were devoted to the construction of a unified trade union movement, the JSP-Sōdōmei and the JCP worked feverishly to cobble their own independent national, industrial, and local organizations. The culmination of this trend occurred in August 1946 when two competing national labor union centers with differing organizational and ideological characteristics, Sōdōmei and Sanbetsu, were formally inaugurated.

After nearly a year of organizing effort, the postwar Sōdōmei held its inaugural convention between August 1 and 3 in Tokyo's Kanda district. According to figures made public by the national center, Sōdōmei represented 850,000 workers in 1,700 locals, with the majority being workers employed in small firms. The organizational center of gravity in Sōdōmei was in the prefectural federations that serviced a large number of small unions in various lines of work in a given geographic area. Sōdōmei also contained four broadly defined industrial unions —in transport and communications, tobacco, textiles, and mining—which were also based in small firms. As in the prewar Sōdōmei, loyalties to individual union "bosses" structured the organization and shaped the decision-making process. The leadership was divided into readily identifiable groupings of social democrats and left socialists.[18] Heading the organization was the prewar social democrat Matsuoka Komakichi. The more numerous social democrats dominated the organization's executive, as they did in the JSP.

Between August 19 and 21 the competing National Congress of Industrial

Organizations, or Sanbetsu, held its inaugural convention in Tokyo's Hibiya district. As interviews with various officials involved make clear, Sanbetsu's formation was closely choreographed by the JCP.[19] Sanbetsu claimed to represent twenty-one industrial organizations with 1.62 million members. In contrast to Sōdōmei, where regional organizations and personal ties held the organization together, Sanbetsu's focal point was to be found in the twenty-one constituent industrial organizations. Unlike Sōdōmei, "industries" in Sanbetsu were rather narrowly defined. In contrast to the small-business base of Sōdōmei, the constituent-unit unions of Sanbetsu's industrial federations were more often than not the enterprise unions of large firms in monopolistic or oligopolistic industries, with the largest of these in the public sector. Given their size and importance to the functioning of the Japanese economy, these unions tended to possess much greater bargaining power than those in Sōdōmei. And thanks to the priority given by the JCP to the speed of organization building over ideological purity, the Sanbetsu unions were considerably more pluralistic politically than those of Sōdōmei, although in many key unions communist cells—often unbeknownst to others in the leadership—were in a position to steer the organization. There had, in fact, been considerable debate inside the JCP while creating Sanbetsu over whether to press for a centralized organization or a loose federation format.[20] The latter course was ultimately chosen on the rationale that a national center with concentrated authority would be more inclined to pursue purely union interests and would for that reason be less amenable to party control. Sanbetsu was therefore organized as a liaison body of industrial federations, rather than as a formally centralized union along the lines of Sōdōmei. In contrast to the seasoned prewar unionists that dominated Sōdōmei's executive ranks, Sanbetsu's staff consisted of a small group of party-affiliated labor movement "amateurs" who had little or no prior experience in the labor movement. The one exception was the assistant director of the Sanbetsu secretariat, Hosoya Matsuta, who had a background of activity in the prewar left-socialist–communist labor unions. It was Hosoya who gradually became the real power inside the secretariat.

The formation of Sanbetsu and Sōdōmei during August 1946 marked a threshold of sorts in the evolution of the postwar Japanese movement. While the coverage of the two national centers was by no means comprehensive (their combined membership perhaps encompassed roughly one-half of unionized workers at that time), the formation of the two national centers symbolized the arrival of a new stage in the evolution of the labor movement. Union organizations were now in place with the potential to mobilize Japanese workers, industry by industry, on a coordinated, national basis. At the same time, by the middle of 1946, it was evident that, instances of united political action notwithstanding, the dream of the "one big union" for the labor movement had not been attained.

Forging a popular front: the People's Democratic League

In early 1946, the prominent left-socialist theoretician Yamakawa Hitoshi published two widely read pieces that appeared to many to have captured the essence of Japan's postwar condition and outlined a compelling political agenda for responding to its dictates. The first was an early January 1946 newspaper appeal entitled "A Proposal for the Immediate Establishment of a Popular Front," and second a widely read article published the same month in the magazine *Kaizō*. Using the Marxian conceptualizations that were the lingua franca of the labor movement, Yamakawa began from the proposition that "a political revolution is accomplished through the disarmament of the old ruling class and the destruction of the apparatus of its rule." Applying this to Japan at the time, he interpreted the occupation forces' disbanding of the Japanese military, the dissolution of the internal security police apparatus, the arrest of war criminals, and the purging of militarists to be developments that assured Japan's old ruling class was being disarmed and its apparatus of rule weakened. Yet, despite this, according to Yamakawa, the apparatus of government was still in the hands of "remnants of the old ruling class." Regarding why this peculiar sociopolitical stalemate prevailed, Yamakawa had the following to say:

> This is occurring because a powerful democratic force capable of taking over the governmental authority seized from the old ruling has yet to emerge from among the people. Therefore, the most pressing task at the current stage of our democratic revolution is to consolidate the desire for democracy that is springing up everywhere among all strata of the people and mold it into a powerful democratic political force —in other words, to establish a popular front. Only through the appearance of a new force of this kind will the government end up where it needs to end up. Only with the establishment of this new government will the people themselves be able to promote the democratization of the new Japan, only then will our democratic revolution be put on the right track, and only then will we be able to take the first steps toward addressing the food problem and other tasks relating to Japan's economic reconstruction.[21]

Yamakawa therefore called for the establishment of what he labeled the Democratic People's League (DPL), or Minshu Jinmin Renmei, to eliminate this critical roadblock that was obstructing the consummation of Japan's democratic revolution. What Yamakawa was proposing, in effect, was a reverse engineering exercise in which Japan would build, ersatz, a political vehicle under the conditions of a postwar occupation that would act as the functional equivalent of what had evolved through the armed resistance struggle in Western Europe. Indeed, the parallels with the Western European situation were explicitly drawn in a number of editorials in Japan's leading dailies written in response to Yamakawa's proposals. Heartily endorsed by the press, Yamakawa's appeal proved to be extremely popular across a wide spectrum of the politically active population. Endorsement of Yamakawa's proposal came from individuals, groups, and interests ranging from the liberal economist Ishibashi Tanzan on the right to leading communists on the far left. This reception highlights how the notion of a broad-based popular front of "resistance" against the "forces of reaction" was a formulation that, as in many other postwar societies, matched the ethos created by the postwar condition.

Japan's political situation clearly contained features that provided grounds for using the popular-front/resistance metaphor. As mentioned earlier, the regime based on the Meiji constitution was still in place. Although not fascist, perhaps, there was a decidedly reactionary quality in the incumbent government of Shidehara Kijūrō. A baron and ex-foreign minister, Shidehara was selected as prime minister by a closed circle of Imperial advisers, as were the members of his cabinet. Certain members of his cabinet, furthermore, had made a number of widely publicized antilabor and antiopposition statements, including a threat to use police force against workers engaged in labor dispute actions. Furthermore, the cabinet presided over an increasingly dysfunctional food distribution system and a hyperinflationary trend that was imposing severe hardship on the general population, but rather than advancing economic policy in a "progressive" socialistic direction, the Shidehara government insisted on scrapping economic controls and implemented a number of other policies that were perceived to favor *zaibatsu* interests. With the authoritarian Meiji constitution still operative and the occupation forces publicly declaring that economic policy was not an area where they would intervene, there was arguably little recourse outside of a show of political unity both inside and outside the Diet if populist policies were to be implemented.

The JCP immediately declared its wholehearted support for Yamakawa's DPL initiative. Spurred by Nosaka Sanzō's return from Yenan, the party's fifth congress, between February 24 and 26, 1946, established a program built around popular-front tactics. As students of the postwar JCP emphasize, the organizing theme in the platform was the so-called lovable JCP line. As succinctly phrased in the congress' declaration, the essence of the new line was that "the Japan Communist party holds as its basic objective for the time being to be the completion of the bourgeois democratic revolution that is currently under way in our country through peaceful and democratic means."[22] The concrete tactic that would be used in the party's pursuit of "peaceful democratic revolution" was to be a popular front linking workers and "democratic elements" from other classes. And, in a move aimed at aligning the party's basic stance with that which was palatable to the other political forces that would cohabit a popular front, the JCP dropped its long-standing demand for the immediate abolition of the imperial institution, since the reduced significance of the emperor in the democratized postwar polity had eliminated the need. Whatever the degree of guidance involved, it is noteworthy that in presenting the new policy line, JCP officials too made a point of drawing parallels between the Japanese situation and that in Europe. As such, the new policy indicates a belated integration of the party and its policies to the international communist movement.[23]

The JSP, by contrast, had a much harder time formulating a response to Yamakawa's initiative. The JSP's left-socialist contingent was enthusiastic about the prospect of having the party participate in the DPL, but the dominant social democrats were reticent. They instinctively distrusted the communists. Under ideal circumstances, they would clearly have preferred to proceed without the JCP, but an outright rejection of a socialist-communist coalition would both alienate the left socialists and dilute the JSP's bargaining leverage vis-à-vis the "bourgeois" parties and interest groups.[24] Caught in the cross fire, the JSP eventually decided to forgo participation in the DPL "for the time being."

After weeks of planning and networking, a preparatory meeting for DPL's establishment was at last held, on April 3. Demonstrating the continuing popularity of the idea, the meeting attracted representatives from over 100 labor unions, farmers' unions, and cultural organizations. Four days later those involved in the preparatory committee organized a rally. The rally was reportedly attended by 70,000 unionists and individuals from other groups. This was followed by a 50,000-strong march to the prime minister's residence to deliver the resolution adopted at the rally.

Meanwhile, General MacArthur ordered the Japanese government to call an election, which was subsequently scheduled for April 10. The election led to substantial changes in the composition of the popularly elected lower house of the Diet. First, as a result of the election, the JSP now held 92 of the 464 seats in the House and was the number-three party behind the "bourgeois" Liberal and Progressive parties (140 and 94 seats, respectively) in a Diet where no single party came close to a majority. The results were a tremendous improvement over the proletarian parties' prewar record (at their peak, in 1937, they had together held 37 seats). More proximately, it made the JSP a player to be reckoned with. In the words of Nishio, "from that day [the day of the election] on, the JSP . . . became in one big leap a powerful, established presence in the Japanese political world."[25] Second, the 5 seats that the JCP won meant that it too was a player in the parliamentary arena—in its case, for the first time. Third, the labor parties were not in a position to construct a majority on their own and would have to enter into a coalition with at least one of the "bourgeois" parties in order to do so. Of the two leading nonlabor parties, the Liberal Party under the prewar-party politician Hatoyama Ichirō was clearly preferable to the inappropriately named Progressive Party, which was unacceptable because it had a larger contingent of Diet members who had actively collaborated with the wartime regime and went on to offend the left's sensibility even more by naming Shidehara its party president.

Technically, with the Meiji constitutional system still in place, the election results did not in and of themselves determine who would become prime minister or who would be included in a new cabinet, as this was a prerogative of the emperor. Shidehara, in fact, embarked on a series of initiatives aimed at retaining his office.[26] This spurred the "popular" parties represented in the Diet—the Liberal Party, the Cooperative Party, the JSP, and the JCP—to form a joint committee to oversee a campaign to force Shidehara's resignation in accordance with "democratic principles." The coordinating committee used the language of popular-front resistance struggle to describe their efforts. Theirs was "a major popular movement inside and outside of the Diet" directed against the "reactionary elements . . . that are attempting to nip the construction of a democratic Japan in the bud."[27] The parties worked with the DPL organizing committee to plan a mass rally to be held on April 28 to demonstrate popular support for an "overthrow" *(datō)* of the Shidehara government. This two-pronged application of pressure proved successful. Shidehara announced his resignation on April 22. The scheduled DPL-sponsored rally was canceled.

With this, the four-party committee was turned into an instrument for forging a "popular democratic" government. However, it quickly became apparent in the committee discussions that there was little hope a formal coalition including all four parties could be forged. The Liberals insisted that a coalition including Communists was out of the question. The left socialists inside the JSP pressed for the JCP's inclusion, as did the JCP, of course. After extremely intricate and difficult negotiations, a two-part compromise arrangement was reached on the construction of a new "democratic" cabinet government. The JSP and the small centrist Cooperative Party agreed to back a single-party government led by the Liberal Party's Hatoyama Ichirō. Outside the Diet, the Communists would be included along with the Socialists in an extra-parliamentary committee that Hatoyama agreed to consult with in formulating policy. Although disjunctured and convoluted, as Takahashi Hikohiro argues, the arrangement did represent a loose "popular front" in that it enveloped political elements similar to those that were behind the Resistance cabinets of France and Italy. When the parties had ironed out the agreement they took it to Shidehara, to whom palace insiders had delegated the task of arranging a successor cabinet. Shidehara then began the process of getting formal imperial approval for the transfer of the reins of government to Hatoyama.[28]

Before Shidehara could submit a memorial to the emperor that would have validated the transfer of power, however, MacArthur threw a wrench into the works. In a move that illustrated how the task of purging Japan of its ostensible militarists was beginning to weigh more heavily in occupation policy than in internal politics, SCAP, spurred by the foreign press corps' discovery of a prewar book ghostwritten for Hatoyama in which support for Japan's war effort was expressed, issued a directive ordering Hatoyama's purge from public office, thereby effectively precipitating the collapse of the painfully crafted "popular democratic" coalition government. A second set of negotiations ensued, and at one point a single-party government of the JSP backed by the four parties was put forward. The party, however, was paralyzed by a three-way split of opinion between proponents of a coalition with Liberals that excluded the JCP (primarily social democrats), a popular-front-style coalition government built on a JSP-JCP entente (left socialists), and a middle-ground position of a single-party minority government of the JSP. In the meantime, the Liberal Party had replaced Hatoyama with Yoshida Shigeru, another conservative, nonelected ex-diplomat with an inbuilt distaste for the labor movement. The upshot was a single-party Liberal minority government headed by a nonparty prewar figure, established on May 23, with the backing of the other conservative party, the Progressives. Thus, thanks to occupation intervention and the absence of a balance of power that would compel an entente with the JCP, an entire month of delicate negotiations and mass demonstrations had produced not a popular-front-style government but another government built on more or less the same model as the preceding government. Both the JSP and JCP promptly labeled the Yoshida government as "reactionary."

With the Yoshida government's establishment, the various factions in the labor movement were once again faced with the task of devising a strategy to overthrow a reactionary government, and all wings declared once again that the appropriate line was to forge a popular-democratic front. But in doing so they were confronted with the delicate issue of whether parliamentary or extra-parliamentary tactics should take priority. Given that the movement was occurring under peacetime conditions and under circumstances in which the parliamentary process was operational and that the occupation forces appeared willing to make sure the Japanese government did not resort to heavy-handed repression, establishing an answer was not nearly as straightforward as when forging a popular resistance movement under wartime conditions. Unfortunately for the coherence of the movement, this was also an issue that hit at fundamental differences in worldviews. The communists in particular promoted initiatives focusing on the extraparliamentary front by organizing mass demonstrations to press populist economic demands and undermine the Yoshida government politically. Tokuda of the JCP and Takano of the Sōdōmei left-socialist wing were prominent among the organizers of a series of massive antigovernment rallies that climaxed in the 1.25-million-strong (500,000 in the capital alone) May Day rally and the 250,000-person "Food May Day" rally on May 19.[29] The demands put forward were identical in spirit to those being put forward by the left on the European continent: "the exclusion of monopoly capital from the democratic people's government and the construction of a planned economy," "voice for labor unions and the establishment of industrial democracy," and "economic recovery and assistance to the unemployed, returning soldiers, repatriates from overseas, injured soldiers, and surviving families paid for by capitalists and large landlords."[30]

The parliamentary-process-oriented social democrats, in the meantime, put forward an initiative intended to co-opt the drive for a popular front for their own purposes when, in late May, they announced their intention to form a Democratic League to Save the Country (Kyūkoku Minshu Renmei). The platform of the new league echoed the basic themes propounded by Yamakawa's DPL but was distinguished by its greater emphasis on the importance of parliamentary processes as a vehicle for assuring progressive political change.[31] In the end, the left socialists, though not entirely happy with the tone of the Democratic League chose to go along, and even convinced the DPL organizing committee to announce a merger with it. This time, the JCP refused to participate.[32] The JSP-sponsored league, however, did little that was of substance, and over the course of the summer gradually disappeared from the scene.

Resistance: the general-strike drive

In an insightful comment years later, Yamakawa Hitoshi, the original architect of the Democratic People's League, assessed the accomplishments of that movement on behalf of a postwar popular front as follows:

> Had the democratic forces coalesced during this period when, under the initial occupation policies, democratic fervor flared up among the masses—and this period was a very short one—it would not have been impossible for them to take the government. However, the correct left-wing forces were too hopelessly small to take full advantage of the circumstances. This was perhaps to be expected since the situation at the time was one in which the forces that had existed before the war had been completely destroyed and nothing was there.[33]

By the fall of 1946, however, significant progress was being made in overcoming the shortcomings of organization among the "correct forces" that Yamakawa pointed out, and nowhere was this more apparent than in the labor unions. By the end of the summer of 1946, unionization had progressed to where 4 million workers were organized. A considerable proportion of these unions were now consolidated nationally in industrial federations. Two national centers further consolidated these unions across industries. Labor-movement-affiliated political parties had been established and now held seats in the Diet. The present question was to what purpose would these new labor movement organizations be put?

The parliamentary elections of April 1946 had left the JCP with 1 percent of the seats in a Diet chamber. Clearly, parliamentary maneuvering held little prospect of providing the party with its primary source of political clout. For the moment, at least, any such clout that the party might hope to obtain had to be derived primarily from extra-parliamentary sources. Such a course, in any event, coincided with the party's natural inclinations.[34] Following a SCAP warning against mass political demonstrations in the wake of the May 19 Food May Day, the JCP's emphasis began to shift from organizing mass demonstrations to harnessing the labor unions. Thanks to the establishment of nationwide industrial organizations in key industries and sectors, industrial federations appeared particularly attractive as a target for a JCP initiative. As for the modality through which this would be done, the term "general strike" began to appear with increasing frequency in party pronouncements and deliberations.

The term "general strike" had been used as a label for planned strikes of Japan National Railway (JNR) and the seamen's union during the summer. On July 24 the government announced plans to dismiss 75,000 redundant railway workers. A week later the quasi-governmental shippers' association revealed plans to dismiss 65,000 ship workers. The respective unions responded by announcing their intent to launch industry-wide "general strikes" to oppose the proposed dismissals. Despite the internal turmoil in both Kokurō and the seamen's union, both unions ultimately won retractions of the planned dismissals.[35] While it is difficult to objectively gauge the extent to which the communists' militancy influenced the settlements, the fact that the JNR and the seamen's union dispute ended in a clear victory for the unions encouraged the JCP and enhanced its reputation as a political force willing to confront the government.

Tokuda and the communists decided to apply the general-strike tactic on a wider scale in what came to be labeled the October Struggle. According to the testimony of communist officials directly involved in the planning of the offensive, it was intended by Tokuda to be a "political struggle" that would commemorate the first anniversary of the reconstruction of the JCP.[36] It was to be an orchestrated wave of strikes by Sanbetsu-affiliated unions, mainly in the private sector. However, the communists and Sanbetsu had trouble getting unit enterprise unions to carry out the scheduled strikes, and the number of strikers in a given industry fell far short of even the number of unionists who were members of the industry's Sanbetsu federation. The following description by an American observer of the communist-led offensives over the course of the summer and fall (which also refers to the Kokurō and seamen's disputes) helps place the effort in a more objective frame of reference: "The movement can be described as a strike wave only in a limited sense. There were, indeed, a great many strikes, usually local in character, and generally short. Threats of strike action were loud and frequent, but they were not always carried out. A strike of seamen was called in September, which was only partly effective owing to an intra-union conflict. The government railway workers called a 24-hour strike for September 15 but an agreement was reached before the deadline. The press-radio strike in October fizzled badly. A five-day strike in October closed most Hokkaido coal mines but not those in Kyushu. . . . At the October strike peak only 1.21 percent of total man-days available were lost by strike actions."[37] When looked at from a business unionist perspective, the results of the October Struggle were a decidedly mixed bag. On the one hand, the unions enjoyed an impressive degree of success in attaining demands relating to wages and working conditions. The settlement that Densan, the electric power workers' union, reached with the electric power industry—in which wage levels were derived from the cost of basic living expenses and pegged to inflation—was widely adopted as a model in subsequent collective bargaining. On the other hand, the offensive also saw the collapse of one of Sanbetsu's most important organizations, the newspaper and communications workers' unions.[38]

The social democrats and the left socialists based in Sōdōmei condemned the October Struggle on two grounds. One, emphasized more in statements by social democrats, was that using strikes for such nakedly political purposes was a violation of principled unionism, and that the primary modality for engineering political change should be the ballot box. The other, more characteristic of left socialists, was that when Japan was facing severe crisis of production, neither labor nor the economy could shoulder the disruptions that use of the strike entailed. Despite these objections, in the wake of the October Struggle, Sōdōmei and the JSP joined the JCP and Sanbetsu in a loosely integrated "resistance" aimed at toppling the Yoshida government, one of the most prominent features of which was a massive general strike. An underlying factor leading to this development was the rapidly deteriorating economic situation: Inflation had worsened significantly, and accelerating prices stimulated labor unrest as workers desperately sought wage increases to allow them to sustain their purchasing power. This translated into a dramatic jump in the number of labor disputes and strikes. The growing estrangement between the Yoshida government and the JSP was another factor. Stimulatory financial policies insistently pursued by the Yoshida cabinet finance minister Ishibashi Tanzan, over the objections of prominent economists and the JSP, were rightly perceived as having exacerbated the roaring inflation; production increases were stymied by lack of resources and inputs. A third factor was what appeared to be highly autocratic and reactionary behavior by the government, and Prime Minister Yoshida in particular.

The JSP's minority left socialists pointed to the mounting labor unrest and used it as justification for their long-standing claim the party needed to enter into a coalition with the communists. According to Sanbetsu's Hosoya, the JCP leadership was aware of what was going on inside the JSP and had thus assigned him the job of linking up with the Sōdōmei left wing's Takano Minoru as a step toward consummating a left-socialist–communist entente.[39] In late November, stimulated into action by sharpening antagonism between the JSP and the Yoshida government and acting in accordance with popular-front sensibilities, the left-socialist chair of the JSP's labor committee, Katō Kanjū, brought together representatives from Sōdōmei, Sanbetsu, and Nichirō Kaigi, the last a newly formed national center representing about 400,000 workers in "neutral" unions not affiliated with the other two national centers. The purpose of the meeting was to organize a campaign of union-led extra-parliamentary demonstrations in support of a drive inside the Diet to pass a vote of no confidence against the cabinet and force its resignation.[40] A second meeting of the same group on December 2 resulted in a resolution to hold a set of union-sponsored overthrow-the-cabinet rallies around the country on December 17, and these rallies were duly held with a reported attendance of 500,000. Parallel rallies were held in Yokohama and Osaka, with attendance reported to be 30,000 in each of these cities.

Simultaneous to this, growing antagonism within the Yoshida government was creating a second front between unions and the government. The deteriorating economy caused acute difficulty for public-sector workers because the cumbersome budgetary process, tight fiscal constraints, and a lack of institutionalized collective-bargaining procedures to negotiate the government employee wages made it extremely hard to adjust public-sector wages to the rapidly changing circumstances. Over the course of late summer and fall, the newly formed national federations of the government railway workers, postal workers, teachers, and other public-sector employees had presented demands for wage increases to the government, but in no instance did the government's offers even begin to approach what the unions considered a reasonable settlement. Frustrated, the government-sector unions, on November 26, coalesced into the National Government Agency Joint Struggle Committee representing 520,000 national railway workers, 380,000 postal and communications workers, 330,000 teachers, 300,000 other government employees, dubbed Zenkankōchō (Zenkoku Kankōchō Kyōdō Tōsō Iinkai). Consolidated bargaining with the government proved no less rocky than when the respective unions bargained independently. At one point in the process, government negotiators, having arrived an hour late and apparently tipsy for a scheduled bargaining session, got into a shouting match with the union representatives. Following angry exchanges, the government negotiators walked out.[41] Whereas the parliamentary drive to topple the Yoshida government was a JSP-centered initiative, the public-sector worker drive was JCP-led. Unbeknownst to most observers at the time, the communists had effectively infiltrated the public-sector workers' bargaining committee with three out of the five seats on the committee taken by members of the JCP.[42]

It was not just in the public sector, however, that wages had not kept up with the galloping inflation. Sōdōmei's more moderate stance on wage issues had meant that wages in its unions tended to lag behind Sanbetsu's. This became particularly conspicuous in the wake of the wage gains made by Sanbetsu unions in the October Struggle, placing Sōdōmei under great pressure to follow suit with a wage offensive of its own. The upshot was Sōdōmei's November 3 announcement of a "year-end struggle" for a substantial increase in wages and the conclusion of collective-bargaining contracts where these were not yet in place.

Under the combined weight of these nominally independent political and economic campaigns, events moved toward a major political and economic showdown between the labor movement and the Yoshida government during the final weeks of 1946. The joint union committee that had organized the rally against the Yoshida government met on December 24 and approved a proposal to form a new committee whose purpose would be to demonstrate the support of as wide a range of unions as possible for two interconnected goals. One was the success of the public-sector unions in their negotiations with the government. The second was the replacement of the Yoshida government with a "democratic government." The latter was defined as a government that would fulfill three conditions. It would be a popular-front-style government resting "on a foundation of all of the opposition parties with the JSP at the center." It would be a government from which the "conservative reactionary forces centered around the Liberal and Progressive parties" would be excluded. And, finally, it would be "a government that would...quickly implement the demands of the public-sector workers' unions."[43] The target date of January 15, 1947, was set for the formal establishment of this new committee, to be christened Zentō (Zenkoku Rōso Kyōdō Tōsō Iinkai, or the National Labor Union Joint Struggle Committee).

With the arrival of the new year, several unforeseen developments added further fuel to the fire. One of these was a New Year's radio broadcast by Prime Minister Yoshida in which he blamed the unions for the current economic crisis and labeled the union leaders involved in these various campaigns "outlaw gangs" *(futei no yakara)*. The term used by Yoshida, it should be noted, had connotations of lese majesty and treason and had a record of use by the prewar establishment in conjunction with prewar repression against the left. This use of the term seemed to highlight the anachronistic authoritarian character of the Yoshida government, precipitating a groundswell of popular resentment. Several weeks later, Sanbetsu president Kikunami Katsumi was knifed by a gangster who happened to be a member of a Liberal Party auxiliary organization, adding further to the government's undemocratic image.

Until the end of 1946, the anti-Yoshida extra-parliamentary mobilization had unfolded more or less in accordance with the left-socialist game plan of labor-union-organized mass demonstrations to put pressure on the Yoshida government to resign. However, this began to change during the first weeks of January. The JCP leadership apparently came to see the developments as constituting a momentous revolutionary upsurge that would allow the party to leapfrog the handicap that it faced in the arena of parliamentary bargaining and install its leadership firmly in a dominant position in a socialist-communist government. A "general strike" of the public-sector unions and other sympathetic unions on the massive scale that now seemed possible, it reasoned, would create a level of disruption and turmoil that would provide the opportunity for a seizure of power by a "democratic people's government" in which the JCP, with the leverage fostered by its control over the most powerful unions, would be a leading player. It would fill in the missing link by the mutually reinforcing circle of labor-party-government coalitions that were the mark of the Resistance governance in Western Europe. Testimony by former Communists recalls a party leadership, intoxicated by the prospect of imminent "revolution," already discussing which party officials should get what cabinet post. The JCP leadership hastily called a secret conference of party operatives from around the country, which met between January 6 and 9. In that meeting, local party officials were explicitly urged to concentrate their energies on turning the current public-sector workers' wage dispute into an interindustry political strike that would precipitate the formation of a "people's government."[44] Following the conference, party operatives returned to their respective cells and fractions and proceeded to engage in agitation and propaganda along the lines that Yoyogi had outlined.

Zentō was formally established on January 15 as a body linking the public-sector wage drive and the extra-parliamentary movement to force the Yoshida government to resign. Comprising representatives from the three national centers, the public-sector workers' alliance, and thirty other union organizations, Zentō constituted an impressive coming together of unions spanning the length and breadth of the labor movement. With its formation, the basic framework that would allow the JCP to turn the public-sector workers' strike into a political general strike was now in place. Three days later, the communist-controlled public-sector workers' negotiating committee announced that it had scheduled a general strike for midnight, February 1. Technically, under Zentō's bylaws, the decision over whether or not to enter into a strike along with the public-sector unions was left up to individual unions, but in the meantime, JCP operatives worked furiously to make sure that as many unions as possible would join in. Care was taken in the planning process by the various unions involved to assure that essential services to the occupation forces were not disrupted (e.g., Kokurō planned an abbreviated production control in which trains to the occupation forces' facilities would be kept running, and Densan was to assure that electric power continued to be delivered). The JCP, wrongly as it turned out, seems to have been confident that the occupation forces would not intervene. Adding to its confidence was a December 24 release by the Far Eastern Commission (FEC)—the newly established multinational body of the Allied representatives whose function was to oversee the occupation—of a list of sixteen principles of trade union policy to be adhered to under the occupation.[45] Prominent among these were the assurance of freedom of expression for the labor movement, its right to engage in strikes and other dispute activity (to the extent that these did not interfere with the occupation), the right of unions to support political parties of choice, and an admonition against government and police interference in legitimate trade-union activity. The FEC announcement was significant because one of the unresolved questions at the time was whether a "general strike" would constitute grounds for occupation intervention. The FEC's Sixteen Principles were interpreted by the JCP as an indicator that the occupation forces would not intervene or, if it did, that this intervention would later be undone by the Allied council.

The party, however, had badly misread SCAP's intentions. The latter, anticipating a near complete breakdown of social order once the strike was called, had concluded that the general strike was a breach of occupation policy and moved to suppress it. What turned the entire episode into an extremely convoluted exercise was SCAP's insistence until the last minute—apparently out of a desire to maintain a democratic gloss and to avoid back home the negative publicity that would be generated by an overt suppression of the strike—on pressuring the unions to call the strike off "voluntarily." A curious ten-day-long behind-the-scenes standoff between SCAP and the predominantly communist union leaders was initiated on January 22. On that day, fifteen union officials involved in the general-strike movement were marched into the office of General W. F. Marquat, chief of the occupation forces' Economic and Scientific Section (ESS), which had jurisdiction over labor affairs, and were read a statement that Marquat claimed was signed by MacArthur. The statement warned the unionists that a "general work stoppage" would not be permitted. Marquat then told the unionists that they were to return the following day with a written response to "these instructions." They were not given copies of the statement, were told that they were authorized to "communicate the gist of the statement within the union for discussion purposes . . . and . . . could take notes on his statement," but were then ordered not to make the statement public.[46] The unionists insisted that they required a written order before they could call off the strike. At this point Sōdōmei announced that it would respect the general-strike cancellation order. The JSP declared that everything possible needed to be done to avoid the strike. The JCP and the JCP-controlled public-sector unions, however, were adamant, and the ensuing days were punctuated by repeated exchanges in which the occupation forces' officials attempted to pressure union officials behind the scenes, and the unions refused to back down until a written order was given. The deadlock was not broken until January 31, just hours before the strike was scheduled to begin, when MacArthur issued a written cancellation order. MacArthur's formal order was followed by a tearful radio broadcast by Zenkankōchō head Ii Yashirō announcing the strike's cancellation.

Considerable controversy surrounds the JCP leadership's role in the hours leading up to MacArthur's announcement of the cancellation, particularly with regard to the question of exactly when and how Tokuda gave Ii the go-ahead to announce the cancellation. It is clear, however, that the party continued to agitate on behalf of the strike until the final hours before the cancellation was announced. In one infamous incident, the Central Labor Relations Board, the tripartite commission created to oversee mediation of disputes, extracted a settlement from the government that met virtually all of the union demands. Tokuda, who was a member of the CLRB, volunteered to communicate the offer to the unions. However, instead of explaining the offer before the assembled unionists, he spent his time inciting them to carry out the strike.[47] Having devoted so much effort to inflaming sentiment in favor of the strike, the party's efforts to halt the strike following its eleventh-hour acceptance of the cancellation order was not easy nor entirely successful as subsequent scattered incidents of strike actions indicate. The strike's cancellation took root nonetheless. The public-sector workers, with the help of SCAP's prodding of the government, eventually reached a settlement.

Resistance governance attained? Zenrōren, April 1947 election, and the establishment of center-left coalition governance

The 2.6 million public-sector workers that were represented by the February 1 general-strike organizing committee constituted a force over six times the size of the total number of unionized workers in Japan at its prewar peak. If we add to this the other unions affiliated with Zentō either directly or through a national center, the total rises to approximately 4 million, or roughly 80 percent of the total unionized workforce at the time. As loose, as tentative, and as disjunctured as it was, the scale and degree of unity in action that the labor movement had attained in its confrontation with the Shidehara and Yoshida cabinets was unprecedented. The spectrum of labor union ideology that stretched from the moderate social democrats on the right to the communists on the left that was brought together in the movement also matched precisely the ideological spectrum found in the WFTU as well as—if one ignores the Catholic wing, which was not a major presence in the Japanese context—the Resistance coalitions that had emerged in France and Italy.

Zentō was dissolved on February 1, the day that the general strike had been scheduled. According to those attending the council's last meeting that day, a rather somber atmosphere prevailed until one of the participants voiced the opinion that it would be a shame to allow to dissipate the solidarity that had been attained among the various currents in the movement. The speaker went on to urge the group to use Zentō as a base for establishing a successor organization that could serve as a permanent vehicle for coordinating joint action among the organizations represented there. The proposal led directly to a series of negotiations among representatives of Sōdōmei, Sanbetsu, and Nichirō Kaigi to create an organ of this kind. These negotiations proved to be exceedingly difficult, however, with the social democrats in Sōdōmei proving to be extremely reluctant to work with the communist elements in Sanbetsu. This opposition was eventually overcome. It is interesting and to some extent symbolic that an important catalyst in breaking the deadlock appeared in mid-February when Japanese unionists learned from GHQ about an upcoming visit to Japan of a delegation from the WFTU. In Japan, as was true elsewhere, the WFTU was looked upon as both a model of labor movement solidarity to strive for and a purveyor of international legitimacy for local movements. Japan was not represented in the WFTU—indeed, as a former Axis power it was at the time deliberately excluded by the organization—but the desire to be part of the international federation was strong among Japanese unionists. One of the WFTU's principles was that each nation should be represented by only one labor union organization and that this organization should represent as broad a spectrum of unionized workers as possible. In light of this, the idea began to circulate that a show of solidarity on the part of the Japanese movement would pave the way for a Japanese bid to become a member of the international organ, and the negotiations relating to the formation of a permanent joint council at the national level gathered new momentum.

The upshot was the inauguration on March 10 of a new umbrella council for the three national centers and a number of unaffiliated industrial organizations that was christened Zenrōren (from Zenkoku Rōdō Kumiai Renraku Kyōgikai, the National Liaison Council of Labor Unions). Zenrōren was deliberately structured as a loose organization in order to gain the approval of Sōdōmei's skittish social democrats. Its articles of incorporation defined it as a "liaison and consultation organ [renraku kyōgi kikan] that respects the autonomy of labor unions," and in order to operationalize this, its statutes required a unanimous vote for any decision.[48] The declaration adopted that day had the following to say about the new council: "The National Liaison Council of Labor Unions that is being established today is not ideal in form, but it is an attempt by the Japanese labor unions, which have gathered together, to advance their historical mission on the basis of class fraternity and loyalty while mutually respecting their differences of stance and opinion." It also pointed to the ongoing need to struggle against the "conservative reactionary forces" behind the Yoshida government.[49]

In the middle of these developments, and in a move that echoed his intervention a year earlier as the Democratic People's League was getting under way, General MacArthur directed this "struggle" into an electoral channel. That is, following upon his cancellation of the February 1 strike, on February 6 MacArthur ordered in a letter to Prime Minister Yoshida that Yoshida call a general election following the close of the Diet session under way at the time. "It is necessary," the letter stated, "to obtain another democratic expression of the people's will on the fundamental issues with which Japanese society is now confronted."[50] The general election held on April 25 was the first to be held under the terms of the new constitution. It was accompanied the same month by elections to fill the newly established and popularly elected House of Councilors and a local election to fill positions in the newly democratized system of local government. The electioneering by the parties and the angle adopted in the press depicted the election as a contest between socialism and capitalism. The stances adopted by the campaigning parties and the realignments that occurred indicated quite clearly that the center of gravity in public discourse was tilting decisively in the direction of socialism toward some form of modified capitalism that incorporated socialistic elements. The JSP, backed by Sōdōmei, proclaimed in its election platform that if it were given a mandate to govern, it would "resolutely implement socialist policies," including state economic planning, public ownership, and democratic operation of basic industries.[51] The JCP and Sanbetsu too shifted their attention to the task of election campaigning in anticipation that the results would pave the way for the realization of the "people's government" built on the socialist-communist coalition that had been nipped in the bud by the general strike's cancellation.[52] On the other side of the class divide, a realignment of the "bourgeois" camp occurred. A party espousing "modified capitalism" was formed when remnants of Shidehara's old Progressive Party and a group that bolted from Yoshida's Liberal Party joined together in the Democratic Party (Minshutō), allegedly with the backing of the progressively oriented business association Keizai Dōyūkai. The party, it declared, would "move in the direction of breaking away from the deeply rooted evils of capitalism while modifying the unrealistic attributes of socialism." Its platform committed the party to "strive for a rapid recovery via the democratization of industry on the basis of a comprehensive economic plan" and, in the area of labor relations, to seek a "separation of capital and management in large firms, seek partnership between management and workers, and in particular respect the important role of labor by making use of managerial councils and establishing a system of profit sharing."[53] Elsewhere, a survey of corporate executives and business owners in the capital region, taken in March by the Kanto Employers Association, showed that 21 percent of respondents favored a JSP government while another 14 percent favored a JSP-conservative coalition.[54]

The election gave the JSP a plurality in the House of Representatives, with its share of seats increasing from 94 to 143 seats out of 466 (or 31 percent of the total). The Democrats obtained 121 seats (26 percent) while the Liberal Party dropped from 141 to 131 (28 percent of the total). Contrary to the party's expectations, the number of JCP seats actually shrank from 5 to 4. The April 20 House of Councilors election produced similar results, with the JSP obtaining a plurality there as well. If the election was a battle between capitalism and socialism, then neither capitalism nor socialism had received a clear mandate. In parliamentary terms the April elections clearly strengthened the position of the center-left in the parliamentary arena at the expense of the right and extreme left. A round of coalition talks from which the JCP was excluded led to an agreement that the next government would be headed by JSP Chair Katayama Tetsu and backed by a coalition of the Liberal Party, the Democratic Party, the Socialist Party, and the small and centrist People's Cooperative Party. On May 16 a policy accord was concluded and signed by the same four parties.[55] An expanded central committee meeting of the excluded JCP held between May 18 and 20 declared that it would support the coalition government even though "it is not a popular democratic government" as long as the Liberals were excluded.[56] It is unclear to what extent the JCP announcement was a motivating factor, but the Liberals subsequently opted out of participation in the cabinet, even as they pledged to back policies based on the four-party agreement. Receiving support from all of the major parties in the Diet, Katayama was chosen as prime minister by a near unanimous vote of 420 out of 426 votes in the House of Representatives and 205 out of 210 in the House of Councilors. The Katayama Cabinet was established on June 1, with ministers brought in from the JSP, the Democratic Party, and the PCP at a 7-7-2 ratio, respectively. Thus emerged a three-party center-left coalition government (Democratic, People's Cooperative, JSP) flanked by two "silent partners," on the left and the right.

As for the WFTU mission that had been greeted with such enthusiasm on the part of the labor movement, a delegation headed by Louis Saillant toured Japan between March 24 and April 7 (the first contingent of the mission arrived on March 17). The visit took place at a point in time when the international labor movement was beginning to feel the effects of the budding East-West tensions of the Cold War, the impact of which will be discussed in greater detail in subsequent parts of this book. GHQ had in fact been reluctant to authorize the WFTU delegation's visit. In one widely noted incident, the members of the delegation, under circumstances that remain murky, stood up a gathering of some 50,000 unionists. When approached later by the rally's organizers at his hotel, Saillant gave a noncommittal answer that has been interpreted by many historians of Japanese labor as alluding to intervention on the part of SCAP. The WFTU delegation did, however, encourage Japanese unionists to send observers to the scheduled June meeting in Prague. SCAP did not authorize the visit.[57] On the other hand, the WFTU delegation's mysterious behavior may have had something to do with the fact that Cold War rifts were beginning to appear around that time that would eventually precipitate a split. Indeed, increasing differences within the mission members that reflected the growing tensions inside the international movement made it impossible for the mission members to write a common report upon their trip to Japan.[58] There was thus great irony in that, just as the Japanese labor movement was beginning to edge toward organizational unity in the form Zenrōren and other initiatives, the unified international labor movement from which it sought inspiration was falling apart.

Of all the wings of the labor movement, it was arguably among the communists that the differences in historical context between Japan, on the one hand, and the Western European counterpart cases with which we have been dealing, on the other, were most consequential. Participation in the wartime resistance, as traced in chapter 3, was critical for Western European communists because it was through their active participation that they were able to build a solid organizational presence, reverse their tarnished popular image, and emerge from the war with a strong base of mass support. Organizationally, the wartime resistance constituted an environment that was particularly conducive to communist methods of expanding influence and control. As a result, by the end of the war both the PCF and the PCI had established a solid presence not only in the trade union and partisan branches of their respective national labor movements, but also in the arena of government through the party's participation in postwar coalition cabinets. In Japan, as noted, the socialists and left socialists had a head start in organization building, and by the time the JCP was in a position to build a presence of its own, the other two wings were already well along in setting up a national organization. It was not a mere coincidence that whereas communists and socialists resided in a common national union organization in France and Italy, JCP overtures for entry into Sōdōmei were rejected and the Japanese communists were effectively prevented from duplicating the French and Italian models. On top of this, in contrast to the top-down vector by which the postwar French and Italian labor movements came into being, Japanese communists faced a highly decentralized and atomized structure of labor union organization that was difficult to control and manipulate. The relatively small party membership, which was itself an outgrowth of the the lack of a resistance movement, meant that the party was not in a position to enhance its image and popular support in the manner that its French and Italian counterparts were able to do.

Further reinforcing this relative weakness of the JCP's position was its delayed exposure to the popular-front tactics that were at the heart of the international communist movement's wartime and immediate postwar strategy worldwide.[59] The incarceration of the party's postwar top leadership, for instance, predated the French Popular Front and the Comintern's seventh congress of 1935. As students of Japanese communism stress, the program with which the party leadership were working upon their release from prison was the so-called 1932 thesis that directed the party to abolish the emperor system and emphasized violent tactics. Given the fact that during incarceration the communists had little opportunity to interact with the international communist movement (and the Comintern itself had been disbanded by this time), it is hardly surprising that a gap existed between what was accepted practice at the level of the international communist movement, on the one hand, and the understandings of the leadership of the JCP, on the other. While the Japanese communist leadership was certainly aware that postwar conditions were radically different from those to which the earlier thesis was directed and it did make an effort to adjust its tactics, as demonstrated by their continued harsh attacks on the "social fascists" in the JSP and Sōdōmei during the last months of 1945, they had not yet mastered popular-front tactics. The cumulative effect of these relative handicaps that the JCP faced as consequence of the absence of a resistance movement in Japan was brought home by the results of the April 1946 general election. The 4 percent of the vote (and 1 percent of the Diet Lower House seats) held by the JCP put the party in a very different position from that of the PCF and PCI with their 25 and 20 percent, respectively, of the vote and comparable portions of seats. Where the latter parties were major presences in their respective partisan politics arenas and in a position to send ministers to the cabinet, the JCP was simply not in a position to participate in government.

If the lack of a resistance experience handicapped the communists relative to their Western European counterparts and prevented their placement in a common political framework with their social democratic and left-socialist colleagues, it was also true that tendencies toward fusion in the repeated efforts to forge a resistance-style popular front during the period of transmuted "resistance" characterized the first year and a half following surrender. These included, along with the various unconsummated bids to unite the communist and social democratic/left-socialist wings in a common national center, the bid for a people's democratic front associated with the DPL, the expansive loosely integrated struggle that fed into the ultimately aborted February 1 general strike, and, in the spring of 1947, the formation of Zenrōren and the partisan and government coalitions associated with the Katayama cabinet. Compared to the French and Italian examples, the Japanese resistance-coalition government that eventually emerged under JSP prime minister Katayama was noteworthy for the tenuousness—or, alternatively, the minimalism—of its "inclusion" of the JCP. Likewise, though Zenrōren might have brought the communists and the socialists together in a common labor union organization, it was an organization in which binding of the political factions was extremely weak and that failed to overcome the essential organizational autonomy of its constituent units. All of this would profoundly affect the dynamics of Japan's postwar "battle for production" that is the subject of the following chapter.

Chapter 5

Organizing the "Battle for Production" in Japan, 1945–1947

J apan's postwar condition, like Europe's, catapulted the interrelated themes of economic recovery and institutional reform to the forefront of both the labor movement's and the general public's agenda. The concern with economic recovery is readily understandable, as basic livelihood commodities were in extremely short supply and frequently available only at high, unaffordable prices on the black market. A massive portion of the population suffered from unemployment or, more commonly, underemployment. Even for those with jobs, the postwar inflation made wage bargaining a desperate cat-and-mouse game in which the purchasing power of even the largest of wage hikes was lost seemingly instantaneously. Aggregate statistics confirmed what was felt directly in daily lives. The population of the home islands increased by 9 million (or by about 12 percent) as a consequence of the repatriation of nationals from overseas. Against the increase in demand, 80 percent of Japan's shipping capacity, 34 percent of its industrial machinery, and an estimated 25 percent of its national wealth had been destroyed. Highly punitive reparations policies, which would later be rolled back, idled the most productive plant and equipment out of production. The rice harvest in 1946 was just 60 percent of the prewar norm. Mining and manufacturing in 1946 was 21 percent of 1934–1936 levels. With estimated per capita GNP just 66 percent of 1934–1936 levels, the economy was simply not producing what was needed.[1] As was true in Continental Europe, the immediate postwar years were permeated by the idea that it was essential that the labor movement play a leading role in this process. Collaboration with the wartime regime had discredited Japanese management, and an outright vacuum in managerial authority was deliberately created in Japan's leading enterprises by the occupation forces' "business purge," first as part of the *zaibatsu* dissolution program in late 1945 and then in the form of a blanket purge of about 3,200 business executives with positions in 278 corporations in January 1947. Even when they remained in control, Japan's employers did not appear to many to be capable of overseeing a just economic recovery. Postwar inflation made it frequently more profitable to sell hoarded materiel and commodities to the highest bidder on the black market than to actually process them. A new term, "production sabotage" *(seisan sabo),* was in fact coined to characterize Japanese management's unwillingness to restart production under these conditions. Outside of the factory, delays in the distribution of already meager food rations, often by up to several weeks, meant that urban populations had little choice but to spend a great amount of time, often work time, desperately foraging in the countryside for food that farmers were willing to barter for clothing or some other possession. Though essential for survival, such activities diverted the labor force that might have otherwise been more productive. Frustration with this state of affairs was high. In the words of one prominent labor figure: "The workers before us . . . wanted to apply their skills vigorously to the task of starting up a broken electrical generator, to take that piece of scrap steel that was sitting there, shape it and put it to productive use."[2]

As in Western Europe at the time, the core challenge was to find a way to increase the production of goods while assuring that basic livelihood needs were met. One "answer" on the part of Japanese workers was "production control" *(seisan kanri),* or the labor dispute tactic in which workers simply took over operations and ran an enterprise without management.[3] As one sympathetic occupation official observed:

> To the worker, production control seemed a "natural" way to avoid undue pressure on a tottering economy and interference with the production and transportation of the necessities of life. The new union leaders were eager to prove themselves responsible people. Finally, where so many enterprises were operating at a fraction of capacity for lack of fuel or raw materials, a work stoppage would not penalize management much. On the contrary, it could help the owners by relieving them of the obligation to pay wages on time. . . . For them, a standard strike would be a welcome excuse to close their doors.[4]

The production control tactic made its initial appearance in late 1945, and by the spring of 1946, labor statistics indicate that it had become the most commonly used tactic in labor disputes.

If the fundamentals of the Japanese economic situation were similar to those in France and Italy, there were nonetheless important differences in the logistics of the battle for production. This stemmed from the fact that during the initial eighteen months following Japan's surrender, it was not a Resistance coalition dominated by the labor movement and oriented toward socialistic policies that was in power, but a string of conservative, bureaucratic governments with a penchant for laissez-faire economics, which were exceedingly hostile toward even a modified capitalist modality of economic recovery. In February the Shidehara government issued a statement declaring production control a violation of property rights, also threatening to crack down on workers utilizing the tactic. GHQ, however, failed to back the government, and production control continued to spread. Along with the formation of enterprise unions in conjunction with which this often occurred, production control represented the functional counterpart of the postliberation workplace committees and factory takeovers in France and Italy, and the initiatives pursued at the grass-roots level by works councils in Germany. Production control, however, was at best a stopgap measure. A full-fledged economic recovery was widely understood to require systematic restructuring of economic institutions in order to facilitate production and allocate consumption in a socially equitable manner. The question was what the political and institutional format should be in doing so.

Beyond this, of the three Western European countries discussed directly in chapter 2, Japan's situation most closely resembled that of West Germany. As in the latter, domestic initiatives in the area of economic institutional reform were subject to the review and redirection of Allied—and most specifically, American—authorities. And as in West Germany, this process was one in which the state-oriented, socialist vector of domestic reform efforts was dampened in favor of a more autonomous and decentralized system of industrial relations, along with a labor movement that was more decentralized and less party-centered than in the post-Resistance movements of France and Italy.

Visions of recovery

It was de rigueur in the post-surrender period for Japanese labor-movement organs to stress their intention to focus on the "battle for production." For instance, the proclamation adopted on October 10, 1945, at the first national meeting of the group of social democratic and left-socialist unionists who reestablished Sōdōmei, specifically mentioned "the recovery of Japanese industry" as a core task of the postwar labor movement.[5] The point was reiterated in the platform adopted at Sōdōmei's inaugural convention in August 1946.[6] Likewise, Sanbetsu took the opportunity of its inaugural convention to declare in a more militant tone that it too would "fight for the economic recovery and cultural construction of Japan."[7]

Despite profound differences in ideological orientation among the competing currents, common themes pervaded the proposals and pronouncements of Japanese labor leaders regarding production recovery. One was that the "capitalistic" recovery being promoted by the incumbent conservatives was a wholly inappropriate response to Japan's socioeconomic situation.[8] The essence of the critique was that by giving priority to financial concerns, the government's strategy sought recovery at the expense of the worker and ignored real economic needs. The labor movement was critical of the callousness with which employers imposed unspeakable hardship on the working class as they sought to "balance the books" by resorting to dismissals of "redundant" workers. Such acts appeared all the more galling because these redundancies were seen as the product of the employers' collaboration with the militarists in the first place. The corollary was the claim that capitalist economic recovery with its stress on profitability and financial soundness needed to be replaced by a socialistic recovery strategy that would maximize employment and make full use of available physical resources and production capacity. Workers and their organizations were seen as the natural vehicle for leading the latter type of economic recovery strategy because worker-based initiatives "by nature cannot but include a transition to an economy that is not premised on unemployment."[9]

Implicit in the idea of a worker-oriented recovery was the principle that the market mechanism needed to be augmented by more of "a democratic" administration of the economy. As in Europe, the socialization and economic democracy were presented as pillars for achieving this democratization. Sōdōmei's 1946 movement policy thus called for "the socialization of the financial system and full-fledged state management of production, collection, and distribution system."[10] The conception of labor's role in economic recovery as outlined in Sōdōmei's proposal revolved around a system of worker "participation in enterprise" (*kigyō sanka*) to be implemented using a system of *keiei kyōgikai,* or management councils.[11] *Keiei kyōgikai* were presented as joint consultation organs consisting of equal numbers of labor union and management representatives, often supplemented by representatives of third-party groups, whose function was to discuss production issues and other matters of mutual concern to labor and management. Primary *keiei kyōgikai* would be established in the enterprise, but other *keiei kyōgikai* were to be organized at the regional, industrial, and national levels and would deal with issues that were broader in scope than those that could be effectively encompassed in an enterprise-based *keiei kyōgikai.* The substance of the Sōdōmei policies thus lay in a vision of production recovery as a joint labor-management exercise in which the two sides would be given more or less equal voice. Formal initiatives on behalf of a worker-led production recovery "movement," efforts in which left socialists played a particularly active role, were in evidence as early as mid-January 1946 when the Kanto Metalworkers Union announced an "industrial recovery movement." A resolution drafted by Takano Minoru calling for what was labeled a "break through the production-crisis industrial-recovery movement" (seisan kiki toppa sangyō fukkō undō) was adopted at his initiative at a meeting of the preparatory committee for the Sōdōmei's postwar inaugural convention. The resulting resolution was unanimously approved at Sōdōmei's convention proper that began on August 3.[12]

Sanbetsu in its Fundamental Policy on Industrial Recovery demanded "an annual industrial recovery plan that would comprehensively raise production in all industries." While calling for management and capital participation in the process, the vision of economic democracy that was prevalent in Sanbetsu contrasted with that of Sōdōmei's in its strict insistence that recovery be worker-led in a more literal sense. One of the earliest concrete manifestations of Sanbetsu's approach to economic recovery was the Coal Industry Recovery Conference that was convened on July 29, 1946, by the Sanbetsu affiliate in coal mining, Zentan, and which served as the model for a broader Sanbetsu-sponsored "industrial-recovery movement" that was formally approved at Sanbetsu's inaugural convention in August. Sanbetsu's industrial-recovery movement was distinctive in that great care was taken to preserve an adversarial relationship between labor and management. A distinction was made between functions to be performed by industrial-recovery conferences (sangyō fukkō kaigi) and industrial-recovery committees (sangyō fukkō iinkai). As outlined in the Sanbetsu policy document, industrial-recovery conferences consisting of workers, farmers, and small and medium-sized enterprise operators, but not capitalists, were to draft industrial-recovery plans aimed at rebuilding industries along "popular" lines. The delegates to these conferences were to tap the expertise of scientists and technicians who were not beholden to capital in drafting their plans. What the conferences were intended to produce was a kind of popular front in miniature on behalf of production recovery. It was only after this process was completed that these plans were to be passed on to "industrial recovery committees"—in essence, keiei kyōgikai—in which labor and "capital" would have equal representation for the purposes overseeing their implementation.[13] Sanbetsu convened in Tokyo on October 7, 1946, a nationwide, pan-industrial industrial-recovery conference based on this model with the participation of Sanbetsu- as well as non-Sanbetsu-affiliated labor organizations. The national conference was followed during October through December by more-narrowly focused industrial-recovery conferences devoted to electric power, housing, food, motion pictures, and education. A handful of enterprise and company-level conferences were also convened.[14]

This confrontational stance on the part of the Japanese communists contrasted with the behavior of the French and Italian communists. The difference was attributable to the differing political economic context. In the French and Italian cases, the communists were a part of the ruling coalition. In Japan prior to mid-1947, the left was in a struggle to replace the existing "bourgeois" regime in favor of a "popular" one. The significance for party officials like Chairman Tokuda Kyūichi of a worker-led recovery movement lay primarily in its utility in expanding the party's influence. As one of Tokuda's top lieutenants recalls, "Tokuda would always point out the importance of amassing strength. By strength he was referring to the organizational strength of the party and labor unions. . . . It was building this strength—organizational strength—that would determine the Japanese revolutionary strategy."[15] The promotion of worker-led recovery came to be understood as an opportunity to create an extra-parliamentary "industrial democratic front" *(sangyō minshu zensen)* consisting of workers, farmers, petty bourgeoisie, intellectuals, and various "victims" of the war like the homeless, the evacuees, and the returned soldiers, that could be wielded against the "old ruling classes" (i.e., "monopoly finance capital" in league with bureaucratic government) and their allies in the Diet, which would further the "bourgeois democratic revolution" the party was promoting.[16] To those who shared this perspective, it was critical that the recovery movement not result in a labor-management "cease-fire." Rather than consensus building, the *keiei kyōgikai* needed to be maintained as sites of institutionalized adversarial confrontation comparable to an American courtroom. The outcome was not consensus so much as a resolution of differences, framed by the balance of power existing at the moment, after which the contending parties were expected to continue in their pursuit of their respective agendas. The JCP leadership in particular was fearful that a privileging of the expertise of technicians and managers in the resolution of production-related problems would result in workers losing sight of the larger political objectives that needed to be pursued. The party's stress on recruiting for the industrial-recovery conferences technicians who were tied to the party and its front organizations rather than the factory or company was a direct outgrowth of such concerns. The communist insistence that participation in *keiei kyōgikai* did not in any way compromise the right to strike was also an outgrowth of this logic.[17]

These competing visions of worker-based recovery differed significantly with respect to goals and tactics, but they did have a common denominator. This was the importance attached in all cases to the institutionalization of a system of representing workers in production-related decision making at various levels of economic organization, beginning with the enterprise and extending to the heights of economic administration at the elite level. There was support for such an arrangement within the management camp as well, as the same situational imperatives that gave rise to the idea of a worker-oriented production recovery in the labor movement led some corporate executives to embrace similar formulations. The primary agent for this impulse was the association of younger corporate executives mentioned in chapter 4, the Keizai Dōyūkai (Japan Committee for Economic Development).[18] Formed on April 30, 1946, the Dōyūkai characterized itself as an organization of "progressive top managers." In a series of widely publicized reports and statements over the spring and summer of 1946, not all of them formally approved by the association, the Dōyūkai mapped out a stance on production recovery that dovetailed with formulations being put forward by Sōdōmei. A core foundation for the stance adopted by the Dōyūkai was a new conception in which corporate management's role was divorced from that of the capitalist. Where top executives in the prewar years were quite comfortable with the term *shihonka* (capitalist), Dōyūkai executives preferred such formulations as *keieisha* (top managers), *keiei ginōsha* (managerial technicians), and *keizaijin* (economic men). Underlying this shifting nomenclature was an understanding that the times and progress demanded that top management in Japanese enterprise apply itself in a calling different from that of the prewar years:

> Under prewar capitalism, profit served as the motive to operate businesses rationally, but today that is not possible. Today new economic men are burning with a passionate entrepreneurial drive and brimming with dynamism. This is because they are aware that their destiny lies in an era in which a separation of capital and management will be promoted and a new vocation of entrepreneurial technician is being established. The passionate desire to reconstruct the motherland's economy will replace the stimulus of the profit motive as the foundation for entrepreneurial drive.[19]

The idea that management constituted a vocation independent of capital allowed Dōyūkai members to comfortably entertain eventualities and proposals that were deeply troubling to their more conventional-minded colleagues. This could be seen, for instance, in the Dōyūkai's stance on production control. Whereas most businessmen saw production control as a gross violation of fundamental property rights, the Dōyūkai issued a statement declaring that production control was justifiable in the context of the distorted economic situation like the one currently being faced. A report on labor issues released by a Dōyūkai committee argued that employment maintenance should be given higher priority than returns to capital. And the Dōyūkai repeatedly expressed its readiness and ability to work with labor unions on behalf of economic recovery within the framework of a "democratized" labor-management relationship. Joint management of enterprise via *keiei kyōgikai* was welcomed as a way to assure the effective operation and the fulfillment of the social responsibilities of an enterprise.[20] Whether deserved or not—for the Dōyūkai's "right wing" was uncomfortable with the "excesses" of its "left wing"—the "modified capitalism" associated with the Dōyūkai was greeted favorably by both the unions and the press. The Dōyūkai, an editorial claimed, had positioned itself on a middle ground somewhere "to the left of capitalism and to the right of socialism," and in so doing was opening up an avenue of escape from Japan's debilitating economic crisis.[21]

In both theory and practice—as the Allies had vested virtual dictatorial powers over Japan in the Supreme Commander of Allied Powers—General MacArthur and his GHQ were the ultimate arbiters of what would and would not be allowed with respect to any programs of reform pursued by domestic groups in Japan. Thus, as in Germany, the policies adopted by the occupation forces, and the ways in which these were implemented, shaped, by commission or omission, the institutional environment in which the Japanese labor movement operated. Within GHQ it was the labor division of GHQ's Economic and Scientific Section (ESS) that was charged with implementing the occupation forces' labor reforms, and it became the organ that had the most direct impact on the course of reform in the area of labor institutions. Most of the Division's chiefs had backgrounds in the AFL, as did the staff itself, although the CIO was also represented in its staff to some extent. Theodore Cohen, the Labor Division's second chief, who served during the period when the occupation reform program was at it peak, had worked closely with Irving Brown, who was serving at the time as the point man for the AFL's aggressive anticommunist drive in Europe.[22] Given this, it is not surprising that GHQ labor officials as a group were philosophically predisposed toward the kind of unionism embraced by the more conservative, apolitical wing of the comparably conservative and apolitical American unionism. In line with this, the general thrust of SCAP reform policy in the area of industrial relations was to foster a system of independent collective bargaining in which the state would play a generally unobtrusive role as an unbiased referee enforcing the rules of play, and unions themselves would appeal to the state only as a last resort. As was generally true of the occupation, the Labor Division preferred to keep the reform process as "democratic" as possible by stepping aside and letting the Japanese initiate the drafting of reform legislation and policies. However, the Division was not averse to intervening when it was felt that important principles were being compromised. In practice, there was considerable variation among Labor Division chiefs as to what circumstances they judged as warranting intervention. The Division's first chief, William Karpinsky, for instance, was more lenient in enforcing "democratic" unionism than his successor, Cohen. This oscillation in the parameters of intervention left its mark, among other places, on the basic labor legislation upon which the occupation-era industrial-relations institutions were built.

The drafting of the Labor Union Law occurred under Karpinsky's watch, and the Japanese commission charged with coming up with a draft was allowed to operate with only minor intervention from GHQ. The Labor Union Law was the work of a tripartite commission, the Labor Law Deliberation Commission, that was established by the Japanese government even before the SCAP directive was issued ordering the establishment of trade union legislation. As studies by Tezuka Kazuaki and Endō Kōshi make clear, the policy ideal pursued collectively by the Labor Law Deliberation Commission was one in which labor-management relations were conceived as having a strongly *public* character (in this sense running counter to the AFL position, reflected in American labor law in which industrial relations constituted an autonomous arena of *private* relations).[23] This was reflected in a number of places in the Labor Union Law that was ultimately passed. One example is the law's preamble, which states that a basic purpose of labor unions was to "contribute to the welfare of the economy." Another can be seen in the reporting requirements and the numerous stipulations of organizational format and rights and duties of unions. A European-style arrangement was adopted wherein the conditions of employment resulting from collective bargaining in an industry or locality were under certain conditions to be applied to workers who were not party to the contract. The most prominent manifestation of this labor-relations-as-public-endeavor orientation in the Labor Union Law can be found in the law's creation of a system of tripartite national and prefectural labor committees *(rōdō iinkai)*. In the end, however, only a small part of the vision of the Japanese committee ended up being reflected in the Labor Union Law. This was because in the rush to get some form of legislation in place to guide the rapid unionization that was under way, the commission decided to concentrate on the basic organizational structures and to defer the drafting of concrete rules and regulations governing their operation to later legislation.

In contrast to the relatively light touch that GHQ maintained in its oversight of the drafting of the Labor Union Law, occupation officials intervened decisively and dramatically in the nine-month-long preparation of the Labor Relations Adjustment Act (promulgated in September 1946), which was the second major piece of occupation labor-reform legislation. The stimulus for this heavy-handed intervention was the concern on the part of Labor Division officials about the Labor Union Law and more broadly about the direction in which the Japanese drafting committee was taking the legislation. US government officials' dissatisfaction with the Labor Union Law had been expressed through a variety of channels, including a twelve-member advisory commission of prominent American labor experts dispatched to Japan in February 1946.[24] In response to this, Theodore Cohen, the Labor Division chief who took over from Karpinsky in January 1946, decided to take steps to correct this "defective" legislation. Cohen noted that "In traditional authoritarian Japan everything was the government's business; the dividing line between public and private was hardly visible. But in a democratic Japan, the line had to be clear and the barrier erected on it high. If Japanese labor was to be free and collective bargaining genuine, government had to stay out of labor disputes as much as possible."[25] It is interesting to note here that the Japanese labor movement itself was more interested in legislation that would establish state-administered basic labor standards than in labor relations legislation and organized demonstrations to protest the Labor Relations Adjustment Act.[26] This suggests that the unions were more comfortable with a state-mediated system of industrial relations. The mutual incomprehension on the two sides was such that at a critical point in the process, five GHQ Labor Division officials sat down and personally rewrote the Japanese draft of the law that had been presented to them.[27] For this reason, the Labor Relations Adjustment Act, to a considerably greater extent than was true of the Labor Union Law, reflected American sentiments.

A highly illustrative development in this regard was GHQ's rejection of a clause that would have made the establishment of *keiei kyōgikai* mandatory. The centrality of the *keiei kyōgikai* in the Sōdōmei and Sanbetsu economic recovery programs and the support for them found in the Japanese management camp have already been mentioned. The Japanese government, as well, indicated on a number of occasions its enthusiasm for these councils.[28] For example, the National Railway Bureau, the Welfare Ministry, and the Ministry of Commerce and Industry all drafted proposals that included the creation of *keiei kyōgikai*. However, GHQ specifically deleted this clause from the draft legislation that was presented to it.[29] As a consequence, the Japanese were forced to pursue *keiei kyōgikai* without a formal legal mandate. This, they in fact did. On June 13, 1946, the Yoshida government announced its intention to prepare informal and non-compulsory guidelines concerning the *keiei kyōgikai*. It described them as follows:

> What is currently needed most is for management and workers to increase production through democratic cooperation. This is why the government would like to encourage the establishment of a *keiei kyōgikai* in each enterprise. . . .
>
> Management should report and explain the overall plans and financial situation, etc., of the firm before the [*keiei*] *kyōgikai* and also discuss general personnel policies while addressing legitimate requests from the workers in the various areas of firm management wherever possible.
>
> The government desires sincerely that management and labor fully respect and understand their respective situation, make active use of the *keiei kyōgikai,* and strive all the more to increase production.[30]

The significance of the *keiei kyōgikai* from the standpoint of the government is made clear when one considers that this announcement was made on the same day that the cabinet released a statement discouraging production control. When on July 17 the Central Labor Relations Committee announced guidelines that it had been commissioned by the government to prepare, the *keiei kyōgikai* were defined as "permanent consultation organs established by labor-management contracts for the purpose of allowing workers to participate in management in accordance with the spirit of industrial democratization." The document also pointed out that the decisions of the *keiei kyōgikai* should carry the same weight as the labor-management contracts themselves.[31] The situation was similar to that in West Germany, where American intervention emerged as an obstacle to initiatives to formalize a multileveled structure of bipartite and triparatite consultation. What the Americans did emphasize in the Labor Relations Adjustment Act was the institutionalization of a machinery for independent collective bargaining that ultimately took up the bulk of the text in the version of the law that was passed. It is noteworthy in this regard that the labor committee system, which also had the potential to serve as a tripartite consultation forum in line with the economic management visions that had gained extensive support inside Japan, was diverted into a role centered on the supplementary support for independent collective bargaining.[32]

Because the *keiei kyōgikai* were voluntary entities without a formal legal mandate, it is difficult to get an accurate quantitative picture of their presence in the Japanese political economy in practice or of the kinds of powers they were granted and the ways in which they were utilized. According to the statistics compiled by the Welfare Ministry, of the 354 labor contracts reported to it prior to June 1946 when the government made its announcements, 207 contained stipulations relating to *keiei kyōgikai.* By December this figure had grown to 1,588. What these figures indicate, and what anecdotal evidence in individual firms suggests, is that they were being formed, and were especially common in larger firms. The ministry report noted that the contract clauses relating to the *keiei kyōgikai* listed a wide range of issues as falling under their purview, though their extent was usually not very closely defined. Labor analysts have concluded that along with wages and work hours—or matters that under other circumstances would have conventionally fallen under the jurisdiction of collective bargaining—the type of issue on which the *keiei kyōgikai* most commonly exercised significant influence was in personnel policies. Since this typically meant that the union was in a position to block layoffs, it allowed for a "socialistic" element to creep into firm management.[33]

A similar dynamic prevailed with respect to GHQ's role in efforts to socialize the economy, although in delineating this point, it is important to make a distinction between GHQ's support for the adoption of economic controls as a temporary measure and the institutionalization of instruments of state control over the economy on a permanent basis. The example of GHQ's response to the *kōdan* initiative of the Katayama cabinet is illustrative of this point.

Officially, SCAP was not responsible during the initial phase of the occupation for the performance of the Japanese economy or the welfare of the Japanese people. In practice, as insider accounts make clear, economic issues, welfare considerations, and in particular the galloping inflation that Japan was facing, were all very big concerns to occupation officials. As one former ESS official recalls: "A constant awareness of the great inflation . . . pervaded the two governments of the country, the Japanese Government and SCAP. . . . Every one of our ESS divisions, with the exception of the Scientific, spent a good part if not most if its time dealing with the inflation or its direct consequences. The same was true of the Natural Resources Section, with its mining, fisheries and farming interests."[34]

Prior to June 1947 when the "popular" center-left coalition government came into being, GHQ's economic policy and those of the incumbent Japanese governments conflicted.[35] GHQ's contingent of reformist "New Dealers" pushed for extensive government-administered wage, price, and distribution controls designed to distribute the burden of recovery more equitably. In order to implement this, they called on the Japanese government to create a superagency to be responsible for overseeing these controls, which would be placed above the normal government agencies. For a full year and a half, economic policy making was characterized by a behind-the-scenes tug-of-war between ESS officials and the Japanese government over the fundamentals of economic policy. The Shidehara program was derailed by a May 1946 GHQ directive ordering the imposition of a 100 percent tax on government indemnity payments received. The superagency that GHQ had called for five months earlier was reluctantly established by the succeeding Yoshida government in August 1946 in the form of the Economic Stabilization Board (ESB, or Keizai Antei Honbu). However, the Yoshida government continued to undercut GHQ intentions even after the ESB was established. Zen Keinosuke, best known as head of the prewar business association set up to oppose the prewar Labor Union Law, was named director but was replaced on January 31, 1947, by laissez-faire economist Ishibashi Tanzan, who was concurrently serving as Yoshida's finance minister. A series of meetings between ESS officials and Ishibashi produced nothing but discord over the issue of market-oriented recovery versus wage and price controls, and set the stage for Ishibashi's subsequent purge from public office. It was not until May 1, 1947, with a major organizational and personnel reshuffling, that the ESB was placed on a footing acceptable to SCAP. It worked under close ESS supervision thereafter.

With the establishment of the Katayama center-left government, GHQ had in place a political agent substantially more inclined to pursue an economic program of which it could approve. According to the Katayama cabinet's Emergency Economic Policy released on June 2, an effort would be made to "secure the distribution of important commodities such as basic production materials, major consumer goods, important foodstuffs, etc., which require thorough controls through a system of public corporations and *kōdan*."[36] The term *"kōdan"* referred to public agencies that would be given monopoly powers to purchase, distribute, and resell specified items. Ironically, the *kōdan* were an institutional innovation that had been encouraged by SCAP. They had actually grown out of SCAP efforts to eliminate the wartime Japanese government's practice of delegating distribution of state-controlled commodities to private business associations.[37] From an American standpoint this was an undemocratic and illegitimate mixing of public authority and private interests, and for this reason GHQ officials insisted that control be exercised directly by the state. The *kōdan* were developed as a vehicle for implementing this. Thanks in part to the reluctance of the Yoshida government to comply with these demands, at the time of the Katayama government's formation, only ten existed. The vast majority dealt with foreign trade, and few of them played a role in the distribution of goods inside the Japanese economy. What the Socialists proposed to do was to create a large array of *kōdan* across the economy—a *kōdan* system—as a way of assuring that commodities were not diverted from official channels into the black market. For its proponents the beauty of the *kōdan* proposal was that, with the legislative apparatus for the creation of the *kōdan* already in place, these entities could be created via administrative order, and the interparty wrangling that inevitably accompanied new legislation could be avoided.

As Theodore Cohen, who had been transferred from his position as Labor Division chief to that of economic adviser in the wake of the February 1 general strike, recollects, the *kōdan* initiative was seen by him as an unpalatable socialistic exercise:

> With these new proposals, the full force of the phrase "*kōdan* system" struck me for the first time. If all "basic production materials, major consumer goods and important foodstuffs, etc." were placed in *kōdan* hands, what would be left for private wholesalers, and what would become of the free market? Manufacturers would naturally produce what their customers, the *kōdan,* ordered in accordance with government production plans, and consumers could get only what the *kōdan* had. The market economy would be out. Relations between makers and users would be severed at the wholesale level. It sounded very much like the Soviet system. Furthermore, what would become of our JCS 1380/15 order to effect a "wider distribution of the means of . . . trade"? We seemed to be going in the opposite direction.[38]

At Cohen's urging, behind-the-scenes jawboning by GHQ officials was used to quietly quash the *kōdan* system proposal.[39] Although the number of *kōdan* eventually increased to fifteen, the ESB was unable to attain the number it sought and the establishment of those that were authorized did not take place in most cases until December, or too late to be of much use in implementing the policy program announced in the summer. It was by no means a foregone conclusion that the shifting of commodities from the black market to official channels could have been successfully achieved even if the *kōdan* system had been implemented as originally conceived. Without them, however, the Katayama government clearly lacked a powerful instrument on the supply side to use in implementing its recovery program.

The economic recovery conference

With (top-down) socialistic or "modified capitalist" economic planning and administrative controls obstructed by a laissez-faire-oriented conservative government, with the JSP and JCP unable to establish a workable entente, and with the avenue of legally mandating *keiei kyōgikai* blocked by GHQ policy, by late 1946 it appeared that the only remaining option for those who saw the need for the "battle for production" was to rely on voluntary, extra-governmental initiative. It was Sōdōmei and the Keizai Dōyūkai that took the initiative, through a series of talks among representatives of the two organizations over the course of the summer and fall of 1946. On October 25, these organizations sponsored a conference to which representatives of other leading labor and management organizations were also invited.[40] At this conference, it was agreed that a central organ manned by delegates representing business associations, labor organs, and other relevant economic interest groups—to be named the "Economic Recovery Conference" (ERC), or Keizai Fukkō Kaigi—would be established to oversee economic-recovery planning on a national scale along with the voluntary implementation of production increase initiatives. A formal preparatory committee was established in November. Represented on the preparatory committee were the Keizai Dōyūkai, Sōdōmei, Nichirō Kaigi, and the trade-association-based business association Nissankyō.

A December 4 document entitled "The Basic Policy for the Economic Recovery Conference" mapped out the purpose and structure of the ERC. The ERC was to be the lead organization for "a major voluntary popular movement devoted to economic recovery" in which the "rights of management" and the "rights of labor" (*keiei ken* and *rōdō ken*) would be respected. The endeavor had the gloss of a popular democratic front in its characterization as an exercise in "democratic mutual cooperation" between "democratic top managers and the working class" that would advance Japan's "democratic revolution." Labor's cooperation was presented as something that would be rewarded with reform and equity. Organizationally, at the macro-level, a central Economic Recovery Conference composed of top executives, unionists, consumers, academics, and technicians would draft "economic reconstruction plans" to provide a broad, economy-wide framework for cooperation and coordination between the various players and thereby give the movement an overarching rationality and synergy. Similar conferences were to be set up in strategic industries and on a regional basis in order to integrate these efforts at the national and firm levels. The core institution in this arrangement, however, was the enterprise-level *keiei kyōgikai.* These were to be granted jurisdiction over "working conditions (work hours, wage and salary arrangements, conditions of employment, welfare facilities, etc.)" as well as matters relating to "management, supervision, accounting and personnel." As such, they were to serve as a vehicle through which labor-management cooperation on behalf of increased production and production efficiency based on the higher-level plans was to be manifested.[41]

The arrangements outlined in the Basic Policy were themselves relatively uncontroversial. What was controversial was the question of whether or not to invite Sanbetsu to participate in the national ERC. The majority in the Dōyūkai and Sōdōmei were in fact against inclusion, fearing that Sanbetsu would manipulate the movement on behalf of the JCP's revolutionary agenda. However, Nissankyō insisted on Sanbetsu participation as a condition for its own participation. The rationale was that many of the industries most critical to recovery contained strong Sanbetsu-affiliated unions and without them any production effort that the ERC might pursue would not be very effective.

As for the JCP, its motivation to direct its cells to support Sanbetsu's participation in the ERC was explained by Tokuda Kyūichi in a January 14, 1947, report presented at a JCP national consultative conference. According to Tokuda, support for the ERC by workers and farmers was "a primitive, reflexive desire stemming from the difficulties of life that surround them." Primitive though it might be, this support was genuine and therefore had to be "handled carefully." It would not do for the JCP to denounce the ERC movement outright since this would cause the party to "become isolated from the people." The network of managerial councils being envisioned for the ERC by Sōdōmei and the Dōyūkai would only contribute to the co-optation of popular revolutionary sentiment. The appropriate strategy under these conditions, according to Tokuda, was to join the ERC but block the movement's full organizational articulation or, in short, to sabotage the movement from within.[42] Even so, a former Sanbetsu official alleges that Yoyogi was insecure enough about the ERC that on the day before the inaugural convention of the central ERC, it ordered Sanbetsu to cancel its participation. Too much momentum in favor of the ERC concept, however, had already built up in the labor union organ for such an order to be carried out. Sanbetsu officials, perturbed by the possibility that the tremendous effort they had put into arranging participation would come to naught, voiced heated protests, and the order was effectively retracted.[43] This led to a series of negotiations with Sanbetsu representatives. The primary concern voiced by Sanbetsu related to the character of the *keiei kyōgikai:* "It is feared that by granting excessively strong decision-making powers to the *keiei kyōgikai,* a tendency will arise in the *keiei kyōgikai* in which the right to strike and engage in collective bargaining will be diluted as a consequence of pressure from the capitalist side, resulting in a disengagement of labor unions."[44] Sanbetsu also demanded that the concerns of a broader constituency beyond unions and management be reflected in the work of the economic recovery conferences since the *keiei kyōgikai*, as councils with a membership restricted to or dominated by labor and management representatives, were unlikely to perform such a function effectively. Continuing negotiations resulted in agreement on changes to wording in the Basic Policy that reflected Sanbetsu's concerns, and Sanbetsu's participation was eventually finalized with the conclusion of a four-item agreement on December 26.[45] The expanded central ERC that now included Sanbetsu was formally inaugurated a week after the February 1 general-strike cancellation on February 6, 1947. With the emergence of the ERC network, an extra-parliamentary coalition was put tentatively in place through which to organize the "battle for production."

During the first eight months of its existence, the ERC concentrated on assisting the formation of economic recovery conferences at the company, regional, and industrial levels. As of July 1947 ten industry-level and eleven prefectural economic conferences had been established. With respect to the industry-level conferences, the most extensive organization occurred in such priority industries as coal, steel, and mining. Nakakita Kōji argues that the formation of the ERC can be read as a de facto no-confidence vote by both the labor movement and an important segment of the business community against the Yoshida government and its policies.[46]

In contrast to the relatively advanced organization on behalf of cross-class collaboration attained in the ERC, the unity of purpose attained by the political parties was rudimentary, and the Japanese situation constitutes overall a mirror image of the respective arenas in France and Italy. The four-party accord constituting the basis for the coalition that voted in the Katayama cabinet represented a tentative consensus between the JSP and the "bourgeois" parties on the acceptability of a limited socialist—or, alternatively, "modified capitalist"—economic policy agenda. Its various clauses juxtaposed archetypal socialist proposals with qualifiers that blunted their socialistic substance. Exemplary phrases include: "necessary state controls based on comprehensive plans that have as their object existing economic organizational forms [i.e., private ownership would be maintained]"; "priority production policies" in strategic industries that would involve "democratized" state "management" *(kanri)* of industries "where necessary."[47] These were clearly a retreat from earlier JSP proposals, which called for, among other things, full-fledged nationalizations (i.e., outright state ownership as opposed to state supervision of privately owned enterprises as found in the four-party agreement) of basic industries and extensive state control of resource allocation in finance and industry. The accord was also an exercise in minimalism in that it was just nine sentences in length! It consequently constituted a list of generalities profoundly lacking in specifics. This brevity and the lack of specifics highlighted just how fragile the consensus behind the four-party accord was, and how thin the political foundation on which it rested.

Given that its Diet members were serving in the cabinet, resistance to "excessive" socialism on the part of the Democrats made itself felt through less overt channels. The most consequential instance of this occurred in conjunction with the controversy over the imposition of state control over Japan's coal mines. As already noted, the nationalization—that is, the transfer of *ownership* to the state —of basic industries was a prominent part of the JSP platform. The feeling was strong inside the JSP that the party had to implement something that could be billed as a step toward fulfilling the spirit of its election promise. The coal mines were seen for several reasons as a suitable object for this. Coal was the country's primary fuel source at the time. The recovery of coal production was considered a linchpin for production recovery elsewhere in the economy. Production lagged behind target levels despite the industry's being supported by a variety of special subsidies and dispensations, and there were allegations that these funds were being misused and of rampant profiteering. There were also various precedents in Europe, with the British Labour Party's nationalization of coal being particularly influential. The move was also supported unanimously by all of the wings of the politically divided unions in the industry. A bill was therefore drafted, under the auspices of the Katayama government, that would give the state control over mine operations and ensure labor's participation via *keiei kyōgikai.* As expected, the Liberal Party voiced strong opposition to the bill. The Democratic Party was deeply divided over the issue, precipitating a virtual civil war inside the party. Pressed by the antinationalization elements inside the party and an intensive lobbying campaign launched by the owners of smaller mines, the Democrats began to push hard for further watering down of the bill. State supervisory powers were weakened dramatically, the period of state control was limited to three years, and small mines were exempted from the bill's provisions. By the time the legislation was finally passed in December, state control remained in name only. In the end, fifty-six mines, most of them formerly owned by the *zaibatsu,* were placed under nominal state control between 1948 and 1950. The Shidehara faction of the Democratic Party ended up splitting from the party over the nationalization bill and eventually merged with Yoshida's Liberals to form the Democratic Liberal Party (DLP), thereby weakening the Democrats and the governing coalition severely.[48]

The dire economic circumstances and sociopolitical disruptions in Japan in the aftermath of the Second World War propelled the themes of reform and recovery to the center of political life as it did in Western Europe. In the Japanese case it proved exceedingly difficult during the initial post-surrender period to forge the political compromises and establish the organizational and institutional appara- tuses that were necessary for a cooperative, domestically driven program of reform and production recovery. Efforts were made to forge workable cross-class ententes that could operationalize a socialistic—or, alternatively, modified capitalist— production recovery of the sort seen as necessary not just in the labor movement, but also widely throughout Japanese society. Like the efforts to forge a popular democratic front, the "battle for production" in post-surrender Japan was charac- terized by the push and pull of centrifugal and centripetal tendencies set in motion by the way in which the labor movement entered the postwar world. And in Japan, as was true for the popular front, the balance between these tendencies fell on the side of the former, making it exceedingly difficult to implement either a socialistic or modified capitalist economic recovery.

I emphasize here that my argument is not that a socialistic or modified cap- italist economic program would necessarily have been any more effective from an economic standpoint than the motley, unfocused approach ultimately taken in Japan. Rather, it is that the structure of the Japanese labor movement explains a lot about the *form* the economic recovery program took, and that that particular structure can be traced to the global political-historical context. As it turned out, by the time the Katayama coalition government came into being, major changes were already under way that were altering dramatically the international context that would in turn profoundly alter the dynamics in the politics of labor move- ments in Western Europe and Japan.

Part 2

COLD WAR

Chapter 6

The Cold War and the Politics of Labor in Western Europe, 1947–1953

The period between the mid-1930s and the years following the end of World War II saw a trend toward unity and consolidation in European labor movements that culminated, where conditions allowed, in the formation of Resistance coalition governments. By contrast, the period that began in 1947 and lasted until the mid-1950s was marked by deepening internal antagonism and division. In France, communist ministers were dismissed from Paul Ramadier's MRP-SFIO-PCF coalition cabinet in May 1947. Since the removal of the PCF from the Resistance coalition government left the socialists and the MRP pitted against the opposition communists, this act marked the decisive collapse of the popular-front coalition that had defined French labor politics for most of the period since the late 1930s. In Italy the defining event was the ouster later that same month of both the PCI and the PSI from the now DC-dominated government. Parallel splits followed in the trade-union sectors. In France, noncommunist unionists walked out of the CGT in December 1947, leaving the CGT under Communist hegemony. The dissidents subsequently established the CGT-Force Ouvrière (FO) as a competing labor confederation. Since Catholic unionists were already organized in a separate federation, the CFTC, this marked a return of the three-way division of the prewar years. A similar pattern of division emerged in Italy as the result of a twofold split. Catholic unionists walked out of the CGIL in August 1948 to form a competing Catholic confederation (LCGIL, later renamed CISL) while a separate social democratic federation (FIL, later reconstituted as the UIL) was formed in June 1949. As happened with the CGT, these splits left the dominant CGIL with a Communist majority, and with a substantial left-socialist minority.[1] Table 5 portrays schematically the resulting union-party blocs. In Germany the communist-noncommunist division also appeared but in a form defined by competing regimes in East and West Germany, as detailed below.

Divisions and internal antagonisms that emerged in postwar European labor movements were closely intertwined with a fundamental shift in the structure of global international relations then under way—specifically, the bipolar, multi-faceted global conflict known as the Cold War, which pitted the United States against the Soviet Union in a global struggle that, in the currently popular peri-odization, dominated international relations until 1989. During the initial years of the Cold War, between 1947 and 1949, the conflict pivoted around a massive and unprecedented program of American economic aid to Western Europe known as the Marshall Plan (alternatively, the European Recovery Program, or ERP), which was announced in June 1947. In total, some $13.3 billion were pumped into fifteen economies via a multilateralized administrative machinery overseen by the US government. The countries that received the most ERP aid were the UK, France, Italy, and West Germany, together accounting for the majority of the dispersed funds. The Soviet Union responded to the plan by consolidating its grip over Eastern European client states and by mobilizing client communist par-ties in Western Europe against it. Somewhat later, what started out as a struggle

Table 5. Union and party blocs in Cold War France and Italy

Bloc	Ideological category		
	Christian democratic	Social democratic / Left socialist	Communist / Left socialist
FRANCE			
Union	CFTC (Confédération Française des Travailleurs Chrétiens)	FO (Force Ouvrière)	CGT (Confédération Générale du Travail)
Party	MRP (Mouvement Républicain Populaire) —cross-class—	SFIO (Section Française de l'Internationale Ouvrière)	PCF (Parti Communiste Français)
ITALY			
Union	CISL (Confederazione Italiana Sindicati Lavoratori)	UIL (Unione Italiana del Lavoratori)	CGIL (Confederazione Generale Italiana del Lavoro)
Party	DC (Democrazia Cristiana) —cross-class—	PSDI (Partito Social-Democratico Italiano)	PSI*-PCI (Partito Socialista Italiano, Partito Communista Italiano)

* Left socialist

centered on an economic recovery program became militarized and consequently shifted focus to the remilitarization of Western Europe.

Over the years the causal links, or lack thereof, between the splits in the labor movement domestically and the global-level East-West strategic conflict have been the subject of considerable scholarly debate.[2] During the 1970s and 1980s, studies relying heavily on American diplomatic documents emphasized the centrality of external intervention in inducing the labor movement splits, suggesting that, in France and Italy in particular, US intervention played a decisive role in precipitating the splits. Proponents of this view contend that threats and moral, logistical, and financial support provided by American government officials and representatives of the American labor movement were a catalyst in the formation of the FO in France and in the split of the CGIL in Italy.[3] On the other hand, more recent studies based on American, French, and Italian sources have tended to emphasize the limits of American intervention and to highlight the significance of domestic politics and preferences. They point out that despite circumstantial evidence suggesting links with American intervention, years of research have produced no definitive "smoking gun" of American direction in the dismissal of the Communists from the French and Italian governments.[4] Irwin Wall adamantly argues instead that for France "the split developed from the internal dynamic process of French labor" and that the CFTC and FO "were always authentic emanations of French working-class traditions, never creations or puppets of Washington."[5] Similarly, Gino Bedani points to the built-in, preexisting tensions inside the unified CGIL as the primary source of the split of the Italian labor movement. Denis MacShane goes even further and argues that "the Cold War was not external to the trade union movement but grew from existing political divisions that resurfaced as soon as the fight stopped in 1945."[6]

For our purpose of making sense of labor movement alignments and their impact on the structure and status of labor movements in national contexts, the issue of whether these splits are best seen as the product of external intervention or internal factors is less important than ascertaining the patterns and dynamics of the splits. Indeed, it is possible to conceive, as done in this chapter, of the national-level and international-level developments associated with these realignments as aspects of a common geostrategic process in which three causal vectors converged. These are the collapse of the socialistic economic arrangements established by the Resistance coalition governments, the resurfacing of ideologically based rivalries in both the trade union and political party segments of the labor movements, and the transition from Allied-Axis to Cold War alignment at the international level. The present chapter traces this convergence as it unfolded in the archetypal French and Italian contexts. It then looks in more detail at the way in which the international context affected realignments within the labor movements in the two countries. The consequences of the resulting realignments in the national labor movements are then shown in the context of a new phase of the Cold War—the militarization of the conflict—that came to the fore, from 1949 onward, which is then followed by a review of how these forces played out in the distinctive context of occupied Germany.

The Marshall Plan and French and Italian labor-movement realignment

In strict chronological terms, the first of the three causal vectors to emerge was the rivalries among competing segments of the labor movement. Although the Resistance and the battle against fascism had reduced the relevance of long-standing differences over principles and policies among the various currents in European labor movements, they did not eliminate the associated ideological identities. In the Italian movement, the Catholics, socialists, and Christians all maintained their separate identities as political parties and as distinct factional groupings within the CGIL. The situation was similar in France, but with the Catholic unionists ensconced in an independent union organization. In the case of the CGT, even at the height of the Resistance-era socialist-communist unity, noncommunists chose to maintain an independent identity through their publication of a journal entitled *Resistance Ouvrière.* The postwar context, in which the more disciplined communists expanded their influence at the expense of other groups through the frequent use of high-handed tactics, gave added relevance to the differences over issues that had until then been expressed in a largely theoretical context. That the emergent tensions resonated with the traditional differences in principles between social democrats and the communists in France is evident in this statement by Robert Bothereau, one of the key leaders of the FO: "For some trade-unionism is a means of obtaining political power and, once that power is obtained, a method of keeping it. For others, trade-unionism represents an economic power which on the whole should keep its distance from political power. Our comrades cannot see the rise to power in all levels of the movement of trade-union activists obedient to Communists without some concern. The movement risks being at the service of a single party."[7] Stimulated by the sometimes heavy-handed tactics of the communists, the FO elements within the CGT coalesced into an increasingly active intra-organizational faction and began to challenge the dominant communists by running separate slates in union elections. The impetus for these initiatives often came from below, at the rank-and-file level, rather than from among the noncommunist union leadership within the CGT, who were more inclined to search for means of accommodating the communists for the sake of sustaining the popular front.[8]

In Italy, the influence of the Catholic Church remained much stronger than in France, and in consequence the Vatican constituted a powerful ideological pole around which labor movement activity coalesced. As a result the more conspicuous division in the CGIL was that which pitted the Catholics against the communists. An important stimulus for the Catholic wing's increasingly vehement anticommunism was the Vatican under Pope Pius XII, which, alarmed by the rise in communist influence, began to actively intervene in Italian politics after mid-1946.[9] The classic issue of whether or not trade unions should be allowed to mobilize for direct political action was the subject of heated debates at CGIL conventions during 1945–1946, with the Catholic wing attempting to disallow union political action mainly out of concern, it seemed, that it was being directed against the Christian Democrats, whom the Church generally supported.[10]

The competing pulls of the Catholics on the right and the communists on the left, in turn, reawakened differences in outlook and sensibility between social democrats and left socialists inside the socialist contingent. In Italy, the "class versus mass" debate that unfolded at party conventions and in other forums of the PSI in 1945–1946 vividly illustrates this point. Guiseppe Saragat, who served as the primary spokesperson for the social democrats, argued to grant highest priority to the defense of democracy and individual liberty. In Saragat's view, communist totalitarianism shared an essential similarity with fascist totalitarianism and as such constituted a similar threat to these core values. He therefore called on the party to constitute itself as a "mass party" that would reach out to the middle classes and enlist them in defense of the liberty and democracy that he saw as fundamentally necessary for the advancement of the working class.[11] Against this, left-socialist ideologue Lelio Basso, basing his argument on the Marxist tenets, argued for a "class party" focused exclusively on the pursuit of the interests of the working class. Basso opposed Saragat's "mass party" strategy of reaching out to the middle classes, because it would weaken the party's defense of working-class interests and dissipate its progressive impetus. Maintaining a class-party character, in turn, implied privileging the PSI's relations with the other class party, the PCI, over those of the other, nonworking class parties. In Basso's case, he went so far as to argue for a "Bolshevization" of the party in order to make it better able to fulfill its class mandate.[12] After increasingly heated debates between the two sides at party conventions, the party finally split over the issue in January 1947, after which the social democrats established a new party, which they named the Partito Socialista dei Lavoratori Italiani or PSLI (later renamed PSDI). They took with them 52 of the 155 PSI deputies in the constitutional assembly. In France, too, the compromises that the SFIO, the French socialist party, was forced to swallow in order to sustain a coalition that included mutually antagonistic partners on the left, and the right reestablished the salience of ideologically based differences between the social democrats from the left socialists. It did not result in a formal split of the party, but a debate that was similar to the Italian mass-versus-class debate unfolded in the SFIO, pitting social democrats like Leon Blum and Daniel Mayer against left socialists led by Guy Mollet. At the September 1946 party convention the left-socialist forces gained sufficient support to install Mollet as head of the party, thereby shifting the balance in the party in a leftward direction.[13]

The internal tensions generated by the differing ideological outlooks extant in the French and Italian movements were exacerbated by the second causal vector, namely the collapse of the socialistic moral economy that was at the heart of the Resistance coalition's economic-recovery strategy. The mechanics of this process can be summarized as follows: The "battle for production" in France and Italy was built on the imposition of economic sacrifices on the part of workers; the economic logic for this was that to peg wages well below prewar levels in real terms it was necessary to restrain consumption and through this to generate the surplus needed to invest in expanded production capacity. These working-class sacrifices were to be made tolerable by mechanisms that would guarantee workers a minimum level of livelihood commodities and give them a sense that the burdens of recovery were being distributed in a socially equitable way. In France this was to be done through the rationed and controlled distribution of basic livelihood commodities, while in Italy a centrally negotiated standardized wage indexed to prices was used. In both instances, various sociopolitical reforms were to be served up as rewards for worker cooperation. The fundamental problem was that in both France and Italy it proved impossible to maintain adequate consumption levels. The winter of 1946–1947 was one of severe weather, dropping farm production, coal shortages, shortages of industrial inputs, disruptions of transport and communications systems, and, externally, severe balance of payments crises. In France, basic livelihood commodities were simply not available in allocated quantities at official prices, and the rationing and distribution system was collapsing. Urban dwellers found it impossible to survive without turning to the black market, where prices were several times higher than the official prices and skyrocketing.[14] In Italy inflation was so rapid that, indexation notwithstanding, wages simply could not keep up with prices. Not surprisingly, these conditions created mounting rank-and-file-worker dissatisfaction in both countries that was seized upon by dissident groups as an ax to wield against the communists. In France wildcat strikes supported by the FO and other dissident elements began to crop up, while in Italy spontaneous local-level protests and strikes that were not authorized by the CGIL were used as fodder in the infighting becoming endemic in the Italian labor movement.

The rising rank-and-file dissatisfaction placed the communists particularly in a difficult position. The communists' suppression of expressions of this dissatisfaction had been instrumental in sustaining the French and Italian economic programs, and the ability to perform this function was a result of a distinctive combination of credentials—that is, the communists' status as a "genuinely revolutionary" party, the patriotism that they had demonstrated during the antifascist struggle, and the top-down internal discipline that they were capable of maintaining over their rank-and-file. This made them, in effect, the linchpins that held in check the centrifugal tendencies that would have otherwise caused the collapse of the Resistance coalition's programs of reform and production recovery. But, as George Ross said with regard to the PCF: "In all this there was an implicit threat as well. The battle for production was to prove in part that the PCF and CGT could discipline the entire French working class. This meant also that party and union might lead the French working class into battle against any government which strayed too far from the behavior which they desired."[15] For the communists, the mounting rank-and-file unrest was a sign that this delicate balance between threat and cooperation they were attempting to maintain was coming undone. On the one hand, the unrest threatened the party's credibility vis-à-vis its coalition partners as a force capable of restraining the working class, and, on the other, its radical credentials in the eyes of the rank-and-file workers. The mounting labor unrest in the face of a collapsing economic recovery program was read as a sign that the point had been reached where moderation on behalf of the battle for production was bringing diminishing political returns. This alerted the party to a need to recalibrate its position in the battle for production.

What brought this point home in France was a set of wildcat strikes that broke out on April 25, 1947, at the Renault plant in Billancourt outside of Paris. The fact that the strike had broken out in the Billancourt plant was significant because this was a recently nationalized plant that was supposed to be a stronghold of the PCF. In addition to highlighting the seriousness of the economic grievances that workers harbored, the strike initiative, which bubbled up from the rank-and-file, was seen as symbolic of a widespread and growing resentment against the high-handed tactics being pursued by communist union leaders as they concentrated their energy and effort almost solely on the "battle for production." Fearing loss of control over the unions, the PCF made a belated about-face and backed the strikers. This move, however, put the party in the position of directly challenging the government, and communist ministers were accordingly expelled from the cabinet on May 4. These strikes proved to be the opening shot for a wave of wildcat strikes in various sectors in the months that followed. In contrast to their earlier stance, the PCF and CGT now consistently supported the strike initiatives that emerged from below over the summer of 1947.

It is important not to overstate the depth of the socialist-communist split at this juncture, although it was clearly deepening. Historians who have looked carefully at the actual behavior of the PCF during the spring and summer of 1947

have noted the reluctant and decidedly delimited quality of the PCF's oppositional status. It is noteworthy, for instance, that the PCF ministers in the Ramadier cabinet did not walk out but were dismissed and indeed bucked custom by
trying to hold on to their ministerial posts even after they had voted against a
major policy initiative of the government that they were a part of. Maurice
Thorez, the PCF leader, specifically declared that "we intend to work with the government for all measures in favor of the working class, although we are momentarily outside the government." He then emphasized, "and be sure to note that I
say 'momentarily.'"[16] In the unions, the communists championed the demands
for measures that would ease the economic distress of striking workers against a
government attempting to hold the line on wages, but also conspicuous in their
behavior were attempts to broker settlements that would demonstrate their utility as a medium through which to deal with a disgruntled working class. There
is ample evidence, in others words, to suggest that during the summer of 1947
the communists saw their oppositional status as a temporary setback and fully
intended to reenter the government when the opportunity presented itself after
having demonstrated that they were indispensable in the task of governing the
French working class.

The situation was similar in Italy. Accelerating inflation during 1946 caused
a deterioration of living conditions, and unauthorized wildcat strikes began to
unfold. Communist efforts to enforce moderation for the sake of the "battle for
production" began to wear thin as continuing compromises with the DC, the
Church, and big business in the name of coalitional unity undermined the PCI's
claim of being the defender of working-class interests. There were vociferous
complaints about the failure of a party that was supposed to be the most radically
committed to working-class interests to press harder for reforms and political
gains.[17] The confusion extended even within the ranks of the party itself, as one
study of grassroots political dynamics in Milan points out: "The PCI's simultaneous stress on broad political unity and military insurrection created great problems after the war. This public stress on unity often led to disorientation, as many
workers believed it to be a temporary façade for public consumption—even
though it was a genuine strategy for the party leadership—workers interpreted
it as a tactical ploy normally defining it as doppiezza, i.e. 'double track' thinking
or 'duplicity.'"[18] Amid the escalating tensions, Christian Democrat Premier
Alfredo De Gasperi dismissed the PCI from his coalition government on May 31,
1947, along with the PSI which, thanks to the departure of the social democrats
to the PSLI, was all the more wedded to a policy of cooperation with the communists. Even so, it was not until August that the communist majority in the
CGIL turned against the government and over opposition from noncommunist
unionists called a nationwide strike. As with the PCF, the pronouncements and

behavior of the PCI suggested that the party leadership considered the exercise a temporary realignment of its position in preparation for a reentry into the government, and its militancy was delimited accordingly.[19]

Domestic-level context strongly influenced the way in which France and Italy digested the European Recovery Program. The receipt of Marshall Plan funds was made contingent upon economic stabilization—that is, taking measures to bring inflation to a halt—and the integration of a country's economy into the more open and liberalized international trade and financial regimes that the Americans were in the process of constructing. Both would clearly require a rollback of various economic controls that propped up these economies and increased pressure on wages, employment, and working conditions. It was clear, furthermore, that participation in the Marshall Plan would require a greater or lesser scaling back of socialistic arrangements that had been instituted or were under consideration even as it presented the possibility of an escape from the debilitating political and economic gridlock that these countries faced. Just how much of a rollback would be involved was heavily dependent on the partisan makeup of governments and the stance adopted by the socialist wings in response to it. Throughout the period of state-communist confrontation over the Marshall Plan in France, the government was in the hands of a Christian-socialist coalition. The MRP-SFIO cabinets carved out a position in the center of the political spectrum as an ostensible "third force," which toed a policy line midway between capitalism and communism. Sustaining this truncated Resistance coalition in a context in which the Cold War was rapidly polarizing opinion was not an easy task. These governments were not popular, and both parties suffered declines in support at the polls. Within the coalition, the MRP was under pressure from conservative Catholics to abandon their ties with the traditionally anticlerical socialists. Inside the SFIO the 1946 capture of key positions within the party by left-socialist elements put pressure on the party to adopt stances in cabinet formation and in policy-making that were more in accord with a militant class line, including demands that the party abandon its ties to the "bourgeois" MRP and link up with the "proletarian" communists.[20] Thus, despite their nominal unity, recurrent confrontations and crises over issues of state-Church relations and over the level of generosity toward working-class interests in government budgeting plagued the third-force cabinets. The SFIO stuck it out nonetheless. Marshall Plan aid appears to have played an important role keeping the socialists on this course. On the one hand, Marshall Plan aid helped to relieve the budgetary pressures that would otherwise have forced the government to adopt harsher economic policies that could have resulted in the left socialists linking up with the communists as happened in Italy (see below).[21] France's ambitious state-led modernization drive, which was generally supported in the SFIO as a "progressive" effort, was bankrolled to a considerable extent by

Marshall Plan aid. At the same time, US support for the third-force cabinets as a bulwark against feared Soviet expansionism encouraged the third-force governments to adopt a harder line against the communists than they might have otherwise, thereby driving a wedge between the left socialists and the communists. In addition, as Irwin Wall argues, Marshall Plan aid effectively allowed the French to finance the colonial wars in Southeast Asia and Algeria that they would not have otherwise been able to afford.[22] This, too, had the effect of helping to keep the left socialists inside the governing coalition, since a key point of difference between the socialists and the communists was communist opposition to the maintenance of France's colonies.

In assessing the way in which the Marshall Plan impacted Italy, it is important to highlight certain situational factors that encouraged a divergence from the French pattern. By far the most important of these was the greater relative size and strength in Italy of the conservative Catholic constituency. With backing from the Vatican and the United States, the DC was able to secure a parliamentary majority in the 1948 election and as a result was given a free hand to implement the policies of its choice. The policy that it chose in the economic arena was a fiscally conservative, laissez-faire-oriented retrenchment presided over by Finance Minister Luigi Einaudi. Where the centerpiece of the French economic policy under the ERP was a "soft landing," the "Einaudi Plan," built on the twin pillars of a drastic halting of banking credit and a strict budgetary retrenchment, was very much a "hard-landing" approach to stabilization. The DC government also adopted a harsh line in dealing with the unrest that inevitably resulted from these policies. As one source describes it, under Interior Minister Scelba's direction, "not only were the police and the Carabinieri purged of former partisans, but they were encouraged to intervene decisively and brutally against all working-class or peasant protests that transcended certain narrow boundaries. Scelba's infamous *celere* (flying squads) were to have a place all of their own in popular recollections of the period."[23] In dialectical fashion, the harshness and conservatism of the DC adjustment to the Marshall Plan political economy intensified left-right tensions and tilted the balance of influence in the PSI leftward. Under these circumstances, as far as the bulk of the left was concerned, the DC coalition was *the* threat from the right. Although a small minority of social democrats (the UIL-PSDI bloc) ended up aligning with the pro-United States DC-dominated government, the majority of the Italian socialists aligned with the communists in opposing both the incumbent regime and the Marshall Plan with which the retrenchment plan was associated. The PSI, in fact, went so far as to establish a joint list of candidates with the communists in the 1948 election.

In both France and Italy the failure of modified capitalist economic-recovery efforts and the consequent unpopularity of the parties associated with their implementation led to a severe drop in support in the polls. The economic effects of stabilization policies, in turn, affected employment and led to a parallel drop in the number of union members. These, in turn, added an element of severe destabilization to increasingly divided labor movements.

International currents and realignment in France and Italy

It was at this point that international developments and the third causal vector entered the picture. US officials found the interrelated political and economic crises being faced in France and Italy to be highly troubling. Having been confronted with what was perceived to be Soviet expansionism in Iran and Greece, US government officials now feared that the Soviet Union would exploit Western Europe's dire economic straits to expand its influence, at the expense of democracy and individual liberty, and its strategic and economic interests in the region. In announcing the ERP in a famous June 1947 speech at Harvard, US Secretary of State George C. Marshall explained the rationale of the proposed aid program by pointing out that the dire economic conditions were providing fertile ground for the expansion of pro-Soviet communist influence. "Europe's requirements for the next three or four years of foreign food and other essential products —principally from America—are so much greater than her present ability to pay that she must have substantial additional help or face economic, social, and political deterioration of a very grave character."[24] Not only would it help Europe to obtain the means to import essentials, he argued, but it would help Europe buy the American goods it needed by relieving the serious "dollar gap" that these economies faced.[25] Against this, the USSR's Stalin came around to the view that the Marshall Plan, which both Western and Eastern European countries were initially invited to participate in, constituted an "aggressive attempt" by the United States to "wrest from Moscow economic control over Eastern Europe."[26] The Soviets subsequently pressured the Eastern European governments they dominated to pull out of a preliminary ERP conference that met in July. On September 21, on the very day that would-be Marshall Plan aid recipients were meeting again to discuss arrangements for a common recovery program, the Soviets summoned representatives of the communist parties of the Eastern European countries with communist governments (Poland, Romania, Bulgaria, Hungary, Yugoslavia, and Czechoslovakia), and two key countries in Western Europe (France and Italy) to an eight-day meeting in Szkalaraska Poreba, Poland. One outgrowth of this meeting was the formation of the Cominform, or Communist Information Bureau, as an ostensibly non-obligatory, nonbinding organ for exchanging information among communist parties and a de facto pared-down successor to the prewar Comintern. (Tito's Yugoslavian party was expelled in 1948.) Another was instructions to the parties to mount a militant campaign against the US imperialism in

their respective countries. In the words of the "Manifesto of the Cominform":
"Communists will form the spearhead of a resistance against plans for imperialist expansion in the political, economic, and ideological fields, and will rally all the democratic and patriotic forces of the nations to which they belong."[27] The French and Italian communists were singled out and berated for having pursued an excessively moderate, parliamentarist strategy up to that point.

The effect of this Cominform criticism on French trade-union behavior became amply apparent in November when communists in the CGT took the lead in fomenting a massive national-strike wave that reportedly involved 3 million workers. Several features distinguished the communist role in the strike wave from those of the late spring and summer. The first was the prominent role that political incidents played as catalyst for the strikes. The first strikes were called, for instance, to protest the arrests of demonstrators in Marseilles and subsequent clashes of communists with right-wing Gaullists and police. The wave spread to the coal mines of Northern France over the dismissal of a communist official who refused a government order to raise coal prices. The second was the refusal of the strike's communist leaders to even consider government offers as a basis for negotiation. This sent the message that the communists were not interested in promoting economic grievances but rather were using the strike to make a political point. In reaction, noncommunist unionists in the CGT chose to go back on the job. Western European governments, in the meantime, were under pressure from the United States to demonstrate that they were getting their economic houses in order and on a market-oriented footing. The depth of the antagonism in the resulting three-way confrontation involving striking communist workers, nonstriking noncommunists, and the government was vividly described by Braunthal: "The Communists occupied factories, railway stations and mines to prevent the resumption of work, and troops were called in to clear occupied premises. In the mining areas striking miners clashed with troops in heavy fighting, street battles were fought in Lyons when about 1,000 Communists tried to storm the central police station; the Paris-Lille express was derailed by sabotage and twenty lives were lost. At the end of November, the government counteracted by introducing an emergency Bill which imposed heavier sentences for acts of sabotage for a limited period, at the same time it called up 80,000 reservists. By early December the strikers' determination was exhausted and two-thirds of them had returned to work. On 9 December the communist-dominated national strike committee at last called off the strike; in order, it said, 'to gather our strength for the hard struggles which lie ahead.'"[28] In the wake of the general strike, the fissure that had been developing between the antigovernment communists and the pro-government socialists reached the point where the antagonism between the two sides was intense enough to break the union. A group of noncommunist unionists walked out of the CGT in December 1947 and subsequently established the CGT Force Ouvrière (FO) as an independent national labor organization with close ties to the French socialist party, leaving the CGT under solid communist hegemony.

Although the PCI's Togalitti maintained a more independent stance toward the Soviets than did the PCF's Thorez—indeed, unlike Thorez, Togliatti did not attend the meeting personally but sent representatives in his place—the PCI's behavior and that of the communists inside the CGIL also changed in quality following the Szkalaraska Poreba meeting. And as in France a communist-led political strike—an "insurrection" in some accounts—in the following year provided the catalyst for the split of the CGIL into separate communist and noncommunist wings, a process in which American government and labor officials played a role, much as they did in France.[29]

As the preceding descriptions of developments during the latter half of 1947 make clear, the American Marshall Plan initiative intersected with deteriorating economic conditions and the revival of internal tension in Western European labor movements to dramatically alter labor movement alignments in France and Italy. During this same period, tensions that were rooted in similar ideological differences and politico-strategic competition were precipitating an effort to realign the international labor movement in a joint, government-backed drive on the part of the British TUC and the American AFL and CIO to split the WFTU.[30] The issues propelling the initiative were analogues of those that were driving the communist-noncommunist confrontations at the national level—specifically, the deepening control by the communists over the WFTU apparatus and the differences over organizational principles that pitted the centralized and politicized communist model against the more decentralized model of union-party relations preferred in particular by the social democrats. Complaints about the behavior of communist unionists in the WFTU were present from the start and grew in intensity as time passed. Reflecting the philosophical differences behind the clashes, a key flashpoint was the international's relationship with the International Trade Secretariats (ITS) that organized unionists in given industrial sectors at the international level. The communists preferred a top-down arrangement that made the ITSes branches of the WFTU, while American, British, and other groups sympathetic to them insisted on an arrangement like that governing the prewar IFTU in which the international and the ITS were linked by a consultative relationship among formally independent organizations. With neither side wanting to appear to have provoked a split of the WFTU, the issue remained unresolved for some time.

As was the case at the national level, the trade-union response to the Marshall Plan brought matters to a head. A proposal by the British and American trade-union representatives to use an upcoming WFTU meeting as a forum for discussing the trade-union response to the Marshall Plan was rejected by the communist-dominated executive. After several confrontations, the frustrated sponsors of the effort went on to establish the forum outside of the WFTU umbrella in the form of the Trade Union Advisory Council for the European Recovery Program (TUAC/ERP) that was convened in London on March 9, 1948. Despite the breakdown of trust, it took some time for the deteriorating relations to precipitate an actual split of the organization. This eventually did happen, on January 17, 1949, when the American, British, and Dutch walked out of a WFTU board meeting in Paris after an acrimonious confrontation over he WFTU executive's activities. This was followed by preparations for the establishment of a competing labor international that culminated in the inaugural congress of the International Confederation of Free Trade Unions (ICFTU), in London on December 7. In keeping with their stand on a key issue that led to the break with the WFTU, the founders created an organization in which the ITSes remained formally independent of the confederation. The autonomy of member organizations was maintained, and decentralization was implemented through a well-developed system of regional organs. Ideologically, the ICFTU was committed to opposing all forms of totalitarianism, including communism. In the preparatory conference, the gathered national representatives went as far as to commit to assisting recovery of Europe through the Marshall Plan and to back regional arrangements like NATO for the defense of democracy. In the meantime, the WFTU proceeded to establish a system of industrial organs directly responsible to it.

The Americans were eager to demonstrate trade-union support for the European Recovery Program and the ICFTU. Membership in the Trade Union Advisory Council attached to the ERP and in the ICFTU were seen as the perfect vehicles for doing this. In this view, the two international labor organizations were bottles into which Americans were anxious to pour the appropriate wine. The ICFTU establishment effort, together with the associated TUAC/ERP, induced the American government to recruit noncommunist confederations from each of the leading nations to populate these organizations. The US government recruited American labor-union officials in this effort, with the most active being Jay Lovestone, Irving Brown, and others associated with the AFL's Free Trade Union Committee (FTUC). Anthony Carew suggests that the peak of such government-subsidized activity was the period that began in 1948 during which the WFTU was breaking up and the ICFTU was getting off the ground.[31] In France the split of the FO in December 1948 presented these officials with something they could use. Italy, by contrast, presented a problem, for the three leading currents at that time in the Italian trade unions were still housed in a common organization, the CGIL, dominated by the communists. Some sort of realignment was therefore seen as necessary.

In Italy the American project to create a confederation to represent Italy in the TUAC/ERP and ICFTU was a joint project of US embassy staff in Rome and representatives of the international bureaus of the AFL and CIO. A trip to the United States was arranged for three leading noncommunist unionists—Guido Pastore of the Catholic wing, Giovanni Canini of the social democrats, and A. Claudio Rocchi, a Republican. The trio's visit began on March 10, 1948. Following their return, on April 12, they distributed an estimated 500,000 copies of a report that made the case for aligning with the United States on the Marshall Plan.[32] However, the Italian labor movement proved to be much less malleable than the Americans had hoped. For one thing, even when key leaders were willing, many lower-level followers were reluctant to abandon the CGIL and the unprecedented organizational unity that it represented. Even among those who were deeply resentful of communist manipulation it was felt that a wiser strategy would be to work to expand noncommunist influence within the framework of the CGIL and redirect the labor movement using the extant CGIL organization. Furthermore, the clerical-anticlerical division remained strong, and the deep mistrust between unionists subscribing to Catholic unionism and those who did not proved to be yet another obstacle. American impatience with the inability of noncommunist groups to coalesce did not help matters. Driven by the TUAC/ERP and ICFTU calendars at the international level, American union representatives adopted what has been described as "a hasty, very undiplomatic way of operating." A US State Department review of the project was later forced to acknowledge that shortcomings in the US effort included "underestimating the importance of political traditions and party groupings in Italian unions and, to a lesser extent, to the fact that the agreements were limited to the leadership of the organizations concerned without sufficient preparation to make it possible to carry them out."[33]

The upshot was a brittle and incomplete process of realignment shaped as much by internal developments as it was by external intervention, and leaving the noncommunists fragmented. The issue of participation in the TUAC/ERP was taken up at the CGIL congress on March 2, 1948. Following fiery debate, a vote was taken and a resolution was passed opposing participation in the TUAC's inaugural meeting. A group of noncommunist leaders went to the London meeting anyway, forcing the communist CGIL leader Di Vittorio and left socialists to tag along to argue the majority's case. The CGIL held together despite this blatant breakdown in organizational discipline. In mid-July, the PCI's Togliatti was nearly killed in an assassination attempt carried out by a right-wing extremist. In protest against the assassination attempt the CGIL executive called a general strike. This provided the catalyst for a formal split in the CGIL's ranks. Declaring themselves to be outraged by this blatant use of the strike for political purposes, a group of Catholic union officials left the CGIL. Despite urging from the Americans, key social democrats refused to follow the Catholic unionists' lead. The dissident Catholic contingent regrouped three months later to form a new

Catholic labor confederation, the Libera Confederazione Generale Italiana del Lavoro, or LCGIL. In May of the following year, a violent clash between communist and social democratic workers in Emilia became the straw that finally broke the camel's back for a group of social democratic leaders in the CGIL. The group bolted to form the Federazione Italiana del Lavoratori, or FIL, a few weeks later, ostensibly as a temporary organizational receptacle for socialist unionists until such time as a formal merger with the Catholic LCGIL could be arranged. However, many social democratic refugees proved reluctant to support the proposed merger because of their distrust of the Christian unionists and fear that they would end up as a voiceless minority in an organization dominated by a much larger Christian bloc. The establishment of the ICFTU, in December 1949, with accompanying urgings from the Americans, put the proposed social democratic–Catholic merger on a concrete track toward implementation. The LCGIL and FIL each held congresses in February where a merger of the two organizations was formally approved. The new federation, dubbed the Confederazione Italiana Sindicati Lavoratori, or CISL, held its inaugural convention on May 1, 1950. This achievement was spoiled, however, by its inability to attain the comprehensive coverage that had originally been sought. Most obviously, the largest group of socialist unionists, namely the left socialists that remained in the CGIL, continued to align themselves with the communists and were opposed to the project. In addition a substantial number of social democratic unionists who had split from the CGIL refused to go along with the LCGIL-FIL merger and ended up establishing their own confederation, the Unione Italiana del Lavoratori, or UIL, in March.

Pacifism and neutralism

An important change in the character of the US containment policy began in mid-1948, specifically, the shift in emphasis from economic recovery and political neutralization of communism inside allied countries to containment of the Soviet Union through military means. Although a changing emphasis was already apparent during the Soviet blockade of Berlin (summer 1948 to late spring 1949), the events that decided the shift to a militarized policy were the Soviet detonation of an atomic bomb in the summer of 1949, the "loss" of China to a communist regime that October, and the Korean War that broke out at the end of June 1950. The Truman administration asked Congress for a vastly expanded military budget, began concluding anticommunist security alliances with noncommunist governments around the world, and urged alliance partners to rearm and host US troops. Perhaps nothing better symbolizes this shift from economic aid to military confrontation than the reorganization of the ERP's Economic Cooperation

Administration (ECA) into the Mutual Security Agency (MSA). The alliance of the United States and its military allies, the North Atlantic Treaty Organization (NATO), was concluded in April 1949. France and Italy were founding members. West Germany joined in 1955.[34]

Militarization of US Cold War policy and the associated armed confrontations between the two camps generated a palpable fear of another world war, this time accompanied by wholesale nuclear annihilation.[35] The United States encouraged this reaction by adopting a "new look" strategic policy that called for massive nuclear retaliation against a communist attack. The fear stimulated a rise of popular movements around the themes of disarmament, peace, and neutralism in various Western European countries. This reaction to the militarization of containment in Western Europe was not restricted to any particular class. Pockets of support were to be found in the working class, the bourgeoisie, the petite bourgeoisie, and professionals, although the most visible and vocal spokesmen for the movement were intellectuals. Support also spanned across the traditional Christian, social democratic, left-socialist, and communist ideological divisions. Strikingly similar stands were taken by groups as diverse as French opponents of the movement against the organized European Defense Community, minority Bevanites in the British Labour Party, and intellectuals associated with the West German antinuclear "Paul's Church movement." These attributes of the peace-and-neutralism movement were such that it did not fit comfortably into the traditional class-based divisions or the preexisting structure of ideological cleavages that were believed at the time to animate politics.[36]

The disjuncture was aggressively seized upon by the communist parties. Under conditions where the communists were in retreat politically, and in the trade unions, the broad sociological and political base of the peace movement was quickly identified as a vehicle through which to expand both the party's influence and the effectiveness of its resistance against Western governmental policies of alignment with the United States. The Cominform, accordingly, adopted a resolution that called on communist parties around the world "to make Communist-led peace campaigns their top priority," adding that "the paramount task of the Communist and Workers' parties is to draw the broadest sections of the working class into the ranks of the fighters for peace."[37] The resultant communist peace campaign was launched at an international meeting of prominent scientists held in Poland in August 1948, sponsored by the international communist movement and given the title World Congress of Intellectuals for Peace. This was followed by the much larger World Peace Congress held in Paris in April 1949. A permanent committee was established at that time to oversee the communist "peace offensive." The most ambitious action of the campaign was the so-called Stockholm Appeal of 1950 that called for the banning of atomic weapons. The campaign's sponsors claimed to have collected 500 million signatures from seventy-nine countries, including 14 million in France and 17 million in Italy. It seems clear that these figures were exaggerated. Nevertheless, a very large international campaign had clearly garnered support from a broad segment of opinion that extended well beyond the communist core of the movement.

Using the example of France, Ross describes the logic behind the peace offensive as follows: "It banked on the hope that large numbers of French people, of all classes and persuasions, would be sensitive to the danger of war and respond to the agitation of peace-oriented mass organizations. The focus on the peace tactic was ideological, designed to influence the climate of ideas in France through propaganda. The desired results would follow when a sufficiently strong peace sentiment was aroused. Then, presumably, French governments would be forced by public opinion to move away from their pro-American foreign policy."[38] By the same token, for the nonpartisan activists in the peace movement, the communists offered an institutionalized mass-organizational base that they did not possess. As Kuisel notes about the relationship between the PCF and the *compagnons de route* (fellow travelers) and "philo-Communists"—that is, prominent noncommunist intellectuals and artists who were willing to align themselves with the PCF: "Such intellectuals looked with favor at the PCF not because they were captivated by the party's doctrinal eminence but because of its record in the Resistance and its strategic political position. Even if its program was a hodgepodge of Soviet-inspired homilies, the Communist party was the most powerful party on the left."[39]

By far the most useful resource possessed by the PCF in mobilizing the peace campaign was its dominance in the CGT, and the PCF consequently mobilized the union to the hilt on behalf of its "peace offensive." The CGT called strikes to protest France's entry to NATO. Communist dockworkers refused to unload military equipment. Other political strikes were called. It has been estimated that there were some 1,500 "work stoppages and other actions to disorganize military production and transport" in France between 1949 and 1951.[40] Parallel actions were instituted in Italy.[41] In addition to the repertoire of communist-led union actions described for the PCF-CGT, the CGIL under Giuseppe Di Vittorio approved the Piano del Lavoro (Labor Plan) that was made public at the CGIL's October 1949 congress. Countering arguments that Italy needed US military aid in order to sustain itself economically, the plan offered a set of policies that were purported to present an avenue by which Italian economic growth and social equity could be sustained outside of an alliance with the United States and without having to integrate into the Western economic bloc.[42] Like the peace campaigns of the PCF and PCI, the political function of the Piano del Lavoro, in addition to solidifying support within the labor movement, was to expand CGIL influence through an appeal to the nationalism and the fears of entanglement in war shared by a broad segment of the Italian population.

From a purely ideological standpoint, given their straddling of the communist and noncommunist camps in the labor movement and their long association with pacifism, it would have appeared natural for the left-socialist wing of the labor movement to have been at the helm of the peace movement in Europe. As a point of fact, there was considerable support for a neutralist stance in the Cold War on the part of left socialists in various countries, and left socialists were drawn to the peace campaign. The Italian PSI under Pietro Nenni had staked a neutralist stance as early as 1947, or shortly after their expulsion from the De Gasperi government. Left socialists in the SFIO (and the social democrats as well, initially) characterized themselves and the centrist cabinets that they supported as constituting a "third force" in the Cold War in addition to marking the halfway point between socialism and capitalism. And when the European Defense Community came to a vote in the French national assembly, the left socialists defied party discipline to cast "no" ballots. Two interrelated factors, however, made it difficult for left socialists to play a distinct leadership role in the promotion of the pacifist neutralism despite their natural affinity to the position. One was the weakness of the left socialists' mass base relative to that of the much better organized communists, with their firm control over the leading trade-union centers, the CGT and CGIL. The second was the zero-sum nature of the Cold War climate itself. For proponents of neutralism in a country that was being incorporated into the Western containment apparatus, and which was simultaneously the site of a large-scale communist peace offensive, it was virtually impossible to maintain equal distance between the two camps. In the words of one student of the phenomenon, "since most of the countries—or groups within a country—which stand for 'neutralism' had been considered as forming part of the Western camp, and since their defection, or even resistance, for ideological motives would weaken that camp, neutralism has . . . come to take on the tangential meaning of fundamental opposition to American policy."[43] The fortunes of the PSI under Pietro Nenni illustrate the perils of the situation for a left-socialist neutralist course. The PSI linked up with the communists as a means of leveraging their neutralist position and to broaden the mass base of their opposition to Italy's participation in NATO.[44] The problem with the strategy, as numerous analysts have argued, was that in the process, the PSI lost its neutral identity, as it was extremely difficult to convincingly sustain a neutralist stance while allied to a party widely believed to be taking orders from one of the primary belligerents in the bipolar Cold War.[45] And even if a group were to actively attempt to maintain an equidistant stance, it still faced a climate in which "it was usual to attack an opinion not because it was believed to be mistaken in itself, but because 'objectively' it gave comfort to the 'enemy.'" Thus, "many of those who campaigned for peace in the 1950s were regularly criticized thereafter, not on the grounds that pacifism was wrong, but on the quite justifiable grounds that their position 'objectively' helped the foreign policy aims of the USSR." As Sassoon concludes, "Trapped in this logic there was nothing the West European Left could do to disentangle itself."[46]

Even when pulled off, however, continued utilization of union organizations for the peace movement was difficult since enthusiasm in unions for purely partisan political action not directly tied to economic concerns was a perishable commodity. Ross notes for France: "Locally, as the limited amount of organizational energy available to the CGT was shifted from trade unionism to peace action, the CGT became a 'peace committee' rather than a union. . . . Party and mass organization began de facto to merge, violating the CGT's integrity as an association where workers of all political opinions could expect to have their interests protected. Moreover, since France's other major union confederations, *Force Ouvrière* and the CFTC, were on the other side of the Cold War issues, the growing identification of the CGT with the PCF—and both, in turn, with the broad goals of Soviet foreign policy—had the effect of ruling out trade-union unity-in-action." With spontaneous rank-and-file enthusiasm for the peace movement in increasingly short supply as time passed, union officials were forced to adopt increasingly heavy-handed mobilizational tactics, which exacerbated tensions and resentments within union organizations.[47] As Ross concludes, the upshot was that "by neglecting its union duties in the interests of Cold War politics, and by stressing just those issues which were most likely to divide the CGT from other unions, the Confederation was making a very large contribution to the paralysis of rank-and-file union life in France."[48] These divisions, occurring as they did amid an attempt by management to seize an expanded freedom of action, set in motion a steady decline in union membership. Suffering defeat after defeat in the face of management intransigence, the 1950s proved to be hard years for both French and Italian unions.

The Cold War and the German labor movement

If the French and Italian examples highlight the multiplicity of ways in which international and domestic politics intertwined during the Cold War's initial years, the German situation during the same period illustrates how a different set of circumstances gave rise to a reduced set of forces and factors. As with their French and Italian counterparts, the German labor-movement activists at the end of World War II found unity a central theme for rebuilding the movement. This goal proved highly elusive for the German movement, as it did in France and Italy, and amid accelerating economic crises and heightened East-West tensions, the German movement experienced deepening division as well. And as in the other countries, the most fundamental differences dividing the communists and noncommunists were those over basic labor-movement principles, dating back to the 1920s. In the German case, however, the primary site for manifestation of such differences was in the interzonal meetings held to discuss reunification of the movement on a national basis.

In the Soviet sector, despite initial claims to the contrary, government officials intervened extensively in the process of reconstructing the labor movement. The Soviets made sure that the leadership of labor unions was firmly in the hands of communists, and when a new labor confederation, the Federation of Free German Trade Unions (Freier Deutscher Gewerkschaftsbund, or FDGB), was established, they made sure the organization was given a highly centralized structure in keeping with Marxism-Leninism. True to communist organizing principles, the German Communist Party (Kommunistiche Partei Deutschlands, or KPD) maintained a transmission-belt relationship with the union organ. In the political party sector, the SPD was forcibly merged with the KPD in April 1946 to form the Socialist Unity Party (Sozialistische Einheitspartei Deutschlands, or SED). After obtaining a majority in the October 1946 elections, again with the help of Soviet authorities, the SED proceeded to implement under Soviet direction a program of Stalinization in the Eastern economic zone.[49] What made the entire process particularly galling for the noncommunists was that it was clear the noncommunist social democrats and left socialists had a majority rank-and-file support, a condition that was itself a product of the absence, as profiled in chapter 3, of a full-fledged resistance coalition within which the communists could gain the legitimacy and political and organizational strength that the French and Italians communists were able to cultivate. The totalitarian excesses of the Communists in East Germany, and the predatory behavior of Soviet troops with which they were associated, made the KPD unpopular. As a result, the party was able to make only the most limited of inroads in the labor movements of the Western sector, and the few free elections held in East Germany prior to the October elections indicated that the SPD was far ahead of the KPD in popular and rank-and-file support. From very early on, noncommunist officials in the Western zones were made aware of the incompatibilities in their respective approaches and ideals vis-à-vis the communists.

Having said this, it is important to note that the actual instances of confrontation between the two camps in the labor movement were relatively few. The format of direct Allied occupation put management of both the economy and the reform process in the hands of the occupation governments. When added to the fact that day-to-day interaction among officials in different zones—particularly between East and West Germany—was very limited, there were few opportunities for such differences to manifest in practical issues. As MacShane points out, "it was only when the issues beyond those of day-to-day existence and organization came on to the union agenda that the divergence of socialist and communist views would surface."[50] One site that provided an opportunity was the interzonal discussions periodically held to discuss the unification of the various zonal union organs. When such differences did come up, they resonated with classic issues that dated back to the 1920s and even further. Thus, "The January 1948 interzone meeting saw the Western representatives putting forward a set of political principles which any new all-German federation should adopt. These included a commitment to free elections, unions to be independent of party control, and the state to respect individual freedom and other norms of liberal democracy. The communists replied with their demands that the new federation should call for state planning and the nationalization of banks, and, in an evident reminder of the language used in Weimar Germany, insisted that the new union should be a *Kampforganization* (a fighting union)." Not surprisingly, the meetings saw a growing estrangement between the unions in the Western and Soviet zones. As in France and Italy, the differences came to a head when the Cold War began to intervene. After the Marshall Plan was placed on the agenda of an interzonal trade-union conference in June 1948, official contact between unionists in the Western and Eastern zones ended. The interzonal split and the subsequent founding of the Federal Republic had the effect of firmly entrenching the hegemony of the noncommunists in the West German labor movement and of the communists in the east. The unions of the British, French, and American zones combined in December of that year. The founding of the Federal Republic of Germany (West Germany) as an independent state based in the Western zones, in September 1949, was followed in October by the creation of the German Labor Federation (Deutscher Gewerkschaftsbund, or DGB) as the common labor-union confederation of the newly created Federal Republic, representing 4.2 million blue-collar workers, 530,000 white-collar workers, and 270,000 civil servants. Despite the existence of a very small communist minority until a later ban on the party, this was essentially a social democratic, Christian democrat, left-socialist organization.[51]

Thanks to the absence of a sizable communist contingent, within the narrower context of West Germany, the labor movement was spared the convulsions over the Marshall Plan that wracked movements in which the communists were a major force. The relatively uneventful internal history of the West German labor movement during this period provides a sharp contrast to the turbulence in this area experienced in France and Italy. The stance adopted by the dominant socialist contingent of social democrats and left socialists in the West German labor movement vis-à-vis the foreign and economic policy aspects of the Marshall Plan and the emerging Cold War conflict can best be described as one of minimal engagement. Not in a position to influence the course of events, the West German labor movement concentrated on gathering resources while biding its time until the restoration of civil government would allow it to play a meaningful role in the

Federal Republican polity. In the area of foreign economic policy, it supported acceptance of Marshall Plan funds but remained ambivalent about it nonetheless. When forced to "decide between the Marshall Plan and the Molotov Plan," to use the characterization of a leading German unionist, German labor leaders chose the former. German unionists expressed their strong desire to participate in the Marshall Plan implementation process, but were rebuffed. The vision that they hoped to pursue was laid out at the DGB's founding congress. As neatly summarized by a European trade union organ on the DGB's fiftieth anniversary:

> As a fall back position, West German unionists made plans to press for the passage of legislation that would institutionalize labor's participation in management through a codetermination law applied across West German industry and in fact launched their drive on behalf of codetermination right after West Germany regained its national sovereignty.
>
> Viewing the Federal Republic's Basic Law (constitution) to be a temporary document that would lose its relevance once Germany was reunited, and not wanting to delay the ending of the Occupation, the labor movement made only minimal effort to embed the social rights that it sought during the process of drafting the document. In economic policy both the SDP and the DGB continued to embrace the vision of a socialized economy . . . that they had adopted during the initial post-Surrender months. . . . There were, in particular, three principal demands in the first DGB basic programme:
>
> 1. "socialisation" of key industries such as mining, iron and steel, chemicals, electricity and banking;
> 2. national planning of economic development through national trade-cycle and investment policy; and
> 3. economic democracy through far-reaching co-determination rights.
>
> To sum up, the first DGB basic programme contained an idea of democratic socialism which [at] that time was seen as a kind of "third way" between capitalism and Soviet state socialism.[52]

This disengagement proved costly for the West German labor movement. Although somewhat less draconian than Einaudi's "hard landing" in Italy, the economic-stabilization policies imposed on Germany under the tutelage of the occupation governments' special adviser Joseph Dodge (who would later administer the same medicine in Japan), a June 1948 currency reform was adopted that forced the abrupt dismantling of wage, price, and distribution controls and put the West German economy on a market-oriented capitalist recovery path. The reform quickly reduced the amount of currency in circulation. Wage and price controls were lifted while unemployment more than doubled, from 442,000 to

937,000 over six months.[53] In turn, the currency reform and the associated retrenchment laid the foundations for a "capital offensive" aimed at rolling back union influence in production decisions. On November 12, 1948, over 9 million West German workers walked out in frustration in a general strike. As Andrei Markovits notes, "The Allies permitted the strike because they were convinced of its tameness, due to its strictly economic character. There is no doubt that this assessment of the German labor movement in 1948 was largely correct."[54] What this confrontation revealed was another major difference in attributes of the West German movement that the distinctive postwar context in Germany created relative to those of France and Italy. Structurally, unions in the Western zones were not well-suited organizationally for mobilization on behalf of partisan goals. Having been organized from the bottom up in a context where politicization had been discouraged, they lacked the interlocking directorates and overlapping ties at the top between unions and parties that were so central to labor movements of the French and Italian variety. The organizing principle of the unitary, nonpartisan union (*einheitsgewerkshaft*)—made sustainable by the absence of a Cold War–inspired communist-noncommunist split—militated against direct partisanship. The internal political loyalties in fact tended to pull the DGB in opposing directions, with the socialists aligned with the opposition SPD, and the minority Christian subgroup aligned with the governing Christian Democrats. These unions were not organized effectively on a nationwide basis, either, since it was not until late in 1949 that the DGB and its member industrial unions were at last established.[55]

Given the leftward shift in the ideological center of gravity throughout Europe during the initial postwar years, the SPD had anticipated that it would do well in Bundestag elections and would be in a position to form a government that would implement its socialization program. However, the East-West polarization of the Cold War had brought about a rightward shift in the popular opinion in Germany. Furthermore, the unpopularity of the Soviet Union led to a discrediting of socialism in the minds of many. As a consequence, it was the Christian Democrats under Konrad Adenauer, who had abandoned their earlier socialistic Ahlener Progam in favor of a minimally modified market capitalism known as the "social market economy," that emerged victorious in the first Bundestag election. Although it might have entered into a coalition government through compromises, the left-leaning reaction in the party to the frustrations of the rightward swing in the political center of gravity in society at large motivated the SPD to stay out of the government and to push even harder for its leftist program. To their chagrin, when it came time to realize the socialist vision of Western German political economy that they had harbored over the course of the occupation, the SPD and the DGB were not in a position to do so. While they were able to win parity codetermination in the coal and iron and steel industries in a famous compromise with the CDU/CSU premier Adenauer, both the parity provisions and the limitation of the industries covered were interpreted as major losses for the movement.

In the foreign-policy arena, the SPD, with backing from the socialist contingent in the DGB, went along with the creation of the Federal Republic but insistently maintained a neutralist stance in the Cold War on grounds that committing West Germany to the West would jeopardize Germany's future unification. In the absence of a strong communist party on the left inside the Germany policy, the SPD was spared the identity confusion that plagued the Italian left socialists. Its neutralism appeared considerably more credible as a result. Nevertheless, negotiating the currents of the Cold War militarization proved to be a delicate task for the DGB's leadership. On the one hand, the issues of West Germany's rearmament and its entry to NATO stimulated powerful demands from below for the DGB to play an active role in opposing Germany's incorporation into the US camp in the Cold War and to back the SPD, which had adopted a neutralist line and opposed the CDU-CSU government's foreign policy. Popular-opinion surveys indicated that there was strong support for the SPD's neutralism among German workers.[56] Furthermore, "with the exception of the ultimately insignificant secession by a small minority of Christian unionists, no topic of the period elicited a more spirited discussion and unified response on the part of organized labor than the issue of West Germany's remilitarization in preparation for its joining the North Atlantic Treaty Organization. Still bearing the traumas associated with the Kapp Putsch and deeply suspicious of the profoundly anti-democratic tradition of the old German military establishment, the unions developed an almost instinctive fear of the reintroduction of a major military force in the Federal Republic. Many unionists were convinced at the time that the creation of the Bundeswehr would severely endanger—perhaps even eliminate—the feeble democracy which was gaining stability and legitimacy for the first time in German history."[57] Unionists forged links with anti-rearmament extra-parliamentary groups and were an important pillar of the alliance of protest groups that constituted the Paulskirche Movement for the Unification of Germany and Against Rearmament. A similar rise in protest greeted the controversy over the introduction of nuclear weapons into West Germany, in 1957–1958. At the same time, however, the fact remained that the DGB was politically divided between a larger segment of SPD supporters and a minority of Christian unionists that backed the government party. The problematic nature of political involvement was illustrated by the loss of support and the political isolation of DGB president Walter Freitag after he openly supported the SPD in the 1953 Bundstag elections. Thus, if in France and Italy communist control of the labor movement presented an obstacle to effective left-socialist harnessing of the latter, in West Germany the coexistence of left-socialist tendencies and social democratic and Christian democratic norms presented other problems when efforts were made to link the peace and labor movements. However, the nonpartisan norms of the *einheitsgewerkshaft* prohibited on general principle the use of the union on behalf of overt political goals, and despite strong appeals from the SPD and occasional minor lapses, the DGB proved wholly unsuited as a vehicle for positive neutralist mobilization.[58]

As for the impact of the onset of the Cold War, one can liken it to a magnetic field. The conflict in the international arena created powerful polarities that reordered the politics of the labor movements to varying degrees in Western Europe. In France and Italy in particular, the war and immediate postwar years produced labor movements highly susceptible to this magnetic effect. This sensitivity's source was the intertwining of ideological identity, union structures, and political party organizations that the Resistance experience had produced. Effects of the polar attraction of the bipolarized international arena were felt most strongly and directly at the two opposite ends of the labor movement—that is, by its communist and its Christian wings. Depending on one's frame of reference, the Cold War's magnetic-field effect was either more or less powerful in Germany. It was more powerful in the sense that it tore asunder the German labor movement, creating two separate movements residing in separate nation-states. Ironically, the very strength of this force was such that once the two German movements were segregated, a kind of cocooning effect emerged that sheltered the respective national labor movements from the internally divisive impact of international developments associated with the Cold War.

Having said this, it is also important to note that the foreign-policy-linked polarization between communists and anticommunists is not the full story of the Cold War's impact. Intertwined with the politics of East-West confrontations in the labor movement were a number of critical issues relating to the type of political economic order the respective countries would adopt, and the status and role of the labor movements there. Of central significance here are such issues as the fate of the socialistic reforms that had been instituted in the pre–Cold War postwar years and the terms under which labor would "participate" in the process of capitalist economic expansion that the United States was hoping to foster in these countries. In addition, there were the issues of labor movement principles and basic questions about the nature and role of labor unions in society that once again came to the fore, issues that predated the emergence of the Cold War. They were salient, however, because they overlapped with core issues that were at the heart of the international conflict.

Chapter 7

Division and Confrontation, 1947–1949

From late 1947 onward, national level politics became increasingly entangled with the bipolar Cold War struggle unfolding in the international system, though the form this entanglement took locally depended greatly on particular circumstances. In France and Italy, the Cold War–period labor movement became a proxy war in which communist parties and the labor unions they controlled confronted segments of the movement maintaining close ties with one or more parties in incumbent governments that were, whatever gloss they might wish to put on it, aligned with the United States. In Germany the two sides were geographically isolated from each other in separately administered military-occupation zones, creating in the labor movement a situation in which the bipolarity of the Cold War was manifested primarily through institutionalization of radically different organizations in the respective zones. Like Germany, Japan was occupied, but in a context in which the competing wings of the labor movement were allowed to organize more or less freely. Additionally, in geopolitical terms, Japan was not until 1950 in a part of the world in which the Cold War was considered to be under way. Although the communists confronted the "American imperialism" directly, neither side overtly acknowledged a formal struggle.

Studies of policy making in Washington, DC, during the period when the European Recovery Program was being formulated reveal that US government officials had begun to view Japan through a Cold War lens.[1] But due to Washington's preoccupation with the European situation and the fact that the communist threat in the Far East was not seen as imminent, this did not precipitate a whole-sale policy shift along the lines of the Marshall Plan. A series of high-profile delegations from Washington did, however, visit Japan during the first half of 1948, and they recommended a number of significant policy changes to facilitate economic recovery there. A threshold of sorts was then reached when, in mid-December, Washington issued the directive to MacArthur to begin administering what came to be known as the Nine Point Economic Stabilization Program, or, in effect, a version for Japan of the stabilization policies being demanded of ERP aid recipients. In order to complete this stabilization, Washington policy-makers sent to Japan the following spring Joseph Dodge, the conservative Detroit banker who oversaw Germany's currency stabilization. Core components of the resulting policy package that Dodge oversaw, known as the Dodge Line, consisted of a balanced national budget, a cutback of government credit, the abolition of government subsidies to private firms, and the establishment of a single exchange rate. The imposition of the Dodge Line quickly brought inflation under control and eliminated most of the modified capitalist arrangements associated with the Katayama economic-recovery program. Although there was an increase in the amount of aid Japan received from the United States, there was nothing on the order of that associated with the ERP. From a comparative standpoint, what Japan got in effect from Washington was stabilization without the Marshall Plan.

As they did in France and Italy during 1947, preexisting tensions between communists and noncommunists intensified in Japan's labor movement as resent-ment built up against communist control and communist tactics in labor unions. Although there was no expulsion of the communists from government (the Japa-nese communists were not in the government), there was a shift from a position of communist support of the Katayama government's economic program to one in which the party attempted to position itself as the voice of rank-and-file worker dissatisfaction produced by economic decline. These developments intersected with deterioration in the economy, producing a reversal of the trend toward a common agenda among the competing wings of the Japanese movement that had only begun to get off the ground in Japan with the formation of the center-left Katayama cabinet. In Europe, as discussed in the preceding chapter, the Soviet Union reacted to the Marshall Plan by directing Western European communist parties to use the labor movements in these countries to agitate against the plan's implementation that autumn. Shortly thereafter, the JCP also adopted a line of active opposition to US "imperialism," which was congruent with the inter-national communist movement's Cold War line. Unfortunately, based on available information it is impossible to say definitively whether or not the JCP was given specific orders from Moscow to adopt a policy of resistance similar to those being pursued by the French and Italian communists. Even if there was no direct guid-ance from Moscow, however, given the party's awareness of developments in the international arena—and the discussions of these events in JCP publications make it clear that the party was familiar with the unfolding Cold War—it was entirely possible for party leaders to have consciously attuned on their own initiative their actions to the trends in the international communist movement. In the process, relations between the communists and the US occupation authorities grew increasingly confrontational between 1947 and 1950. What all of this—that is, a growing emphasis on economic recovery in US occupation policy, increasingly open agitation against communist control in the trade unions, and the concurrent adoption of an anti-imperialist line by the Japanese communists—added up to was a situation in which the basic ingredients of the French and Italian labor politic intertwined in the context of Allied occupation similar to that in West Germany.

The roots of the Mindō movement

The process by which the JCP expanded its influence in the Japanese labor movement following the release of its leadership from prison in October 1945 was outlined in chapters 3 and 4. As noted there, this expansion of communist influence took place in the absence of a wartime resistance, and as a consequence of this historical distinction, the Japanese communists were at a relative disadvantage in their quest to secure control in the trade-union sector when compared with the French and Italian efforts. As noted in those chapters, although they were not part of a united trade-union center along the lines of the CGIL or a common socialist-communist organ like the CGT, they were able to establish a separate national labor-union center, Sanbetsu, over which they exercised considerable control, as well as to extend their influence over other union organizations, particularly from the spring of 1946 onward, in the public-sector unions and elsewhere through the implantation of communist cells.

As recollections of individuals who were involved in the labor movement during the early postwar years spell out, tactics used by Japanese communists to exercise their control over unions could be extremely harsh and heavy-handed. Violence and intimidation were used frequently—and often successfully—in attempts to reverse unwanted decisions on the part of union governing bodies. A concrete illustration of how this worked was seen during the struggles of the railway workers during the summer of 1946. On July 24 the government announced plans to dismiss 75,000 redundant railway workers. As noted in chapter 4, the union responded by announcing its intent to launch an industry-wide general strike. The railway workers' union, Kokurō, reached a last-minute settlement in which the government retracted the dismissals. Kokurō president Suzuki Seiichi, who also chaired the strike committee, then canceled the general strike that the union had set for September 13. Shortly after his announcement, a crowd of JCP loyalists, most of whom were from outside Kokurō, who wanted to see the strike implemented irrespective of a settlement, as a demonstration of labor's power, confronted Suzuki and a couple of other Kokurō executives. The group physically encircled Suzuki and his companions and attempted to intimidate them into retracting the strike cancellation by shouting at them at the top of their lungs. This "mortar conference" *(suribachi kaigi)*—so named because the seated Suzuki and companions, surrounded by the standing JCP contingent, looked like something at the bottom of a mortar about to be ground down by a pestle—had been preceded by an earlier incident in which communist "youth action brigade" members and members of the women's auxiliary packed a meeting of the Kokurō strike committee and engaged in similar intimidation tactics.[2]

A major base of opposition to expanding communist influence and control in the trade unions could be found, naturally enough, among the social democrats in Sōdōmei. It could also be found among other noncommunist unionists in unaffiliated unions. And in the wake of the general strike of February 1947, it was made apparent that the reaction against communist tactics had even permeated the JCP-dominated Sanbetsu organization. The poor showing of the JCP in the April 1947 parliamentary elections despite the great effort that the Sanbetsu organization had put into election campaigning (for instance, none of the Sanbetsu-affiliated candidates obtained a seat in the general election), coming on top of the general strike's humiliating cancellation, precipitated a groundswell of criticism against the JCP and the Sanbetsu executive. Key enterprise unions in a number of Sanbetsu's industrial federations withdrew or threatened to withdraw their affiliations. These developments induced the leadership of several of Sanbetsu's industrial federations to demand that the national center revamp its strategy and tactics as a means to stem the tide of secessions. Alarmed, the Sanbetsu secretariat staff, led by the deputy general secretary (and JCP fraction captain) Hosoya Matsuta, announced on May 12 that an emergency "self-criticism" convention of the confederation would be convened in the near future.[3] The self-criticism convention was scheduled for July 10 through 14. The Sanbetsu secretariat then drafted a self-criticism and made it public on May 15. The document implicitly criticized the JCP for its extreme militancy and excessive intervention in union affairs. Three days later, the party put forward its own self-criticism at an expanded central-committee meeting. The tenor of the party's document was rather different from that of the trade-union confederation. Its main point was that the party had focused too much on the pursuit of visible material gains and not enough on political education.[4] The differing emphases in the party's and union confederation's self-criticisms revealed significant differences between the party and the labor-confederation secretariat—differences that were at the heart of the classic debate over where cues should originate for labor unions, the rank-and-file or the vanguard party.

The party leadership appears to have been sensitive to the implications. On July 9, the day before Sanbetsu's scheduled self-criticism convention, Tokuda called a meeting of the Sanbetsu party fraction. At this meeting, Tokuda responded to the charge that the JCP had promoted an excessively militant line. He claimed that the public-sector raises granted in the wake of the general strike's cancellation were granted precisely because of the threat of a general strike and that it was therefore wrong to consider the strike movement a failure. "Only a Philistine who does not fully understand class struggle," Tokuda is alleged to have importuned, "would say that the February 1 strike was a failure!" Regarding Hosoya, whom he saw as the instigator of the Sanbetsu self-criticism, Tokuda is alleged to have declared: "Hosoya Matsuta is moving in the direction of Nishio Suehiro. We must take care of him!"[5] The next day, in a move that was apparently choreographed beforehand by the JCP executive, a motion was made to select one delegate from each of the leading industrial organizations to man a committee that would rewrite the movement-policy draft prepared by the Sanbetsu secretariat. Six of the ten members chosen for the committee were known to be card-carrying party members. The rewritten movement program rejected the soft tone of the earlier draft and emphasized the need to "struggle" to protect the interests of workers and small businesses. It was approved by the convention the following day. The convention also approved a substantial change in Sanbetsu's leadership lineup. Kan Makoto of the Sanbetsu metals federation, who was popular among both the communist and noncommunist factions in the organization, replaced as president Kikunami of the newspaper and broadcasting union, but party members were selected to fill other key positions. Perhaps the most significant of these was the appointment of Yoshida Sukeharu, a party veteran from the 1920s who had spent twelve years in prison with Tokuda, to the position of general secretary. This was accompanied by the abolition of the position that Hosoya had held since Sanbetsu's founding.[6]

Despite the muzzling, Hosoya and his associates continued to push for greater independence of the unions. Among other things, the Sanbetsu secretariat failed to take concrete action to give substance to the party's increasing emphasis on antigovernment struggle. This inaction, in turn, stimulated the JCP to take further steps to tighten its control. Procedures were revamped to enhance the supervisory capacity of the JCP-dominated executive board over secretariat staff. A particularly significant change could be found in the role played by the general secretary. Whereas the previous incumbent had been content to serve as a figurehead, the recently installed general secretary, Yoshida, began to actively intervene in the daily affairs of Sanbetsu headquarters.[7] The result, in the words of one of the principals, was that a "cold-war-like ill will" began to pervade relations between a key segment of the Sanbetsu staff loyal to Hosoya and JCP loyalists.[8]

The confrontation between the two sides once again came to a boil at Sanbetsu's third convention, held in November, where the JCP used the same tactics it had used at the July self-criticism convention, to quash an initiative promoted by the Hosoya group.[9] At this point Hosoya was ordered to resign from Sanbetsu staff entirely and was sent to work at JCP headquarters, where the party could presumably keep a closer watch over him. Hosoya, however, renounced his party membership a few days after the convention. In the meantime, a number of high-ranking officials of Sanbetsu-affiliated industrial organizations who were also offended by the JCP's tactics quietly established contact with the dissident elements in the secretariat. In February of the following year, these two groups joined forces in creating an informal association of dissident Sanbetsu unionists, which referred to itself as the Sanbetsu Mindō, or Sanbetsu Democratization League (Sanbetsu Minshuka Dōmei). The composition of the resulting factional grouping was reported as follows: four industrial-federation-based members of the Sanbetsu executive board, around thirty other individuals from Sanbetsu-affiliated industrial organizations, and seven individuals from the Sanbetsu secretariat.[10]

Hosoya and his group's struggles with the JCP in Sanbetsu were paralleled by rebellions against the party in other union organizations. The most widely noted of these was the Kokutetsu Anticommunist League (Kokutetsu Hankyō Renmei) formed in mid-October in the massive national railway workers union, Kokurō. The league's formation was inspired by a successful bid by a JCP-led group to replace a movement policy drafted by the union's executive supporting the Katayama wage-price guidelines (see below) with an amended version in tune with the policies of the JCP. The fractious controversy temporarily split the union. Like the original draft of the Sanbetsu self-criticism, but in considerably harsher language, the manifesto of the Kokutetsu Anticommunist League railed against the manipulations of "a minority element that dances to the directives of the JCP."[11] Sōdōmei's central committee declared its intention on January 13, 1948, to lead a "labor union democratization movement" of its own. The impetus for this decision came from its Osaka federation, which had a reputation as being a "fortress of anticommunism," where the leadership found that some of its enterprise-level organizations had been infiltrated by communist activists. Shocked, the federation leaders constituted themselves as a "labor-union democratization federation" whose purpose was to systematically root out JCP influence. The concept was then taken to the Sōdōmei central committee, where it was upgraded to a status of confederation-wide policy.[12] Seizing a perceived opportunity to expand its influence, Sōdōmei, as described in the Ministry of Labor's (MOL) compendium of developments in the Japanese labor movement for 1948, "moved aggressively to designate for itself the role of organizing this anticommunist movement on a nationwide basis and turning it into a major current."[13]

Over the course of 1948, these disparate and independent reactions against communist control and tactics developed an identity as a common initiative that stretched across the existing organizational boundaries aimed at "democratizing" the Japanese labor movement. The Sanbetsu Mindō played a pivotal role. In a practice that raised the hackles of the JCP and the communists in Sanbetsu, representatives of anticommunist elements from non-Sanbetsu organizations were invited to Sanbetsu Mindō gatherings. One of the earliest of these was held on February 24, 1948. Attendance was estimated at between two hundred and three hundred. Along with dissidents from virtually all of the major Sanbetsu unions, present at the meeting were Sōdōmei officials (notably, social democrat Hara Toraichi and left-socialist Takano Minoru) and officials from independent unions like the recently formed Tanrō (Coal Miners' Union), Nikkyōso (Teachers' Union), and Nippōrō (Broadcasting Workers' Union). A second gathering in May was a similar panoply of unions. In addition, Hosoya, who was now leading the Sanbetsu Mindō full-time, began to work closely with individuals in the JSP's left-socialist wing and the party's youth organization.[14] A good indicator of the growing consciousness of a common Mindō identity was the adoption by the Kokutetsu Anticommunist League of a new name, Kokutetsu Mindō.

The breakdown of the "battle for production"

The core of the Katayama cabinet's economic-recovery program was made public on June 11, 1947. Like those of its Western European counterparts at the time, the Japanese government's program was built around a quid pro quo in which the state intended to trade a guarantee that basic worker-consumption needs would be met in exchange for production increases. Under the program the government would "stabilize wages at or slightly above their existing level . . . but . . . increase their purchasing power by making more goods available at official prices" through strengthened state controls over the economy. In order to effect this, the plan included a list of wage guidelines based on price surveys taken in January. "Standard wage rates were announced for 35 industries, ranging from ¥1,124 per month in raw silk to ¥2,440 in freight and shipbuilding. Textiles averaged about ¥1,230 per month, chemicals ¥1,600, food processing ¥1,600, printing ¥1,900, machinery and tools ¥2,181, electric power ¥2,200, metallurgy ¥2,350, freight and transportation ¥2,400." The overall average was 1,800 yen, and this figure was used as a benchmark. On the other side of the equation, sizable increases in official commodity prices were announced "in order to divert goods from the black market." In line with this, "official commodity prices were raised in amounts ranging up to 200 per cent. Rice went up from ¥36 to ¥99 for ten kilograms, and other food prices from 18 to 27 per cent. The price of coal received by producers was lifted from ¥346 to ¥956 per ton; the price paid by essential industries went from ¥200 to ¥400, and that of other consumers from ¥400 to ¥1,208." The Katayama price scheme set the average price level at sixty-five times their 1934–1936 levels while wages were set at twenty-eight times. The 2.3 to 1 disparity between prices and wages translated into a corresponding reduction in real consumption relative to prewar levels, with the gap to be gradually filled through increased production and productivity.[15]

There were a number of problems in the system of wage-price guidelines. For one thing, the announced wage levels were guidelines for calculating wage costs and not part of a program of compulsory state wage regulation. Unions and management were free to negotiate higher wages. As one observer correctly noted, "the government in effect asked labor to give this program a chance by agreeing to voluntary wages ceilings. Meanwhile the government would try to stabilize prices and to make more supplies available in the legal market . . . . Labor was also urged to help the government by boycotting the black market and to apply its effort to increasing production."[16] Beyond this, the pricing data on which the guidelines were based was six months old by the time they were released. Under conditions of rapid inflation this gap implied a substantial disparity between the purchasing power assumed in the guidelines and real purchasing power on the street at the time of the plan's release. Sanbetsu claimed that a more realistic figure for the average wage would be 3,000 yen rather than the officially proclaimed 1,800. The guidelines also assumed that controlled commodities would be available in required quantities at official prices. This assumption was at odds with reality. The most important controlled commodities for the urban worker were, of course, food items. Not all food items needed by urban households were being rationed or controlled, and even those that were, were not necessarily available in required quantities through government channels. The implications were cogently described as follows: "The government's proposal on food policy makes it clear that late deliveries of rations cannot be avoided. In other words, it is saying it can distribute only so much food in the way of food rations, so you will need to find and eat [the rest] on your own, and it will hold down a portion of the cost of living but there are times when it won't be able to do this. In those instances, you will have to make purchases on the black market, and you will need to make do with a monthly wage of 1,800 yen. Under these conditions, many workers will not be able to meet their needs."[17]

Buoyed by the novelty of a government in which the socialist party participated, the first months of the Katayama cabinet were a honeymoon period that saw a significant drop in the number of labor disputes. Shortly after the economic program was announced, the government organized a conference with representatives of the leading labor organizations where it formally requested their cooperation. Not surprisingly, Sōdōmei was the most enthusiastic backer of the Katayama program and issued a statement promising support. Although the tone was less enthusiastic, Sanbetsu pledged its support as well.[18] The ERC proved to be equally supportive and in fact adopted for itself a role in mobilizing support for the program on behalf of the ESB, the government agency for overseeing the recovery program. A series of meetings were held over the course of the summer and fall between ERC officers and various ministers and economic bureaucrats. Prominent ERC officials were assigned key positions in the ESB. Sōdōmei's Watanabe Toshinosuke, for instance, became the ESB's labor bureau chief. A number of prominent Dōyūkai affiliates associated with the ERC were drafted to staff positions in other ESB bureaus.[19]

Bad harvests, corruption, bureaucratic mismanagement, and a variety of other factors, however, exacerbated the difficulties that the government faced in administering its economic-recovery program. The official rations were meager to begin with, but during the summer of 1947, thanks to missed deliveries, the distribution of food rations was, as we noted earlier, twenty days behind schedule in Tokyo and as high as ninety days in Hokkaido. The nondelivery of food rations naturally created even greater demand for black-market goods. Government surveys indicate that the overall black-market price index in Tokyo rose by 79 percent between January and July. For food items this increase was 130 percent. Prices for black-market food were twice as high in Osaka and Kyushu.[20] In August the food situation was relieved somewhat by the release of emergency-aid food provided by the US government. Even so, the ESB calculated that the budget of the average household would suffer a 160 yen deficit that month, thanks largely to the cost of black-market food.

Statistics on the number of labor disputes indicate that the deteriorating food situation and the rise in black-market prices was causing labor unrest. In strategic industries in the private sector, these "disputes" were frequently what was labeled "*avec* struggles," or bargaining in which labor unions and management tacitly cooperated in putting pressure on the government to increase the subsidies needed to cover wage hikes.[21] On the other hand, as the public-sector worker-led February 1 general strike had already demonstrated, the cumbersome budgetary process and the partisan fragmentation associated with public-sector wage determination made it impossible for public-sector wages to adjust to inflation in a timely manner. The deteriorating situation produced spontaneous wildcat strikes and walkouts by public-sector workers over the course of the summer and fall. It is interesting to note that in many instances these involved demands for advance payment of future wages to tide things over until a wage hike was gained or the food situation improved, and as in the private sector, managerial staff often complied with these demands. Among the most prominent hotbeds of these local wildcat strikes were the poorly paid urban postal workers affiliated with Zentei, the postal and telephone workers' union.[22]

Regarding the partisan context within which the effort to implement the Katayama economic-recovery plan was unfolding, it is essential to note that as a result of the creation of the JSP-PCP-democratic cabinet, a pattern of centrist interparty alignment was created in Japan comparable to that emerging at roughly the same time in France as a result of the dismissal of the communist ministers from government. The JCP had tentatively granted its support for the Katayama Cabinet and its economic program, but since it was not part of the coalition, it did not have any formal responsibility for the Katayama program's success. When it became clear that the program's failure to halt inflation was generating rank-and-file unrest, the party was in a position to easily shift to an oppositional stance. This is precisely what the party did. Over the course of the summer of 1947, articles in the JCP's daily, *Akahata,* grew increasingly strident in their criticisms of the cabinet, with the primary theme in the JCP's attacks being that the cabinet was engaging in a revival of capitalism at the expense of worker livelihoods. Newly installed Sanbetsu president Kan accused the government of engaging in "a capitalistic rationalization of enterprise that preserves the profits of finance capital while compelling worker dismissals." The Katayama wage-price guidelines, in his words, constituted a "severe de facto reduction of real wages" that was causing a "collapse" of worker livelihoods.[23] And by the fall of that year, it was readily apparent the party was actively fomenting strikes that would wreck the economic program.

In addition, in a set of developments that paralleled the pattern of internal tensions in the SFIO in France, the failing economic program gave rise to dissidence among left socialists in the JSP that was directed against the more moderate social-democratic leadership. The JSP's left socialists, increasingly frustrated by the inability of the economic program to deliver concrete improvements in the economic situation of Japanese workers, used the public-sector wage issue to attack the moderate social democrats. The key problem in the eyes of the left socialists was failure of the social democrats in the party to press hard enough on behalf of the working class, and the social democrats' consonant willingness to compromise with their "bourgeois" partners at the expense of worker needs. The limits of the left socialists' tolerance was reached toward the end of 1947 as the issue of public-sector workers' salaries was taken up. The cabinet had decided to accept a proposal in which it would pay government workers a special bonus worth 2.8 months' salary to tide them over until a more permanent settlement could be reached. Two months' worth was paid out with the remaining .8 month to be paid later, once legislative arrangements were made to finance the remaining expenditure. The government then introduced legislation to the Diet that would use revenue generated by an increase in rail and postal rates as a way to cover the costs of the wage bonus. The JSP left socialists insisted that the bonus be financed through some means other than what amounted to a tax on the working masses. They also argued that the burden the wage-price scheme was forcing on the working class was now intolerable and called for a revision of the July 1947 wage-price schedule in a manner that would raise real consumption levels. The resulting deadlock between the cabinet and the JSP left socialists ultimately precipitated Katayama's resignation, on February 10. After a month of painstaking negotiations, a successor cabinet based on the same three-party coalition was established under Ashida Hitoshi, president of the Democratic Party, in which prominent left socialists were given key cabinet posts. Thus, as happened in the French socialist party, the deterioration of economic conditions set the stage for a rapid growth in the influence of the left-socialist contingent inside the socialist party and a leftward shift in the center of gravity in the party. This would culminate in the party's 1949 convention, in which the left socialists gained majority control over the party executive. While the issue of financing the government workers' allowances was ultimately addressed by an inflation-assisted natural increase in government revenues that obviated the need for a fare increase, the ongoing dispute over government wages was left for the Ashida government to deal with.[24]

Polarization

As detailed in the preceding chapter, the drama associated with the American announcement of the Marshall Plan and the Eastern bloc's rejection of it unfolded in Europe over the summer of 1947. The Cominform was established in September and initiated an international struggle directed against the Marshall Plan and, more broadly, US "imperialism." In Japan in late 1947, JCP strategy moved in a parallel direction as the primary target against which the JCP's confrontational tactics were to be directed was shifted to GHQ. Specifically, as detailed by Araki Yoshinobu in a recent study, just before the party's sixth congress, held December 21–23, Chairman Tokuda secretly gathered about a third of the convention delegates and indicated to them that the United States, and by extension the occupation forces, were now part of the forces of imperialism and were to be considered the enemy. This point was alluded to at the convention itself during a discussion in which party members were urged to forge a "democratic national front" *(minshu minzoku sensen).* Official endorsement of this line was subsequently granted in February of the following year at a central committee meeting. The new line also appears to have been communicated formally to the communist cells in the leading labor organizations, although former party officials admit that it was not necessarily fully understood. The apparent reason for the secrecy, according to later testimony of JCP officials, was the probably accurate assessment that openly proclaiming a struggle against the United States would only invite occupation forces repression.[25]

Around the time that the JCP's stance toward the United States was undergoing a change, SCAP was receiving signals that Washington expected it to take a harder line against the communists and to attain better results in the area of economic recovery. In a celebrated speech given in January 1948, US Army Secretary Kenneth Royall asserted that Japan should be made a "bulwark against communism in the Far East." Pointed condemnations of the coddling of radical, communist unions and expensive socialistic experiments by occupation officials began appearing in the US press. In March, George Kennan, a State Department official who was one of the primary architects of US Cold War strategy, visited Japan to discuss policies with officials in Tokyo, as did a separate delegation of businessmen led by Army Undersecretary William Draper and Percy Johnston, chairman of Chemical Bank. The latter, in particular, proved to be a source of encouragement for the Japanese business community when they "accepted the testimony of corporate leaders that radical labor unions, reparations, the deconcentration law, and the purge must all be swept away." Mission members conveyed to Japanese business leaders the point that "Japan must be made economical[l]y self-sufficient as soon as possible" and that "by scrapping controls and providing a half-billion dollars in new aid, they would assist the former enemy to reemerge as the 'workshop of the Far East.'"[26]

The primary arena in which the changing communist stance and the altered expectations of the occupation clashed was, naturally enough, the labor movement. Around the time of the sixth JCP congress, the JCP adopted the "local people's struggle" *(chiiki jinmin tōsō)* as its preferred tactical modality for conducting wage offensives. The local people's struggle was designed to get around SCAP's ban on "general strikes." Under this tactic, instead of having a centralized committee or council call a nationwide general strike from the center, an act that would clearly violate GHQ's ban, the party would foment multiple "independent" local-level strikes. Properly orchestrated, such struggles would presumably serve as the functional equivalent of a traditional general strike but without breaking the letter of the SCAP prohibition. A secondary purpose behind the tack was to use the strikes as opportunities to forge local-level "united fronts" linking workers and individuals from other classes. The local people's struggle tactic was systematically applied in the so-called March Offensive of 1948 over public-sector wages. As in the February 1 general-strike movement a year earlier, a council of public-sector workers' unions, the Zenkoku Kankōchō Rōdō Kumiai Renraku Kyōgikai, or Zenkankō, which included non-Sanbetsu unions, provided the organizational vehicle for putting pressure on the government to institute badly needed increases in public-sector wages. Zenkankō's mixed political coloring made it difficult to achieve a consensus inside the organization on the appropriate tactics to pursue. In this context, the JCP used Zentei, the union that organized workers in the state-operated postal and telephone systems and where the communists had control over the executive, to orchestrate and lead a campaign of strikes in the public sector.

The occupation forces, however, were not interested in allowing the strike wave to play out to its conclusion. On March 29, just before a second wave of Zentei-led centrally called strikes was scheduled to start, General Marquat of ESS ordered its cancellation on grounds that the strikes violated SCAP's general-strike directive. The communists in the public-sector unions responded by canceling the planned "national" strikes and switching to a wave of "local people's struggles" in which local units began to "spontaneously" engage in wildcat strikes. A tactical problem that cropped up as de facto authority to call strikes was transferred from the national leadership to the local level was that communist control was decidedly uneven across the country and there were numerous locals controlled by noncommunists who were unwilling to participate in the campaign. The way in which the JCP got around this was described by the JCP's Hasegawa: "It was possible to conduct [strikes] in work sites where there were JCP cells, but . . . there were many district headquarters with work sites where we didn't. In these instances we would conduct federated strikes. That is, several locals where the JCP was in control would get together and establish a branch. Or else the district headquarters and the prefectural federation would intervene and issue a directive [calling a strike]. The end result was the [recalcitrant] union would have no choice but to join in a unified strike."[27] The communist-dominated Zentei central also directed its locals to coordinate their efforts with communist-controlled locals of the national railway union (Kokurō) wherever possible since the Kokurō national organization, where noncommunists had gained a majority, had declined to participate in the Zentei-led strike wave. GHQ, however, set up a further roadblock on March 31, when it explained that coordinated local work stoppages also fell under the purview of the general-strike ban. This GHQ intervention broke the back of the Zenkankō drive. Negotiations continued with the government and by mid-April only Zentei and Zenzaimu, the communist-dominated tax collectors' union, had not agreed to settle with the government.

Zentei and Zenzaimu both ultimately caved, and an agreement was signed with the government. This settlement was not, however, the end of the drama. During the early summer, Zentei sought to revive the Zenkankō movement in a "summer struggle" that was once again ordered to a halt by GHQ. Even worse from the union's perspective, after what was said to have been a heated six-hour-long debate inside GHQ on July 21, General MacArthur drafted a letter to Prime Minister Ashida ordering him to take away the right of public-sector workers to strike entirely.[28] The prime minister responded on July 31 by issuing a special government ordinance, Ordinance 201, retracting public-sector-worker collective-bargaining and strike rights. This was later codified in legislation passed by the Diet in a revision of the Civil Service Law.[29] (The Public Corporation and National Enterprise Labor Relations Law of December 1948 returned to designated public corporations the right to bargain collectively, but not to strike.)[30]

The JCP maintained that the occupation's increasingly harsh stance was proof that the democratic-national-front strategy needed to be carried out with even greater zeal. Even before the issuance of the MacArthur letter, the JCP was preparing the public-sector workers' unions aligned in the Zenkankō labor council for a further struggle built on the democratic-people's-front strategy, this time centered on the national railway union, where the communists had regained control over the executive in late May. Throughout, the JCP took care to contextualize these actions as part of a larger international anti-imperialist struggle. At a meeting of local delegates from Zenkankō-affiliated unions held in June, JCP Chairman Tokuda cited the European Marshall Plan as an illustration of how the world was experiencing the unfolding of a global struggle between the forces of monopoly finance capital and proletarian forces. He then noted how the Ashida government's plans to introduce foreign capital into Japan demonstrated that these contradictions were present and how internal problems in the Ashida cabinet provided the perfect context in which to bring down the government, under conditions where global revolutionary forces were on the rise. In addition to agreeing to demand a 5,200 yen base wage, the conference placed the toppling of the Ashida government on Zenkankō's list of demands.[31]

From around this point onward, the JCP's labor interventions dropped all pretense of being focused on wage issues. The JCP-dominated Sanbetsu responded to the MacArthur-ordered government retraction of public-sector-worker strike rights and the consequent halting of the various mediation and arbitration procedures that were under way by referring to the Potsdam Declaration, the FEC's sixteen labor principles, and the Japanese constitution and arguing that the measures were illegal. It then called for a locally based "popular struggle" to rectify the situation: "We will resolutely protest the unconstitutional actions and fascistic tendencies of the government, engage in direct action, and will organize strikes, people's rallies, demonstrations and so forth around the country."[32] Both Kokurō and Zentei issued "emergency declarations" of similar content.[33] What these emergency declarations showed, however, was that the communists were rapidly losing support. An American observer described the situation as follows: "The call of leftist leaders for 'struggle tactics' against the new legislation and the Ashida cabinet produced, on the whole, little response, but some disturbances resulted, particularly among government railway and communications workers." Sporadic locally implemented "mass absenteeism" occurred in areas where communist unionists were influential. The occupation forces and the Japanese government were quick to respond in kind. All told, "by September 21, 383 railway workers had been arrested, 954 had been discharged, and 633 had suffered pay cuts; over 600 had returned to work."[34]

Massive layoffs in the public and private sectors that were implemented during the spring and summer of 1949 provided the catalyst for yet another wave of JCP-led actions marked by equal parts of overt radical anti-imperialism and desperation. At a central-committee meeting held on February 7 of that year, the JCP offered the "national industrial defense struggle" as the new reigning tactical concept. The defining feature of the industrial-defense struggle was its emphasis on the mobilization of local interests affected by mass dismissals in protest actions aimed at inducing local governments or local-level or district-level management to adopt ameliorative policies, which would simultaneously serve as the building blocks of a broad popular front of national resistance. In an interesting inversion of the earlier Sōdōmei-sponsored economic-recovery-conference idea, "industrial defense conferences" were convened in a number of areas around the country to which unionists, politicians, and representatives of "national capital" (that is, any business interest not tied to foreign capital) were invited.[35]

Events surrounding the so-called people's train incident of June 1949 provide a concrete illustration of what the national industrial-defense effort meant in practice. The proximate catalyst for the incident was the adoption of a new rotation schedule for train conductors by the Japan National Railways (JNR) authorities, which was to be implemented on June 1, the first day of JNR's reorganization as a public corporation.[36] The new schedule extended the shifts of conductors in ways that would, among other things, reduce staffing requirements by about 10 percent and was therefore interpreted as a precursor to the implementation of the much larger staff reductions that the government had announced. Kokurō locals in Eastern Kanagawa and Chiba refused to honor the new schedule and continued to work in accordance with the old one. Officials of the JNR threatened to take punitive action against violators, but those involved continued to defy management's work order. On the morning of June 9, JNR management fired nineteen officials of the two locals. The firings precipitated an unauthorized walkout by conductors in the Eastern Kanagawa railway district that brought rail service to a standstill.

That afternoon, members of JCP-controlled unions like Toshiba, Densan, and Zenjidōsha (Zen Nihon Jidōsha Sangyō Rōdō Kumiai, the All Japan Automobile Workers' Union), along with individuals from nearby JCP-affiliated front organizations such as Chōren (League of Korean Residents in Japan) and Minshō (a JCP-sponsored organization of small businessmen), came to the assistance of the striking conductors and organized a five-hundred-member-strong "JNR defense corps." At 4:00 P.M. representatives, primarily from JCP-affiliated organizations in the area, held a meeting and resolved to institute "people's control" over JNR trains. In the meantime, approximately two hundred police officers who had been called in confronted the picketers, but eventually left. A "train riders' rally" was convened at 8:00 P.M. in front of East Kanagawa Station, where it was resolved that the assembled riders would support the strike and contribute to the strike fund in exchange for a resumption of operations of the stalled train line, after which workers from the locals made two runs. The strike spread on the tenth to other railway districts in the Tokyo area. Management of JNR attempted to keep the trains running by using workers from other railway districts but were obstructed on key railway lines by unionists and JCP front-organization members who sat on the rails, or by workers who blockaded crews in station buildings. There were, however, several "people's trains" operated by "defense unit" members that were able to make their runs.

On the morning of the eleventh, JNR management issued a return-to-work order and fired forty-seven more unionists, deemed responsible for the wildcat strikes. This induced other district locals to join the strike, which continued through the day. At one point a "people's train" began a journey out of East Kanagawa Station but stalled when JNR authorities cut off power. Occupation officials, by this time under great pressure to show results in economic recovery in Japan, then stepped in by issuing a prohibition against the unionists' strike actions. The GHQ Labor Division chief, Robert T. Amis, called the JNR president, Shimoyama Sadanori, and Kokurō representatives into his office, where he allegedly directly ordered the unionists to halt all strike actions immediately, and Shimoyama to refrain from negotiating with the unions until the strikes were called off. Confronted with a direct order from occupation officials, Kokurō's central-struggle committee ordered all workers, including those who had been dismissed, to return to work. Train operations returned to normal on the twelfth. Prime Minister Yoshida, in the meantime, declared the Kokurō wildcat strikes to be part of a JCP "revolutionary plot."

Other "popular" struggles conducted by the JCP at this time included the organization of protests by unemployed workers against local offices of the Employment Security Bureaus and incidents like the Taira Incident, wherein a group of protestors that included unionists and students acting under JCP direction attacked and temporarily seized control of a police station in the city of Taira in Fukushima prefecture. The JCP was also believed by many to have played a role in three unresolved instances of murder—the death of the JNR chief Shimoyama, an apparently deliberate derailing of a freight train that subsequently crashed into Mitaka Station in Tokyo and killed six people, and the blowing up of a JNR freight train on the Tohoku main line near Matsukawa that killed three—although other theories claim that these were government or occupation forces' frame-ups.[37]

Unfortunately for the JCP, the increasingly violent nature of the JCP's labor policies derived from its democratic-national-front strategy led to a figurative meltdown of the apparatus of influence that the party had built up in the labor movement. Defections during the latter half of 1949 caused a dramatic drop in the number of unionists affiliated with Sanbetsu. Between the confederation's fourth convention, in November 1948, and its fifth convention a year later, affiliated membership dropped by 40 percent, from a reported 1.25 million to 770,000. Similarly, Zenrōren, the loosely organized and now JCP-controlled council of unions that included a large number of independent unions which were not part of Sanbetsu or Sōdōmei, lost membership during the same period. The grass-roots-level membership of Zenrōren was reported at 3,810,986 in June 1949. A year later this figure had shrunk to a mere fifth of this. Zenkankō, the JCP's other pillar of influence in the labor movement, collapsed as well. Kokurō withdrew from the council on October 14, and Zentei withdrew on October 22, while Nik-kyōso did the same on November 11. In all cases, these actions were preceded by Mindō elements gaining control of union executives that had previously been dominated by communists. With its largest and most strategically significant members no longer in the organization, the council led a quiet existence until it was dissolved the following year.

Even this, however, proved not to be the end of the story as Cold War–induced international developments pushed the JCP into one final ratcheting up of its tactical militancy. A set of events followed that echoed what happened to the French and Italian parties just over two years earlier. On January 6, 1950, the Cominform journal, *For a Lasting Peace, For a People's Democracy!* attacked the JCP for pursuing an insufficiently militant line against US imperialism. The Cominform's critique was seconded a week later by China's *Jen-min jih-pao* (People's daily). These criticisms were taken to heart and the party began pursuing a policy of "armed struggle." The upshot of the new policy was a handful of "armed" clashes between JCP members and the police. The process of the JCP's rapid decline into political irrelevance on the Japanese scene was capped in June by SCAP's "Red Purge"—the purge of JCP officials, the banning of the party organ *Akahata,* and the forcible dissolution of the already moribund JCP-controlled labor council, Zenrōren—in June.[38]

As in Europe, the impact of the Cold War began to be felt in Japanese labor politics during 1947–1949. And as in the Western European cases, the international impact of the budding bipolar conflict intertwined with domestic sociopolitical developments in complex ways. From a comparative standpoint there were certain distinctive features in the way in which the Cold War magnetic field's polarizing effect was transmitted in the two settings. Among the various players involved, this effect seems to have most strongly and directly affected the behavior of the JCP. While it is impossible to say definitively based on the available information whether this was a product of Cominform direction or independent initiative, the policies of the JCP and its actions in the labor movement arena became infused with the rhetoric, rationales, and tactics of the Cold War in a way that brought it into increasingly direct conflict with GHQ and American policies toward Japan. Ultimately, this would have devastating consequences for the party and for its influence in the labor movement. Under attack both from within and from without, and pursuing a policy line that can only be labeled unrealistic and ineffective, its organizational strength and influence were sapped to the point that by 1950 it had ceased to be a major player in Japanese labor politics. This was most apparent in the rapid shrinkage of the Sanbetsu organization, but could also be seen in the broader context of the Japanese labor movement as a whole. By the time that MacArthur formally outlawed the party in mid-1950, the communist labor movement had already reached a point where it was nearing virtual irrelevance. This, of course, contrasts sharply with the situation in Italy and France, but resembles the West German situation in terms of outcome.

Chapter 8

Reorganization and Realignment, 1948–1950

The collapse of the Katayama cabinet and its replacement a month later by the cabinet of Democrat Ashida Hitoshi, on March 10, 1948, were accompanied by a shuffling of personnel overseeing the government's program for economic recovery.[1] The most visible change was largely cosmetic. At the top a JSP prime minister was replaced with a Democratic one. Below him, however, the same three parties that had constituted the coalition supporting the Katayama cabinet continued to provide the partisan foundation for the Ashida cabinet. Furthermore, the basic structure of the Ashida economic program was identical to that of Katayama's—that is, wage-price schedules, efforts to redirect commodities from the black market to ration-distribution channels, and subsidies to stimulate production in priority industries. A more significant change could be seen in the fact that the four-party accord of the Katayama program was replaced by a three-party accord of those in the cabinet coalition—that is, the Democrats, the JSP, and the People's Cooperative Party. This was significant because it removed from the policy accord a party, the laissez-faire-oriented Liberals, whose ideological outlook was fundamentally at odds with the modified-capitalist or socialistic outlooks of the other parties. There had also been a shake-out in the Democratic Party in the wake of the controversy over the coal industry nationalization, which resulted in the more conservative of the party's Diet members leaving the party under the leadership of Shidehara. This group subsequently joined Yoshida Shigeru's Liberal Party in the formation of the Democratic Liberal

Party. This left the Democratic Party with a leadership more solidly committed to modified capitalism. Furthermore, with the Liberals out of the picture, the rationale for keeping the left socialists out of the government disappeared and two members of the faction—Labor Minister Katō Kanjū and Minister of State Nomizo Masaru—became members of the Ashida cabinet. The upshot was a coalition base comparable to a French third-force cabinet. While this narrowed the range of ideological currents housed within the coalition, it was also like the French third-force cabinets, an arrangement that confronted forces fundamentally hostile to its program on the left (the JCP) and the right (Yoshida Shigeru's Democratic Liberals).

The months straddling the Ashida government's formation were characterized by anticipation and excitement at the prospect of *gaishi dōnyū,* or "the injection of foreign capital." "Foreign capital" in this context referred both to private-sector foreign investments and, more importantly, to loans disbursed through US aid programs like the Government and Relief in Occupied Areas (GARIOA) and the Economic Recovery and Occupied Area (EROA) funds. For the same reasons that Western European governments sought Marshall Plan aid, the "injection of foreign capital" was seen by Japan as an attractive way out of the "stagflationary" trap in which it was mired. As in France under the Monnet Plan, external capital was desired for modernization of equipment to increase production without squeezing domestic consumption. Politically, it was seen as a mechanism to help alleviate the social tensions and divisions created by the need to suppress consumption for the sake of production as the Katayama economic program did. The immediate impetus for this expectation that "foreign capital" was forthcoming— the Ashida cabinet had earned the sobriquet of "the *gaishi dōnyū* cabinet"—was word received by the Japanese government that plans were afoot in Washington to double the aid to Japan in the upcoming fiscal year, and indications from GHQ that it would be removing restrictions on foreign investment in the country. More generally, this expectation can be seen as a response to broader changes in the international system wrought by the Cold War and, more narrowly, by the example of the Marshall Plan. One of the policies adopted by the JSP at its third party convention, in January 1948, for instance, called for "the promotion of the reconstruction of industry through the application of the European Marshall Plan to Japan and the Far East." The position was also taken that "we must consider the reconstruction of Japan and political and economic movements of all sorts within the framework of our clearly residing within the sphere of influence of the United States and in active connection to the United States." Similarly, in its official journal, Sōdōmei drew an unambiguous connection between Cold War–related developments like the Marshall Plan, the establishment of the Cominform, and the emergence of the Eastern and Western blocs, on the one hand, and the changing context of economic recovery in Japan, on the other. The enthusiasm was even greater in the business community and the bourgeois parties. What is fascinating is that the discussions on how the expected recovery aid would be used envisioned a rather hefty role for the state in the process of economic recovery.[2] In this sense, it appeared that the Ashida government was working the same dirigiste political-economic territory that the French third-force coalitions were.

These dreams of a third-force-administered economic recovery financed through US aid proved, however, to be a chimera. One reason for this is the fall of the centrist coalition government and its replacement by a majority conservative government under the Democratic Liberal Party's Yoshida Shigeru. But a more fundamental reason is that the economic stabilization the US imposed on occupied Japan was closer to the model of West Germany than France. As a result of the stabilization, the intricate framework of wage- and price controls and subsidies that supported the Katayama and Ashida cabinets' economic programs was destroyed, thereby shifting the Japanese economy from a state-controlled, modified-capitalist arrangement to a market-based footing.[3] Together with the collapse of the communists, detailed in the preceding chapter, these developments provided the context for a complex process of realignment and reorganization of the Japanese labor movement between the latter half of 1948 and early 1950 that produced a new hegemonic confederation, Sōhyō (Nihon Rōdō Kumiai Sōhyōgikai, or General Council of Japanese Trade Unions).

The rise of the left socialists

The immediate catalyst for the Ashida cabinet's fall was a series of corruption scandals that came to light over the course of 1948. In June of that year, Nishio Suehiro, who was chief cabinet secretary and a social democratic stalwart in both the JSP and Sōdōmei, was accused along with others in the governing coalition of having received illicit funds from a construction company. Nishio acknowledged his receipt of the funds from the contractor but claimed he saw nothing wrong with having received them, given that they were "political contributions." A scandal of even bigger proportions in which Nishio and a large number of other leading lights in the Ashida government were implicated surfaced soon thereafter in the Showa Denkō scandal. The scandal involved the efforts of a fertilizer manufacturer to secure loans from a government bank by wining and dining and generally greasing the palms of politicians in the ruling center-left coalition. Nishio's arrest in conjunction with the Showa Denkō scandal precipitated the resignation of the Ashida cabinet, on October 7, 1948. What made the fall of the centrist coalition permanent was a drop in public support for the governing parties and their economic programs, which benefited the conservatives now ensconced in the recently formed Democratic Liberal Party under Yoshida Shigeru. The minority government of Yoshida that took over from Ashida capitalized on the resentment that had built up against the center-left governments, and captured a solid parliamentary majority in the general election held on January 23, 1949. The JSP had already lost a number of seats as a result of a walkout by a group of far-left, pro-communist left socialists who proceeded to form the Labor Farmer Party. The election reduced the figures further, from 118 before the election to just 48 seats. Key party leaders, including Katayama and Nishio, failed to get elected, as did 14 out of the 26 members of the party's central executive committee. The losses tended to be heavier among the social democrats than among the left socialists. Although it was impossible to know this at the time, the election and the subsequent formation of a third Yoshida Democratic Liberal government marked the start of forty-five uninterrupted years of conservative government in Japan.

The recriminations set in motion by the Ashida cabinet's fall and the election results led to a leftward shift in the balance of power inside the JSP. This occurred at the party's "reconstruction" convention held in April. In a development that echoed what occurred within the SFIO when it shifted to the left as public resentment against France's economic-recovery program grew, the highlight of the convention was a passionate debate between Morito Tatsuo of the JSP right, who urged the party to become an all-embracing "mass" party, and Inamura Junzō of the left, who countered with the argument that the JSP needed to become a more sharply defined "class" party. Although the movement policy's designation of the party as a "class-based mass party" camouflaged the outcome, the leadership elections made it clear that the pendulum had swung in favor of the left socialists. Suzuki Mosaburō, the leading light of the left socialists, was elected party chair by a vote of 390 to 261, and the left wing also gained a dominant position on the central executive committee.

It deserves special note that activists from all of the branches of the Mindō movement (Sanbetsu Mindō, Sōdōmei, Kokurō, etc.) worked closely with the JSP's left wing in wresting control over the party leadership from the right at the 1949 JSP convention. Mindō leaders urged their followers to take out party memberships, and in a symbolic gesture to promote this, seventeen prominent Mindō union officials visited JSP headquarters on February 22 to sign the papers. Even Takano Minoru, who had earlier demurred despite his active role in the left-socialist wing, became a card-carrying JSP member. A special category was established for union-sponsored convention delegates, and union delegates were greeted with a hearty round of applause as they entered the convention arena. Five of the thirty seats in the party's central executive committee were set aside for representatives of "friendly" unions.[4] The left-socialist-based linkages between the Mindō unions and the JSP that were forged in the period leading up to the fourth JSP convention provided the foundation for a close relationship between the two groups that continued in the decades thereafter.

The scandals that plagued the Ashida cabinet in mid-1948 paved the way for a confrontation not only in the JSP, but also in Sōdōmei. The feeling that the prewar social-democratic leadership was "undemocratic" was widely shared among Mindō activists. The movement policy adopted by the Sanbetsu Mindō, for instance, noted: "Where the abuses of fractions are absent there is a need to engage in a thorough democratization of the union in another sense. That is, the democratization movement is not just an anti-fraction movement. It must also fight against tendencies toward domination by bosses and company unionism."[5] The problem of "domination by bosses" and "company unionism" was associated with the prewar generation of leaders in the Sōdōmei right wing. The basis for this association was the proclivity of Matsuoka Komakichi, Nishio Suehiro, and their protégés to dispense with formal procedures and rely on personal connections and loyalties in administering union affairs. It was customary, for instance, for the leaders of Sōdōmei unions to be chosen by acclimation rather than formal balloting, and the same informality was applied in the process of making important union decisions. Negotiations with managers and other interests outside of unions were typically delegated to the leadership unconditionally, and the outcomes were regularly made official union policy without the benefit of a formal or meaningful ratification process.[6] The feeling that such practices violated the principles of union democracy was widely shared by the generation of unionists that was catapulted into leadership positions for the first time during the immediate postwar years. While one must be careful not to overemphasize the parallels, this reaction against old-guard authoritarian paternalism was not unlike the reaction of the Catholic left against the prewar right leadership in the CFTC. On this point, the anti-leadership group in Sōdōmei was in agreement with opinion in GHQ, for GHQ reformers from the earliest days of the occupation had voiced complaints about "labor bossism" on the part of the prewar generation of Sōdōmei leaders.

Nishio's fall from grace provided an opportunity for the left-socialist element to launch a "democratization" of Sōdōmei through a leadership bid. His arrest on corruption charges was portrayed as indicative of a willingness of the social-democratic Sōdōmei leadership to sell out to the bourgeoisie. At the Sōdōmei convention in October, the left-socialist wing demanded that Nishio be disciplined for his "anti-worker" indiscretions and as a consequence of left-socialist pressure, the decision was made to formally expel Nishio. The left socialists were also able to secure a dominant position in the executive, including the installation of Takano as general manager (sōshuji)—the equivalent of general secretary—over Matsuoka and Nishio's protégé Hara Toraichi. The rise of the left socialists in the Sōdōmei under Takano thus paralleled the rise to dominance on the part of the left socialists in the JSP.

Conservative stabilization

The occupation-imposed conservative stabilization—the Dodge Line—was implemented in the spring and summer of 1949. Its core components were, as noted earlier, a balanced national budget, the suspension of state-bank lending to industry, the abolition of government subsidies to private firms, and the establishment of a single exchange rate. The Dodge Line was successful in halting inflation as it was intended, but did so at the cost of inducing a brutal recession. Between April 1949 and April 1950 the number of designated raw materials decreased from 233 to 48, the number of commodities subject to distribution controls from 57 to 15, and the number of goods subject to price controls from 2,128 to 531. Along with the controls themselves went the administrative machinery for their implementation.[7] Deprived of their supporting subsidies and with a severe drop in demand, Japanese firms were forced to adjust their operations, and most did so by closing plants, dismissing employees, and cutting wages on a massive scale in both the public and private sectors. In the public sector, retrenchment legislation passed on May 30, 1949, and a plan to dismiss 240,000 of the 1.65 million employees on the government payroll was announced on June 2. In the private sector, the result was delays in wage payments, factory closings, and dismissals. Official MOL figures put the total number of employees dismissed as a result of corporate rationalization policies during 1949 at 435,466. Ministry officials themselves admitted, however, that its accounting was incomplete and knowledgeable experts placed the figure at around 1 million.[8]

The economic-stabilization program had a tremendous impact on the labor movement. Even before formal instructions were issued by Washington, GHQ began to more aggressively "housebreak" labor unions out of concern that excessive labor unrest would disrupt GHQ's program for economic recovery. By late 1948, SCAP officials were not only intervening in strikes, but also calling union officials into the Labor Division prior to a strike and jawboning them into canceling their plans on grounds that a strike would be "unpatriotic."[9] In November, GHQ's intervention was extended to wage-setting when it issued a directive, aimed at the coal mines, forbidding the use of government subsidies to cover wage increases, thereby amending an important political economic pillar of the Katayama-Ashida program. Both the Labor Union Law and the Labor Relations Adjustment Act were revised during 1949, under the supervision of GHQ, and passed by the Diet. Among other stipulations, the amendments prohibited employers from paying the salaries of full-time union officers, made it illegal to pay workers during strikes, and expanded the range of company positions that were defined as nonunion. The legislation shifted the balance of power in industrial relations in favor of management by instituting provisions that made illegal practices that had earlier been a source of union control over work sites. Even more significant in the short term than the provisions themselves was that the passage of the amendments nullified existing collective-bargaining contracts and made it necessary for unions to renegotiate them in an economic and political context that was extremely unfavorable.[10]

If the general thrust of GHQ's realignment of labor policy was clearly disadvantageous to the labor movement, it would be incorrect to attribute all antilabor outcomes directly to GHQ policy initiatives. The softening of the previously antibusiness orientation of SCAP encouraged Japanese employers to strike out on a much more militant antilabor line, or "capital offensive," as unionists chose to describe it. Perhaps the most concrete indicator that such a shift in employer attitude was underway could be seen in the founding of Nikkeiren (Nihon Keieisha Dantai Renmei, or Japan Federation of Employers Associations) in April 1948. Quickly dubbed "Fighting Nikkeiren," the new employer federation declared itself committed to regaining "managerial rights" *(keiei ken)* and made it a policy to dispense information, advice, and encouragement to employers generally, and to provide direct assistance to management in fighting strategically and symbolically important battles with militant unions.[11]

Under these circumstances it is not surprising that relatively few labor contracts were successfully renegotiated in the wake of the implementation of the revised labor laws. According to Labor Ministry estimates, as late as May 1950 only 37.2 percent of all unions and 44.9 percent of all unionized workers were covered by collective-bargaining agreements. Among the remaining unions not covered by agreements, the ministry could detect signs that a resolution was reachable in only about 40 percent of the cases.[12] The cause of the slow progress was not just union members who were unwilling to lose the gains made in the immediate post-surrender years. Reflecting prewar attitudes, many managers in fact openly expressed the opinion that having no agreement was preferable to having one, since the former arrangement granted them a free hand in managing the firm.[13] The development that ultimately broke the stalemate was, once again, GHQ intervention. In the face of this stalemate, GHQ Labor Division Chief Robert Amis called together union and management representatives on April 7, 1950, and demanded that they quickly conclude new agreements in a "businesslike" manner. This was followed on May 22, 1950, by a Ministry of Labor notice encouraging the swift conclusion of agreements, after which the ministry unfolded a public-relations campaign aimed at accomplishing just that.[14] The contracts that were concluded, however, almost invariably rolled back union rights and privileges.

Statistics make it clear that that unions were weakened significantly over the course of the Dodge Line's implementation: Ministry of Labor figures show the number of unionized workers to have peaked in March 1949 at 6,909,542 in 36,482 unions. By June of the following year, these figures were down to

5,773,908 unionized workers in 29,144 unions. The estimated rate of unionization had dropped 10 percentage points, from 55.7 percent in 1949 to 45.9 percent in 1950.[15] Another important casualty of the rollback against labor was the budding movement toward industry-wide collective bargaining. The immediate postwar period had, of course, produced a system of collective bargaining rooted in the enterprise unions, while the period of wage- and price controls had encouraged more centralized or industry-wide approaches. Most of these industry-level bargaining practices disappeared.

Coming on top of the divisive internal clashes of 1948–1949, the stabilization process, over which the labor movement had no voice, and the outcomes of the process, which the movement could hardly be happy with, forced the labor movement leaders to confront the question of how the movement might best reorganize itself and what sort of strategy and tactics might be most appropriate under the circumstances. What might be done to mold the scattered fragments of the Mindō movement into a coherent whole for the benefit of Japanese workers? How ideologically inclusive or exclusive should a new consolidated organization of the movement be? Should existing organizational units be allowed to keep their current identities, or should they be merged in a single consolidated organization? Should there be a strict litmus test to insure that any new organization that might be created consisted of like-minded unionists? Or should ideological pluralism be tolerated in order to maximize inclusivity? What should be the principles governing its relationship with working-class political parties? What should the new organization's relationship with the government be? Should its mission be the pursuit of larger class-wide interests, or should it worry only about the narrower organizational interests of its membership? Various answers were put forward for each of these. Multiple rallying points grounded in competing unification initiatives were offered. And while there was clearly no consensus, strangely enough a new hegemonic confederation emerged out this morass of competing and contradictory pressures.

From Mindō to Sōhyō

The earliest initiative aimed at bringing about a noncommunist-led realignment of the labor movement emerged toward the end of 1948, out of the Mindō's struggles with the communists, and was grounded in what had until then been the traditional mode of thought about unionism in the prewar years, namely, the organization of unions based on their ideological and political coloring. The initiative, which called for the creation of a new confederation, was promoted by Sanbetsu Mindō's Hosoya Matsuta and by Takano Minoru of Sōdōmei's left-socialist wing and was rooted in what was referred to as the "midpoint stabilization thesis" *(chū-kan antei ron)*.[16] The basic thrust of the thesis was that the realignment of the labor movement should revolve around a new organization built out of the current Sanbetsu and Sōdōmei once they had "cut off the left and cut off the right," with the last phrase referring to the exclusion or marginalization of the communist element in Sanbetsu and the prewar right in Sōdōmei. The anticipated salutary outcome of a realignment along these lines was that it would remove the ideological currents that had contributed most to the destabilization of the movement, and stabilize the movement around a centrist line of "democratic" unionism. Doing so, it was felt, would attract the large number of "independent" unions that had opted out of affiliating with a national confederation.

Although perhaps easy to approach conceptually, in practice "cutting the left" proved to be a somewhat less than straightforward process for activists in the Sanbetsu Mindō, for the initiative was put forward at a time when—and actually was motivated by the fact that—the communists and the Sōdōmei right still maintained a strong position in their respective organizations. On the left, the communists' March Offensive of 1948 had energized the Sanbetsu Mindō. Activists saw in the communists' excesses an excellent opportunity to attract support, as Hosoya recalls: "Around this time, we at Sanbetsu Mindō headquarters sought the most effective means of propagandizing. We . . . made it a practice to pitch the message of Sanbetsu Mindō at the conventions of powerful industrial unions whether we were invited to or not."[17] He goes on to describe how he was welcomed by pro-Mindō elements at all of the national union conventions that he attended but was also consistently met by fierce opposition and catcalls from communist elements. The net result was a series of advances and setbacks. The Mindō forces were able to gain a foothold in the JCP stronghold in Zentei, but control of the union executive remained in the hands of pro-JCP elements. The story was similar at Nittsū and Densan. Following a complicated set of maneuverings and realignments, the Newspaper and Broadcasting Workers' Union, the founding industrial federation of the Sanbetsu organization, was ultimately reorganized into separate organizations for newspapers and for broadcasting, both of which were controlled by Mindō elements.[18] The intensity and byzantine quality of the infighting is hinted at in the Sanbetsu Mindō movement policy: "Democratization is the objective but the tactics and methods used to attain this need not necessarily be democratic in a formal sense. The reason is that as long as the opponent is a secret organization of a party inside a union, democratic methods based on argumentation alone will constitute democracy in a formal sense but will not only not be useful for attaining true democratization of the unions, it will actually cause harm."[19]

A major step in "cutting the left" was taken following the November 19–22

Sanbetsu fourth convention, the first since Sanbetsu Mindō's inauguration, although strictly speaking the process was more akin to a cutting off of the Sanbetsu right. At the convention, communists in the executive easily blocked a bid for the leadership by Sanbetsu Mindō elements. They then managed to turn the tables by censuring Sanbetsu Mindō for "anti-worker" activities and passed a resolution demanding the dissolution of the Sanbetsu Mindō organization. This precipitated a walkout by fifty-two Sanbetsu Mindō–affiliated delegates. At the second Sanbetsu Mindō general meeting, held on December 10–11, a movement policy was approved that outlined the intent to create a "new Sanbetsu" *(shin sanbetsu)* as a confederation that would serve as a receptacle not only for refugee unions escaping the old Sanbetsu but for other unions sympathetic to the Sanbetsu Mindō line.[20]

In the meantime, Hosoya's and Takano's vision of a labor movement realigned in accordance with the "intermediate stabilization thesis" was further concretized when steps were taken to create a new confederation slated to be called Zenrō Kaigi. The Zenrō Kaigi proposal was first floated publicly in the Kokutetsu Mindō in late October 1948. The effort was pursued at the initiative of Kokutetsu Mindō's Hoshika, Sanbetsu Mindō's Hosoya, and Sōdōmei's Takano.[21] The proposed council was envisioned as a replacement for the national labor council, Zenrōren, which, as noted in the preceding chapter, was being used in an effort by the communists to maintain their influence. Like Zenrōren, Zenrō Kaigi was intended to bring together the two national centers, Sanbetsu and Sōdōmei, and the various independent unions that had opted out of national-center membership, only in this case on the basis of Mindō principles. As was true in Zenrōren, the idea was, functionally, to provide a framework for united efforts of the labor movement that extended beyond the boundaries of the rival national confederations while allowing each constituent organization to retain its organizational and ideological shadings.

Proponents of the intermediate stabilization thesis had assumed that it would be possible to attract independent unions if only the right ideological parameters for the organization could be defined and maintained. But their expectations were disappointed. A "preparatory inaugural convention" of Zenrō Kaigi was held on February 12, 1949, in the presence of delegates from the three core organizations—Sōdōmei, Kokurō, and Sanbetsu Mindō—and a host of observers from neutral unions. Total attendance was reported to have been five hundred. The meeting itself proceeded with a minimum of controversy, and the proposed platform and manifesto were adopted without protest. Zenrō Kaigi proved unable, however, to get the large, independent unions and industrial federations to join, and the initiative quickly lost its momentum.[22] In the meantime, the Sanbetsu Mindō group under Hosoya, which had been ousted from Sanbetsu and left without a prospective home thanks to the collapse of the Zenrō Kaigi initiative, took steps to create a confederation of their own, which they decided to call Shinsan-betsu. The intermediate stabilization thesis was revived once again, in the fall, when Takano proposed an immediate merger of Sōdōmei and Shinsanbetsu, but this also failed to generate interest on the part of the unions and was soon over-taken by a different initiative based on somewhat different organizational princi-ples. A clear signal that the Zenrō Kaigi–led unification proposal was falling by the wayside was the embrace of this new, qualitatively different approach by one of the intermediate stabilization thesis' proponents, Takano Minoru. Hosoya per-severed and the new confederation, Shinsanbetsu, held its inaugural convention in December and elected Hosoya its president.[23]

During the latter half of 1949, as it was becoming clear that the Zenrō Kaigi initiative did not have the traction that its proponents had anticipated, a slightly different initiative was proving more successful in rallying the population of unions that Zenrō Kaigi had hoped to attract. This particular initiative was an outgrowth of an effort by younger Mindō activists in the public-sector unions, where Mindō elements had managed to gain control, to forge a strategy to deal with the issues without resorting to the kinds of tactics the communists had pur-sued. The primary issues involved were the massive rationalizations and layoffs that were under way in the public sector and, in wage negotiations, the govern-ment's outright refusal to disburse the wage increases reached in an arbitrated agreement. Having been recently deprived of the right to strike but unwilling to break the law, these activists decided to concentrate on putting political pressure on the government through lobbying in the Diet combined with extra-parliamen-tary protest actions. The most widely covered of the latter was a hunger strike by leading public-sector union leaders that took place in the Ginza district in down-town Tokyo. As the public-sector union leaders pursued their drive, they discov-ered their effort dovetailed with interests of the major private-sector industrial federations in mining, electric power, transport, and broadcasting that were fac-ing layoffs and wage cuts as a consequence of the Dodge Line–induced ending of subsidies and economic controls in their respective industries. These were pre-cisely the organizations that Zenrō Kaigi had unsuccessfully tried to attract. The rapidly expanding initiative culminated in the formation, on October 3—one week before the opening of a new parliamentary session—of a Diet Joint Strug-gle Committee (Kokkai Kyōtō Iinkai). Takaragi Fumihiko, a Zentei Mindō activist and key organizer of the Joint Struggle Committee, estimated that dele-gates from thirty-seven organizations gathered at the Asakusa post office, where the Zentei headquarters was located, in response to the call. He fondly recalls:

> Stimulated by the opening of the sixth extraordinary Diet session toward the end of 1949, we ignored the Sanbetsu Mindō, Sōdōmei, and Nichirō Kaigi organizations and put out a call to create an organization to be called the Diet Joint Struggle Commit-

tee on an industry-federation-by-industry-federation basis that would focus on the two struggles of wage increases and revisions of the labor laws. This succeeded. . . .

The fact of the matter was that an organizational body of 5.2 million had been created. It occurred to me that the Diet Joint Struggle Committee might become the foundation for the unification of Japan's labor front. I still remember how, when it was inaugurated at Zentei headquarters, we bought teacups full of liquor and brought in 30-yen bowls of noodles to celebrate.[24]

In addition to demonstrating the centrality of politics in the activities of the public-sector unions, what the Diet Joint Struggle Committee seemed to demonstrate, in other words, was that the big "neutral" industrial federations in the private sector would be willing to coalesce in an industrial organization built around "non-ideological" objectives.[25]

Formally speaking, the Diet Joint Struggle Committee was a task-specific organization not directed at engineering a realignment of the labor movement. The success of the initiative, however, inspired the same unions to coalesce on similar grounds in an organ that was. This occurred on November 11 when leaders of some of the leading independent unions established a committee, dubbed the National Labor Union Unification Preparatory Committee, or Zenkoku Rōdō Kumiai Tōitsu Junbikai, that declared its goal as being "to organize a unified body of powerful democratic labor unions," and to do so along somewhat different lines from that of Hosoya's and Takano's "midpoint stabilization thesis."[26] The common denominator among the sponsoring unions was that none had participated in the Zenrō Kaigi preparatory committee. In most cases this was because the federation faced a stalemate internally between pro-communist and pro-Mindō unions, which made a neutral stance a necessity for the sake of organizational integrity and coherence. The fact that the unification initiative was taken by a group comprising heads of leading *independent* unions in the private sector—a group that came to be dubbed the "presidents' group"—was significant in that it freed the project of the kind of political baggage that had derailed the earlier effort led by Hosoya and Takano.

A second feature of the National Labor Union Unification Preparatory Committee—not explicit during the committee's formation but increasingly evident over time—was the desire by its primary proponents to make the nationwide industrial federation the primary unit of membership in any new confederation that might form. This dimension of the proposal was significant because it manifested a conceptualization of the labor movement alien to most mainstream prewar unionists and demonstrated how the American-inspired occupation-period labor reforms that sought to facilitate emergence of "free" unions had, as in West Germany, given birth to an organizational milieu distinguishable from the politically grounded identity-driven format that predominated in France and Italy.

Powerful industrial unions that organized an entire industry irrespective of ideological and political coloring was the implicit ideal. They saw in national industrial federations of enterprise unions the potential for solid organizations with bargaining power in the labor market and in political affairs in their own right, even as they were aware that the present decentralized and disaggregated structure of the Japanese enterprise-union-based system did not measure up to the ideal. Given the disjuncture between this type of unionism and the sensibilities of the prewar unionists, it is not surprising to find that support for this model of confederation was most conspicuous among the postwar activists who had risen to the top of the large industrial federations with little or no experience in the prewar movement. Takano Minoru, acutely sensitive to changes in sociopolitical currents, quickly jumped on the bandwagon and, by the spring of 1950, had produced a detailed blueprint for a wholesale restructuring of the Japanese labor movement round a system of consolidated industrial federation level along product category lines. Known as the Takano Plan, the proposal aimed to create industrial organizations that would eliminate the earlier ideologically based organizational identities.[27]

It was along the tracks laid out by the Takano plan and the National Labor Union Unification Preparatory Committee that the work to establish a new confederation proceeded. The initial meeting of the committee on November 1 established a solid consensus among the "president's group." With this core consensus as a foundation, the circle of discussion was gradually expanded over the course of the various meetings that marked the organizational process (see table 6). The unification drive then moved with impressive rapidity, and within a few months the inaugural convention of the new national center Sōhyō had been scheduled. By the time of the March "preparatory meeting," Sōhyō as an organization had been more or less fully fleshed out. That the new organization was being constructed on a paradigmatic foundation differing from the Hosoya and Takano's intermediate stabilization thesis is highlighted by the fact that the most intense and time-consuming debate during the process of establishing Sōhyō concerned the organizational structure of the new confederation. The majority of those involved supported the principle that industrial federations should be the basic unit of the new confederation. It was agreed that membership should be granted to existing confederations and regionally based organizations in order to expedite Sōhyō's formation, but this was done with the understanding that these would be dissolved and amalgamated into industrial organizations at some future date. There was strong opposition to this basic principle on the part of some involved in the negotiation, notably from Hosoya. Unwilling to concede on this point, Hosoya pulled his newly created Shinsanbetsu confederation out of Sōhyō. A similar reaction later occurred on the right when the Takano plan was brought to a Sōdōmei convention.

Table 6. Associations and meetings leading up to Sōhyō

Organization	Affiliation 12/1/49	Membership 12/31/49	National Labor Unification prep. meeting 11/1/49	National Labor Unification prep. meeting 11/14/49	Sōhyō formation meeting 3/11/50	Sōhyō inaugural convention 7/11/50
Zennichiro	National center	435,000	X	X	X	
Tanro	Independent	420,000	X	X	X	X
Kaiin	Independent	145,000	X	X	X	X
Shitetsu Soren	Independent	130,000	X	X	Ob*	
Zennitsu	Independent	103,000	X	X	Ob*	
Zenko	Independent	78,000	X	X	X	
Ryuroren	Independent	42,000	X	X	Ob*	Ob*
Sodomei	National center	1,104,500		X	X	X
Kokutetsu	Independent	470,000		X	X	X
Zensen Domei	Sodomei	257,400		X	X	X
Zentei	Independent	200,000		X	X	X
Shinsanbetsu	National center	196,500		X		
Zensanshi	Independent	72,000		X	X	X
Tororen	Independent	62,200		X	X	X
Zensenbai	Sodomei	36,300		X		
Zenbiren	Independent	6,200		X		
Judenki	Independent			X	X	X
Zen'onden	Independent			X		
Nikkyoso	Independent	499,000			X	X
Nikko	Sodomei	71,700			X	X
Nikken Soren	Independent	56,300			X	X
Jichi Rokyo	Independent	13,000			X	X
Nipporo	Independent	7,000			X	X
Okura Shokuso	Independent	2,000			X	X
Zennorin	Independent				X	X
Zosen Soren	Independent				X	X
Densan	Sanbetsu	145,600			Ob*	
Nichizai	Independent	17,000			Ob*	
Shinbun Roren	Independent	16,000			Ob*	
Zensekiyu	Independent	13,000			Ob*	
Kosaikai	Independent	8,000			Ob*	
Zen'eien	Independent	3,200			Ob*	
Kotsu Kosha	Independent	2,300			Ob*	

* Observer status
Source: *SRUS* (1949), 421–427.

The place of the ICFTU and the role of GHQ

Even though the Japanese labor movement was not a direct participant in the machinations that led to the split of the WFTU and the formation of the ICFTU, the developments in the international-level movement were nonetheless an important factor shaping the realignment process unfolding in Japan, as it was in Western Europe. Zenrōren officials received invitations to send representatives to the WFTU conventions, and elections were in fact held, in late 1948, to choose the members of a Japanese delegation. The effort remained futile, however, since GHQ refused to authorize travel papers for the would-be union delegations, as it did in conjunction with an invitation that Sanbetsu and Zenrōren received from the Soviet labor confederation. Japanese unions were aware of the divisions that were surfacing inside the WFTU and eventually led to the formation of the ICFTU. Sōdōmei, on its part, opposed Japan's entry into the WFTU on grounds that it was communist controlled. And when in 1949 the WFTU split, the conflict between the camps inside that federation was the object of editorializing in the labor journals and of debate at labor union conventions.[28] Given the ongoing struggle to free their organizations from the grasp of the communists, it is not at all surprising that Mindō activists identified with the pro-ICFTU elements in the international-level conflict. It is also not difficult to see how Mindō leaders might have seen parallels between their own battle with the JCP and the deepening split between communists and noncommunists in the international labor movement that was driving the move to create the ICFTU. More fundamentally, the "free and independent" brand of unionism that was the watchword of the ICFTU seemed to articulate a style of unionism these unionists had sought to embody but lacked the ideological frame of reference that would allow it to be communicated effectively.

The first break in GHQ's enforced isolation of the labor movement occurred during the early summer of 1949 and worked to raise another notch the relevance of developments in the international labor movement to those in the Japanese labor movement. The break involved GHQ allowing Katō Etsuo of the Kokutetsu Mindō (and president of the Kokurō union) to serve as a labor representative in Japan's delegation to the July 1949 ILO general meeting held in Geneva. On the way back from the ILO meeting, Katō was directed to the ICFTU preparatory conference in London, and upon his return to Japan, he waxed enthusiastic about the new organization. Tremendous enthusiasm, in turn, greeted Katō's proposal that the Japanese movement try to join the ICFTU. Within a few short weeks of Katō's return, a local committee to promote affiliation with the ICFTU was created that included, in addition to Sōdōmei and Shinsanbetsu, leading independent unions like Tanrō, Zenkō (Zen Nihon Kinzoku Kōzan Rōdō Kumiai Rengōkai, or All Japan Metal Miners' Labor Union Federation), Shitetsu Sōren (Nihon Shitetsu

Rōdō Kumiai Sō Rengōkai, or General Federation of Private Railway Workers' Unions), and Zennichirō (Zen Nihon Rōdō Kumiai Renmei, or All Japan Labor Union Federation), the successor to the earlier "neutral" confederation, Nichirō Kaigi. At a subsequent meeting, on October 7, the group decided to send a five-man delegation to London, with the composition determined by balloting, and to launch a campaign for contributions to help defray travel expenses. After a certain amount of complication relating to the issuance of travel documents for one of the proposed members, the delegation left Japan on November 23 and arrived in London three days later, just in time for the inaugural convention of the ICFTU that was to begin on the twenty-eighth. In the meantime, groups inside many Japanese labor unions pushed to have their organizations formally declare support for the ICFTU and its principles, and the ICFTU attained a kind of talismanic status for the various currents of noncommunist unionism. Under these conditions, it was also hardly surprising that the National Labor Union Unification Preparatory Committee, too, adopted affiliation with the ICFTU and adherence to its principles to be one of the basic tenets of the unification drive. In keeping with this, once Sōhyō was established, affiliation with the ICFTU was stipulated in its platform.

The five-man ICFTU delegation returned to Japan after spending several weeks in the United States on their return trip. Takita Minoru of Zensen Dōmei (Zenkoku Sen'i Sangyō Rōdō Kumiai Dōmei, or National Federation of Textile Workers' Union), who was one of the five Japanese delegates, provides a fairly detailed account of the Japanese delegation's experience in London. It is noteworthy from the standpoint of subsequent developments that the item of discussion at the meeting that appears to have made the biggest impression on him was the issue of peace.[29] As Takita recollects: "What were the major things that were said at the inaugural meeting of the ICFTU? One of them was the extremely strong consciousness that wars should not be undertaken ever again. The slogan was 'the biggest victim of war is the working class.' This was something that everyone was saying. In addition, it was said that 'war is consumption without production.' These were words that we heard for the first time at that meeting hall."[30] As for the message presented by the Japanese labor delegation, it was that Japan wanted to be recognized as an independent nation as soon as possible. The Japanese delegates also noted that a resolution had been prepared advocating the early independence of Germany but nothing similar had been prepared for Japan, and the Japanese delegation made an appeal for equivalent support for the early conclusion of a Japanese peace treaty that would end the occupation. In an interesting footnote to this development, Takita relates how the delegation had prepared two sets of leaflets in which this pitch was made, but one of them was discovered and seized by GHQ officials. The other was surreptitiously taken to London in the bottom of a suitcase. At the meeting itself, the Japanese delegation successfully persuaded the gathering to adopt a resolution supporting Japanese independence.[31]

As indicated in the preceding narrative, GHQ clearly steered the Japanese labor movement away from the WFTU and toward the ICFTU through its manipulation of its travel authorizations, although it is also clear that there were ample bases for identification with the ICFTU already present in the Japanese labor movement. As for GHQ's role in Sōhyō's formation specifically, analysts who have studied the US role generally conclude, as do the principals themselves, that although GHQ was a part of the process, it would be wrong to consider GHQ intervention the exclusive or even primary cause of Sōhyō's establishment. The most thorough study of this kind is a 1982 work by Takemae Eiji, perhaps the leading historian of the US occupation of Japan. After a careful scrutiny of occupation documents, Takemae notes: "Although it is said that Sōhyō was the 'illegitimate offspring of GHQ' or that GHQ created it, as far as can be discerned from the documents it seems safe to say that the attribute of it being a product of factional rivalry within the Japanese labor movement and the initiative of an autonomous movement is stronger."[32] Similarly, the GHQ official who was most actively involved in Sōhyō's establishment describes GHQ as having "assisted" and of having been "here and there . . . able to exert a certain influence." To say that GHQ "created" Sōhyō, the same official contends, "probably gives us more importance than we really had."[33] Labor historian John Price writes: "My interpretation of the documentation leads me to conclude that . . . SCAP clearly backed the formation of Sōhyō as an 'anti-red' national union federation affiliated with the ICFTU. Having said this, however, it is also clear that SCAP never really controlled the democratization movement nor the process leading to the formation of Sōhyō."[34] Such conclusions parallel recent assessments of the role of US labor and government officials in the realignment of Western European labor unions during the initial Cold War years, discussed earlier, based on comparable documentary sources. Thus, as in the European cases, American intervention was one factor among many that shaped the Cold War–era realignment of the labor movement in Japan.

The key figure on the GHQ side was Valery Burati, formerly associated with the CIO-affiliated Textile Workers' Union and the Amalgamated Clothing Workers' Union. But according to Takemae, it was not until February of 1950, five months before Sōhyō's inauguration and over a year after the initial call for Zenrō Kaigi's formation, that the Labor Division under Burati began to actively intervene in the organizational realignment process.[35] Prior to this, although SCAP had intervened in the area of labor policy—indeed, on many occasions rather heavy-handedly—the evidence suggests that Labor Division contacts specifically with the Mindō movement prior to this was minimal. Labor Division officials apparently did not have prior notice of the inaugural convention of the Sanbetsu Mindō and "had to send an army representative . . . in order to get any information at all about the proceedings." In the case of the formation of the ICFTU committee, documents from the period suggest that Labor Division officials learned of plans among Japanese unionists to take steps to link up with the ICFTU in August, or only after planning had already been initiated. It was at least two weeks later that SCAP received a wire from Washington recommending that a Japanese delegation be allowed to attend the ICFTU's London convention. That this was not expected is suggested by the fact the Washington request required SCAP to subsequently initiate a policy review.[36] By that time, Japanese unionists were already well on their way to establishing a committee to promote ICFTU affiliation. When GHQ did learn of the plan, the primary form of intervention was, apparently, Labor Division officials summoning prominent industrial federation leaders and putting pressure on them to join the new Sōhyō. In Burati's recollection the international alignment of the Japanese labor movement was simply a means to attain the organizational end, rather than the other way around, although he acknowledges that other US officials saw things differently.[37] Burati in fact worked with Takano Minoru and Shimizu Shinzō of the Steel Workers' Federation in preparing the Takano plan that was submitted to the Sōdōmei central committee in May 1950. It is noteworthy, as well, that the most controversial incident associated with the ICFTU delegation selection process was not over *communist* influence, but one in which GHQ obstructed the participation of Matsuoka Komakichi of Sōdōmei, a *right-wing* social democrat, on grounds of being too conservative. This was not an isolated incident, but merely a publicly visible manifestation of a longstanding Labor Division antipathy toward the Sōdōmei-affiliated prewar social-democratic "labor bosses" and a consonant desire to assist the Sōdōmei left socialists in gaining the upper hand in the new national center.[38] This, in turn, led to friction with the AFL, which through its Asia representative stationed in New Delhi, Richard Deverall, attempted unsuccessfully to block the Japanese delegation that Burati had arranged to attend the ICFTU meeting.[39] Relations continued to deteriorate between the Labor Division and the Sōdōmei right wing thereafter, resulting in a further celebrated incident in which social-democratic-right elements in Sōdōmei worked with company management to obstruct a Labor Division project, apparently motivated by a desire to get even after the cancellation of Matsuoka's ICFTU visit, by claiming that a *communist* was being sponsored by *GHQ* for a visit to the United States.[40]

Perhaps the most significant consequence of the ICFTU's creation and GHQ's intervention in the Japanese labor-movement realignment process in the period immediately preceding the formation of Sōhyō can be found in the way that it speeded up organizational consolidation among the competing ideological streams extant in the Japanese movement by imposing a time frame on the realignment process. Ironically, the incompleteness of the movement's consolidation serves to highlight the nature of this GHQ role. At its outset Sōhyō was a motley assortment of qualitatively different constituent units—i.e., a national center (Sōdō-mei), consolidated industrial federations, and as yet unconsolidated industrial organizations that in some cases competed with other federations in the Sōhyō organization. The incompleteness of the amalgamation existed precisely because the formation process was rushed and was the object of outside intervention. Nonetheless, as incomplete as this consolidation was, it brought a near majority (and a majority soon thereafter) of Japan's unionized workers under a single organizational umbrella. As such, Sōhyō, as a fait accompli, constituted an entity with an organizational inertia and momentum that would not have been there had the ICFTU and GHQ's leverage not been present at its creation.

Sōhyō's inauguration in Tokyo's Mita district on July 11, 1950, clearly marked a major milestone in the Cold War–induced realignment of the Japanese labor movement. Seventeen union organizations representing 3.77 million organized workers (3.65 million according to Ministry of Labor figures) were present as members, as were 19 observer organizations, most of whom were in the process of arranging formal affiliations. All of Japan's largest industrial federations were represented.[41] Sōhyō's affiliated rank-and-file probably represented about 60 percent of the unionized workforce at the time. The curtain was thus dropped on the era of bipolar competition within the domestic movement, between Sanbetsu and Sōdōmei, and a new structure had emerged marked by Sōhyō serving as a hegemonic axis around which the labor movement revolved.[42] Organizationally, however, Sōhyō was still very much a work in progress. The complicated currents set in motion in the labor movement had created a vessel into which several competing agendas had somewhat haphazardly been poured. These agendas included the desire to forge a labor movement centered around left-socialist ideological principles, the desire (particularly strong in the public sector) to craft a powerful political presence that could wrest concessions from the government at least until such time as a working-class party could make its way into power that would be more responsive to its needs, the desire to realize a new modality of industry-centered activity and to align the Japanese movement with the "free trade unionism" of the ICFTU and the principles that the international was perceived to embody. Just how these various agendas fit together had yet to be determined. The customary laudatory speeches notwithstanding, the mood at Sōhyō's inauguration was likened to that at a funeral. At the time, many were quite pessimistic that any such consolidation could be attained and predicted that the new confederation might be able to survive for two years at most.[43] Another reason for the dark mood was the fact that war had broken out across the Japan Sea, on the Korean peninsula. As it happened, the outbreak of this war would set in motion a chain of events that would determine Sōhyō's identity and, through this, the fundamental structure and dynamics of the Japanese labor movement for decades to come.

Chapter 9

Peace, Neutrality, and the Takano Years, 1951–1954

Because of differences in the timing of militarization of the Cold War in Europe and in East Asia, a mass-based peace movement inspired by Cold War tensions appeared somewhat later in Japan than in Western Europe, and this difference in timing made for a somewhat different political context. As in Western Europe, it was the communists and prominent pro-communist and noncommunist intellectuals who provided the initial impetus for peace-movement activism in Japan, and they in fact did so more or less simultaneously with their Western European counterparts. But war between the two Cold War blocs appeared a much more distant prospect than was the case in the stark atmosphere that had come to envelope Europe in the wake of the Berlin Blockade. It was not until nearly two years after the blockade that a spark of sufficient magnitude to militarize the Cold War in East Asia and ignite a mass-based peace movement was generated in Japan. The spark was the outbreak of war on the Korean peninsula, on June 25, 1950. In the ensuing months, Japan was turned into a staging area for UN operations in Korea. The United States began to put pressure on the government to support the US-led military operation in a more direct way. This led to the creation of an embryonic Japanese military in July of 1951 under the euphemistic nomenclature of a National Peace Reserve (subsequently, the Self-Defense Forces). Four months later, the Japanese government signed a bilateral security treaty with the United States that formally committed Japan to supporting the US Cold War effort in the East Asia through its provision of military bases for American troops, and a variety of other measures. With this, Japan's position in the international system began to resemble closely that of its Western European counterparts, and in line with this, the Japanese labor movement began to be subjected to political-diplomatic pressures similar to those that were shaping Western European labor politics. Within this parallel context, what was distinctive about the Japanese situation was the balance of forces within the labor movement. In contrast to the continuing centrality of the communists in France and Italy, the JCP had lost by the middle of 1950 its capacity to influence mainstream politics, thereby clearing a "space" for some other political force to mobilize protests of Japan's incorporation into the US containment framework. In the Japanese context, it was the left socialists who took on this role. The prominence of the left socialists and the left-socialist viewpoint during this critical period left a long-lasting stamp on the organizational characteristics, the balance of ideological orientation, and the political and economic roles of the Japanese movement for decades to come.

This chapter traces the dynamics of Japan's labor movement politics in the context of the militarization of the Cold War in the East Asia in the early 1950s and the way in which the reaction against Japan's incorporation into the US containment framework embodied in the controversy over Japan's peace settlement gave birth to a distinctive labor-movement strategy under the initiative of Sōhyō's general secretary Takano Minoru. Takano's pursuit of this strategy dramatically redirected and redefined the Sōhyō movement, one of the more perplexing developments in postwar Japanese labor history—namely, what is often referred to as Sōhyō's turning "from a chicken into a duck," its transformation from an apparently moderate pro-Western labor confederation into a central pillar of a broad-based anti-US mass movement.

The peace treaty issue

The promotion of a "peace movement" constituted a major pillar of the JCP's resistance to US "imperialism" in Japan. While it is not possible now to ascertain to what extent this was a product of directives from Moscow or if it was simply a matter of the JCP taking its cues from developments in Western Europe, there was a remarkable coincidence of timing in the initiation of the European and Japanese communist efforts. The party elaborated its basic stance on the peace issue in a Central Committee document adopted on August 1948, a point in time when the European communist movement was gearing up for the initiation of its "peace offensive." In any event, the European and Japanese efforts became overtly intertwined as the communist-led peace offensive progressed. For instance, a statement issued by the JCP Political Bureau clarifying the party's peace-treaty stance proclaimed that the party "supported the Soviet Union's peace policies."[1]

In early 1949 an invitation to have a Japanese delegation attend the communist-sponsored World Peace Congress in Paris was extended to individuals associated with the JCP-sponsored League for the Protection of Democracy. However, the Japanese side was unable to act on this invitation because the occupation officials refused to grant the would-be delegates travel clearance. As a substitute, the league organized a parallel "peace congress" in Tokyo, timed to coincide with the last day of the congress in Paris. Attendance was estimated at approximately twelve hundred. The rally, in turn, served as the catalyst for the formation of the Heiwa o Mamoru Kai (Association to Protect Peace), which then went on to serve as the Japanese organ for overseeing the petition campaign for the 1950 Stockholm Appeal in Japan. (The association would subsequently evolve into the Japan Peace Committee, or Nihon Heiwa Iinkai.)[2]

Given the important symbolic cache that Japan possessed as the world's first nuclear target, there was keen interest in the communist international peace movement to have Japan involved. This interest, however, was not reciprocated on a mass scale in Japan. Aside from workers affiliated with a handful of communist-controlled unions, labor movement involvement in the peace movement was virtually nonexistent, limited to a small number of left-leaning—but not always communist—intellectuals and scientists. Along with occupation policies that discouraged the spread of information on the effects of the atomic bombings in Hiroshima and Nagasaki, a basic reason for this was that Cold War tensions in the East Asia had yet to jell into open confrontation. In addition, the communists themselves were experiencing a rapid collapse of their influence in the Japanese labor movement, and in Japanese society more broadly, and this, of course, limited their capacity to effectively mobilize a mass movement of any kind.

The outbreak of the Korean War would dramatically reverse this set of circumstances, but even so, it took some time for the repercussions of the war to be felt. Sōhyō, for instance, did not adopt a formal position on the Korean War at its inaugural convention, which occurred two weeks following the North Korean attack. This was perhaps understandable. Many of the delegates in fact learned of the fighting while in transit to the convention site, and even if they were anxious to take a stand (most apparently were not), there was insufficient time for them to sound out their home organizations. When an emergency meeting of Sōhyō's board of trustees (*hyōgikai*) did release a formal statement on the war, on July 25, the position adopted was in line with what one might have expected from an organization that was born of an anticommunist struggle and which had declared its support for the ICFTU. (The ICFTU had declared its enthusiastic backing of the US-led intervention almost immediately.) The Sōhyō statement condemned North Korean aggression and declared that "the basic policy and actions of the UN are consistent with the maintenance of world peace and democracy." At the same time, however, the statement opposed any direct Japanese involvement in the war in light of Japan's new "peace constitution." The Mindō-dominated industrial federations that held conventions during the same months adopted essentially similar positions, and on the whole, the initial response of the Japanese labor movement to the Korean War could be characterized as one of perfunctory acceptance of the legitimacy of the UN intervention.[3]

Outside of the communists, the one notable exception to this general noncommittal support for the UN effort on the part of noncommunist elements in the Japanese labor movement was the neutralist stance taken by Shinsanbetsu at its convention in November. A resolution adopted justified this position, by highlighting the emerging postcolonial character of the Asian context, and embraced a third-force thesis that denied the relevance and appropriateness of the Cold War alignment to the conditions of the region. It claimed that "the conflict between the US and the Soviet Union is nothing more than a rivalry between two imperialisms. The way has been opened for the nationalist movements of Asia, including war-torn Korea and occupied Japan, which have begun to attain the conditions needed for unity, to transcend the competition between the two worlds using the neutralist policies of India as their rallying point."[4] In a related decision, Shinsanbetsu announced that it would reverse its previous policy and would join Sōhyō for the purpose of redirecting the national center's line in accordance with Shinsanbetsu's position.

Rapidly unfolding developments on the diplomatic front subsequently propelled the issue of Japan's role in the Cold War to the forefront of labor's political agenda. In Korea, UN troops landed at Inchon, near the center of the peninsula, in mid-September and by October had managed to capture Pyongyang and were advancing toward the Amur River on the Chinese–North Korean border. This sparked the entry of a massive number of Chinese troops, who pushed the UN forces back down the peninsula. By early 1951 communist forces had retaken Seoul and UN forces were being pushed back to the peninsula's southern tip. What had for a while looked like a short police action was now a full-fledged war that threatened to spill over to Japan. Within Japan, the occupation troops were mobilized for war. Japan itself was rapidly turned into a base of operations for the war effort on the peninsula. In addition to the dramatic increase in troop movements throughout Japan that disrupted the lives of average Japanese in various ways, a flood of orders for war materiel and repair work began to flow into Japanese factories. While this "divine wind" of armaments-related orders boosted profits, eased unemployment, and pulled the Japanese economy out of the post-Dodge slump, it also produced inflationary pressures with which wages failed to keep up. Then, in a move that would ultimately be fraught with tremendous repercussions for the Japanese labor movement, General MacArthur presented two propositions in his customary New Year's address to the Japanese public. First, he announced that efforts would be initiated in the coming year to arrange a peace treaty for Japan. Secondly, he urged Japan to take steps to rearm. Behind these proposals were developments in Washington. Concerned that prolonging the occupation would only lead to a growth in anti-US sentiment and make it difficult to secure continued use of bases in Japan, US officials decided to do what was necessary to arrange a treaty and an eventual return of formal national sovereignty on the condition that the United States retain the use of military bases on Japanese soil and that Japan would rearm. John Foster Dulles was put in charge of laying the groundwork for such a peace treaty. Dulles stopped in Japan in late January to conduct talks with Japanese leaders as part of a larger tour of potential peace-conference attendees. MacArthur, in the meantime, used his status as head of the occupation forces to order the creation of a de facto Japanese military in the form of a "national police reserve."

Taken together, these various developments forced leading political actors in Japan to put forward a formal position on the peace treaty and to frame that position within the context of broader issues of geopolitical position in the Cold War–dominated international order. It was abundantly clear that under existing international conditions, the peace treaty arrangements proposed by the United States would place Japan firmly in the US-led anticommunist camp. Any peace treaty drafted under these circumstances would inevitably be a "partial peace treaty" boycotted by the communist camp. It would not be the "all around treaty" signed by all belligerents, which had been held up as the objective by both the occupation authorities and the Japanese government prior to the outbreak of the Korean War. The Yoshida government and conservatives were willing to go along with the US proposals, albeit with a considerable degree of reluctance. Communist opposition to the peace treaty was a foregone conclusion but was not particularly significant politically given the party's nearly complete incapacitation in the wake of the Red Purge. As the ostensible political voice of the working masses and one that was ideologically situated between the conservatives and the more or less defunct communists, there was keen interest in what position the JSP would take.

As for the JSP's stance prior to these developments, in December 1949 it approved what came to be known as the "three principles of peace"—an "all around" peace treaty, a policy of permanent neutrality, and opposition to the maintenance of foreign bases on Japanese soil. Despite the fierce infighting between the party's right and left wings that was under way at the time, this stance was relatively uncontroversial. It was considered to be consistent with the stipulations of the Potsdam Declaration, which called for a demilitarized Japan that would not threaten peace in the region, as well as with the "peace clause" of the Japanese constitution. Given the historical association of socialism with ideas of international peace and solidarity and in a regional context in which the Cold War division had yet to take hold, the concept of a disarmed and neutral Japan was not a hard sell in the party.

The Korean War and the subsequent moves toward a peace treaty and rearmament radically altered the implications of the stance that the JSP had adopted. A bitter fight erupted over the peace treaty issue at the party's January 1951 convention. The left wing championed what they called the "four principles of peace" —the earlier three principles plus opposition to the new issue of rearmament. Against this, the right wing sponsored a resolution intended to pave the way for the party's acceptance of a partial peace treaty, a limited rearmament for defensive purposes, and through this an alignment of the party with the forces supporting the US-led anticommunist alliance internationally. Impassioned speeches were made by spokesmen for both sides. When the dust finally settled, it was evident that the pro-peace position had carried the day. The four principles of peace were adopted by a majority vote. The right wing's initiative was roundly defeated by a 342–82 margin. The left, which had championed the four principles, gained a plurality in the executive committee, and the left-socialist Suzuki Mosaburō was chosen to be party chairman.

Behind this outcome were the passions aroused in particular among junior-level leaders in both party and union segments of the noncommunist labor movement. The inclinations of their more senior colleagues to engineer a face-saving compromise for the sake of party unity was neutralized by the actions of the party's youth group. Assisting the youth group were similarly politically oriented and impassioned Sōhyō unionists in their thirties whose influence in party affairs had increased dramatically thanks to the Mindō-party linkup at the JSP's 1949 "reconstruction" convention. Accounts and recollections of the principals indicate that in contrast to the pacifism of the communists formulated within the context of a broader political strategy and coordinated globally, the younger, politically inclined unionists' pacifism was a spontaneous, heartfelt one rooted in their direct experience of the ravages, oppression, and ultimate disillusionment during the war. As such, it was a phenomenon that more or less spontaneously spread with great rapidity across organizational and factional boundaries, and without any systematic coordination. Fearing a split of the party, the Sōhyō leadership jumped into the fray and smoothed over the divisions sufficiently to keep the party together.

To the chagrin of the Sōhyō executive, the controversy over the four principles of peace was carried into the Sōhyō's second convention. Pressing labor-market issues notwithstanding, the Sōhyō convention held March 10–12 was almost totally consumed by a heated debate over what stance Sōhyō should adopt vis-à-vis the four principles of peace. Three proposals were initially put before the convention (see table 7). Option A, drafted at the senior leadership level, characteristically attempted to stake out a middle-of-the-road position. While expressing support for the four principles, it was worded in such an ambiguous way that it could be interpreted as not committing the confederation to any significant action on the issue even as it adopted language that demonstrated sympathy toward the principles. (That is, it would "aim" to achieve the four principles but would only "struggle" for an unspecified form of independence.) By contrast, the option B, sponsored by Shinsanbetsu, committed Sōhyō to an active political campaign on behalf of the four principles. Option C, of the social democratic Nikkō miners' union, by contrast, put forward what under the circumstances amounted to a pro-US proposal that supported an "all-around" peace settlement as an ideal but deliberately avoided any mention whatsoever of opposition to rearmament, US

Table 7. Peace policy proposals put forward at March 1951 Sōhyō Convention

	Sponsor	Wording	Votes received
ROUND 1			
Option A	Sōhyō executive	"In line with the intent of the unarmed constitution, we oppose rearmament and will protect Japan's peace by aiming for the realization of the maintenance of neutrality, opposition to the sponsorship of military bases, and an all-around peace treaty, and will struggle for the attainment of independence."	86
Option B	Shinsanbetsu	"We shall deem an all-around peace treaty, the maintenance of neutrality, and opposition to the sponsorship of military bases to be the stance of the Japanese working class and will struggle to oppose rearmament in order to uphold peace and independence."	108
Option C	Nikkō	"We will promote the conclusion of an all-around peace treaty and will struggle for the quick attainment of an independence for Japan in which freedom and equality are assured."	27
ROUND 2			
Option 1	Jichirōkyō	"We will promote the conclusion of an all-around peace treaty and, in line with the intent of the unarmed constitution, will struggle for the quick attainment of an independence for Japan in which freedom and equality are assured."	39
Option 2	Zentei	"We will oppose rearmament, will protect Japan's peace through the realization of the maintenance of neutrality, opposition to the sponsorship of military bases, and an all-around peace treaty, and will struggle for the attainment of independence."	202

Source: Based on *MSRUS,* 3:131–133.

bases, or neutrality. It was the hard-line B option that received the majority of the votes in the initial round of balloting. It did not, however, obtain the two-thirds vote required to alter the confederation's platform. A subsequent round of voting pitted slightly reworded versions of B (option 2) against C (option 1). Option 2 surpassed the two-thirds barrier by a wide margin.

The contest over the four principles was followed by a vote on the related issue of whether or not Sōhyō should affiliate with the ICFTU. Although Sōhyō was ostensibly founded with the intent of turning it into an affiliate of the international, there was now a great reluctance among many union leaders to line up with an organization that had declared unqualified support for the United States in the Korean conflict and for the partial peace treaty. The ICFTU membership bid thus failed to gain the required two-thirds majority.[5] Here, too, maneuvering by politically inclined junior-level industrial-federation officials was instrumental in precipitating this outcome. This time, however, their actions met with a counterreaction in the form of a walkout by delegates representing unions that had sponsored the motion in favor of ICFTU membership. The confrontation over the four principles of peace and ICFTU membership was replayed again and again at the industrial-federation conventions convened over the spring and summer of 1951. Although decisions both for and against the peace principles were made, overall the number of industrial federations supporting the peace principles outnumbered by a large margin those opposed. The fact that in all cases the decisions were made over the objections of vocal minorities demonstrates just how divisive these issues were.

A logical culmination, of a sort, to the spreading Cold War–induced internal rivalry inside the Japanese labor movement—that is, overt, polarized factionalization—emerged in the fall of 1951 as diplomatic negotiations for what became the San Francisco peace settlement, signed in September, were nearing their end. On the left, a trio of junior industrial-federation officials who played a central role in mobilizing support for the four principles of peace at the Sōhyō convention in March—Iwai Akira of Kokurō, Takaragi Fumihiko of Zentei, and Hiragaki Miyoji of Nikkyōso—coalesced into an informal group known as the Suiyōkai (Wednesday Society). Against this, a group of like-minded Sōhyō-affiliated industrial-federation officials who supported the ICFTU line and had spoken out against the adoption of the four principles of peace, linked up with like-minded Sōdōmei unionists and met informally.[6] In September this group took on a public persona with the inauguration of an association they named the Minshu Rōdō Undō Kenkyūkai (Democratic Labor Movement Group), or Minrōken.[7] Spurred by Minrōken's formation, the Suiyōkai solidified into a parallel organization of industrial-federation officials, which they named the Rōdōsha Dōshikai (Worker Comrades Society).[8]

Dissension between the two union factions reached a crescendo at the extraordinary JSP convention held on October 23 and 24. The purpose of the convention was to iron out the party's policy for the upcoming Diet vote on the ratification of the peace and security treaties. In contrast to their role during the previous JSP convention earlier in the year, however, Sōhyō unionists were now actively exacerbating divisions in the party. During the convention, Minrōken and the Rōdōsha Dōshikai set up separate operational bases in nearby Buddhist temples from which they coordinated their agitational forays. The actions of the two unionist factions undermined the frantic efforts on the part of JSP leadership to iron out a compromise, and the party ended up splitting into two separate organizations, the Right Socialist Party and the Left Socialist Party. The party remained divided until 1955.[9] Sōhyō, in which the Rōdōsha Dōshikai position maintained numerical dominance, retained close ties to the Left Socialists.

The Takano line

As indicated by his appearance in the preceding chapters, Takano Minoru was a prominent figure in the union arm of the left-socialist wing of the labor movement who played a key role in the establishment of Sōhyō. While his centrality in the labor movement receded to some extent in the aftermath of Sōhyō's creation, his election as Sōhyō general secretary in early 1951—a position that he would subsequently maintain for four years—thrust him once again into a pivotal position. Although his selection took place amid the heated controversy over peace and security at the national center's 1951 convention, Takano was not directly associated at that time with the junior-level unionists who were instrumental in stirring the groundswell of support on behalf of the four principles of peace and the rejection of Sōhyō's ICFTU affiliation. In fact, because of his frequent contacts with the SCAP Labor Division officials who were attempting to engineer Sōhyō's affiliation with the ICFTU, Takano was widely perceived to be fundamentally pro-American in orientation. It thus came as a shock to many when after his election Takano began to steer the Sōhyō organization in the direction of active opposition to Japan's incorporation into the US containment effort.

Takano's writing during this period suggests that Takano's about-face was not a matter of changing convictions but based on a reasoned rethinking of labor movement strategy from a left-socialist perspective in light of the changed political and diplomatic environment in which the Japanese labor movement found itself. Takano states in the introduction to a book published during this period that "right after the end of the war, the labor movement was able to establish that GHQ's occupation policies were progressive and democratic, and in line with this sought its guidance and helping hand." However, he goes on to state that recent international realignments were now causing US policies to become an obstacle to advancement of the cause of the Japanese working class. Instead of constituting a progressive force, US policies now encouraged reactionary tendencies. Specifically, US efforts to rearm Japan were helping to entrench a coalition of ex-military officers, ex-*zaibatsu* officials, and purged politicians, or, in Takano's analysis, the same combination of forces that had gained control of Japan during the 1930s. Extrapolating from this, Takano predicted dire consequences. As had happened in the period leading up to the war, increased military production would take resources away from the civilian economy and set in motion inflationary pressures that would reduce real wages. American insistence that military procurements in Japan be done on a "commercial" basis was something that would force Japan's uncompetitive manufacturing firms to keep wage levels low. In order to keep the resulting worker unrest in check, the Japanese state would choose to resort to repression.[10]

As dire as this picture was, in Takano's Marxian way of thought, given proper strategy, the very severity of the conditions that confronted the working class provided the mechanism through which to overcome them. Thus, Takano noted that the ongoing deterioration of the workers' situation and that of the Japanese masses more generally was creating a groundswell of politically mobilizable grassroots militancy. As demonstrated by the uproar over the San Francisco peace settlement, concerns about war, peace, and national independence were precipitating a grassroots politicization of the Japanese masses. Takano was particularly impressed by the energy and initiative released during the 1951 Sōhyō convention and saw this as the key to getting the labor movement out of the political and economic cul de sac it found itself confronting in the hostile post–Dodge Line climate. Developments in the labor movement associated with the peace treaty had shown that concerns about threats to peace in Japan had created a basis through which workers could connect politically with a broader stratum of society and build a cross-class coalition of political forces capable of rolling back the Cold War–induced "reverse course" and the intensified oppression of Japanese workers.[11]

As the largest mass organization in the country, Takano argued, Sōhyō was well positioned to serve as a "strategic pivot" *(senryakuten)* for a broad-based popular coalition. He envisioned giving Sōhyō a flexible structure that would be responsive simultaneously to rank-and-file concerns and external political developments. What was needed in Sōhyō, he argued, was "high political capacity, a strong organizational network, initiative on the part of the masses, and unbending fighting spirit."[12] Here, he saw a vital role for the group of younger union officials who had stoked the groundswell of support for the four principles of peace: "What was it that allowed the unified body known as Sōhyō to be strengthened and not disintegrate over the highly political issue of the Japanese peace treaty? I believe it comes down to one thing. This is the fact that a new group of shop-level union officials were able to recognize the growing upsurge in favor of peace that is unfolding in the international arena and, instead of being bound by the limits of the enterprise union, are advancing matters toward a mass struggle."[13] Takano described the tactical significance of Sōhyō's "strategic pivot" role as follows: "A broad united front of peace-oriented citizens centered around the working class would take hold of the topical issue of the day and appear and then disappear, and then just when you thought it was gone, appear yet again in another form to threaten the ruling groups."[14] These were, needless to say, organizational principles and tactics that differed fundamentally from both Sōhyō's original industrial union-centered ideal that had animated the group of industrial-federation presidents during the process of Sōhyō's formation and the party-union transmission-belt-based model of the communists.

Sōhyō's initial efforts, under Takano's stewardship following his election to the position of general secretary at the 1951 convention, to fulfill its mandate on the peace issue provided Takano with the opportunity to apply the strategy and tactics that he was in the process of formulating. Takano's earliest and most direct response to the 1951 convention's decision on the four principles of peace was organization of the Peace Promotion People's Conference (Heiwa Suishin Kokumin Kaigi) on July 18, 1951.[15] The conference was essentially a council that linked Sōhyō with the JSP, women's organizations, religious organizations, and a variety of other mass organizations that could be mobilized in protest actions focused on the peace issue. It sponsored a series of rallies and symposiums designed to demonstrate mass support for the positive neutralist position. The largest was held in Tokyo on September 1 and featured, among other things, a "peace cow" sent by a Buddhist group in India. The conference also promoted the formation of local councils throughout the country in which local-level union councils served as the organizational hub in much the same way that Sōhyō did in the national council. An issue that caused great controversy during the conference's formative phase and which illustrates the tactical logic animating the adoption of this format for Sōhyō's participation in the peace movement was that of whether or not Sōhyō's member industrial federations should participate in the conference as a unit (that is, as Sōhyō) or independently on a federation-by-federation basis. The advantage of the latter arrangement from the standpoint of federations that were not supportive of the four principles of peace was that it would allow them to opt out in much the same way that Sōhyō's rejection of ICFTU affiliation left affiliation with the international confederation up to the individual federations. At Takano's insistence, the former option was adopted, thereby allowing him to mobilize the resources of the entire Sōhyō organization on behalf of the peace council despite substantial pockets of opposition to the confederation's policy.[16]

The Rōtō campaign of 1952 provides further illustration of Takano's ongoing effort to reshape Sōhyō into a "strategic pivot" of the anticonservative opposition. The campaign grew out of the labor movement's reaction to the Yoshida government's drive to ram reverse-course legislation through the Diet and solidify the institutional foundations of conservative government by placing limits and controls on the activities of the left. Two specific sets of legislation were of concern. One was the Subversive Activities Prevention Act (Hakai Katsudō Bōshi Hō, or Habōhō), introduced into the Diet in January, which imposed criminal penalties, including a maximum imprisonment of seven years, against those deemed to have promoted "violent and destructive acts," and granted the state the power to order the dissolution of any organizations doing so. To many unionists, this was tantamount to a revival of the prewar Peace Preservation Law that had been used to systematically repress the left during the prewar years.[17] The second was a package of amendments to existing labor laws, introduced to the Diet in May. The provisions therein deemed most objectionable were (1) a revision of the Labor Relations Adjustment Act that would prohibit strikes in a labor dispute for fifty days and impose emergency mediation where a strike was deemed to have major consequences for public welfare, and (2) a separate piece of legislation that would take away strike rights from local public workers and place them under the provisions that governed national government employees.

The Rōtō campaign stretched from January through July of 1952. Several noteworthy features characterized the campaign. First, like the earlier peace initiative, the campaign featured a Sōhyō-sponsored council in which the labor confederation linked up with a phalanx of concerned organizations and groups outside of the labor movement proper. The coalition ultimately encompassed forty separate citizens' groups, including the Japan Pen Club and the Japanese counterpart of the American Civil Liberties Union. As in the preceding year's peace campaign, the council organized a series of rallies and marches. A second feature was Sōhyō's decision to have district-level labor councils play a more independent role in leading protests, which can be read as an effort on the part of Takano to more comprehensively harness the energy and drive of the "initiative groups" that he saw scattered among the local-level organizational nooks and crannies around the country. A third feature was Sōhyō's willingness to use strikes in pressing its position on the issues. Four waves of intermittent strikes, timed to coincide with the spring wage offensives of industrial federations and stages in the Diet deliberations of the legislation in question, were conducted between April and June. With a claimed 3.4 million workers involved nationwide, the second strike wave marked the biggest wave of political strike actions in Japanese history to that point.[18]

The Rōtō campaign was punctuated by an incident, which came to be labeled the Bloody May Day Incident, that brought unfavorable publicity for the unions. During the preceding year, government authorities had banned the use of a plaza fronting the Imperial Palace where the postwar May Day rallies had traditionally taken place. The ban was extended to 1952. Deeming this an unwarranted action, an apparently spontaneously formed group (though communist agitation was alleged), consisting largely of students, marched from the authorized May Day site to the plaza in front of the palace, whereupon they clashed with police. The ensuing melee resulted in two deaths, numerous injuries, and 1,300 arrests. Among other consequences, the incident helped spur public support for the Subversive Activities Prevention Act.

Although it failed to prevent passage of the legislation, the scale of the Rōtō campaign was such that it established Sōhyō's credentials as a political force to be reckoned with. Internally, the Rōtō campaign capped a decisive shift of initiative inside the Sōhyō organization from the "presidents' group" of moderate private-sector industrial-federation leaders to Takano Minoru and an informal faction of more politically minded industrial-federation officials, many of whom were associated with the Rōdōsha Dōshikai. The incident that more than any other illustrated this shift was the resignation of Sōhyō's President Mutō following the passage of a no-confidence vote against him by elements in the federation who were dissatisfied with his role in pulling Tanrō out of the third wave of Rōtō's strikes.[19] The move was significant because Mutō, as Sōhyō's president, was a key figure in the presidents' group.

One can see a more permanent organizational imprint of the emerging "Takano line" in the rapid spread of Sōhyō-subsidized district councils *(chikurō)* during the 1950s, which coordinated the activities of the various local units of the different unions residing in a given local district. Through the district councils, Takano was able to gain access to a broader network independent of the system of industrial federations that were the original mainstay of the Sōhyō organization. District councils remained permanent fixtures of Sōhyō-led political campaigns well into the 1980s.

Confronting containment

Under US pressure, the Yoshida government proceeded to institutionalize Japan-US defense cooperation in the wake of the peace-and-security treaties' conclusion. US military bases were expanded. Japan's military budget increased. The Yoshida government announced in mid-1953 that it would encase the Japan-US relationship in the framework of an "economic cooperation" agreement based on the American Mutual Security Act (MSA). The expansion of US military bases generated confrontations with groups of local residents and sympathizers. One of the earliest and most widely publicized was over the setting up of the Uchinada firing range in Ishikawa prefecture, where a protest movement that spanned the partisan political spectrum was formed to oppose seizure of the land to be utilized for the range. The Japanese government forced the implementation of the plan, sparking sit-down strikes and confrontations that received widespread coverage in the press. The unfolding pattern seemed to fit perfectly Takano's earlier predictions about the militarization of the Japanese economy under US sponsorship. In the Diet, the minority Socialists were helpless in the face of the conservative majority, neither were they able or, it seemed, particularly inclined to effectively harness the mass energy that Takano saw welling up in the face of the deepening contradictions. At Takano's initiative, Sōhyō stepped in to fill the vacuum in political leadership. When the Uchinada confrontation evolved into a cause célèbre, Takano pledged Sōhyō's support. Sōhyō unions subsequently sent organizers to assist the leadership of the local opposition movement, and rank-and-file unionists were sent in as demonstrators. Sōhyō adopted the same tactics in its assistance of other anti-military-base protest movements, including that at Sunakawa village bordering the large US Air Force base in Tachikawa, outside of Tokyo. All of these seemed to embody precisely the kinds of nationalist confrontations that Takano predicted the Japan-US alliance would generate.

In planning the Sōhyō convention of 1953, Takano made it a point to highlight Sōhyō's role as the "strategic pivot" of the opposition. Nonunion activists from Uchinada and other causes were invited to attend, and the galleries were packed with two thousand observers from a variety of walks of life. Takano reflected on the developments of the convention with great satisfaction: "Never before had 'the suffering of the nation' been brought into the site of a convention by people from all different strata. The Uchinada matter, the matter of leprosy, the matter of children. These were all brought into the convention. Sōhyō made it clear at the convention that it was not just there for workers but is the 'pillar' that represents the 'suffering of the nation,' the suffering of all people from various strata who seek peace."[20] A number of organizational changes were made at the convention that aimed to enhance Sōhyō's ability to play the pivotal role. The number of full-time officials at Sōhyō headquarters was increased from one to eight. Coordination of local-level efforts was enhanced by the institution of regular monthly meetings of regional blocs of district councils.

With regard to Sōhyō's external relations, a particularly critical development around this time was Takano's participation, along with a number of other socialist party and union leaders, in the Asian Socialist Conference held in Rangoon between January 6 and 15, 1953. The conference was organized at the initiative of socialists in India, Burma, and Indonesia, the three countries at the forefront of the budding neutralist movement that would peak in 1955, at the famous Bandung Conference. Dominated as it was by representatives from recently decolonized or decolonizing areas, the meeting was colored by a strongly anticolonial tone that pitted Asian socialists against socialist parties in Western Europe, most of whom were either actively or tacitly supporting continued colonial relationships.[21] The importance of the meeting for the evolution of Takano's labor movement strategy is attested to by the fact that a number of individuals who were close to Takano claimed they noticed a definite change in his thinking and demeanor after he returned. Takano's own writing corroborates this. He characterized the conference as the inauguration of a new "Asian" socialist international: "A number of internationals have been created. In every case these originated in Europe. But this time Asian socialists have given birth to an international in Asia, on Asian land." He states with apparent satisfaction that this "international" represents the emergence of an "Asian political force that is not part of either side" in the Cold War and through this is actively working "to contribute to the maintenance of world peace."[22] From a comparative standpoint, the significance of this linkup with other Asian socialists at the conference on the part of Takano and other Japanese left socialists rests in the fact that the conference provided inter-

Table 8. Major Sōhyō-led mass campaigns 1950–1955

Date	Campaign Organization Name	
SEPTEMBER 1950	Zenkoku Minshu Rōsō Tōsō Iinkai	National Democratic Labor Union Struggle Committee
SEPTEMBER 1951	Heiwa Suishin Kokumin Kaigi	Peace Promotion People's Conference
MAY 1952	Akuhō Hantai Kokumin Undō Renraku Kaigi	Liaison Council for the People's Movement to Oppose Unjust Legislation (the coordinating committee for the Rōtō campaign)
JULY 1953	Minshu Dantai Suigai Taisaku Kyōgikai	Deliberation Council of Democratic Organizations on Flood Damage Countermeasures
JULY 1953	Shokuryō Taisaku Kokumin Renraku Kaigi	Food Countermeasures People's Liaison Council
NOVEMBER 1953	Nitchū Bōeki Kokumin Kaigi	People's Conference on Japan-China Trade
JANUARY 1954	Goken Rengō (Kenpō Yōgo Kokumin Rengō)	People's Alliance to Save the Constitution
JANUARY 1954	MSA Yosan Kumikae Yōkyū Kondankai	Deliberation Council to Demand a Rewriting of the MSA Budget
JANUARY 1954	Shakai Hoshō o Mamoru Kai	Association to Save Social Insurance
MARCH 1954	Gensui Kinshi Undō	Movement to Ban the Hydrogen Bomb
APRIL 1954	Heiwa Keizai Kokumin Kaigi	Peace Economy People's Conference
JUNE 1955	Seikatsu to Kenri to Kokudo o Mamoru Daishūkai	Major Rally to Save Livelihoods, Rights and the Land
JUNE 1955	Zenkoku Gunji Kichi Hantai Tōsō Zenkoku Kaigi	National Conference for the National Struggle to Oppose Military Bases
JULY 1955	Kokumin Bunka Kaigi	People's Cultural Conference

Source: *SYS,* 1:137–138.

national legitimation for the anti-US neutralism that they were pursuing. Where Western European left-socialist neutralism floundered in relative isolation in a bipolarized environment, Japan's neutralism was embedded in a supportive regional context. The fact that the vitality of Asia-centered nonaligned neutralism would not outlast the decade does not reduce the significance of this for the evolution of the Japanese labor movement.

Having said this, it deserves note that one of the complicating factors in the pursuit of a neutralist line in the East Asian context was the ambiguous status of the People's Republic of China. While clearly under the control of a communist regime and, at the time, a Soviet ally (and thus a member of the Soviet camp in the Cold War context), pre-1949 Western imperialism also qualified China as postcolonial. Both the PRC and the leaders of the Asian Socialist Conference recognized this, and a number of friendly diplomatic overtures were exchanged between the two sides in the name of encouraging an independent peace in East Asia. Furthermore, before the war, China had been one of Japan's primary sources of raw materials as well as a primary export market, and for this reason, reestablishing economic and diplomatic relations with the PRC was seen by many (including those in the conservative camp) as necessary for Japan's long-term eco-

Table 9. Confederation-supported Diet members elected in general elections 1952–1955

Date of election	Party-affiliation					Background	
	Right socialist	Left socialist	Labor farmer	Other and independent	Total	Former union officials	Formerly in union-related position
Sōhyō-supported Diet members							
October 1, 1952	1	54	4	3	62	14	5
	(2%)*	(100%)	(100%)	(12%)	(13%)	(3%)	(1%)
April 19, 1953		72	4	1	77	9	10
		(100%)	(80%)	(8%)	(17%)	(2%)	(2%)
February 27, 1955	53	89	4		146	39	
	(79%)	(100%)	(100%)		(31%)	(8%)	
Sōdōmei- or Zenrō-supported Diet members							
October 1, 1952	30				30	4	5
	(53%)				(6%)	(1%)	(1%)
April 19, 1953	27				27	5	2
	(41%)				(6%)	(1%)	
February 27, 1955	59	1			60	11	
	(88%)	(1%)			(13%)	(2%)	

*Percentages, in parentheses, are of total number of Diet members elected from that party or total membership of Lower House.
Source: *MRUS,* 4:43, 85, 221.

nomic viability. And for the left socialists specifically, the reestablishment of economic relations with China presented them with an attractive economic and diplomatic alternative to economic and military dependence on the United States. Induced by these circumstances, Sōhyō actively sought closer relations with China. Thus, at around the time that the Asian Socialist Conference was meeting in Rangoon, Nikkyōso's Hiragaki traveled to China with a delegation to discuss the repatriation of Japanese stranded there after the war. Sōhyō gave Hiragaki a letter to deliver to Chinese officials which said that "Japanese workers know that there is no way to secure the economic independence of and peace in Asia other than for China, India, and Japan to become the core and to cooperate in politics and economics." Hiragaki reported back that the message was warmly received by the Chinese. This was followed by an invitation from the Chinese government to Sōhyō to send a delegation to the May Day celebrations in Beijing, but the Japanese government refused to issue exit papers for the delegation.[23] In subsequent years, Sōhyō and left-socialist elements in the JSP would deepen their relations with the PRC and other Asian regimes. Sōhyō would go on to make several attempts to create an Asian trade-union congress rooted in pacifist neutralist principles. Despite great effort on Sōhyō's part, however, this initiative would in the end remain unconsummated. In the meantime, Sōhyō became securely rooted in an international-relations line that diverged fundamentally from that being pursued by the social-democratically dominated ICFTU and to a lesser extent, from the communist WFTU. It would take nearly three decades before Sōhyō would reorient in international stance and begin actively seeking alignment with the Western European movement and the ICFTU.[24]

A further example of Takano's propensity to attune Sōhyō's actions to what he perceived to be the larger international context was his creation of the Peace Economy Plan. Inspired by the PCI's Piano del Lavoro and the winding down of the special-procurements boom, the goal of the exercise was to devise a viable economic alternative to the war economy based on the Japan-US alliance and rearmament that the conservatives were constructing. A number of prominent Marxian economists were commissioned by Sōhyō for this purpose, beginning in April 1953. Local-level discussion sessions on the plan were also held. In the end, however, the move fizzled before a formal plan could be finalized.[25]

New divisions

Takano's full-bore drive to turn the labor confederation that he led into a strategic pivot of mass opposition did give rise to a variety of organizational and political strains that became amply visible by 1953. Virtually all left socialists in Sōhyō and in the Left Socialist Party were supportive of the notion that they were part of a neutralist third force independent of the Cold War's two camps. Takano's extraordinary sensitivity to the changing international currents, however, caused him to stretch his interpretation of what constituted neutralism to the point where it began to engender opposition even among committed supporters. In his report on the world situation before Sōhyō's fourth convention in 1953, Takano, taking his cue from recent developments in international politics, put forward the idea that on the international scene advancing "peace forces" were reversing the trend toward bipolar conflict, and he included the USSR and the PRC among these forces. This assertion proved to be controversial in the extreme. The report itself went through six drafts, and the final version was considerably watered down from Takano's initial proposal.[26] Objections were raised that this classification violated the tenets of neutralism that Sōhyō was committed to. How could the Soviet Union, which had until now been a force of war, suddenly be counted as a peace force? Takano's response was as follows: "There are no countries that are a peace force in the philosophical sense. It is my view that those who make an effort toward peace at a given point in time are a peace force at that point in time. To the extent that the Soviet Union is advocating an armistice in Korea, it is a peace force."[27] Others, however, found this strategic flexibility difficult to stomach.

The same impulse to use Sōhyō as a dynamic tactical vehicle in advancing the peace movement encouraged Takano to intervene in domestic political affairs even if this meant confronting Sōhyō's partisan ally the Left Socialist Party. One such instance occurred in the period leading up to the 1953 general election.[28] At that time, infighting within the conservative camp that pitted Yoshida loyalists against anti-Yoshida conservatives, many of whom were purged, had grown increasingly heated since the end of the occupation. Confronted with a no-confidence vote, the prime minister dissolved the Diet on March 14, 1953, and called an election. The Yoshida Liberals had already lost their majority through defections prior to the elections. The results of the April 19 election left them once again with less than a majority, and a coalition government was clearly called for. Takano had indicated prior to the election that it should be used as an opportunity to create a coalition that would span the breadth of the political spectrum, from sympathetic conservatives to the communists, and that Sōhyō should play a pivotal role in this process. True to his word, following the election, Takano entered the fray by demanding that the Left Socialists back a non-Yoshida cabinet, based on a coalition of conservative and socialist parties and headed by the conservative Kaishintō's Shigemitsu Mamoru, on grounds that any arrangement to end governance by the antilabor Yoshida government was more desirable than another Yoshida cabinet. He argued that doing so would put Sōhyō in a position to bargain with the government and to extract concessions from it. Concessions sought included the government's withdrawal of legislation limiting strike activities in the coal and electric power industries, a promise not to attempt a revision of the constitution (and thus retain the "peace clause"), and the establishment of commercial relations with mainland China. The move was also justified within the context of his longer-term anti-imperialist strategy. To quote Takano: "The strategy for dealing a decisive blow to the enemy is to bring down the Yoshida government that represents internal and external monopoly capital and American military policy in the Far East. If we bring down the Yoshida government, even if a reactionary government were to take power, it would be considerably weaker than Yoshida's. The core of the current strategy is to create as unstable a government as possible."[29] The leadership of the Left Socialists, on the other hand, were embittered by the experience of the center-left Katayama cabinet and maintained the more conventional and doctrinaire stance that the party should concentrate on marshalling the strength of the left-socialist opposition. They were thus against participation in any coalition government that included the conservatives. Takano and his lieutenants in Sōhyō insistently pressed their point at the Left Socialist convention held in May. This intervention caused resentment in the party over what was felt to be unwarranted interference in party affairs. The convention ignored Takano and ratified a policy of supporting party president Suzuki Mosaburō, rather than Shigemitsu, in the prime ministerial balloting. As a result, Yoshida was duly reelected as prime minister, and the strike control law and related reverse-course legislation proposed by the Yoshida government was passed. In reaction, Takano called the Left Socialist Party, "good for nothing" *(fugainai)*. The incident seemed to have reinforced his belief in the need for Sōhyō to act as political broker:

> I believe that the mission of the labor unions [in Japan] is much more burdensome than in other countries . . . Shouldn't labor unions, which possess a historical function as the national support base for Japanese democratization and as the most organized social category among the nation's masses, consolidate their power and adopt a much, much more aggressive attitude . . . ? Rather than wait for the party to do something for them, shouldn't they advance and ensnare partisan forces? Isn't it the case that it is through the experience of mass struggle that parties develop and labor unions will become stronger? The political activities of the labor unions centered around Sōhyō will fill the political vacuum we have today.[30]

Another confrontation between Takano and the Left Socialist Party occurred the following year over the party's platform, which was being drafted by a party committee formed for that purpose.[31] Takano championed the position that the platform should make anti-imperialist national struggle the highest priority of the party, thereby harmonizing party platform with the strategy that Takano was pursuing in Sōhyō. This intervention once again stirred resentment in the party.

The platform revision submitted by Shimizu Shinzō on behalf of Takano was defeated, and a platform more in line with traditional left-socialist positions was adopted instead. It was also around this time that key figures in the Left Socialist Party began sounding out the Right Socialists on the prospects of reunification.[32]

Takano's intense focus on political mobilization had repercussions for Sōhyō's performance in the collective-bargaining arena. At the conceptual level, Takano's and his lieutenants' proclivity to deduce strategy and tactics from a national- and global-level analysis of the balance and dynamics of class forces resulted in a "wage platform" *(chingin kōryō)*, made public in 1952, in which Sōhyō defined targets for wage demands based on an analysis of macroeconomic variables.[33] Specifically, Sōhyō pointed out in the wage platform that the recovery of wage levels lagged well behind the recovery of Japanese industrial production. Using a "market-basket formula" in which consumption needs were calculated on the basis of the cost of a standard "basket" of goods, the confederation concluded that an average wage level of 70,000 yen was needed in order for a worker and his family to sustain a "healthy and cultured lifestyle." With that as a long-term objective, it then demanded that average wages return right away to prewar levels, or around 25,000 yen in nominal terms. Even the immediate target figure would involve a substantial increase, since it was double the average wage of 12,500 for workers 30 years old in firms of thirty or more employees.[34] Not surprisingly, critics argued that the figure was totally unrealistic given the realities of the Japanese economy.

A number of recurring problems hampered Sōhyō's effectiveness in its pursuit of this strategy and its associated tactics in labor dispute struggles. First, when unions put forward the huge wage demands the Sōhyō's wage platform called for, they met adamant resistance from management, and in many instances management used these demands as an opportunity to "tame" the unions, precipitating intense and prolonged struggles that ended in defeat for the unions. At this point, a second structural problem would come into play, namely the decentralized structure of the Japanese labor movement rooted in enterprise unions. Even if an industrial federation was able to launch a wage struggle on behalf of Sōhyō-defined targets, the enterprise-centered union structure would encourage individual unions to drop out of a strike. Sooner or later, the campaign would deteriorate into a fierce isolated struggle by one or two militant enterprise unions against which the collective resources of management would be concentrated. This occurred, for instance, in the wage campaign on the part of the coal and electric power unions in the fall of 1952.[35] A third problem was rooted in the limited financial and human resources on the part of Sōhyō itself. Financially, Sōhyō simply did not have the strike funds needed to support a prolonged strike at the industry level, and even small isolated struggles by a single enterprise union stretched its resources. The national center attempted to overcome these limitations through organizing fund-raising drives in support of striking unions among its rank-and-file, but the amount of funds raised through this means inevitably fell short of what was needed. The human resources that Sōhyō was in a position to tap were also limited, and the national center simply could not effectively guide large-scale strikes. Resources were stretched all the more when a wage offensive coincided with a major political campaign, as happened during the elections of 1952 and 1953. Attaching highest priority to the election campaign, Takano pulled personnel out of the ongoing wage campaigns and put them in election support activities, generating numerous complaints. All told, the Takano years were marked by a series of spectacular defeats by the unions in collective-bargaining and labor disputes.

One would naturally expect a reaction against Takano's anti-US, anti-ICFTU stance and his mobilization of Japanese unions in overtly political campaigns from the social-democratic element in the Japanese labor movement. Old guard social democrats like Nishio Suehiro and Matsuoka Komakichi were uncomfortable from the very beginning with the growing influence of the left socialists. They had clashed over whether or not to amalgamate constituent organizations with others that were under the Sōhyō umbrella and had split with the left socialists at Sōdōmei's fifth postwar convention in November 1950. The secessionists reconstituted themselves as the "reborn Sōdōmei" six months later, taking a reported 300,000 of the earlier combined organization's 835,000 members.[36] Having gained an independent organizational voice, the reborn Sōdōmei became an independent pole of pro-US social-democratic opposition to Takano's neutralist left-socialist line. The traditionally anticommunist Sōdōmei right maintained a foreign-policy line that was diametrically opposed to Sōhyō's—that is, it advocated a "partial" peace treaty and supported the security treaty with the United States as the only practical solution to Japan's situation in the context of the international political situation at the time. They also declared their unequivocal support for the ICFTU and the Socialist International.

We have already detailed how the 1951 controversy over the four principles of peace produced an informal factional grouping of pro-ICFTU, pro-Western activists inside Sōhyō (Minrōken). Like the reconstituted Sōdōmei, Minrōken's beef with the Sōhyō leadership was of a quintessentially Cold War variety. This was evident, for instance, in the Minrōken "statement of purpose": "Although there are numerous issues that we face, the fundamental one before us that we must address first and above all is that of establishing a democratic foundation for our country's labor movement. In order to do this we must maintain the principle of preserving freedom and democracy, adopt the stance of the Socialist International which has made opposition to communism its guiding policy, make clear our ideological stance regarding the ICFTU, and clarify our organizational links with it. We must realign our country's labor movement both qualitatively and quantitatively on this basis."[37]

The next major reaction came from inside Sōhyō. This was a joint manifesto critical of Takano's leadership, made public on December 25, 1952, that had been prepared by the federation of textile workers' unions, the seamen's union, the broadcasting workers' union, and the motion picture and theater workers' union. These were four Sōhyō-affiliated industrial federations in which younger social democrats dominated the executive. Two hundred thousand copies of the manifesto were allegedly printed and distributed widely.[38] In contrast to Sōdōmei's and Minrōken's politically based differences with the Sōhyō line, their discomfort was rooted more in tactical and organizational concerns. The core of the group's complaint was that the Sōhyō executive was "leading unions in the direction of becoming something akin to the action brigades of an anti-rearmament struggle tied to an idealistic peace thesis." This, it claimed, was causing the national center to become estranged from "the real desires and actions of the union masses." A central problem here was Sōhyō's inability under Takano to effectively address the economic needs of union members, which are the primary organizational function of unions. The manifesto went into some detail illustrating its point, using the concrete example of that autumn's Tanrō and Densan strikes based on Sōhyō's wage platform. The four-federation manifesto lamented that the so-called economic demands being put forward by Sōhyō could not be attained unless the Japanese economic structure were in better shape than it was at the time, and that Sōhyō's tactics and strategy were therefore misguided.[39] Unrealistic demands, it argued, were causing Sōhyō's policies to "inevitably go beyond the limits of economic struggles that are feasible for unions and dragging union members into a quagmire of disputes that are difficult to resolve." It was also leading Sōhyō into adopting tactics that were disturbingly close to those used by the communists that the confederation was presumably formed to eliminate. While granting that the policies of the Yoshida government and Japanese capitalists "were factors that cannot but spur workers into fierce struggles," it insisted that the activities of unions needed to be handled properly.

Contacts among sympathetic unionists within Sōhyō led to the establishment of Minrōren (Minshushugi Rōdō Undō Renraku Kyōgikai, or Democratic Labor Movement Liaison Council) in February of the following year, a national network that brought together dissident social-democratic Sōhyō unionists and elements from Sōdōmei. Minrōren's initial aim was to put pressure on Sōhyō to bring it in line with what they interpreted as the confederation's basic social-democratic platform. Minrōren's own "action program" went into considerable detail in pledging its adherence to a fundamental principle of social democratic unionism, separating the spheres of union and party activity. In order to amplify the organization's influence, local Minrōren branches were set up around the country during the spring of 1954. These then campaigned actively on behalf of Right Socialists in the general election of that year and participated in May Day festivities that convened separately from those of Sōhyō. In a number of notable instances—the infamous Nissan strike of 1953 being a case in point—the Min-rōren organization gave support to breakaway "second unions" formed during confrontations between militant unions and management that was determined to tame its workers.[40]

In a manner that paralleled Sanbetsu Mindō's experience several years earlier, Minrōren began as an organization aimed at reforming Sōhyō from the inside, but subsequently shifted its course and started working toward establishing a con-federational alternative to Sōhyō. The catalyst for this shift appears to have been the group's inability to prevent Sōhyō's July 1953 convention from approving Takano's "labor movement under the MSA" program that many felt was a brazen abnegation of fundamental principles of union organization and behavior. Shortly thereafter, three of the four industrial federations that had sponsored the earlier manifesto—Zensen Dōmei, Zen'eien, and the seamen's union—formally with-drew from the confederation. (In the case of Nippōrō, the executive was unable to gain the needed votes at the federation's convention.)[41] Eight months of fever-ish organizational activity culminated in April 1954 in the establishment of a new national center, Zenrō (Zenkoku Rōdō Kumiai Kaigi, or National Trade Union Congress) on April 23, 1954.[42] Consisting of Sōdōmei and the three unions that had bolted from Sōhyō, the rank-and-file membership affiliated with Zenrō was declared to be 840,000, or slightly over one-fourth of Sōhyō's.

Given the center's roots, it was fitting that Zenrō's founders chose to build into the fundamental institutional arrangements of the new confederation adher-ence to basic social-democratic trade-union principles. Where Japanese labor organizations would typically use functionally differentiated basic documents—that is, a statute *(kiyaku)*, a platform *(kōryō)*, and an organizational policy *(soshiki hōshin)*—these were collapsed into a single document that Zenrō called its "char-ter" *(kenshō)*. "The reason for choosing to call this a 'charter,'" the document stated, was to specify its status as "the constitution *(kenpō)* of the organization." And as stipulated by a "constitution," members were obligated to abide by it. Three basic ideals to live by and promote were listed: freedom, democracy, and social justice. The charter pointedly emphasized the need for self-discipline and self-control on the part of unions. In a passage that perhaps epitomizes the spirit of the docu-ment and the new confederation, the charter stated:

> In addition, for labor unions that have as the primary mission of their organization the economic activities of workers, to focus on political power struggles and engage in political party–like behavior not only violates democracy but will lead to the impairment of their functions as labor unions and will in the end invite the self-destruction of the organization and must be forcefully rejected.

It went on to note that true social justice can only be achieved in a "democratic socialist society" in which "economic democracy and political democracy coexist," and that Zenrō would seek the realization of such a society. It insisted that the advance toward this ideal "in all cases be done through the constitutional and legal order based on the fundamental principles of democracy."[43]

One further Sōhyō "loss" of membership as an apparent consequence of its overt politicization occurred in May 1953 with the consolidation of the industrial federations in the electrical machinery industry, which had earlier been divided into the competing Sanbetsu and Sōdōmei organizations. The result was a new industrial federation representing nearly 100,000 workers. What was disturbing to Sōhyō was that the new organization, Denki Rōren (Zen Nihon Denki Kiki Rōdō Kumiai Rengōkai, or the All Japan Electrical Machinery Labor Union Federation), chose to remain independent. The federation's political stance was more or less identical to that of the Sōhyō mainstream, yet the organization apparently did not find the national center attractive enough to warrant affiliation.

One of the most important legacies of the Takano years was infusion of the values and modalities of positive neutralism into the ethos of the Japanese labor movement. As discussed in the preceding chapters, this internationally shared reaction to the militarization of the US Cold War containment policy occurred at a point when it could take on a pivotal significance in the development of the Japanese labor movement. The somewhat differing nuance of the Cold War conflict in the Asian region when compared to that in Europe meant that the neutralist appeal resonated more widely and deeply in Japan. Furthermore, the peace issue became salient in Japan when the Communist Party and its affiliated wing of labor movement had virtually disappeared from the scene. Peace and neutrality thus became a socialist rather than a communist cause and, as a consequence, was free (relatively but not completely) of the antinationalist baggage that association with the Communists had in Western Europe. The entree of the peace and neutrality movement occurred, as well, in a period when the Japanese labor movement was undergoing a major reorganization and was in a politically weak and vulnerable state. Because of its apparent resonance both among workers and in the broader population, key and eventually dominant elements in the leadership of Japan's newly formed labor confederation embraced it as a way out of the political cul de sac that the movement faced. Ideology and organization were modified to accommodate this embrace. Resistance to the excesses of Takano's drive to wholly transform Sōhyō eventually halted it, but few of the concrete organizational innovations that were implemented under his stewardship were reversed. The apparatus of Sōhyō-led mass mobilization remained firmly in place and continued as a core element of the Sōhyō movement thereafter.

The peace and neutrality movement of the early 1950s was pivotal to the development of the Japanese labor movement in a negative sense, as well. Unionists opposed to the strategy and tactics pursued by Takano pulled out of the national confederation and formed a competing one of their own with the aim of rectifying the movement's course and objectives. The result, of course, was Zenrō, created in 1954, which functioned as the beacon of a moderate, pro-Western organizational and ideological alternative to Sōhyō's militant neutralism and confrontational class politics. At the outset a mere joint council of motley anti-Sōhyō unions whose membership was just one-third of Sōhyō's, Zenrō grew into the full-fledged and consolidated national confederation Dōmei that eventually overshadowed Sōhyō in size in the private sector. The initial peace and neutrality experience also provided negative lessons in another sense, as we shall see in the next chapter. The lessons of the Zenrō split were taken to heart by those in Sōhyō who were basically sympathetic to the goals outlined by Takano. The subsequent leadership of Ōta Kaoru and Iwai Akira, while maintaining the essential political stance laid out by Takano and pursuing extra-parliamentary mobilizations enthusiastically, was sensitive to the limits of Sōhyō's mobilizational capacity and took great care ensuring the organization did not proceed any further once these limits were reached. Such self-limitation, in turn, marks Sōhyō's accommodation to the sociological and ideological makeup of the high-growth–era Japanese polity.

Part 3

BEYOND THE COLD WAR

Chapter 10

Productivity and Industrial Modernization under "Peaceful Coexistence"
Western Europe and Japan

The years of 1953 through 1955 were marked by a number of events that altered the quality of the Cold War even as the essential structure of bipolar conflict remained intact. An armistice was signed in July 1953 that ended the fighting in Korea, while an accord terminating war in Vietnam, for the moment at least, was reached in Geneva the following summer, thereby bringing to an end the two "hot wars" that marred the otherwise cold-war character of the confrontation between the two blocs. Stalin's death, in 1953, and the de-Stalinization process that followed in its wake set the stage for the 1956 announcement of a policy of "peaceful coexistence" by the Communist Party of the Soviet Union (CPSU) first secretary (later Soviet premier) Nikolai Khrushchev. As Michael Kort emphasizes, peaceful coexistence "was less pacific than it sounded. . . . [It] meant only that the two systems would henceforth compete by political and economic means short of war."[1] But the shift from military to political and economic means was nonetheless a highly significant development for labor politics in Europe because it dramatically reduced the salience of international-level Cold War developments on domestic politics. First, at the international level the mid-1950s saw a consolidation and stabilization of the competing systems in the two halves of the continent and the emergence of a mutual hands-off attitude by the United States and the Soviet Union toward affairs in the other's sphere of influence. Specifically, the economic and military integration of Western Europe proceeded apace with the completion of the NATO alliance. In

1955, the same year that West Germany joined NATO, the Soviets demonstrated their determination to maintain a firm grip over their Eastern European client states with the establishment of the Warsaw Pact, the Eastern counterpart of the West's NATO. Concurrently, the Soviets signaled their greater willingness to let matters take their own course in Western Europe when they dissolved the Cominform and granted relative autonomy and independence to the communist parties in Western Europe. The United States signaled its own willingness to follow a hands-off policy in the fall of 1956 by not intervening when the Soviets forcefully suppressed a rebellion against a Soviet client regime in Hungary. These various developments helped solidify the segregation of the two halves of the European continent and thereby helped to reduce the likelihood of cross-border conflagrations. Working in the same direction, the loosened Soviet grip on former client parties altered the environment of Western European labor politics by decreasing the perception of an imminent threat to democracy from the far left that had been a primary factor in its politicization since the Cold War began in 1947.

At the same time that these international-level developments were reducing the perceived salience of a threat to postwar democracy from the left, other developments inside these countries eased fears on the left regarding a threat to democracy from the right. Of the three Western European countries that we have focused on, the fear of a fascist revival was reduced earliest in West Germany. The extreme right was a very small presence in West German politics, and legislative initiatives in the mid-1950s effectively outlawed extreme parties on both the left and the right. In France and Italy, fears of a fascist revival remained a concern on the left for a longer period of time, but even there the way in which key political crises were handled during these years helped to ease such concerns by reassuring many on the left that postwar democracy was now strong enough to withstand foreseeable challenges from the far right. In Italy in 1959, DC leader Fernando Tambroni's flirtation with the idea of forming a coalition that included the neofascist Movimento Sociale Italiano (MSI) brought tens of thousands of antifascist demonstrators into the street, precipitating fierce battles around the country that ultimately led to Tambroni's resignation. The DC subsequently abandoned its pursuit of the extreme right and demonstrated its commitment to a long-term policy of linking up with the left. As Ginsborg points out, the Tambroni incident constituted a milestone in Italian politics: "The Tambroni affair established clearly one of the constants in the political history of the Republic: namely that anti-Fascism . . . had become part of the dominant ideology. Any attempt to move in an authoritarian direction, away from the Constitution and back towards the Fascist regime, was likely to meet with a massive and uncontrollable protest movement."[2] In France, the specter of a reversion to fascism came in the form of the coup attempts and turmoil that accompanied the Algerian crisis in 1957–1958 and in 1961. Paralleling what happened in Italy, there was fear on the left that de Gaulle would form a government with the extreme right. De Gaulle, however, did not and instead defended the Fifth Republic's democratic institutions against the far right's attacks. The core institutional apparatus of the French Republic would remain unchallenged thereafter.[3] Given the left's exclusion from government (as contrasted with the center-left government established by the DC in Italy), the comfort level on the part of the left was arguably weaker in France than Italy, but the fact remained that there was a dramatic reduction in French fears of a far-right threat to democracy. Thus, in all three countries, as representative democracy became more and more firmly rooted, the old rationale that political mobilization of the unions was needed in order to establish and/or defend the democratic institutions grew less and less credible.

A third broad trend that had a profound impact on labor politics in Western Europe from the latter half of the 1950s and into the 1960s was the ongoing modernization of Western Europe's economies and the unprecedented prosperity associated with the region's various "economic miracles." These were forces that pulled labor movements—and their trade-union segments in particular—away from the "high politics" of international relations and regime change and pushed them toward the "low politics" of the labor market. The industrial modernization pursued by Western Europe's captains of state economic planning and big industry involved intensive capital investment and the introduction of new technologies and techniques that raised productivity and production in Western European plants and, in a twist unforeseen by most labor movements, actually tightened the demand for workers. Under these circumstances, sustained engagement in the "politics of productivity" on an economy-wide basis became meaningful and necessary in Western Europe for the first time. Beyond the workplace, sustained prosperity set in motion a variety of profound sociological changes. In the midst of the improving living standards, the increasing educational attainment, and the social mobility that modernization engendered grew new attitudes that loosened the tight binding of class, economic well being, and political activity that had earlier provided the foundation for the labor movements. With the old political and religious identities losing relevance, unions were forced to look to other avenues to appeal to workers. Caught between the push of democratic stabilization and the pull of industrial modernization, unions began to shift their attention away from the arena of partisan politics (but not necessarily politics per se) toward the labor market issues.

At a generalized level, one can speak of two broadly defined tendencies that marked this shift in labor movement strategy. One was the embracing of an adversarial or confrontational modality of labor market action. The other was an accommodationist tendency that focused on cooperation with management and expanding labor participation in economic decision-making. Both tendencies had historical precedents in Western European labor movements, and the responses of different elements within the labor movement of a particular country were filtered through the tendencies of thought that were embedded in the specific sections of the labor movement during the preceding decades.

Western Europe: the productivity movement

Although the controversies over rearmament that animated the peace movements of Western Europe were by far the most visible aspect of US Cold War policy during the early 1950s, there was a second set of policies of a related but qualitatively distinct nature. This was the so-called "productivity movement" in which the United States sponsored technical assistance programs aimed at fostering an apolitical form of business unionism modeled after what was thought predominant in the United States. As Anthony Carew details in a seminal study, the impetus for the productivity movement was dissatisfaction on the part of ERP labor attachés and US union representatives with what they saw as the overly business-oriented thrust of the Marshall Plan. Financial stabilization dominated the ERP's initial years, and there was little in the policy mix that would relieve the hardships that these policies imposed on European workers.[4] This was made all the more frustrating because the ERP was supposed to have assured labor a voice in its administration, but in practice, government officials and business representatives made key decisions with minimal input from labor spokespersons. Annoyance reached the boiling point during the latter half of 1949 and spurred American labor officials into a lobbying campaign to make the ERP more sensitive to labor concerns. The upshot was a major jump in "technical assistance" allocations in the Economic Cooperation Administration (ECA) budget, the centerpiece of which was the funding for "productivity centers" to be created in the various Western European countries.

According to figures provided by Carew, whereas technical assistance for Europe accounted for under $4 million (half of which was spent in Britain) in 1949, by the end of the Marshall Plan in 1952 the total had jumped to $43.6 million. A network of national productivity centers in each of the major countries of Europe was established, and these were supplemented with a European Productivity Agency (EPA) created in Paris in May 1953 to administer $100 million in funds. Other funds averaging $1.5 million annually were made available to the EPA by the US government until 1958, although the level of American funding dropped after 1956 and the EPA ceased operations in 1960.[5] The ostensible aim of these centers was to promote mechanisms for fostering productivity growth in industry, and more specifically to encourage through this a "depoliticized" industrial relations environment built on the rising wages made possible by rising levels of labor productivity of the sort that were believed to have made possible the towering wealth and productivity of the American economy.

The essential logic of the vision of industrial relations promoted under the productivity program is often referred as the "pie theory": "In brief, the theory suggested that managers and workers would do better cooperating to increase the size of the pie of industrial production than forever bickering over how best to divide it. If management and labor recognized their mutuality of interests, worked together to apply the 'neutral' principles of modern management, and submitted to the 'unpoliticized' dictates of technological rationality, productivity could be raised, costs lowered, and returns increased. By 'fairly' apportioning the gains (in the form of higher profits, better wages, and lower consumer costs), the demands of management and labor could be satisfied, and the interests of society at large could be served."[6] Another analyst adds:

> The American project contemplated a constructive interaction between industry and unions on a technical plane in a private rather than public setting. Labor and industry were supposed to negotiate on the basis of a common commitment to growth, a progressive acceleration of productivity, and an equitable and timely division of its benefits. This was supposed to take place against a macroeconomic background determined by the interaction of market forces and government policies that in theory were not to be negotiated among organized interests. The placement of unions in contract mechanisms was supposed to be at the company level or, at most, at the industrial sector level.[7]

And not, it might be added, in contests for control and influence over the state apparatus, as had been characteristic of European postwar labor politics up until that point. There was widespread support for this approach in the American labor movement based on the belief that the high-wage–high-productivity–high-consumption formula that it claimed to be pursuing in the US context constituted a universally valid prescription for the fundamental dilemmas of industrial capitalism.

Over the life of the program, thousands of managers and trade unionists from various European countries visited the United States to observe American industry firsthand. Reports and findings were disseminated via seminars, conferences, and publications made available by the various centers. Technical-assistance officers were sent into the field, and the program sponsored extensive public-relations campaigns that extolled the virtues of an American-style productivity orientation. However, the depoliticized approach to wages and productivity associated with the American model was not something that was easily attainable in the Western European context at the time.[8] To begin with, the American promotion of the productivity movement was in and of itself a highly political exercise, and

European unionists were quite aware of this. US foreign-policy makers believed that the program would make possible an "armed prosperity" that would circumvent negative economic consequences of the Cold War–inspired rearmament that the United States was pushing. Higher labor productivity during a period of rearmament would give an economy the increased production that it needed in order to assure that increased military expenditures did not become mired in the zero-sum trap of reduced expenditures in other areas or a reduction in real consumption through inflation. In other words, it was deemed that under the scheme "'guns and butter' were reconcilable."[9] Furthermore, the productivity movement was believed to be "a potent ideological weapon" for countering communist propaganda and that the Marshall Plan and MSA program were promoting exploitative practices that benefited capital at the expense of workers. It would, in other words, give the noncommunist wings of the European labor movements a means to appeal to rank-and-file workers in their competition with the communists and help to weaken "the pacifist tendencies running through European public opinion."[10]

On the receiving end of the productivity movement's appeals, Western European unions were not in a mood to treat productivity issues apolitically. Communist unions opposed the productivity drive unequivocally for foreign policy reasons, arguing that the program was a smoke screen for US imperialism. They were given a readily visible marker to exploit when, following the demise of the ERP, oversight of the productivity program was transferred to the militarization-oriented MSA program. Catholic unionists, and to a lesser extent social democrats, in turn, seized upon the productivity ideology as a weapon to be wielded against the communists. It was impossible under conditions like those in France and Italy where multiple wings of the labor movement competed for influence at the plant level to conclude meaningful productivity-based bargains. The CGT and CGIL would consistently press for immediate gains of astronomical proportions from management, and in an environment in which there was little credible evidence that management was ready and willing to uphold their end of the productivity bargain, moderate unions would be pressed to join in the bidding in order to husband the support of rank-and-file workers.[11] It was precisely for this reason that the FO, the CISL, and other French and Italian unions initially favorably predisposed to the productivity ideology, later found themselves compelled to reduce their level of open support. On the employers' side, the strength of the CGT worked as a disincentive in taking the productivity movement seriously. Kuisel's description of what happened in a French productivity pilot program is illustrative: "[Employers] knew the non-communist unions were weak—in most of the pilot foundries the CGT was the largest syndicate and the other syndicates were often altogether absent. Thus business leaders in the CNPF and the trade associations saw no value in reaching an accord at the national level with syndicates who could not control the work force at the plant level. The free syndicates were playing a weak hand, perhaps trying to use the productivity program to strengthen themselves vis-à-vis the rival CGT, and the employers knew it. Trade associations thus opposed any contractual agreements that would assure labor bonuses in advance, and the CNPF [the French employers' association] insisted that it could not impose collective bargaining and productivity contracts on either trade associations or on individual firms. Individual employers might be willing to cooperate, but organized business was not."[12]

Reticence about supporting the US productivity initiative also characterized the West German movement, even though a strong communist wing did not exist. While there were elements who were sympathetic toward the general ideas espoused, the US-sponsored program arrived at a time when West German unions, on the one side, and business and the ruling Christian democrats, on the other, were locked in a fierce struggle—and one that the unions ultimately lost—over codetermination. This was not a particularly good moment to ask German unionists to work with management. Beyond this, the fact that West German unions were organized as industrial unions meant that the center of gravity in the trade unions did not correspond to the firm-level locus of productivity decision-making on the management side. While something that amounted to the functional equivalent of the productivity-based industrial relations systems envisioned in the pie theory did emerge in West Germany, this disjuncture made it a less natural development than was the case in the enterprise-union-based Japanese system, as will be discussed below. Although the West German Deustcher Gewerkschaftsbund, or DGB, participated in the West German Productivity Center, this was said to have been as much a courtesy toward the American unions as it was any positive embrace of the productivity movement's principles.

The actual administration of the productivity movement in Europe revealed clearly that the program was ultimately unable to fully overcome the tendency in the American aid programs in Europe to relegate labor interests to a secondary priority behind business and military concerns. By far the largest proportion of those participating in the productivity delegations were managers, and in terms of the practices transferred, it was the importance of "scientific management" and capital investment as a means of fostering higher productivity that received the higher stress. The heaviest impact of the productivity movement occurred among managers in large "modern" enterprises. As for labor unions, it was not coincidental that the greatest relative successes in obtaining support were in countries like the UK or the Scandinavian countries, where the labor movements were unified, union density was high, union bargaining power was great, social democratic governments were in office, and where there was potential for mobilizing the power of the state to compel employers to keep there side of the bargain.[13]

Many analysts have claimed that the ultimate significance of the productivity movement for the evolution of Western European labor movements rested not in its intended short-term and direct impact on industrial relations but in a more diffuse and broader reshaping of attitudes and behavioral patterns in Western European industrial society. Carew, for instance, argues: "In the longer run the cumulative influence of a plethora of Marshall Aid-inspired productivity institutes, business schools, training centers, academic research and the conventional wisdom that they developed was pervasive throughout Europe. Cultural values, norms and expectations in industry were certainly changing by the end of the 1950s, and in this the Marshall Plan programs must be seen as an important conditioning force."[14] Although debts to the American-sponsored movement were almost never acknowledged openly, one can see this in emerging labor-movement strategies that increasingly focused on labor market issues and which, though contextualized in ideological frameworks different from that behind the productivity movement, nevertheless implicitly recognized the basic propositions articulated by the productivity movement's proponents.

Western Europe: the politics of productivity and the politics of confrontation

The unprecedented and sustained economic prosperity experienced by Western European capitalism from around 1950 onward came as a great surprise to many, if not most, labor movement activists steeped in the tenets of Marxism. As perhaps most baldly articulated in the PCF's "pauperization thesis," what most unionists and left-wing partisans expected from a revival of capitalism was a repeat of the instability and turmoil of the interwar years, so it is not surprising that adjusting to the new realities proved to be a considerable challenge. However, for better or worse, the respective wings of the labor movements were forced to adapt to the new reality. Spurred also by the decline in the salience of Cold War issues that occurred in tandem, such adaptation inevitably involved a greater role for labor market issues in the labor movement agendas and action. And when adaptation occurred, it was invariably mediated by the ideological tendencies present, the balance of power among competing wings, and the organizational characteristics found in a particular national movement.

One can usefully begin an outline of the historical trajectory of the West German labor movement by recalling that the end of World War II had left it with an ideological balance in which social democrats and left socialists predominated. A substantial Christian wing did exist, but it was one that was divided into Protestant and Catholic elements, and while influential, its relative weight in the DGB—estimated to be between 10 and 15 percent of the DGB membership—was not one that allowed it to play a defining role.[15] While communist elements were present, their numbers were exceedingly small, and they disappeared almost entirely once the party was ruled unconstitutional in 1956. What is more, the West German labor movement had emerged from the Cold War turmoil with its "organic unity" intact. That is, all of the major political tendencies in the West German labor movement—left socialist, social democratic, and Christian—were organized under the umbrella of a single union confederation. (A smaller Christian Catholic organization did break away from the DGB in the mid-1950s but did not constitute much of a challenge to the DGB.) This organic unity was ultimately highly significant for the West German labor movement's adaptation to the new political economy.

The lens of left-socialist unionism provided a key ideological filter through which the West German labor movement came to terms with the new prosperity. The failure of the DGB's politically focused program to bring about the sought-after social and economic reforms in the late 1940s induced reflection and a rethinking of the confederation's strategy. After becoming convinced that, thanks to capitalism's restoration, the day when social and political transformation could occur had receded for the foreseeable future, a group that came to be known as the "activists" began to advocate a "maximalist" wage policy that eschewed attempts to transform society in the short and medium term (which was to happen when labor grew strong enough to decisively overturn the existing political order) in favor of an approach that "endeavored to maximize the unions' effectiveness *within* the already set social and political pattern."[16] (Italics added.) Just how this was to be done was articulated by Viktor Agartz of the DGB's economic research institute, in an influential December 1953 article. Reinterpreting the experience of the US labor movement through a left-socialist lens, Agartz asserted that wage levels attained by workers were a reflection of the political strength of the working class vis-à-vis capital and, as such, the strengthening of bargaining power of unions equaled strengthening the organizational power of the working class. He also pointed out that the foremost demand of the rank-and-file was higher wages and improved working conditions, and he urged unions to aggressively pursue wage increases on behalf of their members as a way of increasing class power. Under this approach "wage increases should not in principle follow productivity but should exhaust union bargaining power to enlarge the wage share."[17] This, he argued, would have a broader transformative impact socially in that an "expansive wage policy" of this sort would stimulate consumption, increase demand, and serve as an engine for raising the living standards throughout society. Agartz's "radical socialist" wage policy was translated into action by Otto Brenner of IG Metall, the metalworkers' union, in the form of aggressive industry-level bargaining offensives for improved wages and benefits. This approach was supported by the chemical workers', printers', woodworkers', and leatherworkers' unions and was given official approval at the confederational level when the DGB incorporated the concept into an action program of its own, May Day 1955.[18]

The militancy and confrontational orientation of the expansive wage policy, however, was not universally supported inside the DGB. A group that came to be known as the "social partners," led by Georg Leber of IG Bau (the construction workers' union), countered with a labor movement strategy that drew on the traditional orientation toward participatory economic democracy on the part of Christian and social democratic unionists as well as on the tenets promoted under the productivity movement. What they proposed constituted the polar opposite of that put forward by Agartz and Brenner along many key dimensions. Where the activists thought in terms of having the labor movement function as a *gegenmacht,* or "countervailing force," in the West German political economy by maximizing labor's organizational strength and directing it against capital, the social partners sought to turn German labor unions into a "force of order" *(ordnungsfaktor)* that would work with capital in comanaging industry and economy. At the macro level, the social partners claimed that the activists' aggressive wage policy would simply create inflationary imbalances in the economy that would undercut the position of workers in the long run. As an alternative, they urged restraint in the form of moderate wage hikes attuned to "productivity-based or cost-neutral pay guidelines across the entire economy."[19] They also advocated working with employers to establish jointly managed institutional arrangements that would stabilize worker livelihoods and advance worker welfare. Prime examples here are the various labor-management-managed welfare funds created by Leber's construction workers' union. The same line of thinking would subsequently lead the DGB to pursue a scheme in which worker "participation" in industry would be furthered by a program in which union-controlled funds would invest in German industry, along with other schemes for furthering economic democracy.[20] An expansion of codetermination's coverage was also on the agenda.

Inside the DGB the late 1950s and early 1960s were consumed by a contest for hegemony between the social partners and the activists over the direction of the West German labor movement. The contest spanned both the trade-union and the political-party components of the movement since both the activists and the social partners maintained links with sympathetic groups in the SPD, who shared similar ideological perspectives. Ultimately, however, because the various ideological currents in the West German movement were housed in a common confederational umbrella, it was spared the delicate job of institutionalizing a framework for common action among competing independently organized ideological streams that the French and Italian had to confront. As noted, the DGB also possessed a built-in firewall of formal norms of neutrality toward political parties that helped keep partisan politics from disrupting trade-union integrity. Being housed in a common organization meant that the intensity of the confrontation between the activists and the social partners notwithstanding, there were strong centripetal pressures at work, ultimately serving to defuse differences and induce compromise. The intraorganizational contest for hegemony between the two sides within the DGB was ultimately resolved via a platform adopted at the DGB's Dusseldorf congress in 1963. The new platform was heavily imbued with the social partners' perspective but in a way that glossed the core with the more radical language of the activists.[21]

Adaptation to the new political and economic realities proved more arduous under conditions where communist and Christian wings confronted one another, as in France and Italy. Devoted as they were to universalistic doctrines intent on either overthrowing capitalism or protecting society from those bent on precipitating this eventuality, the impetus to seriously analyze the internal workings of capitalism was weak in the communist and Christian wings. As Ross observes about the French communists: "Old habits of reducing everything to politics were deeply ingrained in the CGT, in the leadership, and perhaps even more at the middle levels of the organization where party militants prevailed."[22] The decreased salience of the communist threat proved to be problematic for the Christian wings, and the old guard in particular, since these had put so much stock into the battle against communism. The years of denying the salience of class conflict in light of the essential harmony of labor-management interests had given them little incentive to think about the nature of capitalist industrial relations. As one historian of the subject observes: "Numerous Catholic commentators have pointed out that the CISL's assumptions during the 1950s concerning industrialization as the 'inevitable bearer' of automatic benefits and social improvements for all were accompanied by a lack of social analysis. One looks in vain in CISL documents for any reference to conflicting interests of social groups or forces. Social actors are absent from its discourse, so that power relations and the manner in which these affect social and political relations remain unexplored." In terms of union behavior, this led to a tendency on the part of CISL leaders to cooperate with managers while ignoring the hardships and difficulties that such cooperation generated for the workers involved.[23]

International shifts combined with the altered domestic political economy to initiate a gradual process of alteration among the communists. Ross summarizes how the communist-dominated CGT justified a focus on labor market issues using the observation that French industry had grown larger and more monopolistic with the assistance of the state (i.e., state monopoly capitalism):

As workers and others experienced the costs of monopoly rule in their productive lives they would be moved towards protest in the labor market. Given the tight connection between monopolies and the state, however, such protest, as it developed, would turn of its own accord towards broadly political themes. The CGT did not need to politicize the labor market unduly. The regime had already done this. What mattered for the CGT . . . was simply to promote the broadest possible mass mobilization out of labor-market protest. Working class anti-monopoly protest in the form of defensive, bread-and-butter unionism would, if properly nurtured by trade-union organizations, become the core of a larger social mobilization against the regime.[24]

For the PCI's Togliatti, the preferred formulation for articulating the party's rationale for the increased focus on labor market issues was "structural reform"— that is, that struggles in the labor market would yield incremental institutional reforms that, over time, would add up to a complete, revolutionary transformation of Italian capitalism.[25] The modality of justification mobilized by the French and Italian communists was thus not unlike that of the left socialists in West Germany in the sense that a focus on the labor market was articulated in Marxian terms as a continuation of revolutionary class struggle.

In the Catholic camp, failure by the prewar leadership to effectively deal with new issues led to growing rank-and-file dissatisfaction and defection. Even more problematic for the Catholic wing was the secularization rapidly eating away at its hold over its rank-and-file. The resulting organizational crises opened the way for a younger generation of leaders who, sustaining in a new political economic context the corporatist impulse built into the Catholic movement, promoted a unionism that overlapped with the economic democracy-oriented stance of the West German social partners. Among the schemes advanced by the CISL were plans for worker-savings investment schemes tied to state investment trusts.[26] Since secularization was more advanced in France, the decline of the traditional Catholic movement there was even more precipitous. In 1964 the CFTC underwent a "deconfessionalization," and to mark this change symbolically, it changed its name to the Confédération Française Démocratique du Travail (CFDT), or from the French *Christian* Confederation of Labor to the French *Democratic* Confederation of Labor.

West Germany's labor unions were characterized by an institutional structure that made it possible to "bargain" effectively with capital without the mediation of the state, but this did not hold for the French and Italian situations, and for that reason, labor market demands tended out of necessity to be directed at the state as political demands. As the lowered salience of global Cold War issues induced the Catholic and communist wings of the French and Italian labor movements to focus more on labor market issues, they began to find their objectives overlapping, and the two wings came to the conclusion that mutually agreeable unified action needed to be developed. But unlike West Germany, the competing ideological tendencies in France and Italy were housed in competing organizations. This meant overcoming organizational inertia and long-standing enmities reinforced during the preceding decade, necessitating a greater amount of energy and effort.[27] The communists' decision to loosen their transmission-belt relationship with the unions was an important factor in facilitating these efforts. To take the case of the PCI and its relationship with the CGIL, the party declared its decision to replace the party cell as the primary unit of organization in favor of geographically based organizations in 1956. As the formal affiliation of party cadres was shifted from the party to the CGIL, the number of factory cells declined steadily, and the formal organizational autonomy correspondingly increased. Such weakening of party-union links, in turn, made it easier for CGIL units to concentrate on labor market and industrial-relations concerns. The upshot, in the assessment of Miriam Golden, was that the 1960s proved to be a period in which "the union movement gradually acquired techniques of mobilization and organization appropriate to Italy's recently developed mass manufacturing industries."[28] These tended to be, furthermore, concerns that were shared with trade-union organizations affiliated with competing confederations.

In Italy the Catholic wing was linked to the ruling DC via the arena of party politics. This made the Italian DC governments sensitive to the demands of labor movement and willing to grant some degree of legitimacy to unions, particularly given that, as suggested by various electoral surveys, the DC tended to receive more votes from the working class than the PCI until well into the 1970s.[29] This attitude was especially true after the DC instituted its "opening to the left," which saw, in the wake of the Tambroni affair, establishment of a DC coalition government in late 1963 that included the left-socialist PSI. As one commentator on the process points out, concern with labor issues was very much behind this initiative since it was the belief on the part of the DC that "by involving the PSI in government it could, without conceding too much to a party with modest electoral support, satisfy the political demands of the working class" and, at the same time, "detach the PSI from PCI influence and marginalize the communists in the process."[30] In the meantime, both the CISL and the CGIL were actively promoting decentralized bargaining. The neo-corporatist impulses of the center-left coalition government and the unions' push for effective bargaining dovetailed following the explosion of labor unrest in 1969 when the center-left government, anxious to demonstrate its reformist credentials, passed labor legislation that dramatically strengthened union representation and bargaining at the shop-floor level.

In France the primary union actors in the industrial relations field turned out to be the formerly Catholic CFDT, on the one hand, and the communist-dominated CGT, on the other, rather than the socialist, American-encouraged FO. Over the course of the 1960s both worked aggressively to build a plant-level presence in French industry and to achieve the improvements in wages and working conditions that would allow the unions to attract French workers to their respective organizations. A number of joint actions were implemented from the early 1960s onward, although joint effort was regularly marred by differences over goals, strategy, and tactics. The communists, reflecting a preference for confrontational tactics with political resonance, focused on harnessing worker discontent and channeling these into large-scale national actions and concrete material gains. The CFDT, on the other hand, sought sustained local action and reflected a participatory orientation in its demands for *autogestion,* or democracy-oriented economic reforms that would enhance worker participation in industry.[31] Of the two, it was the communists' strategy that carried greater weight in determining the course of evolution in French industrial relations. Not only was it the bigger of the two unions with a greater presence among blue-collar industrial workers, but the centralized nature of the French political system tended to encourage centralized, state-mediated resolutions over resolutions mediated at the enterprise level. The problem, though, was that the center-right composition of the French political regime made it particularly unwilling to recognize the legitimacy of the communists as the representative voice of the labor movement. At the same time, the French state possessed a variety of powers over prices and wage levels that it chose to use to unilaterally respond to and, where necessary, to unilaterally placate the labor militancy as well as maintain a rough balance between wages and productivity growth in the economy. These factors made neo-corporatist bargaining impossible.

The left-socialist response in Japan: the Ōta-Iwai line and Shuntō

As in Western Europe, the years straddling 1955 saw reduction in East-West tensions that helped reduce the salience of Cold War issues in Japanese labor politics. By far the most important development in this regard was the signing of the armistice that ended the fighting in Korea, in July 1953. Beyond this, the conclusion of a bilateral Mutual Security Agreement during 1954 marked the completion of the basic arrangements for the Japan-US military alliance that would continue to this day. Although Sōhyō's massive extra-parliamentary protest over the revision and renewal of the US-Japan Security Treaty in 1960 would vividly demonstrate that Cold War issues were far from dead, it is noteworthy that the revisions themselves involved relatively minor adjustments to the Japan-US alliance system established in 1951, while the protests were as much about the internal political concerns as they were about foreign relations.[32] In 1956 Japan and the Soviet Union were able to sign a treaty "normalizing" their relations, thereby placing their Cold War conflict into a nonbelligerent framework, even as the formal state of war between the two countries continued.

In the economic arena, in a development that echoed the experience in Western Europe, by mid-decade Japan's economy was moving beyond economic recovery and beginning to experience an "economic miracle" of its own. The year 1955, in fact, is designated by Japanese economic historians as the first year of the "high-speed economic growth" that lasted between 1955 and 1972. During these years, double-digit GNP growth was accompanied by steady increases in labor produc-tivity, wages, and employment levels. In the process, Japan was transformed from a producer of textiles and cheap, labor-intensive manufactured items into a lead-ing exporter of highly capital-intensive goods like steel and shipbuilding and of technologically sophisticated products like automobiles and consumer electronics. It was therefore quite fitting that the government's 1955 economic white paper, alluding to the fact that the economy had put wartime devastation behind it and was embarking on an entirely new phase of economic development, should have declared that it was "the postwar era no longer."[33]

In a broad sense, the Japanese labor movement's response to this industrial modernization and economic prosperity resembled that of West Germany's in that it was a two-pronged reaction, which pitted a left-socialist initiative focused on wage struggles against a response from a segment of unionists who promoted an economic democracy-oriented accommodationism emphasizing working with management in adjusting to modernization while harmonizing the interests of labor and capital. However, rather than unfolding within a common organiza-tional framework and culminating in a synthesis, as in the case of West Germany, in Japan the two tendencies were segregated into competing confederations. And rather than setting the stage for eventual inclusionary governance and neo-corpo-ratist accommodation, the competition, in the context of the enterprise-based structure of the Japanese labor movement, had the effect of sustaining militancy and ambivalence toward Japan's democratic institutions on the left, a hyper-accommodationist stance on the part of the social partners, and division and exclu-sion from government for the labor movement as a whole.

The left-socialist initiative grew out of a reaction that surfaced from within Sōhyō's left-socialist contingent against what were perceived to be the excesses of the Takano line. By 1954 Takano's more extreme tactical maneuvering, the defec-tions from Sōhyō, and the series of defeats in high-profile strikes that occurred as Takano pushed Sōhyō deeper and deeper into Cold War politics began to alarm even those who had been key supporters of his policies. These misgivings burst into the open in the period leading up to Sōhyō's fifth national convention, held in July 1954. At the forefront of the dissident elements was Ōta Kaoru, the col-orful president of the synthetic chemical workers' union (Gōsei Kagaku Sangyō Rōdō Kumiai Rengō, or Gōka Rōren). The essence of Ōta's criticism of Takano's leadership was encapsulated in a policy resolution adopted by the Gōka Rōren central committee the preceding month that touched upon three areas.[34] The first was the place of political mobilization in a union's agenda. According to the Gōka

Rōren resolution, the problem with Takano's effort to make political mobilization the core activity of the Japanese labor movement was that it did not accord with certain basic realities, specifically: "The organizational principles of labor unions and political parties are of a fundamentally different nature. The political aims of workers organized in labor unions, whatever they might be, is not the issue . . . in this sense [a union] differs fundamentally from a political party where adherence to a specific political perspective is a condition of membership." The problem, according to the policy statement, was that "unless this point is properly taken into account during the implementation of political struggles, the two [types of organizational principles] will be confused and the delusion will consequently take hold that it is possible for a labor union to perform both the functions of a political party and those of a labor union." This, they maintained, was precisely what was happening in Sōhyō. The Sōhyō executive "was attempting to use labor unions in which the great majority of workers possess a low level of political consciousness to perform the role [of a political party]." As a consequence the executive tended to "ignore the [task of] guiding and assisting the wage hike and anti-rationalization struggles that are the fundamental struggles of Sōhyō's rank-and-file masses." The resolution went on to claim that these tendencies were exacerbated by the fact that Sōhyō headquarters staff was somewhat removed from the rank-and-file and often "mistook the actions of a limited radical element for an upsurge of the whole," resulting in "policies that went too far." "Even if the basic direction of a campaign is correct, unless it matches the consciousness of the rank-and-file masses and they can digest it fully," the statement warned, "it will not build up real power nor will the movement itself progress one bit." In a clear reference to Takano's recent mobilizations, it added that "if, on top of this, one goes on to initiate a series of campaigns while ignoring these situational realities, the struggle will flounder, and mistrust on the part of the rank-and-file masses toward the apparatus will be encouraged," providing opportunities for those who are against the union to divide and weaken it. The prescription offered was a shift in the focus of Sōhyō's endeavors along with institutional changes to assure that "the will of affiliated industrial federations is correctly reflected" in confederation policy. With regard to the former it stated that Sōhyō needed to devote more attention to the bread-and-butter issues that were closest to the hearts of the rank-and-file. On the latter, it recommended a reversal of current arrangements that gave the Sōhyō executive relative independence from the oversight of the member industrial federations. It proposed specifically that full-time directors be seconded from the industrial federations and assigned to Sōhyō headquarters and that the Sōhyō executive board *(kanjikai)* be filled only by people who were *concurrently* serving as an industrial-federation president.

The second broad area that the Gōka Rōren statement touched on was the way in which Takano had handled the peace movement. The document asserted the essential correctness of Sōhyō's promotion of the four principles of peace since 1951 and took exception to Takano's "peace force" thesis. In doing so it launched its criticism not on foreign-policy grounds or on principle, as in the case of the earlier secessionists, but on grounds that it was counterproductive tactically. The essential problem, it maintained, was that at the rank-and-file level there was little identification with the Soviet Union and therefore a neutralist policy would have considerably more appeal.

In addressing the last area, the Gōka Rōren statement quoted from the movement policy of the Kokurō union: "There will be no progress if all we do is label Zenrō and Shinsanbetsu as traitors and proclaim that not a single worker should be given over to the enemy. We should be unrelenting in pointing out errors, but the organization must always be pointed in the direction of unity. We demand that there be united action and a united front with Zenrō, Shinsanbetsu, other nonaffiliated unions, and unorganized workers." The key to bringing such a front about, it stated, was to establish a graduated approach to the pursuit of economic and political demands. Wage increases and opposition to dismissals, on which all unions can agree, should be put forward as a "minimum platform." Any additions to the platform beyond this—peace-movement-related demands, for instance—"should never involve compulsion" but should instead be addressed "with patience" and developed through a strengthening of joint action among organizations.

Over the course of the spring of 1954, the Rōdōsha Dōshikai, which in 1951 had been at the forefront of the campaign for the four principles of peace, was used as a base of operations for coordinating a campaign to unseat Takano and reorient Sōhyō's direction. Ōta's most prominent collaborator was Kokurō's Iwai Akira. Ōta, Iwai, and sympathetic supporters approached officials in key industrial federations and in mainstream leadership of the Left Socialist Party. The industrial-federation convention season that ran between April and July was punctuated by the adoption of action programs that echoed Gōka Rōren's criticisms of Takano-style unionism "as if agreed upon ahead of time."[35] Takano, who managed to retain the support of Nikkyōso, Zenchūrō, and Tekkō Rōren, countered by establishing a journal entitled *Kokumin* (The nation) that he used as a vehicle for defending his own line.[36] The climax of the contest between the two groups was the fifth Sōhyō convention held July 12 through 15, 1954. Those aligned with Ōta managed to secure key positions among Sōhyō's executive offices. Yet in the penultimate confrontation, the contest for the general secretary's position, Takano beat Ōta by a vote of 140 to 107 (with 12 blank votes cast). Perhaps even more than his electoral victory, it was the reception given to Takano's speech before the convention that suggested the spirit of Takano's politicized unionism still retained strong appeal among the assembled delegates despite the criticisms that had been launched against his leadership. Instead of the catcalls that were customary under such circumstances, Takano's impassioned two-hour-long speech was greeted by repeated rounds of applause from the gallery.[37]

Another part of the effort of Ōta and his allies involved the insertion of a section into Sōhyō's movement policy for that year that called on the confederation to lead a massive general strike for increased wages in early 1955. This they were able to do. Takano, however, was consumed by his Labor Plan campaign and did not act on the mandate. A frustrated Ōta then created an unofficial coordinating committee in which the coal miners' union, the private railway workers' union, Ōta's synthetic-chemical workers' union, the paper and pulp federation, and Kokurō were represented. Takano dismissed their effort as "labor aristocracy" dalliance and demanded that the wage offensive be retooled to reflect a broader, more populist mass base. Takano's own small- and medium-sized enterprise-based metalworkers' federation was then added along with two other federations. In the end, however, the committee's spring wage-bargaining offensive, or Shuntō as it came to be called, was mainly carried out by the original five federations.[38] Although not foreseen at the time, Shuntō rapidly became institutionalized and has served ever since as the primary medium for implementing wage bargaining in Japan.[39] The success of Shuntō, in turn, would propel Ōta and Iwai into the top leadership ranks of the confederation. Iwai was elected to the position of general secretary in a contest against Takano in 1955 and continued in that position until 1970. Ōta first became a vice president, in 1955, and served as president between 1958 and 1966. He remained an influential senior figure in the confederation thereafter. Thus, the period between 1955 and 1970 is rightly described as Sōhyō's Ōta-Iwai era.

In justifying Shuntō, Ōta and Iwai built on the themes that were featured in their campaign against Takano. They argued that rank-and-file-worker political consciousness in Japan was "behind" that of Western Europe and for that reason mobilizing workers politically required that union leaders appeal to a worker's economic self-interest. Economic demands attained through Shuntō, they argued, would demonstrate to the rank-and-file the utility and value of the labor movement, thereby winning their allegiance. Or, as Iwai explained it: "The intellectual framework within which the leadership at the time operated was that by stirring the passions of workers by raising wages dramatically through wage struggles—making them 'hot' was the phrase Ōta used—we could then harness their power on behalf of political issues."[40] It was in keeping with this logic that political demands were customarily attached to lists of Shuntō wage demands, and where possible, Shuntō was orchestrated in such a way that its strike waves could be interpreted as expressions of protests against specific government policies. Overall, Takano and Ōta-Iwai were thus in agreement—and typically left-socialist in orientation—on the point that the ultimate purpose of the labor movement remained that of promoting a larger political agenda. Nevertheless, Sōhyō's embrace of Shuntō implied a highly significant reversal of priorities in tactical terms. In Takano's way of thinking, political line should always serve as the pivot of a campaign and any "spontaneous" demands that might emerge from the rank-and-file, from the bottom up, should be carefully harnessed on behalf of the advancement of the line. Shuntō, by contrast, was orchestrated in accordance with a script written at the top, and spontaneity was deliberately suppressed in favor of regimentation.[41]

As Hiwatari Nobuhiro points out, Shuntō can be considered a functional analog of the centralized industry-wide and national bargaining practiced in many Western European nations in an enterprise-union-populated environment.[42] As such, Shuntō does not replace the enterprise-union-centered collective bargaining that is the core feature of the Japanese enterprise union system. Instead, it enhances the bargaining power of participating enterprise unions through scheduling and coordination. Under the Shuntō system, enterprise unions in an industry discuss their bargaining plans with one another ahead of time and establish a common wage-increase demand, a calendar delineating target dates for reaching settlements, and the timing and length of any planned strikes or other dispute actions. This latter practice accounts for the term "scheduled struggle" that is sometimes used to describe this approach to wage bargaining. This industry-level coordination is aimed at precipitating a pattern-bargaining effect in which high settlements in firms and industries early in the round ratchet up the subsequent settlements of other firms and industries. Shuntō, in short, is designed to compensate for structural weaknesses of enterprise unions in wage bargaining by imposing simultaneity and a cross-firm and cross-industry referencing structure as a substitute for the organizational structure found in a bona fide industrial union. It thereby increases the ability of individual enterprise unions to resist management arguments that an "excessive" wage hike or a strike would threaten the financial viability of the company. Ōta captured the essential logic when he compared the Shuntō process to children (enterprise unions) "holding hands in the dark."[43] Also associated with the Shuntō is the "base-up," which refers to an absolute or percentage increase in the per capita wage. A 10,000 yen base-up would thus refer to an increase in which the rise in a firm's total wage bill divided by the number of workers in the firm equals 10,000 yen. This formula, which carried over from earlier practice, was utilized under the thinking that it was particularly suited to Shuntō-style bargaining since it makes for easy comparisons across firms and across industries.

Despite—or perhaps because of—the blurring of political and economic goals, the scale of the annual Shuntō rounds expanded steadily over the years. From 1959 onward, Chūritsu Rōren joined Sōhyō in orchestrating the annual Shuntō round. The total membership of the unions participating in the 1956 Shuntō round were estimated at 3 million. By 1960, this figure had increased to

4.1 million and five years later to 6.5 million.[44] Public-sector wages were informally incorporated into the Shuntō process when it was agreed at a meeting between Prime Minister Ikeda and Sōhyō's Ōta in 1964 that public-sector wage increases would be indexed to those attained in the private sector. And although not officially acknowledged, Zenrō/Dōmei unions also began participating in Shuntō in a de facto sense when they began to schedule their wage bargaining in the spring and attune their demands to those being put forward by the Shuntō committee.

Japan: the social partners, Zenrō/Dōmei, and the productivity movement

A role similar to the alter-ego role that the social partners played against the activists in West Germany's DGB was played in the Japanese context by unionists associated with Zenrō. In the Japanese version this role was intertwined with a component of US Cold War policy, the productivity movement. Emphasis on economic democracy through participation in enterprise management was visible in Zenrō's founding charter, and the promotion of economic democracy continued to serve as a source of organizational identity and a major point of policy emphasis. Like their West German counterparts, Zenrō's social partners maintained that economic democracy could be attained only under conditions where there was cooperation between management and labor and where unions were sensitive to the objective conditions of industry and the national economy. To quote from the Zenrō charter regarding the latter point: "It is absolutely essential that workers not look only at their own economic and social interests but instead pay attention to the welfare of all citizens, establish various plans and policies appropriately correlated with the national economy, and accompany this with constructive activity that contributes to the raising of production levels and the advancement of industry."[45] Statements of this kind peppered Zenrō pronouncements thereafter. The Zenrō labor movement strategy thus posited an active, facilitative role for unions in economic modernization. Not surprisingly, Zenrō was highly critical of the Shuntō process. According to Zenrō, Shuntō's focus on maximizing wage hikes in the name of class conflict was lacking in even the most basic sensitivity to the needs of the national economy.

As in Europe, the productivity movement came to Japan as a component of the US containment policy—specifically in the MSA program—but in contrast to what happened in Western Europe it had a fairly direct and profound impact on Japanese industrial relations.[46] There are several reasons why the productivity movement was met with a more positive response by the labor movement in the Japanese context. One was timing. Rather than coming at the height of Cold

War militarization, the productivity program arrived in Japan as Cold war tensions were beginning to ease. As a result, its association with the bipolar struggle at the international level, although clearly there, was less prominent than was the case several years earlier in Europe. A second reason is the jurisdiction of the enterprise union coincided in most cases with the unit of economic decision-making in capitalism (i.e., the firm). This meant that Japan's enterprise-based union system was particularly well-suited structurally for the application of productivity-based labor-management bargaining at the heart of the practices promoted in the productivity campaign. Third, Japanese managers proved much more willing than their European counterparts to embrace the kinds of industrial-relations practices associated with the program.

Following through in late 1953 on the administrative framework laid out in the Mutual Security Act and its subsequent guidelines as well as the precedent of American policy in Europe, an official from the US embassy in Tokyo approached Gōshi Kōhei, a Keizai Dōyūkai officer, and solicited his and his organization's cooperation in the establishment of an MSA-sponsored technical exchange program. Approaching Gōshi was fortuitous, for several years earlier he had made a trip to Europe, where he was deeply impressed by the program and was highly enthusiastic about its industrial-relations component. Their meeting culminated, after a relatively short period of time, in the establishment of the Japan Productivity Center (Nihon Seisansei Honbu), inaugurated on February 14, 1955, ostensibly a tripartite "foundation incorporating managers, labor and knowledgeable experts" that would direct "its utmost effort to raising productivity" in the Japanese economy. The JPC appealed to the labor unions by declaring its loyalty to what it called the "three principles of productivity": (1) that increased productivity will, in the long run, increase employment but that measures should be taken to minimize the unemployment that can result in the transition to higher productivity, (2) that methods for increasing productivity should be worked out through deliberation between labor and management, and (3) that the gains from productivity should be distributed fairly among management, workers, and consumer. Sōhyō immediately dismissed the JPC and the productivity movement as disingenuous efforts to further US Cold War aims and to dupe workers into aiding in their own exploitation.[47] Zenrō ultimately demurred on formal affiliation as well, but did agree to cooperate with the JPC. The Seamen's Union, one of Zenrō's key members did, however, agree to "join" the JPC, and two of its officials were put on the JPC's board of trustees in the fall. By around 1958–1959, it was clear that JPC activities involving labor unions had gained a momentum of their own as union participants themselves began to actively spread the principles of productivity that had been hashed out in the JPC. A milestone in November 1958 was the holding of a National Labor Union Productivity Central Debate Gathering (Zenkoku Rōso Seisansei Chūō Tōron Shūkai). Three hundred and fifty union delegates representing 2.5 million union members—approximately one-third of unionized workers at the time—were reportedly present at the conference designed to propagate productivity ideology among Japanese unionists. Furthermore, by the early 1960s it was becoming increasingly clear that the constituency for productivity-oriented unionism had spread beyond its base in Zenrō and Sōdō-mei. An increasing number of Sōhyō-affiliated unionists were in fact taking part in these activities, prompting the JPC's journal to declare: "Although Sōhyō, Zenrō, and the independents might as organizations have different struggle policies, the fact that the labor unions have come to a consensus on the common stage known as the productivity issues represents a completely new direction . . ."[48] Capping this horizontal spread of productivity-oriented unionism was the establishment in 1964 of the International Metalworkers' Federation-Japan Council (IMF-JC) that combined industrial unions—from both Sōhyō and Zenrō's successor confederation, Dōmei—of the electrical machinery, shipbuilding, automobile, steel, and other industries into a single organization under an ideological banner built on the productivity principles.[49]

As in Europe, the primary administered component of the productivity movement was technical exchanges. Between 1955 and 1961, 392 teams consisting of almost 4,000 people were sent primarily to the United States on three- to six-week "productivity tours." Corporate executives constituted the overwhelming majority of those who participated, and when they did they used these opportunities for exposure to advanced US technology and management methods. However, the number of labor union leaders participating grew over time, and by 1961 about one-fifth of the team memberships consisted of labor union officials. Not surprisingly, Zenrō and Sōdōmei unionists made up the bulk of these labor participants, but it is noteworthy that some officials from Sōhyō-affiliated unions were involved as well.[50]

Even more important than the study tours, however, was research and analysis conducted under the auspices of the JPC that aimed to concretize ways to institutionalize the productivity principles. Of particular importance here was the work of the JPC's Committee on Productivity Measurement and Distribution (Seisansei Sokutei Iinkai) and the Special Committee on Productivity Councils (Seisansei Kyōgikai ni Kansuru Tokubestu Iinkai). The most important recommendation to emerge from these discussions was that of using the firm-level *keiei kyōgikai* (labor-management councils) as permanent mechanisms through which to institutionalize labor input during the process of introducing new plants and equipment and in determining how to distribute the increased income that would be generated by the resulting increased productivity. The data does indicate a steady spread of labor-management consultation systems from 1955 onward, with joint consultation more institutionalized in larger firms than in smaller ones. Furthermore, a variety of industrial practices consistent with the tenets of the productivity principles began to be systematically implemented by firms' management.[51]

In the meantime, the ruling conservatives also began to adopt policies that were supportive of the firm-level labor-management accommodation being promoted by the JPC and the productivity movement. Following the resolution of the Security Treaty and Miike crises of 1960, the Liberal Democratic Party, or LDP, under Ikeda Hayato moved away from Kishi's politics of confrontation in favor of maintaining a "low-posture" approach that emphasized economic policy. The centerpiece of this was the so-called Income Doubling Plan in which the government promised to double national income over the course of a decade through massive infrastructural investments that would encourage firms themselves to engage in large capital investments and thereby increase industrial productivity and, through this, the national standard of living. It was also during Ikeda's tenure that the LDP began to work on what emerged in June 1966 as the LDP's "labor charter." Said to have been modeled after the British Conservatives' Butler Charter, the LDP's labor charter, on paper at least, shifted the LDP away from its habit of viewing the labor issue largely as a law-and-order issue. "The goal of our politics," declared the ruling-party charter, "is to strive to stabilize and improve the lives of workers, to guarantee opportunities to freely apply their creativity and effort, and to establish the conditions through which working people can enjoy fulfilling lives as human beings."[52] However, while the LDP might have begun taking a "softer" approach to dealing with labor issues, at no point during the 1955–1965 period did it make any move to institutionalize a system of corporatist consultation. With perhaps the one arguable exception of the 1964 Ōta-Ikeda "summit" that was scheduled under the threat of a Sōhyō general strike, any "accommodation" by the LDP to the labor movement was unilateral in nature.

Japan: continuing division and militancy

At a sufficiently high level of abstraction, it is possible to see an essential functional compatibility between the productivity-oriented unionism centered in Zenrō and the confrontational industry-focused wage struggle of Sōhyō's Shuntō campaigns. That is, the expansion of the "pie" via the smooth implementation of productivity-enhancing investments that the former's accommodationist unionism made possible can be seen as having generated the expanding surplus that was distributed to workers under pressure from the tactics that Sōhyō utilized in its annual wage rounds in a way that leveled wage differentials. The combination can be seen as the two sides of the same Fordist coin or, alternatively, as a kind of functional counterpart of the "dual system" of industry-level wage bargaining and firm-level wage drift that Thelen describes for West Germany.[53] At the level of labor politics, however, this functionality was sustained in an atmosphere of heated recrimination and confrontation between proponents of the two competing approaches. Why? The two tendencies were embedded in separate national organizations, with the competition between them exacerbated by the enterprise-union-based organizational structure of the Japanese labor movement.

At the firm and plant levels during the late 1950s and early 1960s, the internal politics of Japanese enterprise unions was characterized by contestation between competing factions operating according to left-socialist (and communist) class-conflict models and those promoting Zenrō-style accommodation, a situation that Sōhyō described in terms of an "XYZ thesis." According to this thesis, enterprise unions were seen as a battle zone over which pro-labor-movement activists (the X group), and pro-management activists (the Y group) competed for the allegiance of the larger mass of uncommitted members (the Z group).[54] In comparative terms, this was a milieu more like the intercurrent competition found in French and Italian factory councils than the more politically neutral works councils of West Germany. This intra-enterprise competition, in turn, was carried over into battles for control over the industrial federations. Shifting balances of power between X and Y groups in constituent enterprise unions would be reflected in changes in the factional balance inside an industrial federation, or else among federations where more than one existed. This would, in turn, translate into shifts in the balance of power between Sōhyō and Zenrō/Dōmei as these shifting balances at lower levels affected the number of unionists affiliated with one or the other confederation.

Over the long term, the decentralized structure of the Japanese labor movement favored the accommodationists. Because the scope of the enterprise union coincided with the unit of management, competition inside Japanese unions was much more open to management intervention and manipulation than would be the case in, for instance, an industrial union where the headquarters of the union is located outside of the enterprise. Consistent with this logic, accounts of inter-factional competition at the enterprise level during this period describe "informal groups" organized or closely associated with management jockeying for control of unions with militant leftist activists.[55] Furthermore, because "sovereignty" rested at the enterprise level, constituent enterprise unions were in a position to simply ignore the directives from militant industrial federations and adopt a moderate stance. The reverse, however, was not the case since successful militancy was highly dependent on cooperation and solidarity across an industry, thereby putting the advocates of confrontation at a distinct disadvantage. The demographics of the era of high-speed growth, too, worked in favor of the accommodationists. The rapid expansion of private-sector employment in industries dominated by Dōmei unions resulted, in the mid-1960s, in the number of private-sector workers affiliated with the moderate confederation surpassing those affiliated with

Sōhyō. For the left-socialist wing of the labor movement, these circumstances provoked never-ending fears of an accommodationist sellout to management and capital. To use the expression that Ōta and Iwai favored, there was a constant fear that through the advance of accommodationist unionism, enterprise unions, and the Japanese labor movement along with them, would be "reeled into" *(nomeri-komu)* capitalism.[56]

The perception that the labor movement suffered from fundamental weaknesses in both its union and party components, faced a hostile socioeconomic and political environment, and was grounded in a politically unsophisticated rank-and-file had the effect of inducing Ōta, Iwai, and those in the Sōhyō mainstream to put a premium on radicalism in the JSP.[57] That is, where Sōhyō was under siege from the capitalists and the social partners in the trade-union arena and burdened by political functions that could not yet be effectively performed by the JSP, which taxed its mobilizational capacities, a radical stance in the arena of party politics was seen as necessary to counterbalance the capitalist forces that were "reeling in" the labor movement. A vivid illustration of the consequences of this attitude on the part of the Sōhyō mainstream can be seen in their derailing of the JSP's "structural-reform thesis" line.[58] As noted earlier in this chapter, the structural-reform thesis refers to the line of Marxian thinking associated with the PCI that grew out of the party's effort to adjust to the conditions generated in Italy by industrial modernization and the toning down of the Cold War. At the heart of the thesis was the idea that the appropriate path to socialism was through accumulation of incremental reforms achieved within the framework of a democratic and capitalist political economy. Labor movements, in this view, were expected to focus not on constructing or waiting for crisis conditions to foment socialist revolution, but to instead confront capital and the state within the system in order to squeeze out of them "structural reforms" that would gradually limit the power of capital.

The ideas associated with the thesis were introduced into Japanese Marxian circles in Japan and were picked up with particular enthusiasm by the staff of the JSP secretariat. The thesis was in fact formally incorporated into the party's platform in late 1960. Championing the new platform was the acting party chairman, Eda Saburō. Inside Sōhyō there were a number of other prominent champions of structural reform as well, and many of the key proponents were individuals who had until then been strong supporters of the Ōta-Iwai line. The structural-reform line, however, was gradually abandoned by the party, primarily because of opposition by Ōta and other Sōhyō figures who had allied themselves with the radical left-socialist group the Shakaishugi Kyōkai (Socialism Association). Subscribing to the classical Marxian view that true socialist revolution could only be attained through a systemic crisis of capitalism, they thought that until this occurred the best thing for the labor movement to do was to concentrate on raising the political consciousness of the working class. Ōta and Iwai, along with Sakisaka Itsurō of the Socialism Association, published several widely read articles denouncing the structural-reform line.[59] Thanks to the Sōhyō leadership's intervention—the Sōhyō mainstream leadership's voice naturally carried great weight in the party, since they supplied the largest part of the party's funding—by the mid-1960s structural reform, which had at the start of the decade been greeted with great enthusiasm as the vehicle that would take the JSP down the road to governance, was effectively marginalized.

Ironically, Ōta himself—who had visited Italy around this time and conferred with the PCI's Togliatti on the subject—admitted that he was not opposed to structural reform on either philosophical or theoretical grounds:

> I am not opposed to the structural-reform thesis per se or the structural-reform thesis generally. But when there are people in the JSP who are so strongly linked to capitalists that they will take money from them and who are not willing to sacrifice, I maintain that where many lack devotion, structural reform would turn into "reformism."
>
> As for the Sōhyō connection, I thought that if you were to adopt the structural-reform thesis where the JSP would be relying on [private-sector unions] that can't even implement a one-day strike and where public-sector unions won't even pull off a half-day strike because they claim they don't have the right to strike, you would not have much of a struggle.[60]

It was, in a nutshell, the old fear that an organizationally weak and divided labor movement grounded in an ideologically and politically unsophisticated rank-and-file was going to be reeled in by capital. It is revealing in this context to look at how Ōta compared Japanese labor's situation with the conditions extant in the home base of structural reform. At a press conference held upon his return from a forty-day visit to Europe in February 1961, Ōta ventured that "several conditions and experiences are necessary if [structural reform] is to succeed." He then went on to point out basic historical conditions conducive to a successful implementation of structural reform that applied to Italy but not Japan. First, he pointed to Italy's wartime resistance experience. That is, unlike Japan, which was unilaterally liberated by the Allied occupation forces after the end of World War II, the Italians themselves had fought against fascism. He noted that even after the war there were numerous instances where Italian conservatives and progressives had taken joint action in response to pressures from the people. Third, he claimed that thanks to their incumbencies in certain local governments, "democratic forces" had experienced considerable success in implementing Togliatti's Piano del Lavoro. Finally, he pointed out that there had been nationalizations in Italy in the war's aftermath. Although originally intended to assist monopoly capital, democratic forces were now in a position to make structural reform work by using state enterprises to weaken the power of monopoly capital. He also noted that the constitution the Italian resistance coalition had produced was much more progressive in character than Japan's. In the absence of comparable experience in mass action, multiparty coalition joint action, and controls on monopoly capital, any attempt to apply structural reform tactics in Japan would turn into either an empty intellectual exercise or dangerous and counterproductive reformism.[61] It was doubly ironic, then, that many of the leading industrial unions in Sōhyō were themselves pursuing "policy change struggles" *(seisaku tenkan tōsō)* that were organized along the lines of the structural-reform thesis.

In any event, Sōhyō's leadership under Ōta and Iwai consistently pressured the JSP to adopt left-leaning policies throughout the late 1950s and 1960s. This, in turn, drove the phenomenon that came to be known as the JSP's "left-wing spring" *(sayoku bane)*—that is, the characteristic behavior pattern when the party, led by its parliamentary delegation, moved toward moderation, and the activists from Sōhyō and local party branches would protest and push the party back to the left.[62]

Beyond the narrower dynamics of union confederation–political party relations, there were several other systemic factors that contributed to Sōhyō's continuing militancy. First, in contrast to the political fluidity set in motion by peaceful coexistence in Europe, political trends were locked in Cold War confrontation in Japanese party politics at the domestic level. Thus, students of Japanese political history will recognize 1955 as not just a turning point for Japan's economy but as a watershed year in party politics, marking the emergence of the so-called 1955 system that would define Japanese politics for nearly four decades thereafter. The year is perhaps most commonly remembered for the merger of the two leading conservative parties, the Liberals and the Democrats, into the pro-American Liberal Democratic Party (LDP) that occurred in November and launched the latter party's thirty-eight years of uninterrupted majority rule. (This rule in fact continued into the next century, after a brief interruption, via various coalition arrangements.) It is also remembered for a second political milestone that preceded the conservative merger by a month, the reunification of the Right and Left Socialist parties, in October, that created what is considered the pacifist-neutralist alter ego of the LDP. Like the LDP, the JSP as the largest opposition party was a primary fixture of the Japanese political system well into the 1990s. A third, less well known, watershed event that occurred that year in the Japanese party-politics arena was the sixth national conference of the JCP, which marked the de facto return of that party to "legalism." Although present in only embryonic form at the time, the sixth national conference started the party down the road to a Japanese brand of independent Eurocommunism and to a return to being a legitimate player in Japanese party politics. These events together marked the formation of the 1955 political system characterized by continual governance by a conservative majority, and an opposition camp with sufficient parliamentary representation to prevent constitutional revision.

At the international level, even though the mid-1950s had brought relative stability and predictability to Japan's relations with its immediate neighbors, international relations in Asia remained markedly more fluid, complicated, and dangerous than in Europe from the latter half of the 1950s through the 1960s. Even though the Korean War armistice and the Geneva Accords of 1954 had clearly brought about a reduction of Cold War tensions in the East Asia, a variety of potential flashpoints in the form of local insurrections tied to communist groups permeated Southeast Asia well into the 1960s. And whereas Europe was characterized by a bipolar structure of international relations, the regional structure in Asia was better described as tripolar, with the strong current of neutralism led by India's Jawaharlal Nehru and Indonesia's Sukarno adding the third rallying point to the Soviet- and American-led camps. China remained an ambiguous presence as a primary player in both the Eastern bloc and in the nonaligned camps. That East Asia remained an unstable and dangerous neighborhood would be uncontrovertibly illustrated by the US war in Vietnam and the Sino-Soviet split.

If peaceful coexistence helped to decrease the salience of Cold War issues in

Table 10. Major Sōhyō campaigns 1960–1970

Year	Political	Legal	Livelihood
1960	Security Treaty Revision		
1961	Political Violence	Coal Miners'	
	Prevention Law	Reemployment Law	
1962			
1963	Nuclear Submarines		
	(Yokosuka)		
1964			
1965	Japan–South Korea Treaty	Dreyer Recommendation;	
		ILO Ratification, Public Sector	
		Workers' Commission	
1966	Vietnam War (to 1975)	Public Sector Workers'	
		Commission	
1967		Public Sector Workers'	
		Commission	
1968	Okinawa Reversion,		
	Nuclear Submarines	Public Sector Workers'	
		Commission	
1969		Public Sector Workers'	
		Commission	
1970	Security Treaty Revision	Public Sector Workers'	Pollution May Day
		Commission	

Source: *SYS*, 2:332–333.

labor politics in Western Europe and to introduce fluidity to politics domestically, Japan's situation might be best described as one in which the Cold War's impact had been toned down but not so much that it lost its primacy in labor politics. This, in turn, sustained a certain structural rigidity in Japanese labor politics domestically. Specifically, the unstable and conflict-ridden regional environment and the institutionalization of Cold War politics in the Japanese party system combined to create a historical context in which Cold War-related international relations would spur Sōhyō to mount extra-parliamentary political mobilizations with considerable regularity, as table 10 illustrates. Zenrō (after 1964, Dōmei) and its affiliated party, the Democratic Socialist Party (DSP), which split from the JSP under Nishio's leadership in 1960, would then predictably react by denouncing these mobilizations as a blatant violation of fundamental labor-movement principles. Zenrō-Sōhyō enmity was heightened as the JCP shifted to an independent Eurocommunism in the middle 1960s. Its doing so brought the party to a stand in international relations that was not all that different from the left socialists' neutralism and made the party a potentially attractive coalition partner for the JSP. This, however, was an eventuality that the social democrats in Zenrō and the DSP were unwilling to countenance. Finally, the continuing quest by the public-sector unions for a return of the right to strike that MacArthur had taken away from them in 1948 meant that they continued to take a strong interest in assuring that Sōhyō maintained its muscle in the political arena.

Conclusion

D uring the half century that spanned the start of World War I
and the early 1960s, industrial societies and labor movements
wrestled with the question To what end would the newfound power and influence of the organized working class be directed? Would this power be harnessed
on behalf of a transformative sociopolitical revolution aimed at bringing down
the existing sociopolitical order, or would it be contained and delimited within
the parameters of capitalism and authoritarianism, totalitarianism, or pluralist
democracy? Any of these alternatives required an adjustment of the relationship
between existing sociopolitical structures and the ideological and organizational
character of organized labor. As we have seen, adjustments occurred in a complicated context in which globality, ideology, and the political-war mobilization
weighed heavily in the shaping of national-level outcomes. In the case of the pres-
ently advanced industrialized countries of Western Europe, an extended period
characterized by complex and constantly shifting patterns of globally linked political mobilizations of labor was followed by a certain degree of stabilizing—alternatively, a "settling"—of the social, political, and economic roles of national labor
movements as the relevance of global strategic concerns to national labor movements was dramatically reduced.

As detailed in preceding narratives, key features of these stabilizations/set-
tlements can be traced to the distinctive national-level dynamics of a global historical process in which the primary axis of global conflict shifted from the Allied-
Axis conflict of World War II to the East-West conflict of the Cold War. Modes
of thought concerning the social and political significance of the newly emergent
industrial working class that appeared in the nineteenth century had, by the interwar years, solidified into clearly defined, competing approaches to the political
mobilization of labor. These, in turn, were embedded organizationally in political
parties and trade unions and expressed in political action in complex ways, though
the overall geopolitically shaped trend was a shift from ideologically based division to unity in opposing fascism. With capitalism discredited and labor focused

on establishing a broad-based popular front, the immediate post–World War II years saw labor movements play a central role in the reconstruction of national sociopolitical and economic orders devastated by war. One common outcome was the impetus to establish sociopolitical and economic arrangements that hovered between reform and revolution, and added a socialistic or, alternatively, a modified capitalist cast to the Western European political economies. As we have seen, the extent to which these visions were translated into concrete institutional forms was strongly determined by the factor of geopolitical location. The onset of the Cold War from 1947 onward, however, led to a rollback of the fuzzy political compromises of the immediate postwar period. Although substantial divergences from the free-market ideal were tolerated, a US-sponsored recovery program mandated that Western Europe's recovery would occur within an international-trade and monetary regime that was in principle open, liberal, and capitalist. One of the consequences of this pendulum swing in historical direction was that the resulting capitalist restoration was not one that pushed the pendulum all the way back to the unrestrained capitalism of the interwar years but remained informed to a greater or lesser extent by socialistic legacies from the immediate postwar years. These legacies ranged from the constitutional clause that declared Italy to be a "republic of labor" and France's rudimentary welfare arrangements to the institutions of codetermination in the iron and steel industries in contemporary Germany.

Having said this, one must be quick to note that it was a capitalist restoration nonetheless, and to the extent that it was, labor movements in these countries were forced to adapt in some way to the realities of a market economy. Furthermore, the labor politics that emerged, though considerably less dynamic than what was seen in the preceding decades, were not static and continued to be characterized by an evolutionary trajectory driven mainly by the internal dynamics of national labor movements. This transition has often been characterized as a process in which labor movements came to "accept" capitalism. While not patently false, such a blanket characterization masks important nuances and complexities that were a product of the legacies of the preceding decades, which were covered in some detail in the preceding chapters and which are at the root of significant cross-national variations in the structure and behavioral patterns of national-level labor movements. Within the Western European context these included things like the centralized, divided, and partisan but weak-at-the-grassroots organizational format of France and Italy, or the unified, organizationally strong, politically more moderate format of the West German movement.

Clearly some parts of the labor movement "accepted" capitalism. The archetypal example of the abandonment of earlier radical goals can be found in the famous renunciation of Marxism by West German social democrats at the SPD's famous Bad Godesberg conference of 1959 and the DGB Dusseldorf convention of 1963 that paved the way for the West German labor movement to play the role of a core "social partner" supporting the Cold War–era sociopolitical order.[1] But in other instances, as for France and Italy, dominant segments remained fundamentally opposed to capitalism. This, in and of itself, however, did not mean that the order could not be "stabilized," for the geopolitical context allowed for the parts to fall into place in other ways.[2] In the state-centric labor politics of France, as Wall notes, the state quite fittingly took on the role of administering a variety of Fordism by effectively indexing wages—industrial as well as social—to productivity gains in the economy. Ironically, the very political hostility between the state and France's largest union organization worked to sustain the "virtuous cycle" of French Fordism: "These policies were deliberately followed because . . . the government hoped to win workers from the CGT." The CGT was faced with a situation in which it was forced by rank-and-file pressure to go along with the state's "politics of productivity" in the labor market while justifying its existence with political mobilizations directed at the state, and hard political stances that would earn it credit for extracting concessions from the state and capital.[3] Given the parallels with France, it is not surprising to find that the system worked similarly in Italy, albeit under conditions where the Communist-dominated CGIL reacted with considerably more creativity and innovation than did the CGT.[4] Even in the case of West Germany, as discussed in the preceding chapter, the labor movement's shift in course was closer to a reconstitution and redirection of goals of social transformation than it was an outright abandonment of them. And while the various ideological wings of the labor movement adjusted to this new capitalist environment of industrial modernity and worked within that system, their acceptance of its legitimacy varied depending on the ideological heritage of that particular segment.

As we have seen, Japanese labor's transition in the latter half of the twentieth century can also be seen as a product of the same global-historical process. During the interwar years, Japan, too, experienced the emergence of the same intense, ideologically based internal divisions in its emerging labor movement and subsequently the pendulum swing that pushed the Japanese political economy from a modified capitalist basis toward a restored capitalist political economy. Although the details and permutations differed in accordance with the specifics of Japan's geopolitical location within the political-historical space in which the shift from Allied-Axis to Cold War confrontation occurred, similar forces were at work and interacted in similar ways. And, as in the case of the Western European labor movements that have been tracked in preceding chapters, the reduced impact of global-level Cold War conflict in the mid-1950s set the stage for a relative stabilization of the structure, status, and role of the Japanese labor movement. Growing as it did out of the same geopolitical process, Japan's settlement contained many of the same elements found in the French, Italian, and West German stabilizations, albeit combined and integrated in a distinctive way.

The key divergence in the Japanese case was the enterprise-union-based institutional structure that the distinctive geopolitical context of the ending of World War II in East Asia left the Japanese labor movement. From the standpoint of stabilization, the significance of this legacy was that it provided the soil in which a Fordist "politics of productivity" would take root in Japan.[5] The firm-level productivity bargains that began to be struck, symbolically in the JPC and more concretely at the firm level in Japan's major corporations thereafter, can be considered to have roots in the *keiei kyogikai*-centered reconstruction efforts of the 1946–1948 period, which were similar in spirit to counterpart arrangements in Western Europe at the time. The difference between the Japanese and the Western European experience rests in the factors that prevented the Japanese labor movement from attaining the institutionalization of these forms in the early postwar period. Key among such factors were the American occupation's preference for an American model of industrial relations, and the structural decentralization of the Japanese movement itself. Another was political circumstances. With accommodation in the arena of party politics blocked by the polarization over the defense-and-security policy that was also spilling over into public-sector labor relations, the pressure for accommodation between labor and capital was, in effect, forced onto private-sector firms. It was only belatedly—well into the 1970s —that the political environment relaxed sufficiently for it to even begin to openly embrace this accommodation and to expand its application.

In the Japanese instance, the contrasting unionisms of the Ōta-Iwai line and Zenrō, and by extension those of Sōhyō and Dōmei, provided the motor for the Japanese labor movement's "settlement" vis-à-vis mid-twentieth-century Japanese capitalism. The Ōta-Iwai line that dominated Sōhyō drew heavily on the noncommunist left-socialist heritage of the Japanese labor movement, with its orientation toward husbanding the organizational resources and political influence of the working class, but shifted the emphasis therein to union attainment of higher wages. By embracing economism on behalf of political transformation, this effectively redirected much of the organizational power of the labor movement away from the goal of toppling the sociopolitical order while leaving its ultimate revolutionary ideological goals and rhetoric intact. Sōhyō entrenched itself firmly in the role of a countervailing force that kept the conservative government and management on their toes and accommodative toward the more moderate wing of the labor movement. Zenrō/Dōmei unionism, on the other hand, drew heavily on the cooperative social-democratic-right tradition dating back to the prewar Sōdōmei, but "democratized" it and added to it a strong organization-oriented ethos, thereby allowing this brand of unionism to serve as a force pushing the system toward the firm-level accommodations that helped to expand the Fordist economic "pie."[6]

The history of the Japanese labor movement between 1945 and 1955 was in many ways a history of a series of ultimately unsuccessful attempts by national-level union leaders to restructure the movement and place it on an alternative, presumably more effective, organizational footing for promoting the interests of the Japanese working class. Ōta Kaoru's invention of Shuntō marks Sōhyō's de facto acceptance of the status quo of union organization. Effectively abandoning the goal of reconstituting the movement on a non-enterprise-union footing, Sōhyō under Ōta and Iwai worked within the framework of the labor movement's existing organizational structure. Though Ōta himself would later call for an abandonment of Shuntō on grounds that it was not serving the purpose that he had intended for it, the fact that Shuntō as *the* core institution of collective bargaining in Japan continues to survive nearly a half century after its first application underlines just how spectacularly well adapted it was to the socioeconomic and political environment of Japan from 1955 onward.[7]

As this narrative and analysis make clear, the globality of the Japanese labor movement's internal ideological divisions and their various political mobilizations of Japanese labor provide a lens through which we can see the dynamic processes that drove the movement's twentieth-century history. It was not so much that geopolitics at the global level impacted labor movements at the domestic level, as it is perhaps most commonly conceived, but rather a matter of labor movements and their activities having been intimately intertwined with global-level geopolitics in a mutually interactive process. In fact, in key ways, the Cold War divisions that split the globe originated in the divisions experienced in the labor movements of Europe and Japan during the 1920s. And when the bipolar international confrontation took hold in the late 1940s, the object of contestation was the hearts and minds of labor movement activists in Europe and Japan. The Cold War confrontation internationally did not simply impact labor movements from the outside so much as permeate national labor movements from the inside. Clearly, no history of the twentieth-century working-class movements can be complete without taking into account this geopolitical dimension.

Abbreviations

Key for identifiers of dominant tendencies in unions and parties:

CH = Christian   LS = left socialist

COM = communist   SD = social democratic

ADGB	Allgemeiner Deutscher Gewerkschaftsbund [General German Federation of Labor] (Germany; SD-LS)
AFL	American Federation of Labor (US)
ASC	Asian Socialist Conference
CDU	Christlich-Demokratische Union [Christian Democratic Union] (West Germany; CH)
CFDT	Confédération Française Démocratique du Travail [French Democratic Confederation of Labor] (France; CH)
CFTC	Confédération Française des Travailleurs Chrétiens [French Confederation of Christian Workers] (France; CH)
CGC	Confédération Générale des Cadres [General Confederation of Technicians and Supervisory Employees] (France)
CGIL	Confederazione Generale Italiana del Lavoro [General Confederation of Italian Labor] (Italy; all prior to 1948, then COM-LS thereafter)
CGL	Confederazione Generale del Lavoro [General Confederation of Labor] (Italy; SD-LS-COM)
CGT	Confédération Générale du Travail [General Confederation of Labor] (France; SD-COM-LS prior to 1947, then COM thereafter)
CGTU	Confédération Générale du Travail Unitaire [Unified General Confederation of Labor] (France; COM)
CIL	Confederazione Italiana del Lavoro [Italian Confederation of Labor] (Italy; CH)

235

CIO	Congress of Industrial Organizations (US)
CISL	Confederazione Italiana Sindicati Lavoratori [Italian General Confederation of Trade Unions] (Italy; CH-SD)
CLN	Comitato di Liberazione Nazionale [Committee for National Liberation] (Italy)
CNR	Conseil National de la Résistance [National Resistance Council] (France)
Cominform	Communist Information Office
Comintern	Communist International
COMISCO	Committee of International Socialist Conferences
Confindustria	Confederazione Generale dell'Industria Italiana [General Confederation of Italian Industry (Italy)
CPSU	Communist Party of the Soviet Union (Soviet Union)
DC	Democrazia Cristiana [Christian Democratic Party] (Italy; CH)
Denki Rōren	Zen Nihon Denki Kiki Rōdō Kumiai Rengōkai [All Japan Electrical Machinery Labor Union Federation]
Densan	Denki Sangyō Rōdō Kumiai [Electric Power Workers' Union]
DGB	Deustcher Gewerkschaftsbund [German Labor Federation] (West Germany; SD and CH, primarily. The name was also used by an interwar German Christian federation.)
DLP	Democratic Liberal Party [Minshu Jiyūtō]
DNVP	Deutschnational Volkspartei [German National People's Party] (Germany; CH)
Dōmei	Nihon rōdō sōdōmei [General Confederation of Trade Unions] (SD)
DPL	Democratic People's League [Minshu Jinmin Renmei]
ECA	Economic Cooperation Administration
EPA	European Productivity Agency
ERC	Economic Recovery Conference [Keizai Fukkō Kaigi]
EROA	Economic Recovery in Occupied Areas
ERP	European Recovery Program
ESB	Economic Stabilization Board [Keizai Antei Honbu]
ESS	Economic and Scientific Section, SCAP
FDGB	Freier Deutscher Gewerkschaftsbund [Federation of Free German Trade Unions] (East Germany)
FEC	Far Eastern Commission
FIL	Federazione Italiana del Lavoratori [Italian Federation of Labor] (Italy)
FO	Force Ouvrière (France; SD, LS)
FOA	Foreign Operations Administration (US)
FTUC	Free Trade Union Committee, AFL (US)

GARIOA	Government and Relief in Occupied Areas
GHQ	General Headquarters, SCAP
Gōka Rōren	Gōsei Kagaku Sangyō Rōdō Kumiai Rengō [Synthetic Chemical Workers' Union]
Hyōgikai	Nihon Rōdō Kumiai Hyōgikai [Japan Labor Unions Council]
ICFTU	International Confederation of Free Trade Unions
IFTCU	International Federation of Christian Trade Unions
IFTU	International Federation of Trade Unions
ILO	International Labor Organization
IWMA	International Workingmen's Association
JCP	Japan Communist Party [Nihon Kyōsantō]
JCS	Joint Chiefs of Staff (US)
Jichirōkyō	Zenkoku Jichi Dantai Rōdō Kumiai Kyōgikai [Prefectural and Municipal Workers' Union Liaison Council]
JNR	Japan National Railways [Nihon Kokuyū Tetsudō (Kokutetsu)]
JSP	Japan Socialist Party [Nihon Shakaitō]
Keidanren	Keieisha Dantai Renmei [Federation of Economic Assocations]
Kokurō/Kokutetsu	Kokutetsu Rōdō Kumiai [Japan National Railway Workers' Union]
Kokutetsu Mindō	Kokutetsu Minshuka Dōmei [Kokutetsu Democratization League]
KPD	Kommunistiche Partei Deutschlands [German Communist Party]
LCGIL	Libera Confederazione Generale Italiana del Lavoro [Free Italian Confederation of Labor] (Italy; CH)
LDP	Liberal Democratic Party [Jiyū Minshutō]
LSI	Labor and Socialist International
Mindō	Minshuka Dōmei [Democratization League]
Minrōken	Minshu Rōdō Undō Kenkyūkai [Democratic Labor Movement Group]
Minrōren	Minshushugi Rōdō Undō Renraku Kyōgikai [Democratic Labor Movement Liaison Council]
MOL	Ministry of Labor (Japan)
MRP	Mouvement Républicain Populaire [Popular Republican Movement] (France; CH)
MSA	Mutual Security Act/Mutual Security Agency
Nichirō Kaigi	Nihon Rōdō Kumiai Kaigi [Japan Labor Union Conference]
Nikkeiren	Nihon Keieisha Dantai Renmei [Japan Federation of Employers Associations]
Nikkyōso	Nihon Kyōshokuin Kumiai [Japan Teachers' Union]
Nissankyō	Nihon Sangyō Kyōgikai [Japan Council of Industries]

Nittsū	Nittsū Rōdō Kumiai [Japan Express Labor Union]
PCF	Parti Communiste Français [French Communist Party]
PCI	Partito Communista Italiano [Italian Communist Party] (Italy)
PCP	People's Cooperative Party [Kokumin Kyōdōtō]
Profintern	(See RILU)
PSDI	Partito Social-Democratico Italiano [Italian Social-Democratic Party] (Italy)
PSI	Partito Socialista Italiano [Italian Socialist Party]
PSIUP	Partito Socialista Italiano di Unità Proletaria [Italian Party of Proletarian Unity] (Italy)
PSLI	Partito Socialista dei Lavoratori Italiani [Italian Socialist Workers Party] (Italy)
RILU	Red International of Labor Unions (also Profintern)
Rōtō	Rōdō Hōki Kaiaku Hantai Tōsō Iinkai [Struggle Committee to Oppose Labor Legislation Revision]
Sanbetsu	Zen Nihon Sangyōbetsu Rōdō Kumiai Kaigi [National Congress of Industrial Organizations]
Sanbetsu Mindō	Sanbetsu Minshuka Dōmei [Sanbetsu Democratization League]
SCAP	Supreme Commander of the Allied Powers
SED	Sozialistische Einheitspartei Deutschlands [Socialist Unity Party] (East Germany; COM)
SFIO	Section Française de l'Internationale Ouvrière [French Section of the Workers' International] (France; SD-LS)
Shinsanbetsu	Zenkoku Sangyōbetsu Rōdō Kumiai Rengōkai [(New) National Federation of Industrial Organizations] (LS)
Shitetsu Sōren	Nihon Shitetsu Rōdō Kumiai Sō Rengōkai [General Federation of Private Railway Workers' Unions]
Sōdōmei	Nihon Rōdō Kumiai Sōdōmei [Japanese General Federation of Workers]
Sōhyō	Nihon Rōdō Kumiai Sōhyōgikai [General Council of Japanese Trade Unions] The term also refers to a short-lived pre–World War II left-socialist confederation.
SPD	Sozialdemokratische Partei Deutschlands [Social Democratic Party of Germany]
SWNCC	State-War-Navy Coordinating Committee (US)
Tanrō	Nihon Tankō Rōdō Kumiai [Japan Coal Miners' Union]
Tekkō Rōren	Nihon Tekkō Sangyō Rōdō Kumiai Rengōkai [Federation of Iron and Steel Workers' Unions]
TUC	Trades Union Congress (UK)
UIL	Unione Italiana del Lavoratori [Italian Workers' Union] (Italy; SD). This acronym was also used by an Italian fascist labor organization after World War I.

USI	Unione Sindicale Italiana [Italian Syndical Union] (Italy; anarcho-syndicalist)
USPD	Unabhängige Sozialdemokratische Partei Deutschlands [German Independent Social Democratic Party] (Germany; LS)
WFTU	World Federation of Trade Unions
Zendentsū	Zenkoku Denki Tsūshin Rōdō Kumiai [National Telecommunications Workers' Unions]
Zenji/Zenjidōsha	Zen Nihon Jidōsha Sangyō Rōdō Kumiai [All Japan Automobile Workers' Union]
Zenkankō	Zenkoku Kankōchō Rōdō Kumiai Renraku Kyōgikai [National Government Agency Labor Union Liaison Council]
Zenkankōchō	Zenkoku Kankōchō Kyōdō Tōsō Iinkai [National Government Agency Joint Struggle Committee]
Zenkō	Zen Nihon Kinzoku Kōzan Rōdō Kumiai Rengōkai [All Japan Metal Miners' Labor Union Federation]
Zennichirō	Zen Nihon Rōdō Kumiai Renmei [All Japan Labor Union Federation] (neutral)
Zenrō/Zenrō Kaigi	Zenkoku Rōdō Kumiai Kaigi [National Trade Union Congress] Two different labor confederations share the same name. Zenrō Kaigi refers to the confederation proposed in 1948–1949, and Zenrō to the social-democratic confederation created in 1954.
Zenrōren	Zenkoku Rōdō Kumiai Renraku Kyōgikai [National Liaison Council of Labor Unions]
Zensen Dōmei	Zenkoku Sen'i Sangyō Rōdō Kumiai Dōmei [National Federation of Textile Workers' Unions]
Zentan	Zen Nihon Tankō Rōdō Kumiai [All Japan Coal Miners' Union]
Zentei	Zen Teishin Jūgyōin Kumiai (Zen Teishin Rōdō Kumiai from 1957) [All Communication Employees' Union]
Zentō	Zenkoku Rōso Kyōdō Tōsō Iinkai [National Labor Union Joint Struggle Committee]
Zenzaimu	Zenkoku Zaimu Shokuin Kumiai [National Tax Collectors' Union]

Notes

Works frequently cited have been identified by the following abbreviations:

MSRUS   Monogatari Sengo Rōdō Undō Shi Kankō Iinkai. *Monogatari sengo rōdō undō shi.* Vols. 1–6. Tokyo: Daiichi shorin, 1997–1999.

NRKM   Ōkōchi Kazuo. *Nihon rōdō kumiai monogatari.* 2 vols. Tokyo: Chikuma shobō, 1973.

NRN   *Nihon rōdō nenkan,* 1949–1955.

SGS   Sōdōmei Gojūnen Shi Kankō Iinkai, ed. *Sōdōmei gojūnen shi kanko iinkai.* Vol. 3. 1964.

SRUS   *Shiryō rōdō undō shi,* 1945–1955.

SSNS   Ōkōchi Kazuo, ed. *Rōdō.* Vol. 4, *Shiryō sengo nijūnen shi.* Tokyo: Nihon hyō-ronsha, 1966.

SSSS   Sōhyō, ed. *Sōhyō sanjūnen shiryō shū,* vol. 2. Tokyo: Nihon rōdō kumiai sōhyō-gokai, 1986.

SYS   *Sōhyō yonjūnen shi* Hensan Iinkai, ed. *Sohyo yonjūnen shi.* 3 vols. Tokyo: Daiichi shorin, 1993.

TMCS   Takano Minoru. *Takano minoru chosaku shū.* 5 vols. Tokyo: Takushoku shobō, 1976–1977.

ZJS   *Zenrō Jūnen Shi* Hensan Iinkai. *Zenrō jūnen shi.* Tokyo: Zenrō jūnen shi hensan iinkai, 1986.

All quotes from Japanese-language sources are my translations.

Introduction

1. For a comprehensive discussion of this in the European context see Stephen Born-stein, "States and Unions: From Postwar Settlement to Contemporary Stalemate," in *The State in Capitalist Europe: A Casebook,* ed. Stephen Bornstein et al. (London; Winchester, Mass.; and Boston: G. Allen & Unwin and Center for European Studies Harvard Univer-sity, 1984).

2. An ambitious globally contextualized political history of Japan, and an inspiration

for this volume, is Masumi Junnosuke's *Hikaku seiji,* 3 vols. (Tokyo: Tōkyō daigaku shuppankai, 1990–1993). Recent works in English that have adopted an implicitly comparative approach to labor history include Ikuo Kume, *Disparaged Success: Labor Politics in Postwar Japan* (Ithaca, N.Y.: Cornell University Press, 1998); and Andrew Gordon, *The Wages of Affluence: Labor and Management in Postwar Japan* (Cambridge, Mass.: Harvard University Press, 1998).

3. One such effort is described in David Palmer, "Gurōburu undō shi ni mukete: Amerika, nihon, ōsutoraria, aruzenchin, 1890–1960," *Sanken ronshū* (2001).

4. Adolf Fox Sturmthal, *Comparative Labor Movements: Ideological Roots and Institutional Development* (Belmont, Calif.: Wadsworth Pub. Co., 1972), 1.

5. Charles Tilly, *Big Structures, Large Processes, Huge Comparisons* (New York: Russell Sage Foundation, 1984), 14.

Chapter 1: Labor Movements in Europe, 1920-1945

1. For detailed treatments of the pre–World War I period, see Julius Braunthal, *History of the International, Volume One: 1864–1913,* trans. John Clark (New York and Washington: Praeger, 1967); Dick Geary, ed., *Labour and Socialist Movements in Europe before 1914* (Oxford and New York: Berg, 1989); and Dick Geary, *European Labour Protest, 1848–1939* (New York: St. Martin's Press, 1981), 1–33. For a more detailed overview of European labor during and after World War I that parallels the account here, see ibid., 134–172.

2. Martin Conway, *Catholic Politics in Europe, 1918–1945* (London and New York: Routledge, 1997), 36.

3. For an overview of the international dimension of the Christian trade-union movement during the period, see John P. Windmuller, *International Trade Union Movement* (Deventer, Boston, and Hingham, Mass.: Kluwer, 1980), 87–94.

4. Among the best sources on the international labor movement during this period is Lewis Levitzki Lorwin, *The International Labor Movement: History, Policies, Outlook* (New York: Harper, 1953), 97–162.

5. Comintern, "The Twenty-One Points," as reproduced in Julius Braunthal, *History of the International, Volume Two: 1914–1943,* trans. John Clark (New York and Washington: Praeger, 1967).

6. Ibid., 265.

7. Lorwin, *International Labor Movement,* 118–119 .

8. Quoted in Braunthal, *History of the International,* 2:364.

9. Comintern, "The Twenty-One Points," as reproduced in Braunthal, *History of the International,* 2:541.

10. Braunthal, *History of the International,* vol. 1; Adolf Sturmthal, *The Tragedy of European Labor 1918–1939* (New York: Columbia University Press, 1943); and Geary, *European Labour Protest,* 147–155.

11. It might be noted that in using the term "left socialist" we are, for the sake of simplicity, collapsing into a single category what are sometimes treated as two separate groups

—namely, the "center" and the "left" of the social democratic movement. See, for instance, Lorwin, *International Labor Movement,* 133–136.

12. Quoted in Braunthal, *History of the International,* 2:547.

13. Lorwin, *International Labor Movement,* 155–156.

14. Conway, *Catholic Politics in Europe.*

15. Philip Taft, "Germany," in *Comparative Labor Movements,* ed. Walter Galenson (New York: Russell & Russell, 1968), 256–260, 272–278. For more detailed treatment, see Sturmthal, *Tragedy of European Labor,* 58–79; Conway, *Catholic Politics in Europe,* 34–36; and Braunthal, *History of the International,* 2:56–61, 118–132, 213–228, 296–300.

16. Account based on Val R. Lorwin, *The French Labor Movement* (Cambridge, Mass.: Harvard University Press, 1954), 55–65; Val R. Lorwin, "France," in *Comparative Labor Movements,* ed. Walter Galenson, 330–339; and Braunthal, *History of the International,* 2:191–198.

17. John Clarke Adams, "Italy," in *Comparative Labor Movements,* ed. Walter Galenson (New York: Russell & Russell, 1968), 429. Summation based on ibid., 425–431, and Braunthal, *History of the International,* 2:198–213.

18. Sturmthal, *Tragedy of European Labor;* Braunthal, *History of the International,* 2:354–390.

19. Braunthal, *History of the International,* 2:555–559.

20. Ibid., 558.

21. Ibid., 471.

22. *Encyclopaedia Britannica Online,* s.v. "Popular front," http://search.eb.com/eb/article?eu=62410&tocid=0&query=popular%20front&ct=eb, accessed March 12, 2004.

23. Braunthal, *History of the International,* 2:434.

24. Braunthal, *History of the International,* 3:1–14; Braunthal, *History of the International,* 2:507–530; Lorwin, *International Labor Movement,* 197–233; Denis MacShane, *International Labour and the Origins of the Cold War* (Oxford and New York: Clarendon and Oxford University Press, 1992), 30–118; Windmuller, *Labor Internationals: A Survey of Contemporary International Trade Union Organizations* (Ithaca: New York State School of Industrial and Labor Relations, Cornell University, 1969), 185–219.

25. Braunthal, *History of the International,* 3:11.

26. General Secretary of the TUC, Arthur Deakin, as quoted in ibid., 13.

27. Darryl Holter, *The Battle for Coal: Miners and the Politics of Nationalization in France, 1940–1950* (DeKalb: Northern Illinois University Press, 1992), 47.

28. Richard F. Kuisel, *Capitalism and the State in Modern France: Renovation and Economic Management in the Twentieth Century* (Cambridge and New York: Cambridge University Press, 1981), 157–186, reviews the discussions inside the resistance coalition over postwar economic policy.

29. Braunthal, *History of the International,* 3:45–46.

30. Paul Ginsborg, *A History of Contemporary Italy: Society and Politics, 1943–1988,* Penguin History (London and New York: Penguin Books, 1990), 17–23.

31. Charles Maier, "The German Resistance in Comparative Perspective," in *Contending with Hitler: Varieties of German Resistance in the Third Reich,* ed. David Clay Large (Washington, D.C.; Cambridge, England; New York; Oakleigh, Australia: German Historical Institute and Cambridge University Press, 1991), 147.

32. Martin Broszat, "A Social and Historical Typology of the German Opposition to Hitler," in *Contending with Hitler: Varieties of German Resistance in the Third Reich,* ed. David Clay Large (Washington, D.C.; Cambridge, England; New York; Oakleigh, Australia: German Historical Institute and Cambridge University Press, 1991), 27.

33. Detlev J. Peukert, "Working-Class Resistance: Problems and Options," in *Contending with Hitler: Varieties of German Resistance in the Third Reich,* ed. David Clay Large (Washington, D.C.; Cambridge, England; New York; Oakleigh, Australia: German Historical Institute and Cambridge University Press, 1991), 41.

34. Willy Brandt, "Address," in *Contending with Hitler: Varieties of German Resistance in the Third Reich,* ed. David Clay Large (Washington, D.C.; Cambridge, England; New York; Oakleigh, Australia: German Historical Institute and Cambridge University Press, 1991).

35. Maier, "The German Resistance in Comparative Perspective."

36. Rebecca Boehling, "U.S. Military Occupation, Grass Roots Democracy, and Local German Government," in *American Policy and the Reconstruction of West Germany,* ed. Jeffry M. Diefendorf, Axel Frohn, and Hermann-Josef Rupieper (Washington, D.C.; Cambridge, England; New York; Oakleigh, Australia: German Historical Institute and Cambridge University Press, 1993). See also Matthew A. Kelly, "The Reconstitution of the German Trade Union Movement," *Political Science Quarterly* 64, no. 1 (1949): 26–27.

37. Diethelm Prowe, "German Democratization as Conservative Restabilization: The Impact of American Policy," in *American Policy and the Reconstruction of West Germany,* ed. Jeffry M. Diefendorf, Axel Frohn, and Hermann-Josef Rupieper (Washington, D.C.; Cambridge, England; New York; Oakleigh, Australia: German Historical Institute and Cambridge University Press, 1993), 312.

Chapter 2: The Labor Movement in Interwar and Wartime Japan, 1920–1945

1. Andrew Gordon, *The Evolution of Labor Relations in Japan: Heavy Industry, 1853–1955* (Cambridge, Mass., and London: Harvard University Council on East Asian Studies, 1985), 17–50; Stephen E. Marsland, *The Birth of the Japanese Labor Movement: Takano Fusatarō and the Rōdō Kumiai Kiseikai* (Honolulu: University of Hawai'i Press, 1989); Robert A. Scalapino, *The Early Japanese Labor Movement: Labor and Politics in a Developing Society* (Berkeley, Calif.: Institute of East Asian Studies, University of California, Berkeley, Center for Japanese Studies, 1983), 1–26; Stephen S. Large, *Organized Workers and Socialist Politics in Interwar Japan* (Cambridge and New York: Cambridge University Press, 1981); George O. Totten, *The Social Democratic Movement in Prewar Japan* (New Haven: Yale University Press, 1966).

2. Byron K. Marshall, *Capitalism and Nationalism in Prewar Japan: The Ideology of the Business Elite, 1868–1941* (Stanford, Calif.: Stanford University Press, 1967); Thomas C. Smith, *The Native Sources of Japanese Industrialization, 1750–1920* (Berkeley, Los Angeles, and London: University of California Press, 1988), 236–270.

3. Andrew Gordon, *Labor and Imperial Democracy* (Berkeley, Los Angeles and Oxford: University of California Press, 1991), 26–79.

4. Nakamura Takafusa, *Economic Growth in Prewar Japan* (New Haven: Yale University Press, 1983), 147–148.

5. Large, *Organized Workers and Socialist Politics in Interwar Japan;* Scalapino, *The Early Japanese Labor Movement,* 57–68, 97–105.

6. Scalapino, *The Early Japanese Labor Movement,* 38–93; Large, *Organized Workers and Socialist Politics in Interwar Japan,* 17–30. See Gordon, *Labor and Imperial Democracy,* 80–109, for a grassroots-level account of the expansion of the Yūaikai during these years.

7. Quoted in Totten, *Social Democratic Movement in Prewar Japan,* 40.

8. Gordon, *Labor and Imperial Democracy,* 204–209.

9. For detailed discussions see Scalapino, *The Early Japanese Labor Movement;* Large, *Organized Workers and Socialist Politics in Interwar Japan;* Totten, *Social Democratic Movement in Prewar Japan,* 116–121.

10. Regarding the ideological tendencies of the prewar Sōdōmei right see Takagi Ikurō, "Nihon rōdō kumiai undō ni okeru 'uha' no keifu: Sōdōmei gata to jc gata no dōshitsusei to ishitsusei," in *Sengo rōdō kumiai undō shiron: Kigyō shakai chōkoku no shiza,* ed. Shimizu Shinzō (Tokyo: Nihon hyōronsha, 1982); Takahashi Hikohiro, *Gendai seiji to shakai minshu shugi: Mittsu no chōryū to sono jikken* (Tokyo: Hōsei daigaku shuppankyoku, 1985).

11. Gordon, *Labor and Imperial Democracy.*

12. Sheldon M. Garon, *The State and Labor in Modern Japan* (Berkeley: University of California Press, 1987).

13. Scalapino, *The Early Japanese Labor Movement,* 185.

14. Julius Braunthal, *History of the International, Volume Three: 1943–1968,* trans. Peter Ford and Kenneth Mitchell (Boulder, Colo.: Westview, 1980), 213.

15. Totten, *Social Democratic Movement in Prewar Japan,* 270.

16. Quoted in Braunthal, *History of the International,* 3:316. See also Rodger Swearingen and Paul Langer, *Red Flag in Japan: International Communism in Action 1919–1951* (1952; reprint, Westport, Conn.: Greenwood Press, 1968), 7–14. For a review of Comintern theses on Japan, see Germaine A. Hoston, *Marxism and the Crisis of Development in Prewar Japan* (Princeton, N.J.: Princeton University Press, 1986), 55–75.

17. For accounts of the Japan Communist Party's early history, see Robert A. Scalapino, *The Japanese Communist Movement, 1920–1966* (Berkeley: University of California Press, 1967), 1–47; Swearingen and Langer, *Red Flag in Japan.*

18. Given the tight surveillance of the Japanese authorities, maintaining contact with Moscow was difficult, though never impossible. See Swearingen and Langer, *Red Flag in Japan,* 23–24, for discussion of routes of contact. See also Sandra Wilson, "The Comintern

and the Japanese Communist Party," in *International Communism and the Communist International*, ed. Tim Rees and Andrew Thorpe (Manchester and New York: Manchester University Press, 1998).

19. Totten, *Social Democratic Movement in Prewar Japan*, 131–175.

20. Quoted in Scalapino, *The Early Japanese Labor Movement*, 175. Rōnō Taishūtō refers to a short-lived left-socialist party established by Mizutani Chōzuburō in 1929, not to be confused with the antifascist National Labor Farmer Mass Party established two years later.

21. Totten, *Social Democratic Movement in Prewar Japan*, 152.

22. For a concise summation of the basic differences between communist and left-socialist policy, as enunciated by the so-called labor-farmer faction, see Yamakawa Hitoshi, *Yamakawa Hitoshi jiden: Aru bonjin no kiroku, sonota* (Tokyo: Iwanami shoten, 1961), 430–435. For detailed discussion in English see Gail Lee Bernstein, *Japanese Marxist: A Portrait of Kawakami Hajime, 1879–1946,* Harvard East Asian Series 86 (Cambridge, Mass.: Harvard University Press, 1976).

23. On this point see Hoston, *Marxism and the Crisis of Development in Prewar Japan.*

24. Based on Masuyama Tasuke, *Kenshō: senryō ki no rōdō undō* (Tokyo: Renga shobō shinsha, 1993), 59–60.

25. Totten, *Social Democratic Movement in Prewar Japan,* 293, 296.

26. Garon, *State and Labor in Modern Japan.*

27. Masumi Junnosuke, *Postwar Politics in Japan, 1945–1955,* trans. Lonny E. Carlile (Berkeley: Institute of East Asian Studies, 1985), 13. For more detailed discussion and specific cases see Gordon, *Labor and Imperial Democracy,* 270–330; Garon, *State and Labor in Modern Japan,* 187–227; Large, *Organized Workers and Socialist Politics in Interwar Japan,* 128–230; Totten, *Social Democratic Movement in Prewar Japan,* 67–107; Sharon Minichiello, *Retreat from Reform: Patterns of Political Behavior in Interwar Japan* (Honolulu: University of Hawai'i Press, 1984); and Miwa Yasushi, *Nihon fashizumu to rōdō undō* (Tokyo: Azekura shobō, 1988).

28. Large, *Organized Workers and Socialist Politics in Interwar Japan,* 181–185.

29. Suzuki Mosaburō, "Jinmin sensen jiken," in *Shōwa keizai shi e no shōgen,* ed. Andō Yoshio (Tokyo: Mainichi shinbun sha, 1966); Katō Kanjū, "Shōwa shonen no rōdō undō," in *Shōwa keizai shi e no shōgen,* ed. Andō Yoshio (Tokyo: Mainichi shinbunsha, 1966).

30. The prewar Sōhyō should not be confused with the postwar labor confederation of the same name established in 1950. However, it is noteworthy that the name was chosen for the postwar version because of the prewar Sōhyō's antifascist credentials.

31. Suzuki, "Jinmin sensen jiken."

32. Gregory Kasza provides the following list of defining features of an administered mass organization, all of which apply to Sampō:

Organization. The [administered mass organization] is a formal organization with offices and bylaws.

Mass. The targeted membership ordinarily includes all or most people of a particular place of residence, industry, workplace, age, or gender; most members are not regime officials, that is, they do not hold office in the governing party, the military, or the state bureaucracy.

Administered. External agencies of the regime define the [administered mass organization]'s structure and mission and appoint its top leaders, who do not rise independently from within the organization.

Gregory James Kasza, *The Conscription Society: Administered Mass Organizations* (New Haven: Yale University Press, 1995), 7.

33. Miwa, *Nihon fashizumu to rōdō undō,* 276.

34. See Koseki Shōichi, *The Birth of Japan's Postwar Constitution,* trans. Ray A. Moore (Denver, Colo.: Westview Press, 1997).

Chapter 3: Labor Movements in Post-World War II Western Europe

1. Stephen Bornstein, "States and Unions: From Postwar Settlement to Contemporary Stalemate," in *The State in Capitalist Europe: A Casebook,* ed. Stephen Bornstein, et al. (London, Winchester, Mass., and Boston: G. Allen & Unwin and Center for European Studies Harvard University, 1984).

2. Paul Ginsborg, *A History of Contemporary Italy: Society and Politics, 1943–1988* (London and New York: Penguin Books, 1990), 82.

3. "The Strategy and Tactics of the International Labour Movement during the Period of Fascist Reaction" (August 1933) as reproduced in Julius Braunthal, *History of the International, Volume Two: 1914–1943,* trans. John Clark (New York and Washington: Praeger, 1967), 556.

4. Donald Sassoon, *One Hundred Years of Socialism: The West European Left in the Twentieth Century* (New York: New Press, 1996), 60–82.

5. Bornstein, "States and Unions," 85.

6. Val R. Lorwin, "France," in *Comparative Labor Movements,* ed. Walter Galenson (New York: Russell & Russell, 1968), 342, 352. The other small but important organization at the time was the General Confederation of Technicians and Supervisory Employees, or Confédération Générale des Cadres (CGC), which organized white-collar and technical workers.

7. Richard F. Kuisel, *Capitalism and the State in Modern France: Renovation and Economic Management in the Twentieth Century* (Cambridge and New York: Cambridge University Press, 1981), 188.

8. Ibid., 202–211.

9. Jean-Pierre Rioux, *The Fourth Republic, 1944–1958,* trans. Godfrey Rogers (Cambridge, London, New York, New Rochelle, Melbourne, Sydney, Paris: Cambridge University Press and Editions de la Maison Sciences de l'Homme, 1987), 70–71; Adam Steinhouse, *Workers' Participation in Post-Liberation France* (Lanham, Md.: Lexington Books, 2002), 87; and Lorwin, "France," 389–390.

10. See Steinhouse, *Workers' Participation in Post-Liberation France,* 87–111.

11. Quoted in George Ross, *Workers and Communists in France: From Popular Front to Eurocommunism* (Berkeley: University of California Press, 1982), 32–33.

12. Steinhouse, *Workers' Participation in Post-Liberation France,* 143.

13. Lorwin, "France," 377–378.

14. See Ginsborg, *A History of Contemporary Italy,* 39–71, for a concise account.

15. Also included in the Resistance were the smaller and "bourgeois" Action and Liberal Parties.

16. Joanne Barkan, *Visions of Emancipation: The Italian Workers' Movement since 1945* (New York: Praeger, 1984), 21; Daniel L. Horowitz, *The Italian Labor Movement* (Cambridge, Mass.: Harvard University Press, 1963), 199–201.

17. John Clarke Adams, "Italy," in *Comparative Labor Movements,* ed. Walter Galenson (New York: Russell & Russell, 1968), 466–469.

18. Ibid., 462–463.

19. For detailed discussion, see Tom Behan, *The Long Awaited Moment: The Working Class and the Italian Communist Party in Milan, 1943–1948* (New York: Peter Lang, 1997), 145–156.

20. Adams, "Italy," 463–464.

21. Joseph LaPalombara, *The Italian Labor Movement: Problems and Prospects* (Ithaca, N.Y.: Cornell University Press, 1957), 32–33.

22. Ginsborg, *A History of Contemporary Italy,* 99.

23. Barkan, *Visions of Emancipation,* 22–25.

24. Ibid., 16.

25. Ibid., 21.

26. Adams, "Italy," 442–443.

27. Andrei S. Markovits, *The Politics of West German Trade Unions: Strategies of Class and Interest Representation in Growth and Crisis* (Cambridge and New York: Cambridge University Press, 1986), 65.

28. Matthew A. Kelly, "The Reconstitution of the German Trade Union Movement," *Political Science Quarterly* 64, no. 1 (1949): 32–33.

29. Lucius D. Clay, *Decision in Germany* (Garden City, N.Y.: Doubleday, 1950), 289–290.

30. Barbara Marshall, *The Origins of Post-War German Politics* (London and New York: Croom Helm, 1988), 69–70.

31. Lewis Levitzki Lorwin, *The International Labor Movement: History, Policies, Outlook* (New York: Harper, 1953), 234–235.

32. Werner Link, "Building Coalitions: Non-Governmental German-American Linkages," in *The Marshall Plan and Germany: West German Development within the Framework of the European Recovery Program,* ed. Charles Maier and Gunther Bischof (New York and Oxford: Berg, 1991). The AFL actively sought to influence US foreign policy in Europe as well as European unions themselves. In late 1945 Irving Brown, an energetic activist from

the AFL-affiliated International Association of Machinists, was sent to Brussels to act as the federation's European representative while Major Henry Rutz served as AFL representative in Germany beginning in 1946.

33. Markovits, *Politics of West German Trade Unions,* 63.

34. Kathleen Ann Thelen, *Union of Parts: Labor Politics in Postwar Germany* (Ithaca, N.Y.: Cornell University Press, 1991), 72.

35. Clay, *Decision in Germany,* 293.

36. Diethelm Prowe, "German Democratization as Conservative Restabilization: The Impact of American Policy," in *American Policy and the Reconstruction of West Germany,* ed. Jeffry M. Diefendorf, Axel Frohn, and Hermann-Josef Rupieper (Washington, D.C.; Cambridge, England; New York; Oakleigh, Australia: German Historical Institute and Cambridge University Press, 1993), 316, 318–319.

37. Sassoon, *One Hundred Years of Socialism,* 159–160.

38. Quoted in Charles Maier, "The German Resistance in Comparative Perspective," in *Contending with Hitler: Varieties of German Resistance in the Third Reich,* ed. David Clay Large (Washington, D.C.; Cambridge, England; New York; Oakleigh, Australia: German Historical Institute and Cambridge University Press, 1991), 145.

Chapter 4: Uniting the Front, 1945–1947

1. Takano Minoru, *Nihon no rōdō undō* (Tokyo: Iwanami shoten, 1958), 10.

2. Shirai Taishirō, "Nihon rōdō kumiai sōdōmei no undō," in *Rōdō kumiai undō shi,* ed. Okōchi Kazuo and Fujita Wakao (Tokyo: Kobundō, 1962), 94–114.

3. Takemae Eiji, "Early Postwar Reformist Parties," in *Democratizing Japan: The Allied Occupation,* ed. Robert Edward Ward and Yoshikazu Sakamoto (Honolulu: University of Hawai'i Press, 1987), 353–354.

4. Kuroda Hisao, "Shakai tō no kettō," in *Shōwa keizai shi e no shōgen,* ed. Andō Yoshio, 108–109 (Tokyo: Mainichi shinbun sha, 1966). As a face-saving device, "Social Democratic Party of Japan" was selected as the official English translation of the party's name.

5. Takano, *Nihon no rōdō undō,* 11–13.

6. Kasuga Shōichi, "Kantō rōkyō kessei zengo," in *Shōgen sanbetsu kaigi no tanjō,* ed. Hōsei Daigaku Ōhara Shakai Mondai Kenkyūjo (Tokyo: Sōgō rōdō kenkyūjo, 1996), 94.

7. For instance, ibid.; Hasegawa Hiroshi, "Sanbetsu kaigi no kessei to shoki no katsudō," in *Shōgen sanbetsu kaigi no tanjō* ed. Hōsei Daigaku Ōhara Shakai Mondai Kenkyūjo (Tokyo: Sōgō rōdō kenkyūjo, 1996).

8. "Rōdō kumiai ni kansuru ketsugi" (December 1–3, 1945), as reproduced in *SSNS,* 4–5.

9. *MSRUS,* 1:57–58.

10. *SRUS* (1945–1946): 460.

11. Nishio Suehiro, *Nishio Suehiro no seiji oboegaki* (Tokyo: Mainichi shinbunsha, 1968), 55–57.

12. Yamakawa Hitoshi, *Yamakawa Hitoshi jiden: Aru bonjin no kiroku, sonota* (Tokyo: Iwanami shoten, 1961), 449.

13. *MSRUS,* 1:98–99. For a version of the events from the perspective of a left social-ist participant, see Takano, *Nihon no rōdō undō,* 15–18; from the point of view of commu-nist participants, Kasuga, "Kantō rōkyō kessei zengo," 101–103.

14. Hosoya Matsuta, "Sengo minshushugi to rōdō kumiai no seiritsu," in *Shōgen sengo rōdō kumiai undōsh,* ed. Takanashi Akira, 10–11 (Tokyo: Tōyō keizai shinpōsha, 1985).

15. Hasegawa, "Sanbetsu kaigi no kessei to shoki no katsudō," 164–165.

16. Technically, the name of the organization, a federation of various independent regional unions of employees of the Japan National Railway, was Kokutetsu Sōren at that time, and it was only after being reconstituted as a single union, in June 1947, that it took on the name Kokurō.

17. Hasegawa, "Sanbetsu kaigi no kessei to shoki no katsudō," 187–188.

18. See Shirai, "Nihon rōdō kumiai sōdōmei no undō."

19. See various interviews in Hōsei Daigaku and Ōhara Shakai Mondai Kenkyūjo, eds., *Shōgen sanbetsu kaigi no tanjō* (Tokyo: Sōgō rōdō kenkyūjo, 1996).

20. Hasegawa, "Sanbetsu kaigi no kessei to shoki no katsudō," 170.

21. *SRUS* (1945–1946): 916–917.

22. JCP, "Dai go kai taikai sengen," as reproduced in *SRUS* (1945–1946): 925.

23. Araki Yoshinobu, ed., *Senryōki ni okeru kyōsanshugi undō* (Tokyo: Ashi shobō, 1993), 150–156.

24. Nakakita Kōji, *Keizai fukkō to sengo seiji: Nihon shakaitō 1945–1951* (Tokyo: Tōkyō daigaku shuppankai, 1998), 9–10.

25. Nishio, *Nishio Suehiro no seiji oboegaki,* 58–59.

26. For details on this process, see Takahashi Hikohiro, "Senryōka shakaitō seiken no seiritsu: yon tō kyōdō iinkai kara kyūkoku minshu sensen e," *Rōdō undō shi kenkyū* (1974), 55–56; and Masumi Junnosuke, *Postwar Politics in Japan, 1945–1955,* trans. Lonny E. Carlile (Berkeley: Institute of East Asian Studies, 1985), 98–108.

27. *SRUS* (1945–1946): 932.

28. For details on this process, see Takahashi, "Senryōka shakaitō seiken no seiritsu," and Masumi, *Postwar Politics in Japan,* 98–108.

29. John W. Dower, *Embracing Defeat: Japan in the Wake of World War II,* 1st ed. (New York: W. W. Norton & Co./The New Press, 1999), 261, 263.

30. Gekkan Shakaitō Henshūbu, ed., *Nihon shakaitō no sanjūnen* (Tokyo: Shakai shinpo, 1974), 1:70–75.

31. *MSRUS,* 1:148–149.

32. For details, see Joe Moore, *Japanese Workers and the Struggle for Power, 1945–1947* (Madison: University of Wisconsin Press, 1983), 160–184; Masumi, *Postwar Politics in Japan,* 108–111.

33. Yamakawa, *Yamakawa Hitoshi,* 454.

34. Araki, *Senryōki ni okeru kyōsanshugi undō,* 164–165.

35. *MSRUS,* 1:169–179; *NRKM,* 1:163–165.

36. Hosoya Matsuta, *Rōdō sensen no bunretsu to tōitsu* (Tokyo: Kanae shuppankai, 1981), 314.

37. Miriam Farley, *Aspects of Japan's Labor Problems* (New York: John Day, 1950), p. 97.

38. Kawanishi Hirosuke, *Enterprise Unionism in Japan* (London and New York: Kegan Paul International, 1992), 102–104, 141–144; Laura Hein, *Fueling Growth: The Energy Revolution and Economic Policy in Postwar Japan* (Cambridge, Mass., and London: Council on East Asian Studies, Harvard University, and Harvard University Press, 1990), 99–101; Andrew Gordon, *The Evolution of Labor Relations in Japan: Heavy Industry, 1853–1955* (Cambridge, Mass., and London: Harvard University Council on East Asian Studies, 1985), 351–362.

39. Hosoya Matsuta, "Sanbetsu kaigi no kessei to ni-ichi suto," in *Shōgen sanbetsu kaigi no tanjō,* ed. Hōsei Daigaku Ōhara Shakai Mondai Kenkyūjo (Tokyo: Sōgō rōdō kenkyūjo, 1996).

40. The impetus for the formation of Nichirō Kaigi was the decision by the Central Labor Relations Board to allow national umbrella organizations with over 100,000 members to recommend labor delegates on labor relations boards. Nichirō Kaigi was formed out of "neutral" unions out of concern that the politicized Sanbetsu and Sōdōmei would monopolize labor representation in the mediation process.

41. Masumi, *Postwar Politics in Japan,* 122.

42. Theodore Cohen, *Remaking Japan: The American Occupation as New Deal* (New York: Free Press, 1987), 280.

43. *SRUS* (1947): 102.

44. Hasegawa Hiroshi, "Rōdō undō ni kansuru hōkuku," as reproduced in *SRUS* (1946): 63–65.

45. "Far Eastern Commission Policy Statement on 'Principles for Japanese Trade Unions,'" as reproduced in Farley, *Aspects of Japan's Labor Problems,* 245–247.

46. Cohen, *Remaking Japan,* 287; for detailed accounts in English, see 285–297, and Masumi, *Postwar Politics in Japan,* 115–117.

47. Masumi, *Postwar Politics in Japan,* 119.

48. "Zenkoku rōdō kumiai renraku kyōgikai kiyaku" in *SRUS* (1947): 608–609.

49. Zenrōren, "Sengen" in *SRUS* (1947): 607.

50. Douglas MacArthur to Yoshida Shigeru, February 6, 1947, in Supreme Commander for the Allied Powers, Government Section, *Political Reorientation of Japan* (Washington, D.C.: U.S. Government Printing Office, 1949), 2:721.

51. JSP Headquarters (March 28, 1947), "Seiji no minshuka to senkyo-senkyo surōgan," in Nihon Shakaitō Kettō Yonjisshūnen Kinen Shuppan Kankō Iinkai, ed., *Shiryō nihon shakaitō yonjūnenshi* (Tokyo: Nihon shakaitō chūō honbu, 1986), 84–85.

52. Hyōdō Atsushi, "Sanbetsu kaigi minshuka dōmei no seiritsu katei," *Ōhara shakai mondai kenkyūjo kenkyū shiryō geppō,* no. 451 (1996), 22.

53. Tsuji Kiyokai, ed., *Seiji,* vol. 1 of *Shiryō sengo nijūnen shi* (Tokyo: Nihon hyōron-sha, 1966), 337–338. See Masumi, *Postwar Politics in Japan,* 135–138, for a detailed account of the Democratic Party's formation.

54. Nakakita, *Keizai fukkō to sengo seiji,* 50.

55. For accounts of these negotiations, see Masumi, *Postwar Politics in Japan,* 141–147; Kinoshita Takeshi, *Katayama naikaku shiron: Renritsu seikein mondai o chūshin ni* (Tokyo: Hōritsu bunkasha, 1982), 85–105.

56. *SRUS* (1947): 1002.

57. *NRKM,* 1:203–207; *MSRUS,* 2:17–18.

58. Anthony Carew et al., *The International Confederation of Free Trade Unions* (Bern: Peter Lang, 2000), 171.

59. See Araki, *Senryōki ni okeru kyōsanshugi undō.*

Chapter 5: Organizing the "Battle for Production" in Japan

1. Kōshiro Kazuyoshi, ed., *Sengo 50 nen: Sangyō, koyō rōdō shi* (Tokyo: Nihon rōdō ken-kyū kikō, 1995), 3, 202.

2. Takano Minoru, *Nihon no rōdō undō* (Tokyo: Iwanami shoten, 1958), 55.

3. For detailed discussion and cases, see Joe Moore, *Japanese Workers and the Struggle for Power, 1945–1947* (Madison: University of Wisconsin Press, 1983).

4. Theodore Cohen, *Remaking Japan: The American Occupation as New Deal* (New York: Free Press, 1987), 220. For discussion of specific instances of production control, see Moore, *Japanese Workers and the Struggle for Power;* also see Laura Hein, *Fueling Growth: The Energy Revolution and Economic Policy in Postwar Japan* (Cambridge, Mass., and London: Council on East Asian Studies, Harvard University, and Harvard University Press, 1990), 91–94.

5. *SGS,* 3:178.

6. Sōdōmei (August 3, 1946), "Sōdōmei's kessei taikai: Sengen," in *SSNS:* 13–14.

7. "Sanbetsu kaigi kessei taikai: Sengen," in *SSNS:* 15.

8. For instance, Sanbetsu, "Sangyō fukkō hōsaku yōkō an," in *SRUS* (1945–1946): 398–399; Sōdōmei, "Tōmen no undō hōshin," in *SRUS* (1945–1946): 558–559.

9. Takano Minoru, "Shitsugyō hantai tōsō no gutaiteki kōryō," (September 2, 1946) in *TMCS,* 1:293.

10. Sōdōmei, "Tōmen no undō hōshin," in *SRUS* (1945–1946): 558.

11. Nakakita Kōji, *Keizai fukkō to sengo seiji: Nihon shakaitō 1945–1951* (Tokyo: Tōkyō daigaku shuppankai, 1998), 30.

12. Ibid., 29–30; *SGS,* 3:178–181; Hayakawa Seiichirō and Yoshida Kenji, "Keizai fukkō kaigi no soshiki to undō," *Ōhara shakai mondai kenkyūjo kenkyū shiryō geppō,* no. 283 (1982), pt. 1, 3–5.

13. Sanbetsu (August 30, 1946), "Sangyō fukkō konpon hōshin," as reproduced in Hayakawa and Yoshida, "Keizai fukkō kaigi no soshiki to undō," pt. 1, 12–13.

14. Ibid., 16–18.

15. Shiino Etsurō, "Nihon kyōsantō no orugu shidō to zentan no kessei," in *Shōgen sanbetsu kaigi no tanjō,* ed. Hōsei Daigaku Ōhara Shakai Mondai Kenkyūjo (Tokyo: Sōgō rōdō kenkyūjo, 1996), 304–305.

16. Nihon Kyōsantō (October 1946), "Sangyō fukkō undō ni taisuru kihon hōshin," as reproduced in Hayakawa and Yoshida, "Keizai fukkō kaigi no soshiki to undō," 18–19.

17. Sanbetsu, "Sangyō fukkō no konpon hōshin."

18. For more detailed discussion, see William M. Tsutsui, *Manufacturing Ideology: Scientific Management in Twentieth-Century Japan* (Princeton, N.J.: Princeton University Press, 1998), 122–129; Ōtake Hideo, "The *Zaikai* under the Occupation: The Formation and Transformation of Managerial Councils," in *Democratizing Japan: The Allied Occupation,* ed. Robert E. Ward and Yoshikazu Sakamoto (Honolulu: University of Hawai'i Press, 1987), 368–372; Lonny E. Carlile, "Zaikai and the Politics of Production in Japan, 1940–1962" (Ph.D. diss., University of California at Berkeley, 1989), 132–145.

19. Shikanai Nobutaka, "Keizai fukkō kaigi to keieisha," *Tōyō keizai shinpō* (May 24, 1947), as quoted in Hayakawa and Yoshida, "Keizai fukkō kaigi no soshiki to undō," 7.

20. In a formulation resembling German formulations of worker representation in enterprise, Ōtsuka Banjō, a leading figure in the Dōyūkai, went so far as to champion a revision of the Commercial Law to mandate a form of corporate organization in which firms would be run by tripartite boards composed of representatives of stockholders, management, and labor unions.

21. *Asahi shinbun* (May 6, 1946).

22. Howard Schonberger, "American Labor's Cold War in Occupied Japan," *Diplomatic History* 3, no. 3 (1979), 251; Cohen, *Remaking Japan,* 40–41.

23. Tezuka Kazuaki, "Kyū rōdō kumiai hō no keisei to tenkai: Shoki rōdō iinkai no kinō bunseki o chūshin to shite," in *Sengo kaikaku: Rōdō kaikaku,* ed. Tōkyō Daigaku and Shakai Kagaku Kenkyūjo (Tokyo: Tōkyō daigaku shuppankai, 1974); Endō Kōshi, *Nihon senryō to rōshi kankei seisaku no seiritsu* (Tokyo: Tōkyō daigaku shuppankai, 1989).

24. Takemae Eiji, *Sengo rōdō kaikaku: GHQ rōdō seisakushi* (Tokyo: Tōkyō daigaku shuppankai, 1982), 95–100.

25. Cohen, *Remaking Japan,* 227.

26. *MSRUS,* 1:184–185.

27. Cohen, *Remaking Japan,* 225–231; Endō, *Nihon senryō to rōshi kankei seisaku no seiritsu,* 71–136; Tezuka, "Kyū rōdō kumiai hō no keisei to tenkai," 258–265.

28. Account based on Endō, *Nihon senryō to rōshi kankei seisaku no seiritsu,* chap. 3; Hyōdō Tsutomu, *Rōdō no sengo shi* (Tokyo: Tōkyō daigaku shuppankai, 1997), 51–58.

29. Tezuka, "Kyū rōdō kumiai hō no keisei to tenkai," 263.

30. "Keiei kyōgikai ni kansuru shokikanchō danwa," *SRUS* (1945–1946): 804.

31. "Keiei kyōgikai shishin," *SRUS* (1945–1946): 805.

32. Tezuka, "Kyū rōdō kumiai hō no keisei to tenkai."

33. Hyōdō, *Rōdō no sengo shi,* 54.

34. Cohen, *Remaking Japan,* 171–172.

35. My discussion is based on Ōmori Tokuko, "Keizai antei no kihon seisaku ritsuan to keizai antei honbu," *NIRA seisaku kenkyū* 8, no. 7 (1995).

36. "Katayama naikaku keizai kinkyū seisaku," in *Shiryō: Shakaitō yonjū nen shi,* ed. Nihon Shakaitō Kettō Yonjusshūnen Kinen Shuppan Kankō Iinkai (Tokyo: Nihon shakai tō, 1986), 96–99.

37. Chalmers A. Johnson, *Japan's Public Policy Companies* (Washington, D.C.: American Enterprise Institute for Public Policy Research, 1978), 75–79.

38. Cohen, *Remaking Japan,* 330–331. The figures for the number of *kōdan* are based on Johnson, *Japan's Public Policy Companies,* 151–152.

39. Account based on Cohen, *Remaking Japan,* 326–333.

40. *SGS,* 3:187.

41. "Keizai fukkō undō no kihon hōshin," as reproduced in Hayakawa and Yoshida, "Keizai fukkō kaigi no soshiki to undō," pt. 1, 9–11.

42. "Tokuda kyūichi no kenkai" (January 14, 1947), in Shakai Bunko, *Nihon shakai tō shi shiryō* (Tokyo: Kashiwa shobō, 1966), 98.

43. Nakahara Junkichi, "Nakahara junkichi shi ni kiku: Keizai fukkō kaigi no soshiki to undō," pt. 1, *Ōhara shakai mondai kenkyūjo zasshi,* no. 362 (1989), 75.

44. Quoted in Hayakawa and Yoshida, "Keizai fukkō kaigi no soshiki to undō," pt. 1, 23.

45. Keizai Doyūkai, 1956, 52–66; Horikoshi Teizō, ed., *Keizai dantai rengōkai jūnen shi* (Tokyo: Keizai dantai rengōkai, 1962), 1:488–492. "Sanbetsu dōyūkai kondankai ryokai jiko oboegaki," in Shakai Bunko, *Nihon shakai tō shi shiryō,* 97–98.

46. Nakakita, *Keizai fukkō to sengo seiji,* 50.

47. "Yon tō seisaku kyōtei" (May 16, 1947), in Nihon Shakaitō Kettō Yonjisshūnen Kinen Shuppan Kankō Iinkai, *Shiryō,* 87.

48. Hein, *Fueling Growth,* 132–143; Masumi Junnosuke, *Postwar Politics in Japan, 1945–1955* (Berkeley: Institute of East Asian Studies, 1985), 144–146; Cohen, *Remaking Japan,* 317–325; *NRKM,* 1:243–246; Nakakita, *Keizai fukkō to sengo seiji;* Hiwatari Nobuhiro, *Sengo nihon no shijō to seiji* (Tokyo: Tōkyō daigaku shuppankai, 1991), 97–99.

Chapter 6: The Cold War and the Politics of Labor in Western Europe

1. Perhaps the best concise but comprehensive account in English of the complicated process associated with the Italian labor movement realignment during the period can be found in Daniel L. Horowitz, *The Italian Labor Movement* (Cambridge, Mass.: Harvard University Press, 1963), 208–227.

2. See Denis MacShane, *International Labour and the Origins of the Cold War,* chap. 1, for discussion.

3. Ronald L. Filippelli, *American Labor and Postwar Italy, 1943–1953: A Study of Cold War Politics* (Stanford, Calif.: Stanford University Press, 1989); Federico Romero, *The United States and the European Trade Union Movement, 1944–1951* (Chapel Hill: University

of North Carolina Press, 1992); Irwin M. Wall, The *United States and the Making of Postwar France, 1945–1954* (Cambridge and New York: Cambridge University Press, 1991).

4. Irwin Wall, "The Marshall Plan and French Politics" in *The Marshall Plan: Fifty Years After,* ed. Martin A. Schain (New York and Basingstoke, UK: Palgrave, 2001), 170.

5. Wall, *The United States and the Making of Postwar France,* 103, 113.

6. Gino Bedani, *Politics and Ideology in the Italian Workers' Movement: Union Development and the Changing Role of the Catholic and Communist Subcultures in Postwar Italy* (Oxford, and Providence, R.I.: Berg, 1995), 37–50; MacShane, *International Labour and the Origins of the Cold War,* 279.

7. MacShane, *International Labour and the Origins of the Cold War,* 259.

8. Darryl Holter, *The Battle for Coal: Miners and the Politics of Nationalization in France, 1940–1950* (DeKalb: Northern Illinois University Press, 1992), 133–138.

9. Elisa A. Carrillo, "The Italian Catholic Church and Communism, 1943–1963," *The Catholic Historical Review* 78 (1991).

10. Bedani, *Politics and Ideology in the Italian Workers' Movement,* 41–45.

11. Spencer M. Di Scala, *Renewing Italian Socialism: Nenni to Craxi* (New York and Oxford: Oxford University Press, 1988), 47–45, 59–62.

12. Ibid., 53.

13. Bruce Desmond Graham, *Choice and Democratic Order: The French Socialist Party, 1937–1950* (Cambridge and New York: Cambridge University Press, 1994), chap. 6.

14. Jean-Pierre Rioux, *The Fourth Republic, 1944–1958* (Cambridge, London, New York, New Rochelle, Melbourne, Sydney, Paris: Cambridge University Press and Editions de la Maison Sciences de l'Homme, 1987), 122–123.

15. George Ross, *Workers and Communists in France: From Popular Front to Eurocommunism* (Berkeley: University of California Press, 1982), 32.

16. Ibid., 48.

17. S. J. Woolf, "The Rebirth of Italy, 1943–50," in *The Rebirth of Italy, 1943–50,* ed. S. J. Woolf (London: Longman Group, 1971), 230; Paul Ginsborg, *A History of Contemporary Italy: Society and Politics, 1943–1988* (London and New York: Penguin Books, 1990), 105–110.

18. Tom Behan, *The Long Awaited Moment: The Working Class and the Italian Communist Party in Milan, 1943–1948* (New York: Peter Lang, 1997), 15.

19. Horowitz, *Italian Labor Movement,* 210.

20. Against this, the supporters of the third force within the MRP and in the CFTC took pains to placate the left in the SFIO by distinguishing their essentially anticommunist stance from the "negative anticommunism" of adherents of political persuasions further to the right by pointing out that, in the long run, progressive social and economic policies provide the most effective means of rooting out the communist threat. They stressed the need to promote economic democracy, and reformist socialists were put forward as the logical partner in the progressive project being pursued by the coalition.

Samuel H. Barnes, "The Politics of French Christian Labor," *Journal of Politics* 21, no. 1 (1959); Anthony Trawick Bouscaren, "The MRP in French Governments, 1948–1951," *Journal of Politics* 14, no. 1 (1952).

21. On this point see Esposito, *America's Feeble Weapon: Funding the Marshall Plan in France and Italy, 1948–1950* (Westport and London: Greenwood, 1994).

22. Irwin Wall, "The Marshall Plan and French Politics," in Martin A. Schain, ed., *The Marshall Plan: Fifty Years After* (New York and Houndsmills, UK: Palgrave, 2001).

23. Ginsborg, *A History of Contemporary Italy,* 122. See also Bedani, *Politics and Ideology in the Italian Workers' Movement,* 44–47; Horowitz, *The Italian Labor Movement.*

24. George C. Marshall, "Marshall Plan Speech" (June 5, 1947), http://www.oecd .org/about/marshall/speech.htm (accessed May 14, 2000).

25. William S. Borden, *The Pacific Alliance: United States Foreign Economic Policy and Japanese Trade Recovery, 1947–1955* (Madison: University of Wisconsin Press, 1984); Esposito, *America's Feeble Weapon;* Jeremy Isaacs and Taylor Downing, *Cold War: An Illustrated History, 1945–1991,* 1st ed. (Boston: Little Brown & Co., 1998); Michael Kort, *The Columbia Guide to the Cold War* (New York: Columbia University Press, 1998); Charles S. Maier, *In Search of Stability: Explorations in Historical Political Economy* (Cambridge and New York: Cambridge University Press, 1987); Michael Schaller, *The American Occupation of Japan: The Origins of the Cold War in Asia* (New York: Oxford University Press, 1985).

26. Isaacs and Downing, *Cold War,* 52–53.

27. Julius Braunthal, *History of the International, Volume Three: 1943–1968,* trans. Peter Ford and Kenneth Mitchell (Boulder, Colo.: Westview, 1980), 541–551. See ibid., 144–151, for details.

28. Ibid., 43.

29. Horowitz, *Italian Labor Movement,* 210–217; Behan, *Long Awaited Moment,* chap. 7; Ginsborg, *A History of Contemporary Italy,* 112–120.

30. Account based on Carew et al., *International Confederation of Free Trade Unions,* 167–199; Anthony Carew, "The Schism within the World Federation of Trade Unions: Government and Trade Union Diplomacy," *International Review of Social History* 24, no. 3 (1984); Lewis Levitzki Lorwin, *The International Labor Movement: History, Policies, Outlook* (New York: Harper, 1953); MacShane, *International Labour and the Origins of the Cold War;* John P. Windmuller, *International Trade Union Movement* (Deventer, Boston, and Hingham, Mass.: Kluwer, 1980).

31. Anthony Carew, "The American Labor Movement in Fizzland: The Free Trade Union Committee and the CIA," *Diplomatic History* 39, no. 1 (1998).

32. Joseph LaPalombara, *The Italian Labor Movement: Problems and Prospects* (Ithaca, N.Y.: Cornell University Press, 1957), 25.

33. Romero, *The United States and the European Trade Union Movement,* 168, 170.

34. For a detailed review of these and related developments, see Kort, *Columbia Guide to the Cold War,* 29–35; Isaacs and Downing, *Cold War,* 63–121.

35. Perhaps the most comprehensive source on the international peace movement during this period is Lawrence S. Wittner, *The Struggle against the Bomb* (Stanford, Calif.: Stanford University Press, 1993). The narrative here relies heavily on Wittner's work, as well as on John T. Marcus, *Neutralism and Nationalism in France: A Case Study* (New York: Book Associates, 1958).

36. Marcus, *Neutralism and Nationalism in France,* chap. 5.

37. Wittner, *The Struggle against the Bomb,* 180–181.

38. Ross, *Workers and Communists in France,* 59.

39. Richard F. Kuisel, *Seducing the French: The Dilemma of Americanization* (Berkeley: University of California Press, 1993), 41.

40. Ross, *Workers and Communists in France,* 62–63.

41. Joseph LaPalombara, "The Political Role of Organized Labor in Western Europe," *Journal of Politics* 17, no. 1 (1955), 68–69; Horowitz, *The Italian Labor Movement,* 227, 239.

42. Bedani, *Politics and Ideology in the Italian Workers' Movement,* 82.

43. Marcus, *Neutralism and Nationalism in France,* 13–14.

44. Di Scala, *Renewing Italian Socialism,* 67.

45. For instance, ibid.; Ginsborg, *A History of Contemporary Italy,* 194.

46. Donald Sassoon, *One Hundred Years of Socialism: The West European Left in the Twentieth Century* (New York: New Press, 1996), 209.

47. B. Salvati, "The Rebirth of Trade Unionism, 1943–54," in *The Rebirth of Italy, 1943–50,* ed. S. J. Woolf (London: Longman Group, 1971), 206.

48. Ross, *Workers and Communists in France,* 63.

49. For detailed discussion of these developments see Braunthal, *History of the International,* vol. 3, chap. 4; MacShane, *International Labour and the Origins of the Cold War,* chaps. 11–12.

50. MacShane, *International Labour and the Origins of the Cold War,* 225.

51. Dennis L. Bark and David Gress, *A History of West Germany* (Oxford, UK, and New York: Blackwell, 1989), 139.

52. "DGB Celebrates Its 50th Anniversary," European Industrial Relations Observatory, http://www.eiro.eurofound.ie/print/1999/10/feature/DE9910116F.html (accessed September 12, 2003).

53. See Bark and Gress, *A History of West Germany,* 198–209.

54. Andrei S. Markovits, *The Politics of West German Trade Unions: Strategies of Class and Interest Representation in Growth and Crisis* (Cambridge and New York: Cambridge University Press, 1986), 71–72.

55. Ibid., 65–66.

56. Otto Kirchheimer, *West German Trade Unions: Their Domestic and Foreign Policies* (Santa Monica, Calif.: Rand Corp., 1956).

57. Markovits, *Politics of West German Trade Unions,* 88–89.

58. Andrei S. Markovits and Philip S. Gorski, *The German Left: Red, Green and Beyond, Europe and the International Order* (Cambridge, UK: Polity, 1993), 35–45; Markovits, *Politics of West German Trade Unions,* 83–93. See also Hideo Otake, "Defense Controversies and One-Party Dominance: The Opposition in Japan and West Germany," in *Uncommon Democracies: The One-Party Dominant Regimes,* ed. T. J. Pempel (Ithaca and London: Cornell University Press, 1990).

Chapter 7: Division and Confrontation

1. For detailed discussion see Bruce Cumings, "Japan's Position in the World System," in *Postwar Japan as History,* ed. Andrew Gordon (Berkeley, Los Angeles, and Oxford: University of California Press, 1993); John W. Dower, *Japan in War and Peace: Selected Essays* (New York: New Press, 1993); William S. Borden, *The Pacific Alliance: United States Foreign Economic Policy and Japanese Trade Recovery, 1947–1955* (Madison: University of Wisconsin Press, 1984); Michael Schaller, *The American Occupation of Japan: The Origins of the Cold War in Asia* (New York: Oxford University Press, 1985); Michael Schaller, *Altered States: The United States and Japan since the Occupation* (New York: Oxford University Press, 1997).

2. *MSRUS,* 1:172–173.

3. Hosoya Matsuta claims that the JCP's Tokuda told him and others to begin work on a Sanbetsu self-criticism even before this meeting. Hosoya Matsuta, *Rōdō sensen no bunretsu to tōitsu* (Tokyo: Kanae shuppankai, 1981), 333, 337–338.

4. *SRUS* (1947): 1002–1003.

5. *MSRUS,* 2:55–56. Although hardly a disinterested account, a detailed chronicle of developments surrounding the Sanbetsu self-criticism can be found in Hosoya, *Rōdō sensen no bunretsu to tōitsu,* 336–359.

6. *MSRUS,* 2:55–58.

7. Yoshida Sukeharu, "Sanbetsu kaigi no kessei to soshiki shidō," in *Shōgen sanbetsu kaigi no tanjō,* ed. Hōsei Daigaku Ōhara Shakai Mondai Kenkyūjo (Tokyo: Sōgō rōdō kenkyūjo, 1996), 242–243.

8. Hosoya, *Rōdō sensen no bunretsu to tōitsu,* 349.

9. *MSRUS,* 2:84–88.

10. Hyōdō Atsushi, "Sanbetsu kaigi minshuka dōmei no seiritsu katei," *Ōhara shakai mondai kenkyūjo shiryō geppō,* no. 451 (1996): 32–33, n. 95.

11. "Kokutetsu hankyō renmei seimeisho" (October 21, 1947), in *SSNS:* 78.

12. *SRUS* (1948): 574.

13. "Rōdō minshuka undō ni kansuru ken," in *SRUS* (1948): 575–576.

14. *SYS,* 1:121.

15. Miriam Farley, *Aspects of Japan's Labor Problems* (New York: John Day, 1950), 174.

16. Ibid., 174.

17. Sanbetsu, "Chingin an e no sarani daini no atsuryoku o" (July 8, 1947), in *SSNS*: 65–66.

18. Nakakita Kōji, *Keizai fukkō to sengo seiji: nihon shakaitō 1945–1951* (Tokyo: Tōkyō daigaku shuppankai, 1998), 104; Hyōdō Atsushi, "Sanbetsu kaigi minshuka dōmei no seiritsu katei," 27.

19. Nakakita, *Keizai fukkō to sengo seiji*, 96, 105–106.

20. *NRKM*, 1:220, 231.

21. Ōta Kaoru, *Tatakai no naka de: Rōdō undō nijūgo nen* (Tokyo: Aoki shoten, 1971).

22. See Naitō Norikuni and Akita Seishū, "Zen teishin jūgyōin kumiai (zentei)," in *Nihon rōdō kumiai ron*, ed. Ōkōchi Kazuo (Tokyo: Yūhikaku, 1954), for detailed discussion.

23. "Rōdōshō hassoku ni attate sanbetsu kaigi gichō (Kan Makoto) no iken," in *SSNS*: 68–69.

24. Masumi Junnosuke, *Postwar Politics in Japan, 1945–1955* (Berkeley: Institute of East Asian Studies, 1985), 151–155; Farley, *Aspects of Japan's Labor Problems,* 182.

25. Araki Yoshinobu, ed., *Senryōki ni okeru kyōsanshugi undō* (Tokyo: Ashi shobō, 1993), 182–184; *MSRUS*, 2:89.

26. Schaller, *American Occupation of Japan,* 129.

27. Hasegawa Hiroshi, "Sanbetsu kaigi no kessei to shoki no katsudō," in *Shōgen sanbetsu kaigi no tanjō,* ed. Hōsei Daigaku Ōhara Shakai Mondai Kenkyūjo (Tokyo: Sōgō rōdō kenkyūjo, 1996), 192.

28. "Letter from the Supreme Commander to Prime Minister Ashida, July 22, 1948," in Farley, *Aspects of Japan's Labor Problems,* 250–256.

29. *MSRUS*, 2:155–158, 169–170; *NRKM* 1:275–276, 290–292.

30. Farley, *Aspects of Japan's Labor Problems,* 182–186, 189–211; Motoi Hisao, *Shinpan nihon rōdō undō shi* (Tokyo: Rōmu gyōsei kenkyūjo, 1983), 125–126; 178–185.

31. *MSRUS*, 2:152–155.

32. "Sanbetsu kaigi: Shirei" (July 30, 1948), in *SSNS*: 107. See also Farley, *Aspects of Japan's Labor Problems,* 196–199.

33. "Kokutetsu rōso: Hijōji sengen" (July 30, 1948), and "Zentei: Hijōji sengen" (July 30, 1948), in *SSNS*: 107–108.

34. Farley, *Aspects of Japan's Labor Problems,* 200–201.

35. *MSRUS*, 2:205–206.

36. Account based on *NRKM*, 1:327–330; *MSRUS*, 2:210–213.

37. *NRKM* 1:338–346, 350–353; *MSRUS*, 2:214–223, 226–228.

38. Masumi, *Postwar Politics in Japan,* 218–225.

Chapter 8: Reorganization and Realignment

1. The line of argument in my text is based on Nakakita Kōji, *Keizai fukkō to sengo seiji: Nihon shakaitō 1945–1951* (Tokyo: Tōkyō daigaku shuppankai, 1998), 142–146.

2. Ibid., 153–155.

3. This did not in and of itself mean a laissez-faire economy emerged, as the large literature on Japan's postwar industrial policy makes clear. See, for instance, Chalmers Johnson, *MITI and the Japanese* (Stanford: Stanford University Press, 1982).

4. *MSRUS,* 2:200.

5. "Sanbetsu minshuka dōmei dai ikkai zenkoku taikai kettei: Undō hōshin" (June 13, 1948), in *SSNS:* 79–80.

6. See for instance, Shiota Shōbei, "Zen sen'i sangyō rōdō kumiai dōmei," in *Nihon rōdō kumiai ron,* ed. Okōchi Kazuo (Tokyo: Yūhikaku, 1954).

7. Noda Kazuo, *Sengo keiei shi* (Tokyo: Nihon seisansei honbu, 1965), 307.

8. *MRUS,* 2:203.

9. Theodore Cohen, *Remaking Japan: The American Occupation as New Deal* (New York: Free Press, 1987), 444.

10. Ministry of Labor, "Minshuteki rōdō kumiai oyobi minshuteki rōdō kankei no jochō ni tsuite" (December 22, 1948), in *SRUS* (1948): 1030–1031; Nikkeiren, *Nikkeiren sanjūnen shi* (Tokyo: Nihon keieisha dantai renmei, 1981), 206–207.

11. Lonny E. Carlile, "Zaikai and the Politics of Production in Japan, 1940–1962" (Ph.D. diss., University of California at Berkeley, 1989), 276–296.

12. *SRUS* (1950): 797.

13. See Hazama Otohiko, "Shihon kōsei no shokyokumen," *Keiei hyōron* 3, no. 7 (1948).

14. For detailed treatment through primary documents, see *SRUS* (1950): 797–875.

15. *MSRUS,* 2:200–201.

16. Murakami Kanji, *Sōhyō monogatari* (Tokyo: Nihon hyōronsha, 1960–61), 1:32–34.

17. Hosoya Matsuta, *Rōdō sensen no bunretsu to tōitsu* (Tokyo: Kanae Shuppankai, 1981), 384.

18. *MSRUS,* 2:131–139.

19. "Sanbetsu minshuka dōmei dai ikkai zenkoku taikai kettei," 79–80.

20. *MSRUS,* 2:173–174; *NRKM,* 1:295–296.

21. *SRUS* (1949): 380.

22. Murakami, *Sōhyō monogatari,* 1:79–81.

23. *MSRUS,* 2:249–250.

24. Takaragi Fumihiko, "Sōhyō tanjō zengo," in Takanashi Akira, ed., *Shōgen sengo rōdō kumiai undō shi* (Tokyo: Tōyō keizai shinpōsha, 1985), 99.

25. For detailed treatment, see *NRN* (1952): 392–399.

26. *NRN* (1952): 352.

27. For detailed elaboration of the Takano plan, see *SYS,* 1:161–170.

28. *NRN* (1951): 431–435.

29. See transcript of press conference held by the delegation on its return to Japan in *SRUS* (1950): 410–412.

30. Takita Minoru, "Kokusai rōdō undō no chōryū to nihon no rōdō kumiai," in *Shōgen sengo rōdō kumiai undō shi,* ed. Takanashi Akira (Tokyo: Tōyō shobō, 1985), 224.

31. Ibid., 225–226.

32. Takemae Eiji, *Sengo rōdō kaikaku: GHQ rōdō seisakushi* (Tokyo: Tōkyō daigaku shuppankai, 1982), 307.

33. Takemae Eiji, "Sōhyō and US Occupation Labour Policy: An Interview with Valery Burati," *Tōkyō keizai daigaku shi,* no. 97–98 (1976): 256.

34. John Price, "Valery Burati and the Formation of Sohyo During the US Occupation of Japan," *Pacific Affairs* 64, no. 2 (1991): 224.

35. Takemae, *Sengo rōdō kaikaku,* 308–310.

36. Price, "Valery Burati and the Formation of Sohyo," 214–215, 217–219.

37. Takemae, "Sōhyō and US Occupation Labour Policy," 256–257.

38. Takemae, *Sengo rōdō kaikaku,* 310–311.

39. Ibid., 314–316; Price, "Valery Burati and the Formation of Sohyo," 218, 220–222.

40. For a detailed presentation, see Takemae, *Sengo rōdō kaikaku,* 321–331.

41. *SYS,* 1:62–63.

42. Sōhyō's hegemony would erode over time, but it would remain a primary force in the movement until its dissolution, in 1989.

43. Shimizu Shinzō, *Sengo kakushin no hanichikage* (Tokyo: Nihon keizai hyōronsha, 1995), 115–116.

Chapter 9: Peace, Neutrality, and the Takano Years

1. *NRN* (1951): 673.

2. *NRN* (1952): 522–524; Shakai Undō Chōsa Kai, *Sayoku dantai yōren* (1958): 98, 114.

3. *SYS,* 1:66.

4. Quoted in Shimizu Hajime, "Kaisetsu," in *TMCS,* 3:572.

5. *MSRUS,* 3:130–134.

6. For details, see *SRUS* (1951): 743–746.

7. Among the key figures here were Hoshika Kaname and Katō Etsuo of Kokutetsu's Shinsei Mindō, Murata Tetsuo of Zenkō, Saitō Isamu of Zensen Dōmei, Koga Hiroshi of Sōdōmei, and Kanesugi Hidenobu of Zenzōsen. Shimizu Hajime, "Kaisetsu," in *TMCS,* 3:574. See *SRUS* (1951): 746–748, for details.

8. In addition to Iwai, Takaragi, and Hiragaki, figures associated with the Rōdōsha Dōshikai included Kashiwabara Minoru of Shinsanbetsu, Ishiguro Kiyoshi of Tanrō, Ōta Kaoru of Gōka Rōren, Shima Kiyotake of Densan, Shimizu Shinzō of Tekkō Rōren, and Nomoto Shōzō of Zenji. Shimizu Hajime, "Kaisetsu," in *TMCS,* 3:574. See *SRUS* (1951): 748–750, for details.

9. *SRUS* (1951): 742–743; Masumi Junnosuke, *Postwar Politics in Japan, 1945–1955*

(Berkeley: Institute of East Asian Studies, 1985), 218; *NRKM*, 2:73–74; *MSRUS*, 3:162–165.

10. Takano Minoru, *Tainichi kōwa to kongo no rōdō undō* (Tokyo: Gaikoku bunkasha, 1951), 42–52.

11. Ibid., 51–52.

12. Ibid., 4.

13. Quoted in *SYS*, 1:136.

14. Ibid., 137.

15. Shimizu Hajime, "Kaisetsu," in *TMCS*, 3:573. Although one of the declared principles of the conference was the exclusion of communists, and this principle was maintained at the national level, communist activists were in fact active in some of the local chapters.

16. *MSRUS*, 3:155.

17. At one point, the Minister of Labor hinted that the government might be willing to consider revisions to the law that would specifically exempt labor union activities from the provisions of the law, but in the end the Yoshida government did not adopt the proposal. *MSRUS*, 3:191–192.

18. *MSRUS*, 2:201.

19. Differences that emerged among Sōhyō unions over matters of principle, and in particular those associated with the calling of political strikes, became more overt as the campaign progressed. Matters came to a head as discussions were conducted on the choice of targets for the third and fourth strike waves. A group of industrial-federation leaders, including those in the Seamen's Union, the Textile Workers' Union, and the Private Railway Workers' Union argued that it would be a violation of parliamentary democratic principles for the unions to strike against "political" legislation and that, therefore, the target of the strike wave should be limited to the labor legislation package. Other unions insisted on maintaining the element of protest against the antisubversive-actions legislation. The matter was ultimately dealt with by dividing the initially planned wave into two separate waves, one of which was directed of the labor legislation and the other in protest against the Subversive Activities Prevention Act. The number of unions and workers participating in this latter protest was a mere whimper compared to the earlier waves. Shortly before the first wave, Tanrō "postponed" its strike to a later date, while Zenkō, another union associated with the presidents' group, decided to hold workplace rallies instead of a strike. The initial wave on June 7 to protest the labor legislation had 29,000 workers participating in full 24-hour strikes and another 51,000 involved in strikes of a more limited duration. The numbers for the second wave, on June 17, were 17,000 and 26,000, respectively. The Seamen's Union, the Textile Workers' Union, and the Private Railway Workers' Union all "postponed" the strikes that they had scheduled for that day.

20. Quoted in *SYS*, 1:144; *MSRUS*, 4:111–112; *SYS*, 1:98–100.

21. Anthony Carew, *Labour Under the Marshall Plan: The Politics of Productivity and the Marketing of Management Science* (Manchester: Manchester University Press, 1987), 236;

Julius Braunthal, *History of the International, Volume Three: 1943–1968,* trans. Peter Ford and Kenneth Mitchell (Boulder, Colo.: Westview, 1980), 366–374.

22. Takano Minoru, "Moeru ajia: Shakaitō kaigi ga oshieru mono," as reproduced in *TMCS,* 4:252–258.

23. *MSRUS,* 4:78–79; *SYS,* 1:141–142.

24. *SYS,* 2:537–546, 555–560.

25. *MSRUS,* 4:211–213; *NRKM,* 2:170–171.

26. *MSRUS,* 4:11.

27. *SYS,* 1:99; *MSRUS,* 4:111–115; *NRKM* 2:146–147.

28. *MSRUS,* 4:84, 86–90; *NRKM,* 2:128–130.

29. *MSRUS,* 4:88–89.

30. "Yoshida dokusai seiken no genjitsu o miyo," as quoted in *SYS,* 1:144.

31. For an account, see *MSRUS,* 4:147–150.

32. Yamamoto Masahiro, "Sasha kōryō no sakusei o meguru ronsō ten to sōhyō undō e no impakuto," *Kokusai rōdō,* nos. 209, 211 (1988–1989).

33. *SYS,* 2:283–287; *MSRUS,* 2:178–184; *NRKM,* 2:86–89.

34. *MSRUS,* 3:182.

35. *MSRUS,* 4:40–56; *NRKM,* 2:113–117.

36. For details, see *SGS,* 3:637–756; *NRKM,* 2:27–30; *MSRUS,* 3:113–116, 137–141.

37. Minrōken, "Shuisho," in *SRUS* (1951): 747–748.

38. *ZJS,* 82. The text of the statement ("Sōhyō shidō hōshin hihan: Minshuteki rōdō kumiai no tachiba ni tatte") is reproduced in *ZJS,* appendix, 7–15.

39. Zensen Dōmei, Kaiin Kumiai, Nippōro, and Zen'eien, "Sōhyō shidō hōshin hihan" (December 26, 1952), in SSJS, 266.

40. *ZJS,* 83–98.

41. *MSRUS,* 3:116–120.

42. For details, see *ZJS,* 98–104, 124–211.

43. "Kenshō sōan zenbun," in *ZJS,* 211–234.

Chapter 10: Productivity and Industrial Modernization under "Peaceful Coexistence"

1. Michael Kort, *The Columbia Guide to the Cold War* (New York: Columbia University Press, 1998), 40. See also, Jeremy Isaacs and Taylor Downing, *Cold War: An Illustrated History, 1945–1991,* 1st ed. (Boston: Little Brown & Co., 1998), 125–143.

2. Paul Ginsborg, *A History of Contemporary Italy: Society and Politics, 1943–1988* (London and New York: Penguin Books, 1990), 257.

3. George Ross, *Workers and Communists in France: From Popular Front to Eurocommunism* (Berkeley: University of California Press, 1982), 101–105, 107–108.

4. Anthony Carew, *Labour Under the Marshall Plan: The Politics of Productivity and the Marketing of Management Science* (Manchester: Manchester University Press, 1987), 112.

5. Ibid., 158, 167, 184–185.

6. William M. Tsutsui, *Manufacturing Ideology: Scientific Management in Twentieth-Century Japan* (Princeton, N.J.: Princeton University Press, 1998), 137.

7. Federico Romero, *The United States and the European Trade Union Movement, 1944–1951* (Chapel Hill: University of North Carolina Press, 1992), 224–225.

8. William Gomber, "Labor's Participation in the European Productivity Program: A Study in Frustration," *Political Science Quarterly* 74, no. 2 (1959).

9. Paolo D'attore, "ERP Aid and the Politics of Productivity in Italy During the 1950s," EUI Working Paper No. 85/159 (Florence: European University Institute Department of History and Civilization, 1985), 14.

10. Ibid., 15. On these points, see Carew, *Labour Under the Marshall Plan,* passim; Romero, *The United States and the European Trade Union Movement,* passim; Mark Rupert, *Producing Hegemony: The Politics of Mass Production and American Global Power* (Cambridge and New York: Cambridge University Press, 1995), passim; Charles S. Maier, *In Search of Stability: Explorations in Historical Political Economy* (Cambridge and New York: Cambridge University Press, 1987), 121–152.

11. D'attore, "ERP Aid and the Politics of Productivity in Italy," 38.

12. Richard F. Kuisel, *Seducing the French: The Dilemma of Americanization* (Berkeley: University of California Press, 1993), 98.

13. For a detailed account of the British experience, see Carew, *Labour Under the Marshall Plan,* 131–157, 168–171, 200–211.

14. Ibid., 223.

15. Andrei S. Markovits, *The Politics of West German Trade Unions: Strategies of Class and Interest Representation in Growth and Crisis* (Cambridge and New York: Cambridge University Press, 1986), 25.

16. Helga Grebing and Mary Saran, *The History of the German Labour Movement: A Survey* (London: Wolff, 1969), 178.

17. Peter Swenson, *Fair Shares: Unions, Pay, and Politics in Sweden and West Germany,* Cornell Studies in Political Economy (Ithaca: Cornell University Press, 1989), 192.

18. Markovits, *Politics of West German Trade Unions,* 84–86.

19. Swenson, *Fair Shares,* 191.

20. See ibid., 177–223.

21. For discussion, see Markovits, *Politics of West German Trade Unions,* 101–104.

22. Ross, *Workers and Communists in France,* 86.

23. Gino Bedani, *Politics and Ideology in the Italian Workers' Movement: Union Development and the Changing Role of the Catholic and Communist Subcultures in Postwar Italy* (Oxford, and Providence, R.I.: Berg, 1995), 72–73.

24. Ross, *Workers and Communists in France,* 168–169.

25. Don Sassoon, *The Strategy of the Italian Communist Party: From the Resistance to the Historic Compromise* (New York: St. Martin's Press, 1981).

26. Bedani, *Politics and Ideology in the Italian Workers' Movement,* 121–122.

27. For detailed discussion, see Peter Michael Lange, George Ross, and Maurizio Van-

nicelli, *Unions, Change, and Crisis: French and Italian Union Strategy and the Political Economy, 1945–1980* (London and New York: Allen and Unwin, 1982); Ginsborg, *A History of Contemporary Italy;* Bedani, *Politics and Ideology in the Italian Workers' Movement;* Joanne Barkan, *Visions of Emancipation: The Italian Workers' Movement since 1945* (New York: Praeger, 1984); and Ross, *Workers and Communists in France.*

28. Miriam Golden, *Labor Divided: Austerity and Working-Class Politics in Contemporary Italy* (Ithaca: Cornell University Press, 1988), 50. Also, Ginsborg, *A History of Contemporary Italy,* 207–208.

29. Golden, *Labor Divided,* 28–31.

30. Bedani, *Politics and Ideology in the Italian Workers' Movement,* 103.

31. Details in Lange, Ross, and Vannicelli, *Unions, Change and Crisis,* and Ross, *Workers and Communists in France.*

32. For detailed treatment see George R. Packard III, *Protest in Tokyo: The Security Treaty Crisis of 1960* (Princeton: Princeton University Press, 1966).

33. See Kōsai Yutaka, *The Era of High Speed Growth: Notes on the Postwar Japanese Economy* (Tokyo: University of Tokyo Press, 1986), and Nakamura Takafusa, *The Postwar Japanese Economy: Its Development and Structure, 1937–1994,* 2nd ed. (Tokyo: University of Tokyo Press, 1995).

34. Gōka Rōren, "Sōhyō taikai ni taisuru hōshin," in *SRUS* (1954): 836–839.

35. *SRUS* (1954): 833.

36. Among those involved on the Takano side were the noted progressive intellectual Shimizu Ikutarō, Fujita Tōtarō of Shitetsu Sōren, Shimizu Shinzō of Tekkō Rōren, Masuda Tetsuo of the Nissan Union, and Ichikawa Makoto of Zenchūrō.

37. *MSRUS,* 4:187–193; *NRKM,* 2:198–200.

38. *SYS,* 1:235–249; *MSRUS,* 4:222–230; and *NRKM,* 2:218–222.

39. For a concise but comprehensive overview, see Takanashi Akira, *Kawaru shuntō: Rekishiteki sōkatsu to tenbō* (Tokyo: Nihon rōdō kenkyūjo, 2002). In English, Ikuo Kume, *Disparaged Success: Labor Politics in Postwar Japan* (Ithaca, N.Y.: Cornell University Press, 1998); John Price, *Japan Works: Power and Paradox in Postwar Industrial Relations* (Ithaca: ILR Press, 1997); and Mari Sako, "Shunto: The Role of Employer and Union Coordination at the Industry and Inter-Sectoral Levels," in *Japanese Labour and Management in Transition: Diversity, Flexibility and Participation,* ed. Mari Sako and Hiroki Sato (London and New York: Routledge, 1997).

40. Iwai Akira, *Sōhyō to tomoni* (Tokyo: Yomiuri shinbunsha, 1971), 149. For detailed discussion, see Lonny E. Carlile, "*Sōhyō* Versus *Dōmei:* Competing Labor Movement Strategies in the Era of High Growth in Japan," *Japan Forum* 6, no. 2 (1994).

41. *SYS,* 1:304–305.

42. Hiwatari Nobuhiro, *Sengo nihon no shijō to seiji* (Tokyo: Tōkyō daigaku shuppankai, 1991), 119–137.

43. Ōta Kaoru, *Tatakai no naka de: Rōdō undō nijūgo nen* (Tokyo: Aoki shoten, 1971), 103.

44. Takanashi, *Kawaru shuntō,* 5.

45. "Kenshō sōan zenbun," in *ZJS*, 211–234.

46. For treatments of the JPC and the productivity movement, see Lonny E. Carlile, "Zaikai and the Politics of Production in Japan, 1940–1962" (Ph.D. diss., University of California at Berkeley, 1989), 333–425; Kume, *Disparaged Success*, 102–104; Tsutsui, *Manufacturing Ideology;* and Charles Martin Weathers, "Transforming Labor: State and Employer Strategy in Postwar Japan" (Ph.D. diss., University of California, 1995). A comprehensive history can be found in Nihon Seisansei Honbu, *Seisansei undō sanjū nen shi* (Tokyo: Nihon seisansei honbu, 1985).

47. Sōhyō, "Seisansei zōkyō undō ni taisuru kihon taido," in *SSSS*, 1:498–500.

48. *Seisansei shinbun,* quoted in Nihon Seisansei Honbu, *Seisansei undō sanjū nen shi,* 290.

49. Zenrō and Sōdōmei amalgamated their organization in 1964 into a new organization, Dōmei.

50. Nihon Seisansei Honbu, *Seisansei undō sanjū nen shi,* 465–467.

51. Carlile, "Zaikai and the Politics of Production," 412–417.

52. Jiyū Minshutō, *Jiyū minshutō tōshi* (Tokyo: Jiyū minshutō, 1987).

53. Kathleen Ann Thelen, *Union of Parts: Labor Politics in Postwar Germany* (Ithaca, N.Y.: Cornell University Press, 1991).

54. Shimizu Shinzō, *Sengo rōdō kumiai undō shiron: Kigyō shakai chōkoku no shiza* (Tokyo: Nihon hyōronsha, 1982); SYS, 1:265.

55. Andrew Gordon, *The Wages of Affluence: Labor and Management in Postwar Japan* (Cambridge, Mass.: Harvard University Press, 1998); Michael H. Gibbs, *Struggle and Purpose in Postwar Japanese Unionism,* vol. 14 of Japan Research Monograph (Berkeley: Institute of East Asian Studies, 2000); Akira Suzuki, "The Polarization of the Union Movement in Postwar Japan: Politics in the Unions of Steel and Railway Workers" (Ph.D. diss., University of Wisconsin, 1997); Price, *Japan Works.*

56. Iwai, *Sōhyō to tomoni,* 12, 180.

57. Rōdō Dōshikai, "Rōdō undō no zenshin no tame ni," (January 23, 1960) in *SSSS,* 1:391–393.

58. For details see Gerald L. Curtis, *The Japanese Way of Politics* (New York: Columbia University Press, 1988), 138–156, and Masumi Junnosuke, *Contemporary Politics in Japan,* trans. Lonny E. Carlile (Berkeley: University of California Press, 1995), 322–345. In Japanese, see Shinkawa Toshimitsu, *Sengo nihon seiji to shakai minshu shugi: Shakaitō sōhyō burokku no kōbō* (Kyotoi: Hōritsu bunkasha, 1999), 61–64, 75–76.

59. *SYS,* 1:404–413.

60. Ōta, *Tatakai no naka de,* 168.

61. *Asahi shinbun* (February 4, 1961), 1.

62. For a discussion of JSP behavioral patterns during this period, see Satomi Tani, "The Japan Socialist Party before the Mid-1960s: An Analysis of Its Stagnation," in *Creating Single-Party Democracy: Japan's Postwar Political System,* ed. Tetsuya Kataoka (Stanford, Calif.: Hoover Institution Press, 1992).

Conclusion

1. See Volker R. Berghahn, "The United States and the Shaping of West Germany's Social Compact, 1945–1966," *International Labor and Working-Class History* 50 (1996); Andrei S. Markovits, *The Politics of West German Trade Unions: Strategies of Class and Interest Representation in Growth and Crisis* (Cambridge and New York: Cambridge University Press, 1986); Hideo Otake, "Defense Controversies and One-Party Dominance: The Opposition in Japan and West Germany," in *Uncommon Democracies: The One-Party Dominant Regimes,* ed. T. J. Pempel (Ithaca and London: Cornell University Press, 1990).

2. Ross and Gourevitch, "Conclusion," in Peter Alexis Gourevitch, ed., *Unions and Economic Crisis: Britain, West Germany, and Sweden* (London and Boston: Allen & Unwin, 1984), 366.

3. Chris Howell, *Regulating Labor: The State and Industrial Relations Reform in Postwar France* (Princeton, N.J.: Princeton University Press, 1992), 51–60; Irwin M. Wall, "The French Social Contract: Conflict Amid Cooperation," *International Labor and Working-Class History* 50 (1996).

4. Joanne Barkan, *Visions of Emancipation: The Italian Workers' Movement since 1945* (New York: Praeger, 1984); Peter Michael Lange, George Ross, and Maurizio Vannicelli, *Unions, Change, and Crisis: French and Italian Union Strategy and the Political Economy, 1945–1980* (London and New York: Allen and Unwin, 1982).

5. Andrew Gordon, "The Emergence of a Labor-Management Settlement in Japan, 1945–1960," *International Labor and Working-Class History* 50 (1996).

6. See Lonny E. Carlile, "*Sōhyō* Versus *Dōmei*: Competing Labor Movement Strategies in the Era of High Growth in Japan," *Japan Forum* 6, no. 2 (1994), for more discussion.

7. Ōta Kaoru, *Shuntō no shūen: Tei seichōka no rōdō undō* (Tokyo: Chūō keizaisha, 1978).

Bibliography

Adams, John Clarke. "Italy." In *Comparative Labor Movements,* edited by Walter Galenson, 410–479. New York: Russell & Russell, 1968.

Allinson, Gary D. "The Moderation of Organized Labor in Postwar Japan." *Journal of Japanese Studies* 1, no. 2 (Spring 1975): 409–436.

Andō Yoshio. *Kindai nihon keizai shi yōran.* 2nd ed. Tokyo: Tōkyō daigaku shuppankai, 1979.

———, ed. *Shōwa keizi shi e no shōgen.* 3 vols. Tokyo: Mainichi shinbunsha, 1966.

Arahata Kanson. *Kanson jiden.* Tokyo: Ronsōsha, 1961.

Araki Yoshinobu. *Senryōki ni okeru kyōsanshugi undō.* Tokyo: Ashi shobō, 1993.

Ariizumi Toru, Akita Seishu, and Tosaka Arako. "Denki sangyō rōdō kumiai (densan)." In *Nihon rōdō kumiai ron,* edited by Ōkochi Kazuo, 51–150. Tokyo: Yūhikaku, 1954.

Banno Junji. "Senzen nihon ni okeru 'shakai minshushugi,' 'minshu shakai shugi,' 'kigyō minshushugi.'" In *Rekishiteki zentei,* edited by Tōkyō Daigaku Shakai Kagaku Kenkyūjo, 227–261. Tokyo: Tōkyō daigaku shuppankai, 1991.

Bark, Dennis L., and David Gress. *A History of West Germany.* Oxford, UK, and New York: Blackwell, 1989.

Barkan, Joanne. *Visions of Emancipation: The Italian Workers' Movement since 1945.* New York: Praeger, 1984.

Barnes, Samuel H. "The Politics of French Christian Labor." *Journal of Politics* 21, no. 1 (1959): 105–122.

Bedani, Gino. *Politics and Ideology in the Italian Workers' Movement: Union Development and the Changing Role of the Catholic and Communist Subcultures in Postwar Italy.* Oxford, and Providence, R.I.: Berg, 1995.

Behan, Tom. *The Long Awaited Moment: The Working Class and the Italian Communist Party in Milan, 1943–1948.* New York: Peter Lang, 1997.

Berger, Stefan. "Democracy and Social Democracy." *European History Quarterly* 32, no. 1 (2002): 13–37.

Berghahn, Volker R. "The United States and the Shaping of West Germany's Social Compact, 1945–1966." *International Labor and Working-Class History* 50 (1996): 125–132.

Bernstein, Gail Lee. *Japanese Marxist: A Portrait of Kawakami Hajime, 1879–1946.* Harvard East Asian Series 86. Cambridge, Mass.: Harvard University Press, 1976.

Boehling, Rebecca. "U.S. Military Occupation, Grass Roots Democracy, and Local German Government." In *American Policy and the Reconstruction of West Germany,* edited by Jeffry M. Diefendorf, Axel Frohn, and Hermann-Josef Rupieper, 281–306. Washington, D.C.; Cambridge, England; New York; Oakleigh, Australia: German Historical Institute and Cambridge University Press, 1993.

Borden, William S. *The Pacific Alliance: United States Foreign Economic Policy and Japanese Trade Recovery, 1947–1955.* Madison: University of Wisconsin Press, 1984.

Bornstein, Stephen. "States and Unions: From Postwar Settlement to Contemporary Stalemate." In *The State in Capitalist Europe: A Casebook,* edited by Stephen Bornstein, David Held, Joel Krieger, and Harvard University, 54–90. London; Winchester, Mass.; and Boston: G. Allen & Unwin and Center for European Studies Harvard University, 1984.

Bouscaren, Anthony Trawick. "The MRP in French Governments, 1948–1951." *Journal of Politics* 14, no. 1 (1952): 104–131.

Brandt, Willy. "Address." In *Contending with Hitler: Varieties of German Resistance in the Third Reich,* edited by David Clay Large, 9–16. Washington, D.C.; Cambridge, England; New York; Oakleigh, Australia: German Historical Institute and Cambridge University Press, 1991.

Braunthal, Julius. *History of the International, Volume One: 1864–1913.* Translated by John Clark. New York and Washington: Praeger, 1967.

———. *History of the International, Volume Two: 1914–1943.* Translated by John Clark. New York and Washington: Praeger, 1967.

———. *History of the International, Volume Three: 1943–1968.* Translated by Peter Ford and Kenneth Mitchell. Boulder, Colo.: Westview, 1980.

Broszat, Martin. "A Social and Historical Typology of the German Opposition to Hitler." In *Contending with Hitler: Varieties of German Resistance in the Third Reich,* edited by David Clay Large, 25–33. Washington, D.C.; Cambridge, England; New York; Oakleigh, Australia: German Historical Institute and Cambridge University Press, 1991.

Carew, Anthony. "The American Labor Movement in Fizzland: The Free Trade Union Committee and the CIA." *Diplomatic History* 39, no. 1 (1998): 25–42.

———. *Labour Under the Marshall Plan: The Politics of Productivity and the Marketing of Management Science.* Manchester: Manchester University Press, 1987.

———. "The Schism within the World Federation of Trade Unions: Government and Trade Union Diplomacy." *International Review of Social History* 24, no. 3 (1984): 297–335.

Carew, Anthony, Michel Dreyfus, Geert Van Goethem, and Rebecca Gumbrell-McCormick. *The International Confederation of Free Trade Unions.* Bern: Peter Lang, 2000.

Carlile, Lonny E. "*Sōhyō* Versus *Dōmei:* Competing Labor Movement Strategies in the Era of High Growth in Japan." *Japan Forum* 6, no. 2 (1994): 145–157.

———. "Zaikai and the Politics of Production in Japan, 1940–1962." Ph.D. diss., University of California at Berkeley, 1989.

Carrillo, Elisa A. "The Italian Catholic Church and Communism, 1943–1963." *The Catholic Historical Review* 78 (1991): 644–657.

Clay, Lucius D. *Decision in Germany.* Garden City, N.Y.: Doubleday, 1950.

Cohen, Theodore. *Remaking Japan: The American Occupation as New Deal.* New York: Free Press, 1987.

Colbert, Evelyn Speyer. *The Left Wing in Japanese Politics.* New York: International Secretariat Institute of Pacific Relations, 1952.

Cole, Allan Burnett, George O. Totten, and Cecil H. Uyehara. *Socialist Parties in Postwar Japan.* New Haven, Conn.: Yale University Press, 1966.

Congressional Quarterly. *Evolution of Foreign Aid 1945–1965: A Comprehensive Chronology of Foreign Aid Legislation, Highlighting Major Aid Policies, Programs, Congressional Debates, and Government Aid Agencies.* Washington, D.C., 1966.

Conway, Martin. *Catholic Politics in Europe, 1918–1945.* London and New York: Routledge, 1997.

———. "Democracy in Postwar Western Europe: The Triumph of a Political Model." *European History Quarterly* 32, no. 1 (2002): 59–84.

Cook, Alice Hanson. *An Introduction to Japanese Trade Unionism.* Ithaca: New York State School of Industrial and Labor Relations, Cornell University, 1966.

Cumings, Bruce. "Japan's Position in the World System." In *Postwar Japan as History,* edited by Andrew Gordon, 34–63. Berkeley, Los Angeles, and Oxford: University of California Press, 1993.

Curtis, Gerald L. *The Japanese Way of Politics.* New York: Columbia University Press, 1988.

D'attore, Paolo. "ERP Aid and the Politics of Productivity in Italy During the 1950s." EUI Working Paper No. 85/159. Florence: European University Institute Department of History and Civilization, 1985.

Di Scala, Spencer M. *Renewing Italian Socialism: Nenni to Craxi.* New York and Oxford: Oxford University Press, 1988.

Dower, John W. *Embracing Defeat: Japan in the Wake of World War II.* 1st ed. New York: W. W. Norton & Co./The New Press, 1999.

———. *Empire and Aftermath: Yoshida Shigeru and the Japanese Experience, 1878–1954.* Cambridge, Mass.: Council on East Asian Studies Harvard University, 1979.

———. *Japan in War and Peace: Selected Essays.* New York: New Press, 1993.

Endō Kōshi. *Nihon senryō to rōshi kankei seisaku no seiritsu.* Tokyo: Tōkyō daigaku shuppankai, 1989.

Endō Sōkichi. "Nihon kokuyū tetsudō rōdō kumiai (kokutetsu)." In *Nihon rōdō kumiai ron,* edited by Ōkōchi Kazuo, 153–222. Tokyo: Yūhikaku, 1954.

Esposito, Chiarella. *America's Feeble Weapon: Funding the Marshall Plan in France and Italy, 1948–1950.* Westport, Conn.: Greenwood Press, 1994.

Farley, Miriam. *Aspects of Japan's Labor Problems.* New York: John Day, 1950.

Filippelli, Ronald L. *American Labor and Postwar Italy, 1943–1953: A Study of Cold War Politics.* Stanford, Calif.: Stanford University Press, 1989.

Fitzpatrick, Sheila. "Socialism and Communism." In *The Columbia History of the 20th Century,* edited by Richard W. Bulliet, 203–228. New York: Columbia University Press, 1998.

Fujita Wakao. "Zen nihon sangyōbetsu rōdō kumiai kaigi no undō." In *Rōdō kumiai undō shi,* edited by Ōkōchi Kazuo and Fujita Wakao, 25–79. Tokyo: Kōbundō, 1962.

Galenson, Walter. *Comparative Labor Movements.* New York: Russell & Russell, 1968.

Garon, Sheldon M. *The State and Labor in Modern Japan.* Berkeley: University of California Press, 1987.

Geary, Dick. *European Labour Protest 1848–1939.* New York: St. Martin's Press, 1981.

———, ed. *Labour and Socialist Movements in Europe before 1914.* Oxford and New York: Berg, 1989.

Gekkan Shakaitō Henshubu, ed. *Nihon shakaitō no sanjū nen.* 2 vols. Tokyo: Shakai shinpō, 1974.

Gibbs, Michael H. *Struggle and Purpose in Postwar Japanese Unionism.* Vol. 14, Japan Research Monograph. Berkeley: Institute of East Asian Studies, 2000.

Ginsborg, Paul. *A History of Contemporary Italy: Society and Politics, 1943–1988.* London and New York: Penguin Books, 1990.

Godson, Roy. *The Kremlin and Labor: A Study in National Security Policy.* New York: Crane, Russak and Company, Inc., 1977.

Golden, Miriam. *Labor Divided: Austerity and Working-Class Politics in Contemporary Italy.* Ithaca: Cornell University Press, 1988.

Gomber, William. "Labor's Participation in the European Productivity Program: A Study in Frustration." *Political Science Quarterly* 74, no. 2 (1959): 240–255.

Gordon, Andrew. "The Emergence of a Labor-Management Settlement in Japan, 1945–1960." *International Labor and Working-Class History* 50 (1996): 133–139.

———. *The Evolution of Labor Relations in Japan: Heavy Industry, 1853–1955.* Cambridge, Mass., and London: Harvard University Council on East Asian Studies, 1985.

———. *Labor and Imperial Democracy.* Berkeley, Los Angeles, and Oxford: University of California Press, 1991.

———. *The Wages of Affluence: Labor and Management in Postwar Japan.* Cambridge, Mass.: Harvard University Press, 1998.

Gōshi Kōhei. "Seisansei kōjō undō." In *Shōgen: Kōdō seichōki no nihon,* edited by *Ekonomisuto* Henshūbu, 233–242. Tokyo: Mainichi shinbunsha, 1984.

Gourevitch, Peter Alexis. *Politics in Hard Times: Comparative Responses to International Economic Crises.* Ithaca: Cornell University Press, 1986.

Gourevitch, Peter Alexis, and Harvard University Center for European Studies. *Unions and Economic Crisis: Britain, West Germany, and Sweden.* London and Boston: Allen & Unwin, 1984.

Graham, Bruce Desmond. *Choice and Democratic Order: The French Socialist Party 1937–1950.* Cambridge and New York: Cambridge University Press, 1974.

Grebing, Helga, and Mary Saran. *The History of the German Labour Movement: A Survey.* London: Wolff, 1969.

Griffith, William E. "The Diplomacy of Eurocommunism." In *Eurocommunism and Deténte,* edited by Rudolf L. Tökés, 385–436. New York: New York University Press, 1978.

Hasegawa Hiroshi. "Sanbetsu kaigi no kessei to shoki no katsudō." In *Shōgen sanbetsu kaigi no tanjō,* edited by Hōsei Daigaku and Ōhara Shakai Mondai Kenkyūjo, 161–205. Tokyo: Sōgō rōdō kenkyūjo, 1996.

Hayakawa Seiichirō. "Kankō rōshi kankei no seisei to tenkai: Kokutetsu yūsei ni okeru kenri kankei ni tsuite." In *Sengo kaikaku: Rōdō kaikaku,* edited by Tōkyō Daigaku. Shakai Kagaku Kenkyūjo, 309–353. Tokyo: Tōkyō daigaku shuppankai, 1974.

Hayakawa Seiichirō and Yoshida Kenji. "Keizai fukkō kaigi no soshiki to undō." *Ōhara shakai mondai kenkyūjo kenkyū shiryō geppō,* nos. 283, 284, 292 (1982): 1–34, 1–57, 1–22, respectively.

Hazama Otohiko. "Shihon kōsei no shokyokumen." *Keiei hyōron* 3, no. 7 (1948): 18–21.

Hein, Laura. *Fueling Growth: The Energy Revolution and Economic Policy in Postwar Japan.* Vol. 147. Cambridge, Mass., and London: Council on East Asian Studies, Harvard University and Harvard University Press, 1990.

Hiwatari Nobuhiro. *Sengo nihon no shijō to seiji.* Tokyo: Tōkyō daigaku shuppankai, 1991.

Holter, Darryl. *The Battle for Coal: Miners and the Politics of Nationalization in France, 1940–1950.* DeKalb: Northern Illinois University Press, 1992.

Horishoki Teizō, ed. *Keizai dantai rengōkai jūnen shi.* 2 vols. Tokyo: Keizai dantai rengōkai, 1962.

Horowitz, Daniel L. *The Italian Labor Movement.* Cambridge, Mass.: Harvard University Press, 1963.

Hōsei Daigaku Ōhara Shakai Mondai Kenkyūjo, eds. *Shōgen sanbetsu kaigi no tanjō.* Tokyo: Sōgō rōdō kenkyūjo, 1996.

Hosoya Matsuta. *Nihon rōdō undōshi.* Tokyo: Kanae shuppankai, 1981.

———. *Rōdō sensen no bunretsu to tōitsu.* Tokyo: Kanae shuppankai, 1981.

———. "Sanbetsu kaigi no kessei to ni-ichi suto." In *Shōgen sanbetsu kaigi no tanjō,* edited by Hōsei Daigaku Ōhara Shakai Mondai Kenkyūjo, 105–130. Tokyo: Sōgō rōdō kenkyūjo, 1996.

———. "Sengo minshushugi to rōdō kumiai no seiritsu." In *Shōgen sengo rōdō kumiai undōshi,* edited by Takanashi Akira, 1–36. Tokyo: Tōyō keizai shinpōsha, 1985.

Hoston, Germaine A. *Marxism and the Crisis of Development in Prewar Japan.* Princeton, N.J.: Princeton University Press, 1986.

Howell, Chris. *Regulating Labor: The State and Industrial Relations Reform in Postwar France.* Princeton, N.J.: Princeton University Press, 1992.

Hyōdō Atsushi. "Sanbetsu kaigi minshuka dōmei no seiritsu katei." *Ōhara shakai mondai kenkyūjo kenkyū shiryō geppō,* no. 451 (1996): 18–34.

Hyōdō Tsutomu. *Rōdō no sengo shi.* Vol. 1 of 2. Tokyo: Tōkyō daigaku shuppankai, 1997.

Igarashi Jin. *Seitō seiji to rōdō kumiai undō: Sengo nihon no tōtatsuten to nijūisseiki e no kadai.* Tokyo: Ochonomizu shobō, 1998.

Iriye, Akira. *The Cold War in Asia: A Historical Introduction.* Englewood Cliffs, N.J.: Prentice-Hall, 1974.

Isaacs, Jeremy, and Taylor Downing. *Cold War: An Illustrated History, 1945–1991.* 1st ed. Boston: Little Brown & Co., 1998.

Iwai Akira. *Sōhyō to tomoni.* Tokyo: Yomiuri shinbunsha, 1971.

Jiyū Minshutō. *Jiyū minshutō tōshi.* Tokyo: Jiyū minshutō, 1987.

Johnson, Chalmers A. *Japan's Public Policy Companies.* Washington, D.C.: American Enterprise Institute for Public Policy Research, 1978.

———. *MITI and the Japanese Miracle.* Stanford: Stanford University Press, 1982.

Kasuga Shōichi. "Kantō rōkyō kessei zengo." In *Shōgen sanbetsu kaigi no tanjō,* edited by Hōsei Daigaku Ōhara Shakai Mondai Kenkyūjo, 83–104. Tokyo: Sōgō rōdō kenkyūjo, 1996.

———. "Nihon kyōsan tō no saiken." In *Shōwa keizi shi e no shōgen,* edited by Andō Yoshio, 115–130. Tokyo: Mainichi shinbunsha, 1966.

Kasza, Gregory James. *The Conscription Society: Administered Mass Organizations.* New Haven: Yale University Press, 1995.

Katō Kanjū. "Shōwa shonen no rōdō undō." In *Shōwa keizai shi e no shōgen,* edited by Andō Yoshio, 154–170. Tokyo: Mainichi shinbunsha, 1966.

Kawanishi Hirosuke. *Enterprise Unionism in Japan.* London and New York: Kegan Paul International, 1992.

———. *The Human Face of Industrial Conflict in Post-War Japan.* London and New York: Kegan Paul International, 1999.

Kelly, Matthew A. "The Reconstitution of the German Trade Union Movement." *Political Science Quarterly* 64, no. 1 (1949): 24–49.

Kenny, Martin, and Richard Florida. *Beyond Mass Production: The Japanese System and Its Transfer to the US.* New York: Oxford University Press, 1993.

Kindleberger, Charles. "Toward the Marshall Plan: A Memoir of Policy Development in Germany." In *The Marshall Plan and Germany: West German Development within the Framework of the European Recovery Program,* edited by Charles Maier and Gunther Bischof, 71–114. New York and Oxford: Berg, 1991.

Kinoshita Takeshi. *Katayama naikaku shiron: renritsu seiken mondai o chūshin ni.* Tokyo: Hōritsu bunkasha, 1982.

Kirchheimer, Otto. *West German Trade Unions: Their Domestic and Foreign Policies.* Santa Monica, Calif.: Rand Corp., 1956.

Kort, Michael. *The Columbia Guide to the Cold War.* The Columbia Guides to American History and Cultures. New York: Columbia University Press, 1998.

Kōsai Yutaka. *The Era of High Speed Growth: Notes on the Postwar Japanese Economy.* Tokyo: University of Tokyo Press, 1986.

Koseki Shōichi. *The Birth of Japan's Postwar Constitution.* Translated by Ray A. Moore. Denver, Colo.: Westview Press, 1997.

Kōshiro Kazuyoshi, ed. *Sengo 50 nen: Sangyō, koyō rōdō shi.* Tokyo: Nihon rōdō kenkyū kikō, 1995.

Kōzuma Yoshiaki. "Nihonteki rōdō kumiaishugi no teiki to sono nerai." *Gekkan kokusai rōdō undō,* no. 213 (1989): 70–82.

Kuisel, Richard F. *Capitalism and the State in Modern France: Renovation and Economic Management in the Twentieth Century.* Cambridge and New York: Cambridge University Press, 1981.

———. *Seducing the French: The Dilemma of Americanization.* Berkeley: University of California Press, 1993.

Kume, Ikuo. *Disparaged Success: Labor Politics in Postwar Japan.* Ithaca, N.Y.: Cornell University Press, 1998.

Kuroda Hisao. "Shakai tō no kettō." In *Shōwa keizai shi e no shōgen,* edited by Andō Yoshio, 106–115. Tokyo: Mainichi shinbunsha, 1966.

Lange, Peter Michael, George Ross, and Maurizio Vannicelli. *Unions, Change, and Crisis: French and Italian Union Strategy and the Political Economy, 1945–1980.* London and New York: Allen and Unwin, 1982.

LaPalombara, Joseph. *The Italian Labor Movement: Problems and Prospects.* Ithaca, N.Y.: Cornell University Press, 1957.

———. "The Political Role of Organized Labor in Western Europe." *Journal of Politics* 17, no. 1 (1955): 59–81.

Large, Stephen S. *Organized Workers and Socialist Politics in Interwar Japan.* Cambridge and New York: Cambridge University Press, 1981.

Levine, Solomon Bernard. *Industrial Relations in Postwar Japan.* Urbana: University of Illinois Press, 1958.

Link, Werner. "Building Coalitions: Non-Governmental German-American Linkages." In *The Marshall Plan and Germany: West German Development within the Framework of the European Recovery Program,* edited by Charles Maier and Gunther Bischof, 282–330. New York and Oxford: Berg, 1991.

Lipset, Seymour Martin. "Radicalism or Reformism: The Sources of Working-Class Politics." *American Political Science Review* 77, no. 1 (1983): 1–18.

Loriaux, Michael Maurice. *France after Hegemony: International Change and Financial Reform.* Cornell Studies in Political Economy. Ithaca: Cornell University Press, 1991.

Lorwin, Lewis Levitzki. *The International Labor Movement: History, Policies, Outlook.* New York: Harper, 1953.

Lorwin, Val R. "France." In *Comparative Labor Movements,* edited by Walter Galenson, 313–409. New York: Russell & Russell, 1968.

———. *The French Labor Movement.* Cambridge, Mass.: Harvard University Press, 1954.

MacShane, Denis. *International Labour and the Origins of the Cold War.* Oxford and New York: Clarendon and Oxford University Press, 1992.

Maier, Charles. "The German Resistance in Comparative Perspective." In *Contending with Hitler: Varieties of German Resistance in the Third Reich,* edited by David Clay Large, 141–150. Washington, D.C.; Cambridge, England; New York; Oakleigh, Australia: German Historical Institute and Cambridge University Press, 1991.

Maier, Charles S. *The Cold War in Europe.* New York: M. Wiener Pub., 1991.

———. *In Search of Stability: Explorations in Historical Political Economy.* Cambridge and New York: Cambridge University Press, 1987.

———. "The Politics of Productivity: Foundations of American International Economic Policy after World War II." In *Between Power and Plenty: Foreign Economic Policies of Advanced Industrial States,* edited by Peter J. Katzenstein, 23–49. Madison: University of Wisconsin Press, 1978.

Marcus, John T. *Neutralism and Nationalism in France: A Case Study.* New York: Book Associates, 1958.

Marglin, Stephen A., and Juliet Schor. *The Golden Age of Capitalism: Reinterpreting the Postwar Experience.* Oxford and New York: Clarendon Press and Oxford University Press, 1990.

Markovits, Andrei S. *The Politics of West German Trade Unions: Strategies of Class and Interest Representation in Growth and Crisis.* Cambridge and New York: Cambridge University Press, 1986.

Markovits, Andrei S., and Philip S. Gorski. *The German Left: Red, Green and Beyond.* Europe and the International Order. Cambridge, UK: Polity, 1993.

Marshall, Barbara. *The Origins of Post-War German Politics.* London and New York: Croom Helm, 1988.

Marshall, Byron K. *Capitalism and Nationalism in Prewar Japan: The Ideology of the Business Elite, 1868–1941.* Stanford, Calif.: Stanford University Press, 1967.

Marsland, Stephen E. *The Birth of the Japanese Labor Movement: Takano Fusatarō and the Rōdō Kumiai Kiseikai.* Honolulu: University of Hawai'i Press, 1989.

Masamura, Kimihiro. *Sengo shi.* Tokyo: Chikuma shobō, 1985.

Masumi Junnosuke. *Contemporary Politics in Japan.* Translated by Lonny E. Carlile. Berkeley: University of California Press, 1995.

———. *Hikaku seiji.* 3 vols. Tokyo: Tōkyō daigaku shuppankai, 1990–1993.

————. *Postwar Politics in Japan, 1945–1955.* Translated by Lonny E. Carlile. Berkeley: Institute of East Asian Studies, 1985.

Masuyama Tasuke. *Kenshō: Senryō ki no rōdō undō.* Tokyo: Renga shobō shinsha, 1993.

Minichiello, Sharon. *Retreat from Reform: Patterns of Political Behavior in Interwar Japan.* Honolulu: University of Hawai'i Press, 1984.

Miwa Yasushi. *Nihon fashizumu to rōdō undō.* Rekishi kagaku sōsho. Tokyo: Azekura shobō, 1988.

Monogatari Sengo Rōdō Undō Shi Kankō Iinkai. *Monogatari sengo rōdō undō shi.* Tokyo: Daiichi shorin, 1997–1998.

Moore, Joe. *Japanese Workers and the Struggle for Power, 1945–1947.* Madison: University of Wisconsin Press, 1983.

Motoi Hisao. *Shinpan nihon rōdō undō shi.* Tokyo: Rōmu gyōsei kenkyūjo, 1983.

Murakami Kanji. *Sōhyō monogatari.* 2 vols. Tokyo: Nihon hyōronsha, 1960–1961.

Naitō Norikuni and Akita Seishū. "Zen teishin jūgyōin kumiai (zentei)." In *Nihon rōdō kumiai ron,* edited by Ōkochi Kazuo, 223–275. Tokyo: Yūhikaku, 1954.

Nakahara Junkichi. "Nakahara junkichi shi ni kiku: Keizai fukkō kaigi no soshiki to undō." *Ōhara shakai mondai kenkyūjo zasshi,* nos. 362, 366, 367 (1989): 71–80, 60–73, 58–67, respectively.

Nakakita Kōji. *Keizai fukkō to sengo seiji: Nihon shakaitō 1945–1951.* Tokyo: Tōkyō daigaku shuppankai, 1998.

Nakamura Kikuo. *Matsuoka komakichi den.* Tokyo: Keizai ōraisha, 1963.

Nakamura Takafusa. *Economic Growth in Prewar Japan.* New Haven: Yale University Press, 1983.

————. *The Postwar Japanese Economy: Its Development and Structure, 1937–1994.* 2nd ed. Tokyo: University of Tokyo Press, 1995.

Niethammer, Lutz. "Structural Reform and a Compact for Growth." In *The Cold War in Europe,* edited by Charles S. Maier, 271–311. New York: M. Wiener Pub., 1991.

Nihon Rōdō Kumiai Sōhyōgikai, ed. *Sōhyō sanjūnen shiryō shū.* Tokyo: Rōdō kyōiku sentā, 1986.

Nihon Seisansei Honbu. *Seisansei undō sanjū nen shi.* Tokyo: Nihon seisansei honbu, 1985.

Nihon Shakaitō Kettō Yonjusshūnen Kinen Shuppan Kankō Iinkai. *Shiryō nihon shakaitō yonjūnenshi.* Tokyo: Nihon shakaitō chūō honbu, 1986.

Nikkeiren. *Nikkeiren sanjūnen shi.* Tokyo: Nihon keieisha dantai renmei, 1981.

Nishida Yoshiaki. "Labour and Farmers' Movements in Prewar Japan." In *The Political Economy of Japanese Society: The State or the Market?* Vol. 1, edited by Banno Junji, 237–276. Oxford and London: Oxford University Press, 1997.

————. "Senzen nihon ni okeru rōdō undō nōmin undō no seishitsu." In *Rekishiteki zentei,* edited by Tōkyō Daigaku Shakai Kagaku Kenkyūjo, 263–313. Tokyo: Tōkyō daigaku shuppankai, 1991.

Nishimura Hiromichi. "Nihon rōdō kumiai sōhyōgikai no kessei to bunretsu." In *Rōdō kumiai undō shi,* edited by Ōkōchi Kazuo and Fujita Wakao, 151–217. Tokyo: Kōbundō, 1962.

Nishio Suehiro. *Nishio suehiro no seiji oboegaki.* Tokyo: Mainichi shinbunsha, 1968.

Noda Kazuo. *Sengo keiei shi.* Tokyo: Nihon seisansei honbu, 1965.

Okazaki Saburō, ed. *Nihon no sangyōbetsu kumiai: Sono seisei to undō no tenkai.* Tokyo: Sōgō rōdō kenkyūjo, 1971.

Ōkōchi Kazuo. *Nihon rōdō kumiai monogatari.* 2 vols. Tokyo: Chikuma shobō, 1973.

———, ed. *Nihon rōdō kumiai ron.* Tokyo: Yūhikaku, 1954.

———, ed. *Rōdō,* vol. 4. *Shiryō sengo nijūnen shi.* 6 vols. Tokyo: Nihon hyōronsha, 1966.

Ōmori Tokuko. "Keizai antei no kihon seisaku ritsuan to keizai antei honbu." *NIRA seisaku kenkyū* 8, no. 7 (1995): 8–13.

Ōta Kaoru. "Rōdō kumiai kara mita keieisha: Nihon no keieisha wa kindai teki ni nattaka." *Chūō kōron* 75, no. 11 (1960): 166–169.

———. *Shuntō no shūen: Tei seichōka no rōdō undō.* Expanded ed. Tokyo: Chūō keizaisha, 1978.

———. *Tatakai no naka de: Rōdō undō nijūgo nen.* Tokyo: Aoki shoten, 1971.

Otake, Hideo. "Defense Controversies and One-Party Dominance: The Opposition in Japan and West Germany." In *Uncommon Democracies: The One-Party Dominant Regimes,* edited by T. J. Pempel, 128–161. Ithaca and London: Cornell University Press, 1990.

———. "The *Zaikai* under the Occupation: The Formation and Transformation of Managerial Councils." In *Democratizing Japan: The Allied Occupation,* edited by Robert E. Ward and Yoshikazu Sakamoto, 366–391. Honolulu: University of Hawai'i Press, 1987.

Packard, George R. III. *Protest in Tokyo: The Security Treaty Crisis of 1960.* Princeton: Princeton University Press, 1966.

Palmer, David. "Gurōburu undō shi ni mukete: Amerika, nihon, ōsutoraria, aruzenchin, 1890–1960." *Sanken ronshū* (2001).

Paterson, William E., and Ian Campbell. *Social Democracy in Post-War Europe.* New York: St. Martin's Press, 1974.

Pempel, T. J. "Japan and Sweden: Polarities of 'Responsible Capitalism.'" In *Comparative Political Dynamics: Global Research Perspectives,* edited by Dankwart A. Rustow and Kenneth Paul Erickson, 408–438. New York: HarperCollins, 1991.

———. *Regime Shift: Comparative Dynamics of the Japanese Political Economy.* Ithaca: Cornell University Press, 1998.

Pempel, T. J., and Keiichi Tsunekawa. "Corporatism without Labor? The Japanese Anomaly." In *Trends toward Corporatist Intermediation,* edited by Philippe C. Schmitter and Gerhard Lembruch, 231–270. Beverly Hills: Sage, 1979.

Peukert, Detlev J. "Working-Class Resistance: Problems and Options." In *Contending with Hitler: Varieties of German Resistance in the Third Reich,* edited by David Clay

Large, 35–48. Washington, D.C.; Cambridge, England; New York; Oakleigh, Australia: German Historical Institute and Cambridge University Press, 1991.

Piore, Michael J., and Charles F. Sabel. *The Second Industrial Divide: Possibilities for Prosperity.* New York: Basic Books, 1984.

Price, John. *Japan Works: Power and Paradox in Postwar Industrial Relations.* Ithaca: ILR Press, 1997.

———. "Valery Burati and the Formation of Sohyo During the US Occupation of Japan." *Pacific Affairs* 64, no. 2 (1991): 208–225.

Prowe, Diethelm. "Economic Democracy in Post-World War II Germany: Corporatist Crisis and Response." *Journal of Modern History* 57, no. 3 (1985): 451–482.

———. "German Democratization as Conservative Restabilization: The Impact of American Policy." In *American Policy and the Reconstruction of West Germany,* edited by Jeffry M. Diefendorf, Axel Frohn, and Hermann-Josef Rupieper, 307–329. Washington, D.C.; Cambridge, England; New York; Oakleigh, Australia: German Historical Institute and Cambridge University Press, 1993.

Rice, Richard. "Japanese Labor in World War II." *International Labor and Working Class History,* no. 38 (1990): 29–45.

Rioux, Jean-Pierre. *The Fourth Republic, 1944–1958.* Translated by Godfrey Rogers, Cambridge History of Modern France. Cambridge, London, New York, New Rochelle, Melbourne, Sydney, Paris: Cambridge University Press and Editions de la Maison Sciences de l'Homme, 1987.

Romero, Federico. *The United States and the European Trade Union Movement, 1944–1951.* Chapel Hill: University of North Carolina Press, 1992.

Rōmu Gyōsei Kenkyūjo. *Shiryō rōdō undōshi.* Tokyo: Rōmu gyōsei kenkyūjo.

Ross, George. *Workers and Communists in France: From Popular Front to Eurocommunism.* Berkeley: University of California Press, 1982.

Rupert, Mark. *Producing Hegemony: The Politics of Mass Production and American Global Power.* Cambridge and New York: Cambridge University Press, 1995.

Sako, Mari. "Shunto: The Role of Employer and Union Coordination at the Industry and Inter-Sectoral Levels." In *Japanese Labour and Management in Transition: Diversity, Flexibility and Participation,* edited by Mari Sako and Hiroki Sato, 236–264. London and New York: Routledge, 1997.

Salvati, B. "The Rebirth of Trade Unionism, 1943–54." In *The Rebirth of Italy, 1943–50,* edited by S. J. Woolf, 181–211. London: Longman Group, 1971.

Sassoon, Donald. *One Hundred Years of Socialism: The West European Left in the Twentieth Century.* New York: New Press, 1996.

———. *The Strategy of the Italian Communist Party: From the Resistance to the Historic Compromise.* New York: St. Martin's Press, 1981.

Scalapino, Robert A. *The Early Japanese Labor Movement: Labor and Politics in a Developing*

Society. Berkeley, Calif.: Institute of East Asian Studies, University of California, Berkeley, Center for Japanese Studies, 1983.

————. *The Japanese Communist Movement, 1920–1966.* Berkeley: University of California Press, 1967.

————. "Labor and Politics in Postwar Japan." In *The State and Economic Enterprise in Japan: Essays in the Political Economy of Growth,* edited by William W. Lockwood, 669–720. Princeton: Princeton University Press, 1965.

Schaller, Michael. *Altered States: The United States and Japan since the Occupation.* New York: Oxford University Press, 1997.

————. *The American Occupation of Japan: The Origins of the Cold War in Asia.* New York: Oxford University Press, 1985.

Schonberger, Howard B. *Aftermath of War: Americans and the Remaking of Japan, 1945–1952,* American Diplomatic History. Kent, Ohio: Kent State University Press, 1989.

————. "American Labor's Cold War in Occupied Japan." *Diplomatic History* 3, no. 3 (1979): 249–272.

————. "The Japan Lobby in American Diplomacy, 1947–1952." *Pacific Historical Review* 46, no. 3 (1977): 327–359.

Schwabe, Klaus. "German Policy Responses to the Marshall Plan." In *The Marshall Plan and Germany: West German Development within the Framework of the European Recovery Program,* edited by Charles Maier and Gunther Bischof, 225–281. New York and Oxford: Berg, 1991.

Shakai Bunko, ed. *Nihon shakai tō shi shiryō.* Tokyo: Kashiwa shobō, 1966.

Shiino Etsurō. "Nihon kyōsantō no orugu shidō to zentan no kessei." In *Shōgen sanbetsu kaigi no tanjō,* edited by Hōsei Daigaku Ōhara Shakai Mondai Kenkyūjo, 283–306. Tokyo: Sōgō rōdō kenkyūjo, 1996.

Shimizu Shinzō. *Nihon no shakai minshushugi.* Tokyo: Iwanami shoten, 1961.

————. *Sengo kakushin no hanichikage.* Tokyo: Nihon keizai hyōronsha, 1995.

————. *Sengo rōdō kumiai undō shiron: Kigyō shakai chōkoku no shiza.* Tokyo: Nihon hyōronsha, 1982.

Shinkawa Toshimitsu. *Sengo nihon seiji to shakai minshu shugi: Shakaitō sōhyō burokku no kōbō.* Kyotoi: Hōritsu bunkasha, 1999.

Shiota Shōbei. "Zen sen'i sangyō rōdō kumiai dōmei." In *Nihon rōdō kumiai ron,* edited by Okōchi Kazuo, 277–336. Tokyo: Yūhikaku, 1954.

Shirai Taishirō. "Nihon rōdō kumiai sōdōmei no undō." In *Rōdō kumiai undō shi,* edited by Okōchi Kazuo and Fujita Wakao, 81–150. Tokyo: Kōbundō, 1962.

Smith, Thomas C. *The Native Sources of Japanese Industrialization, 1750–1920.* Berkeley, Los Angeles, and London: University of California Press, 1988.

Sōdōmei Gojūnenshi Kankō Iinkai. *Sōdōmei gojūnenshi.* Tokyo: Sōdōmei gojūnenshi kankō iinkai, 1964.

Sōhyō, ed. *Sōhyō jūnen shi.* Tokyo: Rōdō junpōsha, 1964.

————, ed. *Sōhyō sanjūnen shiryō shū.* Vol. 2. Tokyo: Nihon rōdō kumiai sōhyōgokai, 1986.

Sōhyō yonjūnen shi. Hensan Iinkai, ed. *Sōhyō yonjūnen shi.* 3 vols. Tokyo: Daiichi shorin, 1993.

Stebenne, David L. "Introduction." *International Labor and Working-Class History* 50 (1996): 114–115.

————. "The Postwar 'New Deal.'" *International Labor and Working-Class History* 50 (1996): 140–147.

Steinhouse, Adam. *Workers' Participation in Post-Liberation France.* Lanham, Md.: Lexington Books, 2002.

Stockwin, J. A. A. *The Japanese Socialist Party and Neutralism: A Study of Political Party and Its Foreign Policy.* Carlton, London, and New York: Melbourne University Press and Cambridge University Press, 1968.

Sturmthal, Adolf Fox. *Comparative Labor Movements: Ideological Roots and Institutional Development.* Belmont, Calif.: Wadsworth Pub. Co., 1972.

————. *Left of Center: European Labor since World War II.* Urbana: University of Illinois Press, 1983.

————. *The Tragedy of European Labor, 1918–1939.* New York: Columbia University Press, 1943.

Sumiya Mikio. "Sekitan kōgyō no rōdō kumiai: 'Tankō rōdō kumiai rengō' o chūshin to shite." In *Nihon Rōdō Kumiai Ron,* edited by Okōchi Kazuo, 1–50. Tokyo: Yūhikaku, 1954.

Supreme Commander for the Allied Powers. Government Section. *Political Reorientation of Japan.* 2 vols. Washington, D.C.: U.S. Government Printing Office, 1949.

Suzuki, Akira. "The Polarization of the Union Movement in Postwar Japan: Politics in the Unions of Steel and Railway Workers." Ph.D. diss., University of Wisconsin, 1997.

Suzuki Mosaburō. "Jinmin sensen jiken." In *Shōwa keizai shi e no shōgen,* edited by Andō Yoshio, 146–156. Tokyo: Mainichi shinbunsha, 1966.

Swearingen, Rodger, and Paul Langer. *Red Flag in Japan: International Communism in Action 1919–1951.* 1952. Reprint, Westport, Conn.: Greenwood Press, 1968.

Swenson, Peter. *Fair Shares: Unions, Pay, and Politics in Sweden and West Germany,* Cornell Studies in Political Economy. Ithaca: Cornell University Press, 1989.

Taft, Philip. "Germany." In *Comparative Labor Movements,* edited by Walter Galenson, 243–312. New York: Russell & Russell, 1968.

Takagi Ikurō. "Nihon rōdō kumiai undō ni okeru 'uha' no keifu: Sōdōmei gata to jc gata no dōshitsusei to ishitsusei." In *Sengo rōdō kumiai undō shiron: Kigyō shakai chōkoku no shiza,* edited by Shimizu Shinzō, xii, 526. Tokyo: Nihon hyōronsha, 1982.

Takagi Tadao. "Gōka rōren." In *Nihon no sangyōbetsu kumiai: Sono seisei to undō no tenkai,* edited by Okazaki Saburō, 227–249. Tokyo: Sōgō rōdō kenkyūjo, 1971.

Takahashi Hikohiro. *Gendai seiji to shakai minshu shugi: Mittsu no chōryū to sono jikken.* Tokyo: Hōsei daigaku shuppankyoku, 1985.

———. "Mindō to nashonaru sentaa no saihen." In *Sengo taisei no keisei,* edited by Nihon Gendai Shi Kenkyūkai, 187–222. Tokyo: Otsuki shoten, 1988.

———. "Senryōka shakaitō seiken no seiritsu: Yon tō kyōdō iinkai kara kyūkoku minshu sensen e." *Rōdō undō shi kenkyū* 55–56 (1974): 7–40.

Takanashi Akira. *Kawaru shuntō: Rekishiteki sōkatsu to tenbō.* Tokyo: Nihon rōdō kenkyūjo, 2002.

———. *Shōgen sengo rōdō kumiai undō shi.* Tokyo: Tōyō keizai shinpōsha, 1985.

Takano Minoru. *Nihon no rōdō undō.* Tokyo: Iwanami shoten, 1958.

———. *Tainichi kōwa to kongo no rōdō undō.* Tokyo: Gaikoku bunkasha, 1951.

———. *Takano minoru chosaku shū.* 5 vols. Tokyo: Takushoku shobō, 1976–1977.

Takaragi Fumihiko. "Sōhyō tanjō zengo." In *Shōgen sengo rōdō kumiai undō shi,* edited by Takanashi Akira, 77–121. Tokyo: Tōyō shobō, 1985.

Takemae Eiji. "Early Postwar Reformist Parties." In *Democratizing Japan: The Allied Occupation,* edited by Robert Edward Ward and Yoshikazu Sakamoto, 339–365. Honolulu: University of Hawai'i Press, 1987.

———. *Sengo rōdō kaikaku: GHQ rōdō seisakushi.* Tokyo: Tōkyō daigaku shuppankai, 1982.

———. "Sōhyō and US Occupation Labour Policy: An Interview with Valery Burati." *Tōkyō keizai daigaku shi,* no. 97–98 (1976): 253–288.

Takita Minoru. "Kokusai rōdō undō no chōryū to nihon no rōdō kumiai." In *Shōgen sengo rōdō kumiai undō shi,* edited by Takanashi Akira, 209–241. Tokyo: Tōyō shobō, 1985.

Tanahashi Yasusuke. "Shitetsu sōren." In *Nihon no sangyōbetsu kumiai: sono seisei to undō no tenkai,* edited by Okazaki Saburō, 125–148. Tokyo: Sōgō rōdō kenkyūjo, 1971.

Tani, Satomi. "The Japan Socialist Party before the Mid-1960s: An Analysis of Its Stagnation." In *Creating Single-Party Democracy: Japan's Postwar Political System,* edited by Tetsuya Kataoka, 173. Stanford, Calif.: Hoover Institution Press, 1992.

Tezuka Kazuaki. "Kyū rōdō kumiai hō no keisei to tenkai: Shoki rōdō iinkai no kinō bunseki o chūshin ni shite." In *Sengo kaikaku: Rōdō kaikaku,* edited by Tōkyō Daigaku and Shakai Kagaku Kenkyūjo, 245–307. Tokyo: Tōkyō daigaku shuppankai, 1974.

Thelen, Kathleen Ann. *Union of Parts: Labor Politics in Postwar Germany.* Ithaca, N.Y.: Cornell University Press, 1991.

Thurston, Donald R. *Teachers and Politics in Japan.* Princeton: Princeton University Press, 1973.

Tilly, Charles. *Big Structures, Large Processes, Huge Comparisons.* New York: Russell Sage Foundation, 1984.

Tokita Yoshihisa. "Tanrō." In *Nihon no sangyōbetsu kumiai: Sono seisei to undō no tenkai,* edited by Okazaki Saburō, 3–49. Tokyo: Sōgō rōdō kenkyūjo, 1971.

Tōkyō Daigaku Shakai Kagaku Kenkyūjo. *Gendai nihon shakai.* Tokyo: Tōkyō daigaku shuppankai, 1991.

———. *Sengo kaikaku.* Tokyo: Tōkyō daigaku shuppankai, 1974.

Totten, George O. *The Social Democratic Movement in Prewar Japan.* New Haven: Yale University Press, 1966.

Tsuji Kiyokai, ed. *Seiji.* vol. 1. *Shiryō sengo nijūnen shi,* 6 vols. Tokyo: Nihon hyōronsha, 1966.

Tsutsui, William M. *Manufacturing Ideology: Scientific Management in Twentieth-Century Japan.* Princeton, N.J.: Princeton University Press, 1998.

Wall, Irwin. "The Marshall Plan and French Politics." In *The Marshall Plan: Fifty Years After,* edited by Martin A. Schain, 167–183. New York and Basingstoke, UK: Palgrave, 2001.

Wall, Irwin M. "The French Social Contract: Conflict Amid Cooperation." *International Labor and Working-Class History* 50 (1996): 116–124.

———. *The United States and the Making of Postwar France, 1945–1954.* Cambridge and New York: Cambridge University Press, 1991.

Weathers, Charles Martin. "Transforming Labor: State and Employer Strategy in Postwar Japan." Ph.D. dissertation, University of California, 1995.

Weiler, Peter. "The United States, International Labor and the Cold War: The Break-up of the World Federation of Trade Unions." *Diplomatic History* 5, no. 1 (1981): 1–22.

Willey, Richard. "Pressure Group Politics: The Case of Sohyo." *Western Political Quarterly,* December 1964.

Wilson, Sandra. "The Comintern and the Japanese Communist Party." In *International Communism and the Communist International,* edited by Tim Rees and Andrew Thorpe. Manchester and New York: Manchester University Press, 1998.

Windmuller, John P. *International Trade Union Movement.* Deventer, Boston, and Hingham, Mass.: Kluwer, 1980.

———. *Labor Internationals: A Survey of Contemporary International Trade Union Organizations.* Ithaca: New York State School of Industrial and Labor Relations, Cornell University, 1969.

Wittner, Lawrence S. *The Struggle against the Bomb.* Stanford, Calif.: Stanford University Press, 1993.

Woolf, S. J. "The Rebirth of Italy, 1943–50." In *The Rebirth of Italy, 1943–50,* edited by S. J. Woolf, 181–211. London: Longman Group, 1971.

Yamakawa Hitoshi. *Yamakawa Hitoshi jiden: Aru bonjin no kiroku, sonota.* Tokyo: Iwanami shoten, 1961.

Yamamoto Kiyoshi. "'Sangyō saihen' to sho seiji shutai." In *Rōdō kaikaku,* edited by Tōkyō Daigaku Shakai Kagaku Kenkyūjo, 181–244. Tokyo: Tōkyō daigaku shuppankai, 1974.

Yamamoto Masahiro. "Sasha kōryō no sakusei o meguru ronsō ten to sōhyō undō e no impakuto." *Kokusai rōdō,* no. 209, 211 (1988–1989): 62–73, 87–96.

Yanaga, Chitoshi. *Big Business in Japanese Politics.* Yale Studies in Political Science 22. New Haven: Yale University Press, 1968.

Yoshida Sukeharu. "Sanbetsu kaigi no kessei to soshiki shidō." In *Shōgen sanbetsu kaigi no tanjō,* edited by Hōsei Daigaku Ōhara Shakai Mondai Kenkyūjo, 207–248. Tokyo: Sōgō rōdō kenkyūjo, 1996.

Zariski, Raphael. "The Italian Socialist Party: A Case Study in Factional Conflict." *American Political Science Review* 56, no. 2 (1962): 372–390.

Zen Nihon Rōdō Sōdōmei. *Hitosuji no michi: Minshuteki rōdō undō no rekishi.* 3 vols. Vol. 1. Tokyo: Zen nihon rōdō sōdōmei, 1978.

Zenrō jūnen shi. Hensan Iinkai. *Zenrō jūnen shi.* Tokyo: Zenrō jūnen shi hensan iinkai, 1968.

Index

Adenaur, Konrad, 132
AFL, 22, 55, 121, 123, 170
Agartz, Viktor, 207–208
allgemeine gewerkschaft (single general union), 53
Amis, Robert T., 150, 159
anarcho-syndicalism, 16, 30
antifa movements, 26
Arahata Kanson, 35
Ashida cabinet, 153–155; fall of, 155–156
Ashida Hitoshi, 145, 147, 153
Asian Socialist Conference, 185–187

Badoglio, Pietro, 52
Bandung Conference, 185
base-up, 217
Basso, Lelio, 113
battle for production/struggle for production, 47, 52, 53, 55–57, 89–90, 101; failure of in France and Italy, 114–117; failure in Japan, 141–142
Bernstein, Eduard, 44
Bloody May Day Incident, 183–184
Blum, Leon, 21, 114
Bothereau, Robert, 112
Brenner, Otto, 207–208
Brown, Irving, 95, 122, 248n. 32
Buozzi, Bruno, 53,
Burati, Valery, 169–170
Butler Charter, 221

Canini, Giovanni, 123
Catholic Church, 8, 10, 15, 23; in Italy, 52, 113, 118
cells, 67

CFDT (Confédération Française Démocratique du Travail), 210–212
CFTC (Confédération Française des Travailleurs Chrétiens), 45, 47, 109, 111, 157, 210, 255n. 20
CGIL (Confederazione Generale Italiana del Lavoro), 50–51, 52, 116, 204, 231; formation of, 24, 49; internal tensions in post–World War II, 112–113; loosened "transmission belt" relationship with PCI, 211; and "peace offensive," 126; splits of (1948–1949), 109, 111, 112, 121, 123–124
CGT (Confédération Générale du Travail), 17, 23, 24, 45, 47–48, 115, 204–205, 231; internal tensions in post–World War II, 112; role in PCF "peace offensive," 126, 128; split of (1947), 109, 120–121; turn to labor market activism, 209–211
CGTU (Confédération Générale du Travail Unitaire), 17
Christian unionism, 9, 10–11, 15; and fascism, 19; and industrial modernization; in Japan, 28, 31, 209–210
Chūritsu Rōren (Federation of Independent Unions), 217
CIL (Confederazione Italiana del Lavoro), 18
CIO (Congress Industrial Organizations), 22, 121, 123
CISL (Confederazione Italiana Sindicati Lavoratori), 109, 124, 204, 209–210
Civil Service Law, 148
Clay, General Lucius, 54–55, 56
class-versus-mass party debate: in Italy 113–114; in Japan, 156

285

efforts to mobilize international labor movement backing for, 122–123, 130; Japanese reaction to, 154–155; and productivity movement, 202, 204

ESB (Economic Stabilization Board, Keizai Antei Honbu), 99

European Defense Community (EDC), 125

Fascism: defined, 18; fear of revival of, 200–201; impact on European labor movements, 18–26, 57–58; in Japan, 36–40

FDGB (Freier Deutscher Gewerkschafts-bund), 129

FEC (Far Eastern Commission), 80–81, 148

FIL (Federazione Italiana del Lavoratori), 124

FO (Force Ouvriēre), 128; formation of, 109, 111, 112, 121, 204, 211

Food May Day, 74, 76

Fordism, 231–233

Four-party accord. See parliamentary coalitions

four principles of peace, 177, 177–179, 215

fractions. See cells

France interwar period, 17; fascism in, 19; fear of revival of fascism, 200–201; formation of the Resistance, 23–24; impact of Cold War in, 114–116; 1944–1947, 45–49; Popular Front, 21; productivity movement in, 204–205; significance of Marshall Plan, 117–118; stabilization in, 231

Freitag, Walter, 133

FTUC (Free Trade Union Committee), 55, 122

GARIOA (Government and Relief in Occu-pied Areas), 154

Germany: absence of Resistance movement in, 25–26, 54, 59–60; characteristics of the post–World War II occupation of, 26, 53–57; impact of Cold War, 128–134; interwar period, 16–17; politics of productivity in, 206–209; productivity movement in, 205–206

GHQ: economic recovery policies of, 98–100; labor reforms of, 65–66, 95; policy toward production control, 90; release of communists, 63. See also MacArthur, Douglas; Labor Division

globality, 1, 7, 229, 233

Gōka Rōren (Synthetic-Chemical Workers' Union), 213–215

Gōshi Kōhei, 219

Grande, Achille, 53

Great Treason Incident, 28

Hara Toraichi, 141, 157

Hasegawa Hiroshi, 147

Hatoyama Ichirō, 72–74

Heiwa o Mamoru Kai (Association to Protect Peace), 174

Hiragaki Miyoji, 179, 188

Hitler, Adolf, 19, 59

Hoshika Kaname, 162

Hosoya Matsuta: objection to Sōhyō 165; role in Sanbetsu, 77–78, 138–140; and Sanbestu Mindō, 160–163; and Sanbetsu unionization drive, 66–67, 69

Hyōgikai (Japan Labor Union Council), 30–31, 34

ICFTU (International Confederation of Free Trade Unions): formation of, 122–124; and the Japanese labor movement, 167–171, 179, 192; and the Korean War, 174

IFTCU (International Federation of Christian Trade Unions), 15

IFTU (International Federation of Trade Unions), 13–14, 21; increased British influence in, 22

Ii Yashirō, 81

Ikeda Hayato, 218, 221

ILO (International Labor Organization), 33, 167

IMF-JC (International Metalworkers' Federa-tion-Japan Council), 220

imperial democracy, 33

Inamura Junzō, 156

institutional reform: in Japan, 88–90; in post–World War II Europe, 43–44, 58–59

International Workingmen's Association, 16

Ishibashi Tanzan, 71, 77, 99

Italy: fascism in, 19, 24; fear of revival of fascism, 200–201; formation of Resis-tance, 24; impact of Marshall Plan in, 118–119; interwar period, 17–18;

1944–1947, 49–53, 116–117; productivity movement in, 204–205

Iwai Akira, 179, 196, 215–216, 223, 225, 232–233

Japan: absence of resistance movement during World War II in, 39–40; characteristics of post–World War II occupation of, 40–41; Cold War context compared to Western Europe, 135–137, 151–155, 172–173, 186–188, 195–196; economic recovery and institutional reform in, 88–90; impact of "peaceful coexistence" on, 212–213, 225–227; impact of World War I on, 28–29; interwar labor movement of compared to Europe, 35–36; "resistance" milieu that emerges after the end of World War II in, 41, 61–62, 71, 86–87, 104–105; stabilization in, 231–233; timing of industrialization, and industrialization, 27–29

Japan Labor Farmer Party (Nihon Rōdō Nōmintō), 31–32

Japan Peace Committee (Nihon Heiwa Iinkai), 174

Japan Proletarian Party (Nihon Musantō), 38

JCP (Japan Communist Party): democratic national front, 145, 148, 151; and ERC, 102–103; fifth party congress (February 1946), 71–72; and general-strike movement (1946–1947), 76–77, 78–82; labor policies of, 64, 66–68; local people's struggle, (chiiki jinmin tōsō), 146; national industrial-defense struggle, 149–150; near disappearance of influence, 173; and 1947 four-party talks and accord, 85; origins of 31, 84, 154; postwar situation compared with Western European communist parties, 86–87; reestablishment after World War II, 63–64; relations with international communist movement, 34–35, 136–137; relations with Sanbetsu, 138–140; response to Cominform criticism, 151; response to DPL initiative, 71–75; role in peace movement, 172–173; sixth national conference and shift to Eurocommunism, 225–227; sixth party congress (December 1947),

145; stance toward Katayama economic recovery program, 144; tactics used to control labor unions, 137–138; and worker-led economic recovery, 92–93; during World War II, 40

JPC (Japan Productivity Center), 219–221

JSP (Japan Socialist Party): contention over peace treaty at party convention (January 1951), 176–177; establishment of 62–63, 249n. 4; increased left-socialist influence in, 155–157; internal tensions in, 144–145; merger of Right and Left Socialist parties, 225; October 1951 convention and split of, 180; "reconstruction" (fourth) party convention (April 1949), 145, 156–157; relations with Sōhyō, 177–179, 223–227; response to DPL initiative, 72–74; and socialization, 103–104; third party convention (January 1948), 154. See also four principles of peace; structural reform thesis

Kaiin Kumiai (Seamen's Union), 36, 60, 67, 76–77, 193–194, 219

Kamiyama Shigeo, 64

Kan Makoto, 139, 144

Kanto Metalworkers' Union, 91

Karpinsky, William, 95

Katayama cabinet: economic recovery program, 99, 141–144, 153–154; fall of, 145

Katayama Tetsu, 85, 87

Katō Etsuo, 167

Katō Kanjū, 35, 37, 78, 154

keiei kyōgikai (management councils), 84, 91–93, 97–98, 102–103, 220, 232

Keizai Dōyūkai (Japan Committee for Economic Development): and ERC, 101–102; "modified capitalism" of, 93–95, 253n. 20

Kennan, George, 146

Kikunami Katsumi, 79, 139

Kinzoku Rōkyō (Metalworkers' Federation), 216

kōdan, 98–101

kōjō daihyōsha kaigi (factory delegate councils), 64

Kokkai Kyōtō Iinkai (Diet Joint Struggle Committee), 163–164

Kokurō (National Railway Workers' Union),

Nippōrō (Broadcasting Workers' Union), 141, 193–194
Nishio Suehiro, 29–30, 65, 72, 155, 157, 192, 227
Nissankyō (Japan Council of Industries), 101–102
Nomizo Masaru, 154
Nosaka Sanzō, 29, 39–40, 71

October Struggle (1946), 76–77
"one big union," 62, 69. See also *allgemeine gewerkschaft*
Ōta Kaoru, 196, 213, 215–218, 221, 223–225, 232–233

party coalitions: anti-Shidehara of 1946 (Liberal Party, Cooperative Party, JSP, JCP), 73–74; Ashida Cabinet three-party accord of 1948 (Democratic Party, People's Cooperative Party, JSP), 153; four-party talks and four-party accord of 1947 (Liberal Party, Democratic Party, JSP, People's Cooperative Party), 85, 103
Pastore, Guido, 123
Paulskirche Movement for the Unification of Germany and Against Rearmament, 125, 133
PCF (Parti Communiste Français), 17, 23–24, 45, 52, 120–121; pauperization thesis of, 206; and "peace offensive," 126; role in "battle for production" 47–48, 115–116
PCI (Partito Comunista Italiano), 17, 49, 52–53, 116–117; loosening of "transmission belt" relationship with CGIL, 211
Peace Economy Plan, 188
peace force thesis, 215
Peace Police Law, 28
Peace Preservation Law, 34, 183
Peace Promotion People's Conference (Heiwa Suishin Kokumin Kaigi), 182
Peace Treaty. *See* San Francisco Peace Treaty
People's Cooperative Party, 153
People's Train Incident, 149–150
Piano del Lavoro (Labor Plan), 126, 188, 224
politics of productivity. *See* productivity
Popular Front: in France (Front Populaire), 21; in Japan, 37–38, 70–72

Popular Party, 17
presidents' group, 164–165, 184
production control *(seisan kanri)*, 89–90, 94
productivity: pie theory, 203; politics of productivity, 201–202, 231–232; productivity movement, 202–206, 218–221; three principles of productivity, 219
Profintern, or Red International of Labor Unions (RILU), 11, 13, 22
Progressive Party, 72, 74
PSDI, 113, 118
PSI (Partito Socialista Italiano), 49, 52, 116, 118; and neutralism, 127; split of (1947), 113
PSLI, 113, 116
Public Corporation and National Enterprise Labor Relations Law, 148

Red Purge, 151
Resistance, 18, 58–60; coalitions in post–World War II Europe, 43, 45, 49, 51–53
Right Socialist Party, 193, 225; formation of, 180
Rocchi, A. Claudio, 123
Rōdō Kumiai Dōmeikai (Labor Union League), 30
Rōdōsha Dōshikai (Worker Comrades Society), 179–180, 184, 215, 261n. 8, 283
Rōnō Taishūtō (Labor-Farmer Mass Party), 34
Rōtō campaign (1952), 182–184, 262n. 19

Saillant, Louis, 22, 85
Sakisaka Itsurō, 224
Sampō (Industrial Patriotic Associations) movement, 38–39
San Francisco Peace Treaty, 176
Sanbetsu (National Congress of Industrial Organizations), 68–69, 76, 82–84, 90, 142, 148, 167; and ERC, 102–103; fourth convention (November 1948), 159–162; and Katayama economic recovery program, 141, 144; membership decline in, 151; "self-criticism convention" (July 1947), 138–140; third convention (November 1949), 140; and worker-led economic recovery, 92–93
Sanbetsu Mindō (Sanbetsu Democratization

League), 140–141, 156–157, 161–162, 169–170

Saragat, Giuseppe, 113

SCAP. *See* MacArthur, Douglas.

SED (Socialist Unity Party), 129

settlement/stabilization, 229, 231–232

SFIO (Section Française de l'Internationale Ouvrière), 45, 113–114, 117

Shakaishugi Dōmei (Socialist League), 30

Shakaishugi Kyōkai (Socialism Association), 223–224

Shidehara Kijūrō, 71, 73, 104, 153

Shiga Yoshio, 63

Shigemitsu Mamoru, 189–190

Shimizu Shinzō, 170, 191

Shimoyama Sadanori, 150

Shinsanbetsu, 167, 215; formation of 162–163, 165; neutralist position of 175, 178

Shitetsu Sōren (private railway workers' union), 167–168, 216

Showa Denkō scandal, 155

Shuntō, 216–218, 233

social democrats, 11–14, 44–45; in interwar Japan 31, 32–33, 37–38; relations with communists, 64–65, 74–75, 82, 112, 121, 130; relations with left socialists, 113–114; response to fascism, 19

Socialist, or Second, International, 11, 13–14, 192; relations with interwar Japanese labor movement, 33; response to communist popular front initiative, 21; response to Great Depression and fascism, 19–20, 21, 44

socialistic policies. *See* socialization

socialization, 43–44, 59; in France, 45–46, 117; in Italy, 50; in Japan, 84–85, 91, 98, 103–105; in West Germany, 131–133

Social Mass Party (Shakai Minshūtō), 31, 37

Sōdōmei (General Confederation of Labor), 82–83, 154, 156, 170, 220, 232; anti-communist drive of, 140–141; and ERC, 101–102; establishment of pre-war organization, 30–31; and general-strike movement (1946–1947), 77–79, 81; and Katayama economic recovery program, 143; October 1948 convention and "democratization" of, 157; postwar reestablishment of, 62–63, 68,

90, 91; response to fascism, 37; split of at fifth convention (November 1950), 192; worker-oriented recovery plans of, 90–92; and Zenrō Kaigi, 162

Sōhyō (National Council of Labor Unions), 195–196, 213–227, 232–233, *passim;* and China, 187–188; fifth convention (July 1954), 213, 215; formation of, 164–171; fourth convention (July 1953), 194; four-union manifesto, 193; and ICFTU, 168; interwar period, 37–38; and Korean War, 171, 174–175; and peace movement, 182; relations with JSP, 185, 223–227; Rōtō campaign, 182–184; second convention (March 1951), 177–179; wage bargaining under Takano 191–192. *See also* Shuntō

SPD (German Social Democratic Party), 16; Bad Godesberg conference (1959), 230; in East Germany, 129; neutralism of, 133–134; and socialization, 132–133

stabilization. *See* settlement/stabilization

Stalin, Joseph, 20, 21, 119, 199

Stockholm Appeal, 125–126, 174

structural reform: in JSP, 223–225; in PCI, 210

Sturmthal, Adolf, 10

Subversive Activities Prevention Act (Habōhō), 183–184

Sukarno, 226

Suzuki Bunji, 29–30

Suzuki Mosaburō, 35 37, 177, 190

Suzuki Seiichi, 137–138, 156

Taira Incident, 150

Takagari Fumihiko, 163–164, 179

Takano Minoru, 29, 74, 77–78, 92, 141, 173, 215–217; Asian Socialist Conference and, 185–188; elected Sōhyō general secretary, 180; general manager of Sōdōmei, 157; joins JSP, 156; leadership style in Sōhyō, 182–192; and Left Socialist Party, 189–191; and Mindō movement, 160, 162–163; ouster of and left-socialist criticisms, 213–215; peace force thesis of, 188; shifting political stance of, 180–182; social democratic reactions to Takano Line, 192–195; Takano Plan and formation of Sōhyō, 165, 170

About the Author

Lonny E. Carlile received his M.A. from Kyushu University and his Ph.D. from the University of California, Berkeley, both in political science. He has published a number of articles and essays on Japanese labor history, including most recently "The Japanese Labour Movement's Road to the Millennium," in David W. Edgington, ed., *Japan at the Millenium* (2003). He is coeditor (with Mark Tilton) of *Is Japan Really Changing Its Ways?* (1998), and translator of Masumi Junnosuke's *Contemporary Politics in Japan* (1995) and *Postwar Politics in Japan* (1985), and is currently an associate professor of Asian studies at the University of Hawai'i at Mānoa.

Production Notes for Carlile / *Divisions of Labor*

Cover design by Santos Barbasa Jr.

Interior design by University of Hawai'i Press production staff with display type in Avant Garde and text in Garamond Three

Composition by Josie Herr

Printing and binding by The Maple-Vail Book Manufacturing Group

Printed on 60# Sebago Eggshell, 420 ppi